THE SPIRIT IN WORSHIP—WORSHIP IN THE SPIRIT

Edited by Teresa Berger and Bryan D. Spinks

The Spirit
in Worship—*Worship*
in the Spirit

A PUEBLO BOOK

Liturgical Press   Collegeville, Minnesota

www.litpress.org

A Pueblo Book published by Liturgical Press

Excerpts from *Baptism, Eucharist and Ministry*. Faith and Order Paper No. 111. Geneva: World Council of Churches, 1982. Reprinted with permission.

Excerpts from Ephrem the Syrian, in Sebastian P. Brock, *The Harp of the Spirit: Twelve Poems of Saint Ephrem*, Studies Supplementary to *Sobornost* 4. London: Fellowship of St Alban and St Sergius, 1975. Reprinted with permission.

Excerpts from Ephrem the Syrian, in Sebastian P. Brock, "St Ephrem on Christ as Light in Mary and in the Jordan: Hymni De Ecclesia 36," *Eastern Churches Review* 7 (1975): 138. Reprinted with permission.

Worthy Is the Lamb. Words and Music by Darlene Zschech. © 2000 Darlene Zschech and Hillsong Publishing (admin. in the U.S. and Canada by Integrity Worship Music/ASCAP) c/o Integrity Media, Inc., 1000 Cody Road, Mobile, AL 36695. All Rights Reserved. International Copyright Secured. Used by Permission.

Scripture texts in this work are taken from the *New Revised Standard Version Bible* © 1989, Division of Christian Education of the National Council of the Churches of Christ in the United States of America. Used by permission. All rights reserved.

Cover design by David Manahan, OSB. Photo from photos.com; illustration by Frank Kacmarcik, OblSB.

© 2009 by Order of Saint Benedict, Collegeville, Minnesota. All rights reserved. No part of this book may be reproduced in any form, by print, microfilm, microfiche, mechanical recording, photocopying, translation, or by any other means, known or yet unknown, for any purpose except brief quotations in reviews, without the previous written permission of Liturgical Press, Saint John's Abbey, PO Box 7500, Collegeville, Minnesota 56321-7500. Printed in the United States of America.

Library of Congress Cataloging-in-Publication Data

The Spirit in worship, worship in the Spirit.
       p.   cm.
  "A Pueblo Book."
  Proceedings of a conference held in Feb. 2008 at the Yale Institute of Sacred Music.
  Includes index.
  ISBN 978-0-8146-6228-1
  1. Public worship—Congresses.   2. Holy Spirit—Congresses.
3. Pentecostalism—Congresses.

BV15.S65   2009
264—dc22   2009020976

Contents

Contents

vi

Foreword

The Yale Institute of Sacred Music was host to an international conference in February 2008 entitled "The Spirit in Worship—Worship in the Spirit." The present volume emerges from the lectures and conversations at this meeting. As an interdisciplinary graduate center for the study and practice of sacred music, worship, and the arts, the ISM works for both academic and ecclesial communities in support of ministry and scholarship. In any given year the ISM supports events such as this that gather people from across boundaries of tradition, methodology, practice, and nation.

The ISM is a community of musicians and ministers, scholars, and practitioners. As one of the musicians I am drawn to myriad repertoires, including not only my native "Western Classical" tradition, but also American vernacular forms, and world music. I am blessed to be in a place where so much of the world's music is heard, but I confess that "home" for me remains contrapuntal music. For me, the procedure of counterpoint, in all its shapes and sizes, can signal hope for a world in discord. These sounds made of separate strands, artfully knit together, serve as a model that lives can be lived in community.

I am a musician, but I fraternize with theologians—especially the kind who think about the Trinity, straining to talk about the One and Three in terms that, at times, sound to me like groanings too deep for words. The dialogue is difficult some of the time, and abstruse most of the time. Scholars are compelled to "figure it out," even though they know that the Trinity is by nature ineffable. And yet, my theologian friends labor tirelessly.

Sometimes, I just want to play them a Bach fugue . . . like a musical dose of chicken soup: simple, yet thoroughly nourishing. It seems to me that this is a perfectly good way to experience utter distinctiveness, utter unity, utter interunity. One voice is heard in its own peculiar integrity, and yet heard in concert with other voices of equal interest. Sung or played together, these voices exhibit a unity at the subatomic level—a level that lives in the mathematic proportions of sound itself—formed this way at the dawn of creation. You must admit that this is a pretty good "something like . . ." analogy of a Being for whom analogies can never say enough.

The writings that follow serve in elegant counterpoint to scores of studies on creation and liturgy, the place of Christ and the liturgy, eucharistic prayer, and sacraments, because, at last, the Holy Spirit is beginning to receive her due attention in liturgical studies. It is understandable that we have, for so long, been fixated on anything but the Spirit in worship. Academic fields develop as people develop, and since we are finite beings, attention to one thing at a time seems an inevitable way of proceeding. We are learning our lesson, though, and finally giving serious attention to the ways people are naming the work of the Spirit as catalyst of immense growth in the Christian communion (e.g., the Pentecostal movement in Africa, charismatic churches in the States, the church growth movement, etc.). The Spirit is surely blowing powerfully in these corners of the world—powerfully enough to wake those of us who are somnambulant Westerners.

Reading what follows has made me more aware of the Spirit's breath in our own local situation at the ISM: the breath that flows through a young singer's vocal chords, the collective intake of air in a choir, the artist's breath that dries the freshly painted canvas, the wind that blows through a sacred structure and inhabits the bowels of a pipe organ, the groanings too deep for words in our daily prayer. In our meeting, the Spirit was churning the atmosphere wildly as seventy-five scholars from around the world descended upon Yale. Those lectures (and then some) have been winnowed to the finely crafted essays that follow.

Since this volume serves as a kind of window into the workings of the Institute, I know my colleagues join me in thanking the primary framer of this conference, Professor Bryan Spinks, and the primary editor of these papers, Professor Teresa Berger, for their tireless efforts given toward this cause. These two were convinced that not enough work has been done on the Holy Spirit in worship, and they were right.

It is our prayer that this volume will be for liturgical scholars, for scholars of religion, of ecclesiology, and of pastoral theology, a valuable resource of insight and challenge. May it open worlds for students, scholars, and church leaders alike, and enhance all our Spirit-filled work.

Martin Jean, Director
Yale Institute of Sacred Music

Foreword

Abbreviations

BELS   Bibliotheca *Ephemerides Liturgicae*, Subsidia

JPT   *Journal of Pentecostal Theology*

OCA   Orientalia Christiana Analecta

OCP   *Orientalia Christiana Periodica*

PG   Patrologia Graeca

PL   Patrologia Latina

SC   Sources chrétiennes

Teresa Berger, with Bryan D. Spinks

Introduction

it is the Spirit in whom we worship and in whom we pray
Gregory of Nazianzus

ev'ry time I feel the Spirit moving in my heart I will pray
African American Spiritual

Spirit of Love, Great loom of God . . . weave us into one
Shirley Erena Murray

The twentieth century was heralded (in its opening decades, no less) as the "century of the church."[1] Against this backdrop, contemporary theologians might be forgiven for envisioning the twenty-first century as a "century of the Spirit," having witnessed what one theologian aptly described as the "dramatic growth of attention to the Holy Spirit in recent Christian theology."[2] This growth of interest in the Holy Spirit began deep within the twentieth century itself, even while complaints about the occlusion of pneumatology, at least in Western Christianity, were still *de rigueur*. One has only to think of such diverse phenomena as the extraordinary global growth of Pentecostal and charismatic communities, or the vibrant retrieval of pneumatological traditions in older faith communities, or even the multifaceted cultural fascination with all things "spiritual" in order to appreciate the deeper roots of the contemporary interest in the Holy Spirit.

---

[1] Otto Dibelius, *Das Jahrhundert der Kirche* (Berlin: Furche-Verlag, 1928). The same sentiment, if not the exact phrase, can also be found in the writings of, for example, Romano Guardini and Henri de Lubac.

[2] F. LeRon Shults and Andrea Hollingsworth, *The Holy Spirit*, Guides to Theology (Grand Rapids, MI: Eerdmans, 2008), 1. See also F. LeRon Shults, "Spirit and Spirituality: Philosophical Trends in Late Modern Pneumatology," *Pneuma* 30, no. 2 (2008): 271.

In the Roman Catholic Church, for example, one might trace a twentieth-century trajectory from the encyclical of Pope Leo XIII on the Holy Spirit, *Divinum Illud Munus* (1897), to the encyclical *Dominum et Vivificantem* of Pope John Paul II (1998), dedicated to "The Holy Spirit in the Life of the Church and the World." The latter encyclical was a part of the "Year of the Holy Spirit," in preparation for the Great Jubilee Year 2000. In between these twentieth-century papal writings on the Holy Spirit—and more could be cited[3]—there were major theological retrievals. Yves Congar's extraordinary body of work on the Holy Spirit presents an important scholarly milestone.[4] Karl Rahner's meditations signal a poignant attentiveness not only to the workings of the Holy Spirit but also to the spiritual life.[5]

Developing cartographies for the twentieth-century renewal of interest in the Holy Spirit is not without difficulties, of course. The Spirit blows where she wills, after all—even, one must assume, through scholarly attempts at mapping renewed interest in her movements. That said, three areas do stand out in the past decades as peculiarly marked by Spirit-attentiveness. These areas provide the larger context within which the 2008 conference on "The Spirit in Worship—Worship in the Spirit" at the Yale Institute of Sacred Music took place. The present volume gathers the papers from this conference and thus its larger context deserves attention here. The three areas to be highlighted are, first, the pneumatological turn in constructive theology; second, reflections on the Holy Spirit in ecumenical conversations and

---

[3] There is, for example, the oft-quoted prayer of Pope John XXIII that the council be a "new Pentecost." Or, from the years after the council, Pope Paul VI emphasized in a general audience in 1973 that "the Christology and particularly the ecclesiology of the Council must be succeeded by a new study of and devotion to the Holy Spirit, precisely as the indispensable complement to the teaching of the Council" (*Insegnamenti di Paolo VI*, 11 [1973], 477; quoted in English in *Dominum et Vivificantem*, no. 2).

[4] Yves Congar, *I Believe in the Holy Spirit*, trans. David Smith. 3 vols. (New York: Seabury Press, 1983).

[5] See, for example, Karl Rahner, *Erfahrung des Geistes: Meditation* (Freiburg i.B.: Herder, 1977); English: *The Spirit in the Church* (New York: Seabury Press, 1979); *Von der Not und dem Segen des Gebetes*, new ed. (Freiburg i.B.: Herder, 1991), 33–51; English: *Happiness through Prayer* (Westminster: Newman Press, 1957); and the moving prayer to the Holy Spirit in *Gebete des Lebens*, ed. Albert Raffelt (Freiburg: Herder, 1984), 16f.; English: *Prayers for a Lifetime*, ed. Albert Raffelt (New York: Crossroad, 1984), 96.

Teresa Berger, with Bryan D. Spinks

convergences; and third, a growing Spirit-attentiveness in liturgical life. Obviously, these areas are not separate entities but interwoven in multiple ways. We highlight them in turn here primarily for the sake of analysis.

A PNEUMATOLOGICAL TURN IN CONSTRUCTIVE THEOLOGY

Constructive theology—its increasing pluriformity since the mid-twentieth century notwithstanding—has in recent decades witnessed a veritable "pneumatological turn." This turn to pneumatology, interestingly, took place in the midst of other turns[6] that have generally not fostered a lively engagement with traditional doctrinal loci. The (re-) turn to pneumatology, however, has flourished in the midst of contemporary theology, as is evident on a number of different levels. To begin with, there has been a vibrant retrieval of earlier pneumatological traditions, ranging from studies of the Spirit in the scriptural witness and early Christian origins[7] to medieval metaphors for the Holy Spirit[8] to inquiries into the pneumatological thinking of individual theologians of the past.[9] On this level of theological retrieval one might also situate the contemporary constructive pneumatology of Eugene Rogers's *After the Spirit*, which draws on a variety of resources, including theological and liturgical texts, as well as art from "outside the Modern West."[10]

A second site of the pneumatological turn in theology is constituted by the entry into theological conversations of Pentecostal and charismatic voices. Two different publications serve to exemplify this entry: *Pneuma*, the journal of the Society for Pentecostal Studies, began in 1979 with the goal of providing "a major medium for the international discussion of scholarly issues related to Pentecostal and Charismatic stud-

---

[6] One might think here of the linguistic turn, or the turn to the practices of ordinary believers in recent constructive theological work.

[7] The essays in the *Festschrift* for the biblical scholar James D. G. Dunn offer a rich overview: *The Holy Spirit and Christian Origins: Essays in Honor of James D. G. Dunn*, ed. Graham N. Stanton et al. (Grand Rapids, MI: Eerdmans, 2004).

[8] See Elizabeth A. Dreyer, *Holy Power, Holy Presence: Rediscovering Medieval Metaphors for the Holy Spirit* (New York: Paulist Press, 2007).

[9] A succinct map of such retrievals can be found in Shults and Hollingsworth, *The Holy Spirit*, part I.

[10] Eugene F. Rogers, *After the Spirit: A Constructive Pneumatology from Resources Outside the Modern West* (London: SCM Press, 2006).

ies." The spring 2002 issue of this journal, for example, was devoted to the shape of an "ecumenical pneumatology," with articles about Pentecostal and Eastern Orthodox understandings of the Holy Spirit, as well as the pneumatological thinking of major theologians, e.g., Luther and Wesley. Coming from the other side of the long-standing fence between theological scholarship and Pentecostal voices is a collection of scholarly essays edited by Michael Welker, *The Work of the Spirit: Pneumatology and Pentecostalism*.[11] This book contains a section titled "The Spirit in Pentecostal Theology" and essays by both Pentecostal and charismatic scholars as well as scholars of pentecostalism. Both the journal and this collection of essays bridge the divide between Pentecostal voices and theological scholarship. So of course does the present volume, for the field of liturgical studies; more on this below.

A third site of the pneumatological turn in theology is represented by a host of new constructive proposals in light of contemporary planetary issues. These constructive proposals include feminist[12] and liberationist work,[13] the new ecological Spirit-attentiveness,[14] and interfaith and global concerns.[15] The present introduction obviously

---

[11] Michael Welker, ed., *The Work of the Spirit: Pneumatology and Pentecostalism* (Grand Rapids, MI: Eerdmans, 2006).

[12] Elizabeth A. Johnson, *Women, Earth, and Creator Spirit* (New York: Paulist Press, 1993); Rebecca Button Prichard, *Sensing the Spirit: The Holy Spirit in Feminist Perspective* (St. Louis, MO: Chalice Press, 1999); Nancy M. Victorin-Vangerud, *The Raging Hearth: Spirit in the Household of God* (St. Louis, MO: Chalice Press, 2000).

[13] José Comblin, *The Holy Spirit and Liberation*, trans. Paul Burns (Maryknoll, NY: Orbis Books, 1989), and, more recently, Joerg Rieger, "Resistance Spirit: The Holy Spirit and Empire," in *The Lord and Giver of Life: Perspectives on Constructive Pneumatology*, ed. David H. Jensen (Louisville: Westminster John Knox Press, 2008), 129–46.

[14] Mark I. Wallace, *Fragments of the Spirit: Nature, Violence, and the Renewal of Creation* (New York: Continuum, 1996); Denis Edwards, *Breath of Life: A Theology of the Creator Spirit* (Maryknoll, NY: Orbis Books, 2004); Sigurd Bergmann, *Creation Set Free: The Spirit as Liberator of Nature*, trans. Douglas Stott (Grand Rapids, MI: Eerdmans, 2005); Laurel Kearns and Catherine Keller, eds., *Ecospirit: Religion, Philosophy, and the Earth* (New York: Fordham University Press, 2007).

[15] Suffice it here to name but two recent contributions in this burgeoning field: Roger Haight, "Holy Spirit and the Religions," and Amos Yong, "Guests, Hosts, and the Holy Ghost: Pneumatological Theology and Christian Practices

Teresa Berger, with Bryan D. Spinks

is not the place for an in-depth look at these contemporary pneumatological proposals.[16] These proposals are easily accessible in the startling number of collections on pneumatology published since the turn of the century. Thus, 2001 saw the publication of both *Advents of the Spirit: An Introduction to the Current Study of Pneumatology* and *Knowing the Triune God: The Work of the Spirit in the Practices of the Church*.[17] A volume with papers from the College Theology Society appeared in 2004, titled *The Spirit in the Church and the World*.[18] *The Work of the Spirit: Pneumatology and Pentecostalism* (see note 11) was published in 2006. In 2008, the year of the Yale ISM conference on "The Spirit in Worship—Worship in the Spirit," a multi-authored volume appeared, *The Lord and Giver of Life: Perspectives on Constructive Pneumatology*, as well a brief introduction to *The Holy Spirit*, in the series "Guides to Theology."[19] Most recently, a volume on classical and contemporary texts on pneumatology has been published by Eugene Rogers.[20] These collections are only a small part of the many English-language publications on pneumatology. Clearly, we are witnessing a "dramatic growth of attention to the Holy Spirit in recent Christian theology."[21] Sadly, in this theological turn to pneumatology, the study of worship as a site of the Spirit's presence and work remains, for the most part, marginal.[22]

---

in a World of Many Faiths," both in *Lord and Giver of Life: Perspectives on Constructive Pneumatology*, ed. David H. Jensen (Louisville: Westminster John Knox Press, 2008), 55–70 and 71–86.

[16] A wide-ranging, annotated bibliography is available in Shults and Hollingsworth, *The Holy Spirit*, 99–150.

[17] Bradford E. Hinze and D. Lyle Dabney, eds., *Advents of the Spirit: An Introduction to the Current Study of Pneumatology*, Marquette Studies in Theology 30 (Milwaukee: Marquette University Press, 2001); James J. Buckley and David S. Yeago, eds., *Knowing the Triune God: The Work of the Spirit in the Practices of the Church* (Grand Rapids, MI: Eerdmans, 2001).

[18] Bradford E. Hinze, ed., *The Spirit in the Church and the World* (Maryknoll, NY: Orbis Books, 2004).

[19] Jensen, ed., *The Lord and Giver of Life* (n. 15); Shults and Hollingsworth, *The Holy Spirit* (n. 2).

[20] Eugene F. Rogers, Jr., ed., *The Holy Spirit: Classic and Contemporary Readings* (Oxford: Wiley-Blackwell, 2009).

[21] Shults and Hollingsworth, *The Holy Spirit*, 1.

[22] An exception is Susan K. Wood's essay on "The Liturgy," in Buckley and Yeago, *Knowing the Triune God*, 95–118.

THE HOLY SPIRIT IN ECUMENICAL CONVERSATIONS AND CONVERGENCES

The vibrant theological interest in pneumatology has also shaped ecumenical conversations and insights.[23] It is worth remembering here that the Decree on Ecumenism of the Second Vatican Council, *Unitatis Redintegratio*, saw the Holy Spirit at work in the ecumenical movement, describing it as "the movement, fostered by the grace of the Holy Spirit, for the restoration of unity among all Christians."[24] In another key document of the Second Vatican Council, *Lumen Gentium*, the Holy Spirit is understood as vivifying the church with a variety of gifts and charisms, thus enabling the church to recognize authentic Christian values in other ecclesial communities as fruits of the same Spirit.

An example of a bilateral ecumenical dialogue with a particular focus on pneumatology is the 1981 Methodist/Roman Catholic document, *Towards an Agreed Statement on the Holy Spirit*. The statement notes that the doctrine of the Holy Spirit was never a point of division between the two churches; pneumatology was being explored now as a way of encouraging discernment of the workings of the Spirit in the church today.[25] Except for this particular document, most of the bilateral ecumenical conversations have discussed pneumatology only in passing, and most obviously within the context of trinitarian concerns. The 2006 Anglican/Orthodox Dialogue on *The Church of the Triune God* is a case in point.[26] Ecumenical conversations with Eastern Orthodox

---

[23] Important studies on pneumatology in an ecumenical context include Veli-Matti Kärkkäinen, *Pneumatology: The Holy Spirit in Ecumenical, International, and Contextual Perspective* (Grand Rapids, MI: Baker Academic, 2002); D. Donnelly, A. Denaux, and J. Famerée, eds., *The Holy Spirit, the Church, and Christian Unity: Proceedings of the Consultation Held at the Monastery of Bose, Italy, 14–20 October 2002*, Bibliotheca Ephemeridum theologicarum Lovaniensium 181 (Dudley, MA: Uitgeverij Peeters, 2005); and Kirsteen Kim, *The Holy Spirit in the World: A Global Conversation* (Maryknoll, NY: Orbis Books, 2007).

[24] *Unitatis Redintegratio*, no. 1; the English translation used here is that of the Vatican website: http://www.vatican.va/archive/hist_councils/ii_vatican_council/documents (accessed February 20, 2009).

[25] Harding Meyer and Lukas Vischer, eds., *Growth in Agreement* (New York: Paulist Press, 1984) 1:367ff.

[26] International Commission for Anglican-Orthodox Theological Dialogue, *The Church of the Triune God: The Cyprus Agreed Statement* (London: Anglican Communion Office, 2006), sec. 2, 25–38.

Teresa Berger, with Bryan D. Spinks

Churches have tended to concentrate on the problem of the *filioque*, for example, the Orthodox/Old Catholic and the Orthodox/Reformed dialogues. The Orthodox/Roman Catholic dialogue sought to push beyond the problems posed by the *filioque* and identify shared pneumatological convictions: "we can already say together that this Spirit, which proceeds from the Father (John 15,26) as the sole source in the Trinity and which has become the Spirit of our sonship (Rom 8,15) since he is also the Spirit of the Son (Gal 4,6) is communicated to us particularly in the eucharist by this Son upon whom he reposes in time and in eternity (John 1,32)."[27] On the whole, bilateral conversations have tended to concentrate on the relationship of the work of the Spirit and the work of Christ, the Spirit and renewal of life, the Spirit in the sacraments, and the church and ministry.

In multilateral ecumenical conversations, especially as represented by the World Council of Churches, the Holy Spirit has also been the subject of discussion in relation to broader, or indeed other, concerns. Perhaps the most celebrated document (with practical liturgical implications!) was the 1982 text of the Faith and Order Commission, *Baptism, Eucharist and Ministry*. Pneumatological themes are present in relation to sacraments and to ministry, based on a pneumatological understanding of the church. Baptism is said to include the gift of the Spirit, which "nurtures the life of faith in [the believers'] hearts until the final deliverance when they will enter into its full possession, to the praise of the glory of God."[28] Although Christians might differ on their understanding as to where in the rite the sign of the gift of the Spirit is to be found—oil, hand-laying, or the water rite—all agree that baptism is in water and the Holy Spirit. In the Eucharist, the Spirit is said to make present the crucified and risen Christ; the Spirit is the immeasurable strength of love that makes the Eucharist possible and continues to make it effective. The church thus lives through the liberating and renewing power of the Holy Spirit, who bestows on the community diverse and complementary gifts or charisms; those ordained to ministry are appointed through the invocation of the Spirit and the laying on of hands.[29]

---

[27] Jeffrey Gros, Harding Meyer, and William G. Rusch, eds. *Growth in Agreement* (Grand Rapids, MI: Eerdmans, 2000) 2:369.

[28] *Baptism, Eucharist and Ministry* (Geneva: World Council of Churches, 1982), Baptism II.C.5.

[29] *Baptism, Eucharist and Ministry*, Ministry I.3, 5 and II.7.b.

More recent ecumenical discussions have been enriched by the participation of charismatic Pentecostals alongside the older "classical" Pentecostals, and by churches from the global South. At Canberra 1991, where for the first time in an assembly of the World Council of Churches pneumatology was the overarching theme ("Come, Holy Spirit, renew the whole creation"), this enrichment also created contestation. The opening presentation by Parthenios, Orthodox Patriarch of Alexandria and All Africa, treated the Holy Spirit within the mystery of the Trinity. Patriarch Parthenios noted that one of the signs of the Spirit's workings is the search for Christian unity. His presentation has been described by Mary Tanner as a "beautiful, profound meditation on the theme from deep within the Tradition of the Church."[30] The Patriarch's talk was followed by a dramatic presentation by Professor Chung Hyun Kyung, a feminist theologian from Korea; dressed in the attire of a Korean shaman she led an exorcist's dance, and invoked the Holy Spirit together with a number of other spirits—*Han*-ridden spirits that she understood as agents of the Holy Spirit. Both Orthodox and Evangelicals expressed consternation, regarding this approach as a lack of proper discernment of the Spirit in human movements. Instead they stressed the importance of guarding against a substitution of the *Zeitgeist* or other contemporary spirits *en vogue* for the Holy Spirit. Although the assembly at Canberra revealed considerable disunity, it also broadened the conversation partners by adding East Asian as well as charismatic voices to the ecumenical dialogue. When the Thirteenth Conference on World Mission and Evangelism of the World Council of Churches met in Athens in 2005, the theme was "Come, Holy Spirit, Heal and Reconcile." By that meeting a theology of embrace had seemed to replace the contestations of the Canberra assembly. Not least of the reasons for such a shift was the growing movement of interfaith conversations. In these conversations not only has pneumatology emerged as a key theological resource for the Christian conversation partners, but pneumatological differences between Christian communities have also faded into the background in light of a much wider set of faith traditions.

SPIRIT-ATTENTIVENESS IN LITURGICAL LIFE

Given both the pneumatological turn in theology and the ecumenical convergences around the doctrine of the Holy Spirit, it comes

---

[30] Mary Tanner, "Pneumatology in Multilateral Settings," in *The Holy Spirit*, ed. Donnelly et al. (n. 23), 225–43, 236.

Teresa Berger, with Bryan D. Spinks

as no surprise that there has also been a noticeable turn to Spirit-attentiveness in worship. Such Spirit-attentiveness is evident not only in the worship practices of Pentecostal and charismatic communities, which have spread around the globe, but also in a renewed emphasis on invocations and prayers to the Holy Spirit in older ecclesial communities. The introduction of an epiclesis proper into eucharistic and baptismal liturgies in some churches is a case in point.[31] There are, moreover, liturgical materials that easily travel across denominational lines. Among these are the many new hymns to or about the Holy Spirit. "She Comes Sailing on the Wind," by Gordon Light of the Anglican Church of Canada, is one example. This song, which maps the journey of the Holy Spirit from creation to the present, was first published in Canada in 1987 and then widely translated; it is now sung around the globe. Other Spirit-songs have similar appeal, among them "Enemy of Apathy" by John Bell of Iona, "Spirit, I Have Heard You Calling" by Thew Elliot, and "Spirit of Love" by Shirley Erena Murray.[32]

The Spirit also seems to be the face of the Divine Presence most readily visible in the new rituals that have emerged, be they gender-attentive, eco-sensitive, or openly interfaith. Such new rituals often make authorizing appeals to the Spirit as the One who opens space for the new, widens, challenges, and transforms.

Lastly, the Spirit broods in cyberspace. One only has to visit websites such as *Holy Spirit Interactive*, or watch the chants of *"Veni Creator Spiritus"* posted on YouTube, or ponder online the reserved sacrament in the chapel of the Holy Spirit Adoration Sisters[33] to witness the intricate interplay between pneumatology and the internet. At the far end of that interplay stands the Church of Fools, "the world's first

[31] For more on this, see Paul Bradshaw's and Maxwell Johnson's papers in this volume.

[32] Our thanks to Patrick Evans, Director of Chapel Music at Marquand Chapel, Yale Divinity School, for pointers to these songs.

[33] The cloistered community of Holy Spirit Adoration Sisters in Philadelphia had a live webcam focused at the reserved sacrament in the chapel for perpetual adoration. This has, however, now been replaced with (much less direct and compelling) photos in a virtual tour; see "Virtual Tour," Holy Spirit Adoration Sisters, http://www.adorationsisters.org/stories.html (accessed January 23, 2009).

3D online church," as its website claims.[34] This online church allows one to worship interactively by choosing an avatar to enter the online sanctuary, sit or kneel in a pew, key in prayers, and make the sign of the cross. Who would want to argue that the Spirit can *not* be present there? Cyberspace in fact seems to be a prime site for indications of the broader cultural interest in all things "spiritual" and the attendant "implosion of the secular," as Graham Ward has termed it. Cyberspace is also the site where popular agency and religious authorship are visible as never before; appeals to the movement of the Holy Spirit never seem absent in such popular claims to religious authority.

So much for a look at the contemporary renewed interest in the Holy Spirit. This renewed interest forms the backdrop to the present volume. We now turn to the volume's more specific focus, namely, on the Spirit in worship.

THE SPIRIT AND THE FIELD OF LITURGICAL STUDIES

Given the broad-based contemporary interest in the Holy Spirit, what about the field of liturgical studies? Has this field remained undisturbed by the pneumatological turn? Is there a revival of interest in the Holy Spirit among scholars of liturgy? In many ways, *The Spirit in Worship—Worship in the Spirit* can be read as an answer precisely to these questions. The volume demonstrates that the field of liturgical studies is not untouched by the pneumatological turn, that there is a renewed interest in the Holy Spirit among scholars of liturgy, and that this interest is vibrantly interdisciplinary. That said, it is instructive to set the present volume in its context within the field of liturgical studies as such.

A convenient starting point is provided by the Constitution on the Sacred Liturgy of Vatican II and its claim that it was indeed the Holy Spirit who moved in the twentieth-century liturgical movement: "Zeal for the promotion and restoration of the liturgy is rightly held to be a sign of the providential dispositions of God in our time, as a movement of the Holy Spirit in His Church" (SC 43).[35] Six years after *Sacrosanc-*

[34] Church of Fools, http://churchoffools.com (accessed January 22, 2009). Our thanks to Blake A. Scalet, a Yale Divinity School student, for pointers to this website, and to Peter Berger, for help with making the avatar pray.

[35] The English translation used here is that of the Vatican website: http://www.vatican.va/archive/hist_councils/ii_vatican_council/documents (accessed February 20, 2009).

Teresa Berger, with Bryan D. Spinks

tum Concilium, some of the best-known liturgical scholars of the time gathered at the Orthodox Institute of Saint-Serge in Paris for the annual "Week of Liturgical Studies." The theme was "The Holy Spirit in the Liturgy." The conference, both in terms of participation and scholarly topics, was broadly ecumenical—in the traditional sense of the 1960s, that is. Thus, we find presentations on the Syrian, Byzantine, Armenian, Roman Catholic, Lutheran, and Anglican traditions.[36] Pentecostal communities and presenters from the Global South were not part of the conversation; neither were Jewish voices; and all presenters were men. Their studies focused on key public rites and on detailed analyses of liturgical texts. Congregational hymnody was given little attention, popular piety was of no interest, and cyberspace did not yet exist.

Forty years later, the present volume reflects a somewhat different engagement with the same theme, the Holy Spirit in worship.[37] Most noticeably, there has been a broadening of conversation partners and a shift in sites of inquiry. Both these changes are related to wider theological developments, as mapped above. In terms of conversation partners, the scholarly conference on which this volume builds had a particular focus on one lacuna, the divide between scholarly liturgical work on pneumatology on the one hand, and the voices of Pentecostal and charismatic communities on the other hand. This divide had become particularly troubling given the fact that Pentecostal and charismatic movements now encompass roughly one-fourth of the two billion Christians worldwide. Liturgical scholarship, as a field of inquiry that works both theologically and also with an eye to worship as an embodied practice of faith, is uniquely positioned to build bridges here. This is precisely where the conference on "The Spirit in Worship—Worship in the Spirit" came in. Organized by the Yale Institute of Sacred Music and its Program in Liturgical Studies, the conference took place February 21–24, 2008, at Sterling Divinity Quadrangle in New Haven, Connecticut. The conference's main focus

---

[36] The papers from the conference were published as: *Le Saint-Esprit dans la liturgie: Conférences Saint-Serge*, BELS 8 (Rome: Edizioni Liturgiche, 1977).

[37] This is not to suggest that the thirty-five years between the conferences at Saint-Serge and at the Yale Institute of Sacred Music saw no publications on liturgy and pneumatology; see, most notably, *Spiritus spiritalia nobis dona potenter infundit: A proposito di tematiche liturgico-pneumatologiche: Studi in onore di Achille M. Triacca*, ed. Ephrem Carr, Studia Anselmiana 139, Analecta Liturgica 25 (Rome: Pontificio Ateneo S. Anselmo, 2005).

was the divide between liturgical traditions of the historic churches on the one hand, and the worship of the newer Pentecostal, charismatic, and Spirit-focused communities on the other. Yet other divides also were bridged at this conference. Both scholars and practitioners, from as far away as Singapore, Sydney, and South Africa, representing a great many traditions and voices, came together to explore the place and understanding of the Holy Spirit in worship. The present volume gathers the papers from this conference, with the addition of one paper from a speaker at the Liturgy Symposium at Yale in the same year, Matthew Myer Boulton, who seemed to the editors to make a significant contribution to *The Spirit in Worship—Worship in the Spirit*.

The volume is divided into three major sections: foundations, historic trajectories, and newer ecclesial movements. The first section, foundations, presents five essays that lay the biblical, historical, and theological groundwork for the essays that follow. The section opens with a study by the New Testament scholar (now bishop of Durham, England) N. T. Wright, who maps the New Testament intersections between worship and Spirit. Rabbi Ruth Langer, a professor of Jewish studies, explores the rabbinic understandings of how, after the destruction of the Temple, God's immanent presence is seen to continue in worship, on the Temple Mount, in the gathered community, and in the community's place of gathering. Simon Chan, a systematic theologian and ordained Pentecostal minister from Singapore, explores the interrelationship between pneumatology and ecclesiology, with a special focus on how worship is to be understood as the work of the Spirit. Matthew Myer Boulton, a Reformed theologian and professor of ministry studies at Harvard, develops a biblically grounded Barthian-shaped understanding of the role of the Holy Spirit as "adversary" as well as enabler of liturgy. Finally, the historian of liturgy Paul Bradshaw sketches the rediscovery of the Holy Spirit in twentieth-century eucharistic rites, specifically through the restoration of a form of epiclesis in a number of Western churches.

The second section of the volume presents six different ecclesial traditions and their specific understandings of the liturgical work of the Holy Spirit. The section opens with an essay by Simon Jones, chaplain and research fellow at the University of Oxford, who highlights the Syrian baptismal tradition and identifies the incarnational image of the womb as the principal symbolic focus for understanding the activity of the Holy Spirit in baptism. Peter Galadza, a priest of the Ukrainian Greco-Catholic Church who teaches liturgy at Saint Paul University,

Teresa Berger, with Bryan D. Spinks

Ottawa, Canada, writes about the Holy Spirit in Eastern Orthodox Worship, an ecclesial tradition frequently described as deeply
Spirit-attentive. Galadza tests this claim by exploring key aspects of
Byzantine liturgy, both historically and from the perspective of contemporary theology and practice. In the following essay, Teresa Berger,
professor of liturgical studies at Yale, challenges the commonly held
notion of her own Roman Catholic tradition as Spirit-forgetful; she
argues that by shifting what counts as evidence for the Spirit's always-
elusive presence a quite different image of the Catholic liturgical tradition emerges. Maxwell Johnson, a Lutheran liturgical scholar from
Notre Dame, highlights the pneumatology of the Lutheran tradition,
focusing on the recovery of a Spirit-epiclesis in modern baptismal and
eucharistic liturgies. The Ethiopian Orthodox Tradition is the subject
of Habtemichael Kidane's essay, which introduces readers to the little-
known liturgical writings on the Holy Spirit that the Ethiopian Church
has produced. Finally, Melva Wilson Costen, a Presbyterian minister
and professor of worship, sketches African American worship traditions and their multifaceted engagement with the Holy Spirit.

A third and last section presents a look at newer ecclesial communities and movements known for their intensely Spirit-oriented worship practices. Daniel Albrecht, an Assemblies of God scholar from
California, opens this section with an essay on past and present Pentecostal understandings of worshiping in the Spirit. James Steven, from
King's College London, follows this with a study of contemporary
charismatic worship in England, with special attention to the ritual
patterning in the worshiping assembly. Jonathan Draper from the
University of KwaZulu-Natal analyzes the worship practices of some
African Independent Churches, drawing on both historical and field
data; he calls into question attempts to homogenize these worship
practices with more traditional Pentecostalism, arguing instead that
these are creative new indigenous expressions of Christian faith. Finally, Darlene Zschech, the songwriter and worship leader at Hillsong
Church in Sydney, Australia, introduces readers to her understanding
of the role of the Holy Spirit in worship, providing both a look at her
own church's liturgical practices and also a glimpse at forms of liturgical reasoning embedded in these practices.

At the end of these diverse essays, and indeed in light of them,
new questions emerge—which is of course precisely what a vibrant
scholarly conversation should lead to. Among these questions two sets
deserve to be highlighted here, by way of a conclusion. The first set of

questions concerns the interpretive lenses liturgical scholars use: How do we discern the Spirit's liturgical presence *in actu*? What counts as evidence for her presence? What is occluded when the primary focus for a liturgical pneumatology is the presence of an epiclesis, or—to invoke a quite different example—speaking in tongues? Could there be absences that indicate the presence of the Spirit just as powerfully as the epiclesis or the gift of speaking in tongues? How would one know? And, given that the essays in this volume show how quite different traditions (and the liturgical scholars who study them) discern the Spirit's presence in worship, what would constitute a shared core inventory of liturgical witnesses for the Spirit's movement? A second, related set of questions arises regarding the different forms of liturgical reasoning visible in the present volume. Can these distinct and particular forms of liturgical reasoning be brought into actual conversation with each other, that is, truly engage each other, beyond being set side by side? The Yale ISM conference on "The Spirit in Worship—Worship in the Spirit" obviously achieved this *in actu*, especially in the discussions after each paper, in a roundtable discussion among presenters, and in the many conversations outside the individual sessions. Intriguing trajectories and surprising convergences emerged, for example, in challenges to narrowly scholarly-textual approaches to pneumatology that occlude the embodied, participatory knowledge of lived liturgy. However, scholarly conferences and the scholarly volumes they generate by definition will not be the best sites for exploring such challenges more deeply. We can only hope that the present volume will do its share in furthering such explorations.

It remains for us to thank a number of people at the Yale Institute of Sacred Music and at Yale Divinity School without whose unfailing support, hard work, and good spirit neither the 2008 Conference on "The Spirit in Worship—Worship in the Spirit" nor this editorial project would have been possible:

Martin Jean, the Director of the Yale Institute of Sacred Music, for generously hosting the 2008 Conference and for enthusiastically supporting the publication of its papers.

Melissa Maier, ISM Manager of External Relations and Publications, for her care in overseeing the organization of the 2008 conference (especially for "greening" the event) and for managing the publication of *The Spirit in Worship—Worship in the Spirit*. Melissa was ably assisted in all of these tasks by Albert Agbayani.

Teresa Berger, with Bryan D. Spinks

John Leinenweber, ISM Research Assistant, for untiring work in editing, reediting, proofreading, and indexing this volume; and Derek Greten-Harrison, formerly on staff at ISM, for valuable assistance.

Mary K. Farag, a 2009 graduate of Yale Divinity School's MAR in liturgics for superb research assistance throughout.

Last but not least, we are grateful to the dedicated, vibrant, wonderful ISM staff, without whose daily labors the Institute's manifold activities could not flourish: Jacqueline Campoli, Laura Chilton, Andrea Hart, Trisha Radil, and Sachin Ramabhadran.

Finally, it has been a pleasure to work with the editors and the entire staff at Liturgical Press, especially Hans Christoffersen, Peter Dwyer, Mary Stommes, and Colleen Stiller.

We dedicate this volume to the memory of a colleague, friend, and scholar of liturgy who was present at the 2008 ISM conference on "The Spirit in Worship—Worship in the Spirit" but died before this volume went to press, Hieromonk Gregory Woolfenden (1947–2008). We wish to honor Father Gregory's life and work by dedicating this volume to him. Memory eternal.

Part 1

Foundations

N. T. Wright

1. Worship and the Spirit in the New Testament

At first sight, it appears strange that those who have written about the Holy Spirit in the New Testament have not usually given much attention to worship, and those who have written about worship in the New Testament have not usually given much attention to the Holy Spirit. Gordon Fee's massive book on the Spirit in Paul has precisely three pages on worship. Paul Bradshaw's splendid book on the origins of Christian worship doesn't have either Spirit or Holy Spirit in the index. These may be unrepresentative, but I don't think so. Even the Westminster/SCM *Dictionary of Liturgy and Worship* has no entry under Spirit or Holy Spirit. You might have thought it would at least advise us to look under "Pentecost" instead, but it doesn't.[1]

Yet it may not be so strange; or, perhaps the strangeness is located in the material itself. Mostly, when worship is either discussed or evidenced in the New Testament, the Spirit is not mentioned, and mostly when the Spirit is mentioned, worship is not. Obvious exceptions exist, such as 1 Corinthians 14, but when we look at the great references to worship, or the great examples of worship such as the hymns in Revelation 4 and 5, or the poems in Philippians 2 or Colossians 1, the Spirit seems conspicuously absent. Perhaps, after all, the apparent scholarly lacuna reflects, even if accidentally, a gap in the early Christian writings themselves.

A further word about the subject matter. In both cases—"worship" and "Spirit"—there is an implied double focus. As I hinted a moment

---

[1] Gordon D. Fee, *God's Empowering Presence: The Holy Spirit in the Letters of Paul* (Peabody, MA: Hendriksson, 1994); Paul F. Bradshaw, *The Search for the Origins of Christian Worship: Sources and Methods for the Study of Early Liturgy*, 2d ed. (New York: Oxford University Press, 2002 [1992]); *The New Westminster Dictionary of Liturgy and Worship*, ed. Paul Bradshaw (Louisville: Westminster John Knox Press, 2002). Similar remarks could be made about the substantial *Festschrift* for James D. G. Dunn: *The Holy Spirit and Christian Origins*, ed. G. N. Stanton et al. (Grand Rapids, MI: Eerdmans, 2004).

ago, there is a difference between talking about worship and actually doing it, or at least quoting material used in worship. Thus Paul in Romans 1:18-23 refers to the worship that humans ought to be offering to God for his greatness, power, and divinity, but that in fact they refuse. There is no suggestion—at least, I've never met one—that he is there quoting an actual liturgical formula. At the end of Romans 11, when he is praising God for the depth of his wisdom and mercy, Paul is worshiping, whether or not he is using or adapting formulae known from elsewhere. In between these two passages we find those christological poems or hymns that form part of the argument of his letters but that many scholars have assumed were being quoted from the worship of the church. I will be referring to all three of these categories, but it is worth being clear that they are subtly different kinds of things. (All of them, of course, are now embedded in the documents, in Paul's case the letters, that provide a different setting, context, and genre.)

So it is, too, with the Spirit. Many passages talk about the Spirit and the Spirit's work and effects. Depending on your view of inspiration, you may want to say that the whole New Testament is the result of the Spirit's work. Once you step back from individual passages and construct a larger theology of worship, you will undoubtedly want to say that the Spirit is at work in the worship of the church even when that fact isn't mentioned. Again and again the worship offered in the book of Revelation appears binitarian, praising God and the Lamb; only gradually do we understand what becomes clear near the very end, that the Spirit is at work within the church, enabling the worshiping church to be the worshiping church. "The Spirit and the Bride say, 'Come'"; the Spirit enables the Bride to *be* the Bride (Rev 22:17). Once we recognize these dual and indeed multiple foci, our subject matter may appear wider than at first sight.

I don't wish to widen the subject matter too far, however. A good deal written about early Christian worship assumes almost at once that "worship" really means "liturgy," and that liturgy can quite quickly be focused on sacramental liturgy and the like. Now that is hugely important, though again it is interesting how, for example with the New Testament references to the Eucharist, the Spirit is conspicuously absent. (How careless of Paul, we are inclined to think! How much easier he could have made it for himself and for us if only he'd added the pneumatological dimension to 1 Corinthians 10 and 11! There is always John 6, of course, but that brings its own problems . . .) I want to focus, rather, on the fact and act of worship *in itself*, that is, on the

N. T. Wright

4

human activity of giving God the glory, of praising the Creator for his goodness and power, his judgments and his mercy past, present, and future. I want to try to understand how, in the mind of the New Testament writers at least, the Spirit was supposed to be involved in this activity, and where this understanding belonged on the larger map of early Christian theology and practice.

That understanding, it seems to me, was not substantially advanced by the scholarly fad for discovering allusions to, or echoes of, primitive Christian worship in a good many texts of the New Testament. Without prejudice to the question of whether Philippians 2:6-11 was written for church use before Paul incorporated it into his letter as we now have it, labeling such a passage "worship" or "liturgy" is of little help exegetically, either in understanding what the passage itself is saying, or in grasping how it works rhetorically and theologically within the larger unit of the letter itself. The passion for discovering liturgy—what the late, great Charlie Moule characterized as "our professors saying 'worship, worship' where there is no worship"—belongs, strictly speaking, not to the exegetical task but to the attempt to recover, behind the text, something called "early Christian experience" and the like.[2] Not that this is not a proper historical question in itself. I merely think it is a much more uncertain quest than the previous generation of scholars supposed. In particular, the attempt to discover fragments of worship, and signs of the Spirit's inspiration, in the pre-Synoptic tradition, seems to me very tenuous. In fact, both the motivation for such a search and the method by which it worked seem to me flawed beyond repair. I have no doubt that the stories of Jesus were told and retold within the life of the early church. To work back from that and suggest that they were shaped by *worship* as such, however, let alone generated in the course of Spirit-inspired prophecy within such worship, seems to me pure assertion, and I will not be going in that direction in what follows.

Rather, I want to situate my study within the context of the much more historically secure worshiping life of first-century Judaism. This is the subject of another chapter in the present work, so I needn't say much, except to note that of course this worship is focused centrally

[2] C. F. D. Moule, *The Birth of the New Testament*, 3d ed. (San Francisco: Harper & Row, 1982 [1962]), 19. The whole chapter ("The Church at Worship") is instructive, though again there is almost nothing about the Spirit.

Worship and the Spirit in the New Testament

on the Temple, with the prayers, festivals, and particularly the sacrificial cult all prominent. Away from the Temple, synagogue worship would include, centrally, the reading of Torah, the singing of Psalms, and again the prayers, notably the *Shema* and the ʿamidah. And, so as not to keep you in suspense, my somewhat unoriginal proposal is that when we look at the Spirit and worship in the New Testament we find that the early Christians believed that their Spirit-led worship was the new-covenantal form of that synagogue and Temple worship, worshiping the same creator God but filling that worship with new content relating specifically to Jesus crucified and risen—and believing (as, interestingly, did the community at Qumran) that the promised Holy Spirit was leading them in that worship.

With that it is high time to turn to some particular texts. I begin, obvious at one level though not at another, with the book of Acts.

EXEGESIS

Acts

The grand scene of Pentecost in Acts 2, prepared for in the previous chapter with the promise of Jesus, which itself looks back to the words of John the Baptist near the start of the gospel narrative, has been studied so often in connection with the Pentecostal movement and its associated phenomena that we may have missed, or at least sidelined, two things about it that seem to me of great importance.[3]

The first is that this chapter forms something of a parallel, in Acts, to the baptism of Jesus in the gospel, and thus demands to be understood not simply as a fascinating and initiatory incident in the very early life of the church, but as the story that must be held in mind as a kind of running heading for all that is to follow. Just as Jesus' baptism and anointing with the Spirit in Luke 3 is to be understood as standing behind and explaining everything else, from his "messianic" proclamation in Luke 4 to his messianic death and resurrection, so the coming of the Spirit in Acts 2 is to be understood as standing behind and explaining everything else that the church then does, particularly its worship, its mission, and its bold stand in obeying God rather than human authorities. Thus, when Luke later tells us that the Christians gathered together were all filled with the Spirit and spoke God's word with boldness (4:31), this should be understood not as a fresh and mo-

---

[3] Acts 2:1-41; 1:5, with Luke 3:16 and parallels.

N. T. Wright

mentary filling, repeating Pentecost, as it were, on a strictly temporary basis, but as a fresh manifestation of what had been the case all along since Pentecost itself. The church from Acts 2 onward is the Spirit-led church, with worship as an integral part of its proper life.

The second point about Acts 2 is that the sudden filling of the house with the wind and fire is, I suggest, described in such a way as to evoke the various manifestations of the creator God in the Old Testament, not least the filling of the Tabernacle or Temple with God's presence at the end of Exodus, at Solomon's dedication, and at Isaiah's moment of vision and call.[4] The church is thereby constituted as, among other things, the counter-Temple movement. This becomes abundantly clear in the chapters that follow, not just in Stephen's speech, which draws this theme out explicitly, but in the chapters that build up to it, in which the Christians more or less take over Solomon's porch, close enough in to be a threat and far enough out to be an alternative (Acts 5:12f.). There is of course considerable ambiguity and tension inherent in all this, because they still worship in the Temple proper (presumably, though Luke does not say so, offering animal sacrifices). Their characteristic common life is focused, not there, however, but in their various homes, where they devote themselves to the apostles' teaching and fellowship, the breaking of bread, and the prayers (Acts 2:42-47). Here we have the root, I suggest, of that developed Temple-ecclesiology that we will see elsewhere. Because the living God had come to live and work personally and powerfully in their lives and in their midst, the early Christians saw themselves as the alternative Temple, and though it took time for this to be worked out in all its implications, it was present from the very start. This in turn explains the constant counter-Temple theme, whether the Temple in question be that in Jerusalem, as in Acts 7, or those in Athens, as in Acts 17.

In this context, that of the church worshiping in the power of the Spirit, the major new advances in mission take place. Classically, this is expressed at the start of chapter 13, where during worship, prayer, and fasting the Spirit instructs the church in Antioch to set apart Barnabas and Saul for fresh work (Acts 13:2). That work consists, not least, of calling pagans to acknowledge and worship the creator God, the God of Israel. There isn't a direct, simplistic account of the Spirit leading people to worship or calling forth that worship from them. Rather,

[4] Exod 40:34–38; 1 Kgs 8:10f.; Isa 6:4.

Worship and the Spirit in the New Testament

Luke's overall narrative informs us that the Spirit inspires the worship of the church, the worship that stakes the astonishing claim to be the reality to which the Temple-worship was pointing all along, and thereby enables the church to be the missionary community.

John

With John we enter a multitextured and many-layered world in which the Temple and its worship are never far away. Jesus goes to Jerusalem not once or twice but frequently, following the pattern of regular festivals—Passover, Tabernacles, Dedication, Passover again. Jesus, John has told us early on, is the one who has the Spirit and gives it to others (1:33). The regular going up to Jerusalem is the rhythm of worship within the Jewish calendar that Jesus fills, fulfills, and transcends, as he does the six water jars in chapter 2, at which point John gives us a nudge in relation to the Jewish purification customs, implying again that these too are fulfilled and transcended (2:6).

Within that overall context of Jesus' transcending the Jewish life of worship we encounter one of the most spectacular moments of Johannine pneumatology. In chapter 7 Jesus goes to Jerusalem for the feast of Tabernacles, during which water was poured out to symbolize God's provision of water from the rock in the wilderness (the Exodus-motifs are seldom far away from Jewish, or indeed early Christian, worship). Then, on the last and great day of the feast, Jesus takes this central act of worship and transforms it around himself. "Let anyone who is thirsty come to me, and let the one who believes in me drink. As the scripture has said, 'Out of the believer's heart shall flow rivers of living water'" (John 7:37-38).[5] He was speaking about the Spirit, explains John, which those who believed in him would receive; "for as yet there was no Spirit (*oupō gar ēn pneuma*), because Jesus was not yet glorified" (John 7:39). Jesus is himself the source of the water—both the water in the wilderness and also, with a clear allusion, the water promised in Isaiah 55:1. Jesus is the real focal point of the festival, inviting people to "come to him and drink," to give to him the place that YHWH himself would normally take in their worship. The double invitation to "come" and "believe" echoes the previous chapter, where Jesus declared that "whoever comes to me will never be hungry, and whoever believes in me will never be thirsty" (6:35); but this time the

---

[5] Unless otherwise noted, passages from Scripture follow the New Revised Standard Version.

N. T. Wright

result of "coming" and "believing" and "drinking" is not the mere quenching of thirst, important though that is, but the transformation of the believer not only into a receptacle for the living water, as in John 4:10-15 and 6:35, but to a conduit or channel: "out of the believer's heart" (not merely into it) "will flow rivers of living water." Here, offering Jesus the worship that transcends the dramatic retelling of the Exodus story in praise of YHWH *results in* the gift of the Spirit. This happens, John says, not at once, but after Jesus is "glorified," i.e., lifted up on the cross. John 20:19-22 answers to this as the risen Jesus breathes the Spirit onto his rejoicing followers, not for their own sake but to equip them for their otherwise impossible task: "as the Father has sent me, so I send you." The puzzle about the biblical reference in 7:38 ("as the scripture has said") is best resolved, as I think the majority of exegetes agree, by reference to the end of Ezekiel (chap. 47), where the river of the water of life flows out of the renewed Temple to irrigate the surrounding land, making even the Dead Sea (mostly) fresh. At every point this Spirit-and-worship theology is rooted in Temple-theology.

The Johannine theology of the Spirit reaches its full height in the Farewell Discourses, where Jesus promises that by sending the Spirit he will enfold his followers within the intimate personal fellowship that he already enjoys with the Father.[6] Having declared in chapters 2 and 12 that the present Temple is redundant, Jesus constitutes those around him as the community in which the presence of the living God will be known—known by the Spirit, the Paraclete, who will be in them and with them. The so-called High Priestly prayer of chapter 17 then becomes the central act of renewed Temple worship, grounding the worship of Jesus' followers forever afterward in Jesus' own prayer, his own holy self-offering to the Father, and enfolding those followers within his own holiness and offering even as he entrusts them with his own mission. Thus, though the Spirit is not mentioned in chapter 17, this great act of worship and devotion, with Jesus praying for his followers, catches up the promises of the preceding chapters and forms the basis for John's strong, if often implicit, theology of the church's own worship, indwelt by the Paraclete. What the Temple had apparently offered—the presence of the living God and the sacrificial system by which the worshiper was renewed as a member of God's people—is now to be attained by a different route, namely the self-offering of

---

[6] John 14:15-26; 15:26-7; 16:7-11.

Jesus and his resulting gift of the Spirit. The negative verdict on the Temple, already adumbrated in chapters 2 and 12, is sealed with the declaration of the chief priests, "We have no king but the emperor!" (19:15). The positive verdict on Jesus and his followers is established with the resurrection, the gift of the Spirit, and the launching of the worldwide mission in chapters 20 and 21. Just as "the Word became flesh and *tabernacled* (*eskēnōsen en hēmin*) in our midst" (1:14, my translation), so the Spirit now tabernacles within the followers of Jesus, fulfilling all that the Temple had been within a radically new reality.

All this points back to a cryptic but powerful statement in John 4:19-26. The Samaritan woman raises with Jesus, as well she might, given the previous four hundred years of smoldering controversy, the question of the location of true worship: Samaria or Jerusalem? Jesus, while insisting that the Jews have the inside track on worship because they remain the bearers of God's promises of salvation, insists also that the question is wrongly posed. This is not because of some generalizing or Platonizing downgrading of the notion of sacred space, but because of the eschatology now inaugurated around Jesus himself. The hour is coming, and now is, when the true worshipers will worship in Spirit and in truth. (There is, of course, here the question, which we shall meet again in Paul, as to whether Spirit here has a capital or small *s*; I am content to let the question resonate for the moment.) This insistence, before the sequence of festivals has really got under way, means that the reader should already know, on Jesus' subsequent visits, that the program announced in chapter 2, of Jesus replacing the Temple with his own (dying and rising) body, will mean the fresh location of worship itself, not in one geographical spot but wherever people hear Jesus' words, believe in him, and so come to worship the Father.

What then of John 3:1-15, where the language of baptism and Spirit comes thick and fast? In some later traditions, as other chapters of this book explore, a supposedly "Johannine" view of baptism, based on John 3, has sat in uneasy tension with a supposedly "Pauline" view based on Romans 6, with John's language about birth from a mother's womb contrasting with Paul's talk of dying and rising with Christ. This is, I believe, a false antithesis. John 3 needs to be set within the larger context in which believers pass through death to new life.[7] Romans 6, as we shall see, is part of a larger unit in which the idea

---

[7] E.g., John 5:19-29; implicitly already in 3:16.

N. T. Wright

of new birth plays a leading part (8:18-27). What John 3 does give us, within the limits of our present topic, is a statement of baptism and the Spirit that can only be understood in terms of inaugurated eschatology: ordinary human birth, and within that ethnic Jewish birth into the ancient people of God, is not enough, because God's kingdom is coming as a new thing, and God is reconstituting his people around Jesus, who is himself marked out by baptism and the Spirit (John 1:33). This passage thus develops the dense statement in the prologue: the Word was in the world, but the world did not know him; he came to his own, but his own did not receive him; but to all who received him, and believed in his name, he gave the power to become God's children, who were born not by the usual human method, or from a particular ethnic descent, but from God. John 3 is not, strictly speaking within our narrow limits, about "worship" itself, but it explains the ground on which the later passages are standing.

The regular Johannine theme of "receiving Jesus" or "believing in Jesus," which runs from the prologue right through to near the end of the gospel, is ultimately to be subsumed within the larger, though less frequently stated, theme of worshiping the Father. Believing in Jesus in the present will lead to the fresh gift of the Spirit once he is glorified; from then on, all those who believe, whoever and wherever they may be, will worship the Father in Spirit and truth, and will themselves become conduits of the Spirit in an outward flow of world-renewing grace. In this larger picture, framing John himself within the Jewish scriptures he so frequently and hauntingly evokes, we see what has happened on a larger scale still. The purposes of Israel's God in creation, purposes to be taken forward through obedient humanity, purposes borne forward through Israel as representative of that humanity, are now fulfilled in the human life, death, and resurrection of Israel's Messiah, and within that through his personal embodying of the Temple as the focal point of Israel's worship, prayer, and sacrificial self-offering. Those who belong to Jesus, who believe in him and follow him, are constituted as the new or renewed humanity, worshiping the creator God through Jesus in and through the Spirit. By that same Spirit, and in consequence of that worship, they are enabled to be the bearers of new life for the world.

Paul

Taking a flying leap from John into Paul, we note the almost casual reference to Spirit-given worship in Philippians 3:3. Part of the self-definition of God's people in Christ is that they "worship God in Spirit"—as opposed, that is, to boasting in the flesh, in Jewish ancestry, and purity. The question inevitably presses as to whether Paul's primary antithesis here is the standard romantic one of "outward/inward" worship, of going through formal rituals as opposed to worshiping from the heart. If that question had been asked, Paul would of course have insisted (along with many Jewish teachers!) on the heart as opposed to the outward ritual. But along with others in the "New Perspective" reading of Paul, I have come to see his fundamental antithesis not in terms of Protestant or romantic controversies but in terms of his salvation-historical understanding of the single unfolding purpose of the one true God.[8] The God who called Israel, and gave Israel the law, the covenants, the Temple and all that therein was, had now, in paradoxical fulfillment of all that, effected in Jesus and by the Spirit a massive transformation whose primary category was the opening of membership to all people without distinction.[9] Of course Paul's flesh/spirit dichotomy carries resonances in terms of the outward/inward distinction on the one hand, and the ethical consequences on the other, but I remain convinced that his insistence on the Spirit in the antithesis of Philippians 3:3 has as its primary referent the contrast between the ethnically circumscribed worship of Israel and the free offer of the gospel of Jesus to all nations. Everything else flows from this, not least the renewal of humanity, which, long promised by Israel's prophets, had now been accomplished through the death and resurrection of Jesus and the gift of the Spirit.

With that, we move to the Corinthian correspondence, where many readers would naturally go to find Pauline material on worship and the Spirit. But before we reach the obvious passage, 1 Corinthians 14, we must note that Paul has already grounded his theology of Spirit-led worship in the two strong Temple-passages in chapters 3 and 6. In the first of these, the main stress is on unity. Appealing against faction and party spirit, Paul asks, "Do you not know that you are God's temple and that God's Spirit dwells in you? If anyone destroys God's temple, God will destroy that person. For God's temple is holy, and you are that Temple" (1 Cor 3:16-17). Or, perhaps better for *hoitines este*

---

[8] On the various "perspectives" on Paul, see, e.g., James D. G. Dunn, *The New Perspective on Paul*, rev. ed. (Grand Rapids, MI: Eerdmans, 2008 [2005]).

[9] See N. T. Wright, *Paul: Fresh Perspectives* (U.S. title: *Paul in Fresh Perspective*) (London: SPCK; Minneapolis: Fortress Press, 2006), chap. 6.

N. T. Wright

hymeis in 3:17, "and that's the sort of thing you are." The extraordinary claim Paul makes here, especially considering the muddled and fractious state of the Corinthians, is that what one might say about the single, holy Temple in Jerusalem, that it was the unique dwelling place of the one true God, is now to be said of the assemblies of those who meet to worship this God through Jesus and in the power of the Spirit. The Spirit within the church has, in other words, taken the place of the Shekinah within the Temple—a replacement all the more powerful when we consider that nowhere in second-Temple literature do we find the claim that YHWH has actually returned to take up residence on Mount Zion; actually we find strong indications that he has not.[10] Paul's claim fits into this narrative: YHWH has indeed returned, in the person of Jesus himself, but also in the person of the Spirit. Though 1 Corinthians 3 is not about worship per se, it is not too much to claim that when we have such a theology of the renewed Temple we are observing the foundation of all that might then be said about the worship that is offered within it.

This worship then comes into the open, in what we would call an "ethical" context (though that may simply show how narrow our post-Enlightenment categories really are!), in 1 Corinthians 6. Faced with the problem of sexual immorality, Paul builds up a sustained argument through verses 9-20, and as usual we would be right to see his final point as deliberately chosen to round the whole thing off with his strongest argument: " . . . do you not know that your body is the temple of the Holy Spirit within you, which you have [i.e., possess as a gift] from God, and that you are not your own? For you were bought with a price; therefore glorify God in your body" (1 Cor 6:19-20). Here, as in Romans 12:1-2, the Temple is the place of worship. If the living God has chosen to come now to dwell, not in a single house of stone and timber but in the living bodies of human beings, that constitutes a call to worship, to a worship that consists of bringing glory to God in that body, not using the body for purposes that dishonor it, that (in other words) deconstruct the very nature of what humans were made to be and do. That is, of course, in our language, a powerful ethical imperative. It is, for Paul, a matter of transferring the holy worship of Israel from the Jerusalem Temple to the bodies of individual members of the church, even in Corinth—especially in Corinth! Once more, the

[10] Hag 2:7 and Mal 3:1 promise, to the postexilic worshipers, a still-future return of the Lord whose glory ought to be filling the Temple.

Worship and the Spirit in the New Testament

13

Spirit has taken the place of the Shekhinah. Those who by baptism and faith are constituted members of the renewed worldwide people of God are called to a life of constant worship, constant sacrificial devotion to the God who is present to them and within them.

All this, I suggest, must be understood in the background as we turn to 1 Corinthians 12 and 14 (which are not to be understood without a backward look to 2:6-16, for which there is no space here). Let me say from the start that I am innately suspicious of one standard reading of this passage, one that discovers here a priority of free-form, so-called "non-liturgical" worship as the genuine Spirit-led phenomenon, as opposed to liturgical or set forms, deemed to be less fully spiritual. That reading, I fear, is the long product of the muddling up of Reformation theology with romantic and existentialist spirituality and has little to do with Paul. Of course, the passage does indeed give us a picture of the early worshiping church as enjoying considerable freedom; Paul's arguments against chaotic worship would be irrelevant unless there were an openness to fresh revelations of the Spirit that could in principle lapse into complete disorder. His argument for unity despite diversity of gifts in chapter 12 (including a remarkable trinitarian statement in vv. 4-6), and his argument for order rather than chaos in chapter 14, indicate as well that as far as Paul is concerned, genuine Spirit-led worship will have framework and body to it, not just free-floating and unstructured outbursts of praise and prayer. Interestingly, and perhaps despite expectations, chapter 14 actually hardly mentions the Holy Spirit; when Paul speaks of praying and singing with the spirit and with the mind (vv. 14-16), his introductory remark in verse 14 indicates that this is *his* spirit, rather than the Holy Spirit, that he is referring to: "For if I pray in a tongue, my spirit prays but my mind is unproductive." On the positive side, we must of course say that the order he envisages is an order within which all sorts of new and unexpected things can and should happen. We should also note the emphasis on mission: one of the key criteria for authentic worship will be that if an outsider enters, he or she will be confronted, not with chaos and apparent gibberish, but with the clear and convicting message of the gospel. There is also, of course, the famous and tantalizing glimpse of Spirit-led worship at the end of 1 Corinthians, in the cry "Marana Tha!" (16:22). About this I have nothing new to say, merely to observe that it reminds us both of the continuing early Palestinian roots within the developing largely Greek church and of the eschatological context of all early Christian life.

N. T. Wright

14

The place of the Spirit in the complex and overlapping arguments of 1 Corinthians gives way in the second letter to a very different presentation. Paul is here mounting an argument about the nature of his apostleship. Having been rejected by a majority of Corinthian believers because of their adherence to the newly arrived super-apostles, Paul goes back to the cross and resurrection of Jesus and argues that genuine apostleship is modeled on and fashioned by those events, and by them alone. Faced with demands for demonstrations of God's powerful Spirit, he responds with the message of weakness shaped by the cross. Within that, his exposition of the new covenant in chapter 3 forms another perspective on his view of the Spirit and worship. The passage is highly complex, and I have no space here to retrace the steps of the exegesis I have proposed elsewhere.[11] The crunch comes at the end of chapter 3. Paul has been arguing that his ministry is indeed genuine "new-covenant" ministry, and that the evidence for this is the presence of the Spirit. But how do you know that the Spirit is present? Answer: because, when we worship together in the Spirit, we gaze *at one another in the Christian fellowship* and realize that we are gazing at the glory of the Lord, through the Spirit who dwells in you and me alike, in apostle and congregation, teacher and hearers. This, I believe, is the full meaning of the dense statement in 3:18. The unveiled face, the mutual recognition of the glory of the Lord among the worshipers, indicates, far better than any other "letters of recommendation" that Paul might have been able to offer (3:1-3), that he is indeed the Lord's apostle.

Notice what has thereby happened. Paul has here developed and enriched his new-Temple ecclesiology. The Spirit, indwelling believers, enables them to look upon God's glory as Moses gazed upon it in the wilderness Tabernacle, or as Isaiah accidentally saw it in the Temple. The developing argument of chapter 3, in which Paul contrasts his own ministry, which is a life-giving work, with that of Moses—which was (despite his intentions; here we need all of Romans 7 to help us understand what is in Paul's mind) a death-dealing work—indicates that as well as seeing the Spirit as fulfilling the promise of the Temple, Paul sees the Spirit as fulfilling the promise of the Law. With that we move, by implication at least (but it would certainly have been clear

[11] See esp. N. T. Wright, *The Climax of the Covenant* (Edinburgh: T&T Clark, 1991; Minneapolis: Fortress Press, 1992), chap. 9.

Worship and the Spirit in the New Testament

for Paul), from the Temple to the synagogue, but without leaving behind the context of worship. Already by Paul's day the synagogue theology was well developed: where two or three study Torah, there the Shekinah dwells among them.[12] In other words, for those who cannot easily make the journey to Jerusalem, God has provided another way of meeting him in worship and self-offering. The Torah, read and studied and prayed in the synagogue, is the means of God's presence. Now, for Paul, the Spirit picks up both Temple and Torah and, fulfilling both, transcends both. Here we are close to the very heart of Paul's theology of worship and the Spirit.

Before plunging into Romans, where all these themes are drawn out still further, we pause and reflect on Ephesians. (One of the ironies of contemporary Pauline scholarship is that nobody much seems to have noticed that the revolution we think of as the "New Perspective" should have brought Ephesians and Colossians back into play. They only appear as "deutero-Pauline" when seen from within the truncated theological Old Perspective. Another generation may be needed before the penny drops. Such is the power of unthinking theological and exegetical fashion.)

Ephesians offers the most explicit "new Temple" theology in Paul. Developing what we saw in 1 Corinthians 3, Ephesians 2:14-22 provides an extended picture of the coming together of Jew and Gentile within a single structure—which turns out to be the Temple itself, not now with a barrier keeping Gentiles out, or a law that enables Jews and Jews only to stay in, but with a welcome into a single new humanity, a welcome extended through the cross. "[T]hrough him [i.e., Jesus Christ] both of us have access in one Spirit to the Father": "access" is itself a Temple word, with the worshiper approaching the holy place reverently but without inappropriate fear or shame because of the cross.[13] The final emphasis of the paragraph rams home the point: this building, consisting of human beings from every possible background worshiping together, "grows into a holy temple in the Lord, *in whom you also are built together to form a place for God to dwell by the Spirit*" (Eph 2:21-22, my translation). It could hardly be clearer. The Spirit is the Shekinah dwelling in the new Temple, which is the single family of those who are rescued by the Gospel and renewed by the Spirit.

[12] Mishnah *Pirke Aboth* 3.2.
[13] Eph 2:18; cf. 3:12; Rom 5:2.

N. T. Wright

But what does that worship look like, or indeed sound like? Paul does not say "and this is the sort of thing you will say or hear when you are worshiping in this Temple." I think, however, that we are on safe ground if we work back into chapter 1 and see the great opening prayer of verses 3-14 as a classic piece of early Christian worship, rooted in Jewish antecedent, inspired (Paul would undoubtedly say) by the Spirit, and including the Spirit within the narrative of praise for God's mighty acts. The prayer, as is well known, develops the Jewish *Berakah* tradition, blessing God for his acts of salvation, which are cast in the form of a Creation-and-Exodus story: God's people in Christ are chosen before the foundation of the world and rescued through the (paschal) blood of the Messiah, not so that they can escape the wicked world, but so that they can be the advance guard of God's plan to save and reunite the created order, bringing all things in heaven and on earth into a new unity in Christ (1:10). The point of this, in verses 11-14, is that Jew and Gentile alike might together worship the one true God, albeit having come to this position by different routes: the Jewish people were chosen in accordance with God's will; Jewish Christians (1:12) were the first to hope in the Messiah and so live to the praise of his glory, while Gentile Christians, having been brought into the same family through the Gospel, have now received the Holy Spirit so that they, too, can live to the praise of God's glory. Here, explaining how and why this has come about, Paul notes as he does elsewhere that the Spirit is the *arrabōn*, the down payment, of the final inheritance. As the Spirit enables Jew and Gentile alike to worship the living God already in the present, the church experiences a genuine foretaste of the final inheritance, which of course in the light of 1:10 is not "heaven," as so often supposed, but the renewed and rejoined heaven and earth.

It is in this larger context that we must set the other mention of the Spirit and worship in Ephesians, that in 5:18-20. Drunkenness is the low-grade and shameful parody of that genuine self-transcendence, enhancement, and ennoblement of what it means to be human, that can and should be known when the Spirit fills individuals and whole assemblies and enables them to speak to and sing with one another, making melody with the heart to the Lord, and giving thanks in the name of the Lord to God the Father. This, indeed, is one of Paul's more strikingly trinitarian passages, reminiscent of 1 Corinthians 12:4-6, but this time giving not just a parallel between the three members of the Godhead but also a shape and a mutual relation: the Spirit enables

Worship and the Spirit in the New Testament

worshipers to give thanks to the Father in the name of the Lord Jesus. Here we see, unsurprisingly but still importantly, the roots of developed trinitarian worship, not in a formula to be repeated (though there may be some of those too in Paul) but in the theological interpretation of what happens when Christians gather for worship.

All of which brings us at last to Romans. As with so many other great themes of Pauline theology, a good deal comes to clear and almost poetic expression in chapters 5–8. This section is not, indeed, a detached statement either of soteriology or of sanctification. It belongs exactly where it is within the ongoing flow of the letter, yet its formal structures and repeated refrains give it a special quality, marking it out as indubitably the greatest of Paul's sustained pieces of writing. As is well known, Paul has shaped the entire argument in a developing circle, so that the opening statements in 5:1-5 and 5:6-11 are echoed, on the basis of the intervening argument, in the closing stages of chapter 8. This parallel, in particular between 5:5 and 8:28, convinces me that in 5:5 we have a statement not of God's love for humans but of our love for God: in other words, a wholehearted worship that is poured out by the Spirit. Hope does not make us ashamed, *because* the love of God, i.e., our love for God, has been poured out into our hearts by the Holy Spirit who has been given to us. Why this "because"? Paul does not say here, but in 8:18-30 the reason becomes clear: the Spirit is once more the down payment, the gift-in-advance-from-God's-future, the present possession that gives assurance of the future possession of the *klēronomia*, the "inheritance," that, more clearly in Romans 8 even than in Ephesians 1:10, is the entire renewed creation.[14] The whole argument of Romans 5–8 is held within this description of Spirit-led worship, love for God the creator and re-creator. I have argued in various places that this Pauline theme of loving God is in fact Paul's reworking, through Christ and the Spirit, of the great Jewish prayer, the Shema, linking this present passage with 1 Corinthians 8:4-6, Paul's most explicit evocation of the Shema, and also with the theme of "obedience of faith" in Romans 1:5, 3:30, and 16:26. Paul has consistently reworked the worship he inherited—Temple, Torah, prayer—around Jesus and the Spirit.

[14] The "hope of sharing the glory of God" in 5:2 is, I think, another instance of Paul's picking up the Jewish theme of the Shekinah glory returning to the Temple. I hope to pursue this theme more fully elsewhere.

N. T. Wright

Thus, though Paul does not speak in chapter 6 explicitly either of worship or of the Spirit, we can see the substructure of what we have found elsewhere clearly visible in this chapter. The baptismal theology of the first half forms the basis for the ethical appeal of the second half: "having been set free from sin, [you] have become slaves to righteousness"; "as you once presented your members as slaves to impurity and to greater and greater iniquity, so now present your members as slaves to righteousness for sanctification" (6:18-19). More particularly, you have been, he says, enslaved to God (v. 22) and must now serve him. As in 1 Corinthians, though that service looks like what we now call "ethics," it would start with and be framed by what Paul calls "worship." This is already clear from the long argument of 1:18–4:25, which begins with a description of the worship humans should have offered but did not (1:20-23) and the consequent fragmentation of human life, and ends with a description of Abraham worshiping God in the right way and so being given new life (4:17-21). This integration of worship and holiness is borne out further by the opening verses of chapter 12, where Paul echoes chapter 6 but within an explicit appeal: "present your bodies as a living sacrifice, holy and acceptable to God," which is your *logikē latreia*, your "rational worship." Again, the Spirit is not mentioned, but the appeal is unthinkable, in Pauline theology, without the Spirit. The debates about *logikē*, though important, would take us too far afield. Suffice it to say that Paul seems to be implicitly indicating what he elsewhere makes more explicit, the contrast between the sacrificial worship of the Jerusalem cult and the sacrificial worship offered by those in Christ.

But to return to Romans 5–8. Chapter 7 forms, notoriously, Paul's longest and densest argument about the Torah. What is not often noticed is that the language he uses about it is the language of worship: I delight in God's Torah, according to my inner self, even though in my members I see another Torah, making war on that first one and holding me captive. The echoes of 2 Corinthians 3 in 7:4-6, where Paul uses "new covenant" language to contrast the life under Torah with life in the Spirit, give us the clue as to what is going on. Paul looks back on his pre-conversion life and does not suggest that it was misguided, that Torah was not after all worthy of his love and delight. The problem was not with the law, but with the "self" that was, despite God's call and gift to Israel, nevertheless still in Adam. Unredeemed Torah-worship, Paul is arguing, was proper God-directed worship, but it failed to be life-giving as it might have been, not because there was anything wrong with Torah but because "I," the Jew, was still "in the flesh," part of the solidarity of the old Adam that could not help bringing death. The Torah formed, as we have noted, the center of worship in the synagogue, the direct means of God's living presence with his people. Delight in Torah was delight in God. This passage points ahead to 10:2-3: Israel according to the flesh (i.e., Paul in his former life) has "a zeal for God, but it is not according to knowledge."

This theme of worship—rightly directed but frustratingly thwarted—then spills over into the dramatic statement of 8:1-11. God has done what the law could not do, acting through the death of his Son to deal with the long and law-enhanced buildup of sin, and acting through the Spirit to give the life that the law had longed to give but could not because of the raw material on which it was working. Just as the note of worship in chapter 7 often goes unnoticed, so the note of the Torah's fulfillment often goes unnoticed in 8:5-8: the mind of the flesh is hostile to God's law, cannot submit to it, and cannot please God, but (by clear and strong implication) the mind of the Spirit *does* submit to God's law, and can and does please him (again, compare 12:1-2). The Spirit thus enables those in Christ to offer God the worship that Torah wanted to evoke, the reality of which synagogue-worship was a frustrated foretaste.

But it is not only Torah-worship that is fulfilled in the Spirit, according to this passage. Paul speaks once more, as in 1 Corinthians 3 and 6, about the Spirit's indwelling. This was clearly a Temple theme in those passages, and we have no reason to deny that it is so here as well. The Spirit dwells within those who are "in Christ," and the result is that, just as YHWH's indwelling would accompany the rebuilding of the Temple, in Ezekiel and elsewhere, so the Spirit will give life to the mortal bodies of those in Christ, even though they face bodily death because of the continuing entail of sin. Romans 8:1-11 thus offers a spectacular theology of Jewish worship reinvigorated through the Spirit, with Torah and Temple both pointing forward to a new kind of fulfillment in Christ, a fulfillment in which the life that should have followed the worship of the living God is at last brought to reality in the resurrection.

Before we proceed with Romans 8, we note the larger pattern, again centrally characteristic of Jewish worship, that these chapters provide. Think of the story of the Exodus: the children of Israel, in fulfillment of the promise to Abraham, come out of Egypt through the shed blood of the Passover lamb, and then come through the Red Sea, leaving

N. T. Wright

behind the world of slavery so that they can serve their covenant God. They arrive at Mount Sinai and are given the Torah, which proves a hard burden; but God is gracious and goes with them, dwelling in their midst in the tabernacle, leading them through the wilderness by the pillar of cloud and fire, until they come at last to their promised inheritance. As I have argued elsewhere, Romans 5–8 follows exactly this pattern: in fulfillment of the promise to Abraham (chap. 4) and as a result of the blood of the Messiah (5:6-11), God's people come through the waters and so from slavery to freedom (chap. 6), arrive at Mount Sinai and face the puzzle of the Torah (chap. 7), and then are led by the pillar of cloud and fire—i.e., the Holy Spirit—through the present life to the promised inheritance, which turns out to be, not "heaven" as in much popular Christian imagination, but the renewed creation (8:18-26). The Exodus narrative, which forms the backbone of so much Jewish worship, festival, and liturgy, provides the framework for Paul's exposition of what it means to be the single family of Abraham, the people of God in Christ.[15]

That is the context within which we find his most spectacular (if characteristically dense) treatment of worship and the Spirit. First, the Spirit and the cry of the adopted child (8:15-17). "For you did not receive the spirit of slavery to fall back into fear"—in other words, now that you're God's Passover people on the way to your inheritance, don't even think of going back to Egypt—"but you have received a spirit of adoption. When we cry 'Abba! Father!' it is that very Spirit bearing witness with our spirit that we are children of God" (again, like the Israelites, "Israel is my son, my firstborn"); "and if children, then heirs, heirs of God and joint heirs with Christ." A parallel to this passage exists, of course, in the remarkably trinitarian Galatians 4:1-7, again within an implied Exodus-context. Opinion inevitably differs as to whether this cry of "Abba! Father!" is a reference to the Lord's Prayer or something like it, whether it is the spontaneous cry evoked by the Spirit within, or whether it is part of the church's tradition—or whether Paul would not have recognized that disjunction. Perhaps equally important, to set the wider context of this moment of Spirit-inspired worship, is the notion of "inheritance" in terms of the biblical

---

[15] I have elaborated this most fully in my commentary: "Romans," in *New Interpreters Bible* 10 (Nashville: Abingdon, 2003), 508–619, esp. 510–13, and the various articles referred to there.

background: the idea of the Messiah's inheritance takes us back to Psalm 2:8, where it is the nations that constitute that inheritance, and whose leaders are therefore called to do him homage.

This leads directly into the famous triple groaning of verses 18-26. The creation groans in travail. The church groans within creation, awaiting its full adoption. The Spirit groans within the church and is heard by the Father, generating the trinitarian and christological shape and framework of Christian worship: worship of the Creator who will redeem and transform the creation, but worship evoked by the Spirit from the place where the world is in pain; worship offered by those who are discovering in the strange pattern of Jesus' death and resurrection what it means to be younger siblings of the firstborn son (v. 29). The "inarticulate groanings" of verse 26 may or may not be a reference to speaking in tongues—though, if it is, it seems strange to use *alalētos*, precisely "speechless," to describe it. Let me simply repeat my previous exegesis of this passage:

> It is important to say that, if [Paul] is not referring to speaking in tongues, nor is he simply referring to silent prayer such as is commonly practised in private Christian devotion in the contemporary Western world (in Paul's day most people would have prayed aloud, just as people used to read aloud, even when alone). Rather, he is speaking of an agonizing in prayer, a mixture of lament and longing in which, like a great swell of tide at sea, "too full for sound or foam," the weight of what is taking place has nothing to do with the waves and ripples on the surface. Whether Paul expected all his readers to know this experience in prayer (as he seems to have expected them to know the *Abba*-experience) is difficult to judge. Then as now, perhaps, his words may have come as a challenge to a deeper wrestling with the pain of the world and the church, a struggle in which, like Jacob, Christians might discover that they had after all been wrestling with God as well as with their own weak humanness, and had prevailed.[16]

Romans 8 is a fitting climax for this brief survey of worship and the Spirit in the New Testament. There are, to be sure, other passages in this great letter that could be studied. We should note the cry of adoration and wonder at the end of chapter 11, the call for the "living

---

[16] Ibid., 599.

N. T. Wright

sacrifice" and the "reasonable worship" in 12:1-2, and particularly the summons to united worship across traditional boundaries in 15:1-13, which ends—and this is the conclusion of the letter's theological argument—"May the God of hope fill you with all joy and peace in believing, so that you may abound in hope by the power of the Holy Spirit." This is another echo of 5:5, and another indication that for Paul when the church was united in worshiping the one true God this was because God's own Spirit was at work within it.

CONCLUSION

If the topic is enormous, the implications and conclusions are equally so. I have highlighted the way in which the early Christians understood their Spirit-led worship in terms of a Temple theology, and to a lesser extent a Torah theology, in which the tabernacling presence of God was both the object of worship and the enabler of that worship. This has, of course, direct and constant corollaries in terms of the call for holiness and the language of sacrifice in which that call was expressed. (I am aware that I have not even mentioned the letter to the Hebrews; this is not because it isn't relevant at a secondary level, but because it does not make explicit the link between worship and the Spirit.) This wasn't a matter of borrowing Temple liturgies, which are in any case difficult to reconstruct, nor was it simply that the early Christians were thinking of the biblical Temple rather than the actual one they knew in Jerusalem. The earliest Christians were Jews; first-century Jews had Temple worship in their bloodstream, and the first generation saw, from very early on, that in Jesus and the Spirit they had that toward which the Temple had been an advance signpost. Indeed, as we saw, the first Christians discovered this as a daily geographical and political reality. From that root there grew, quite naturally it seems to me, the early liturgies, including sacramental liturgies, in which this was variously embodied. We have seen, as the context for this, the regular retelling of the Exodus story, and the way in which the story of Jesus—more fully, of the Father's work in and through Jesus Christ and then by the Spirit of Christ—was told in those terms and with the intention of evoking that narrative.

All this is to insist once more that we understand early Christian worship as eschatological. Not that early Christians thought the space-time world was coming to an end. As I and others have argued, that is largely a modern construct, a way of parking a problem within

Enlightenment belittlings of early Christianity, a move, moreover, that normally ignores the resurrection.[17] The early Christians believed that they were already living in the time of fulfillment and transformation, in which the great Exodus-shaped story that began with creation itself, and that took a fresh turn with Abraham, had reached its appointed goal, and was now bearing fruit in a quite new way. Early Christian worship was thus characterized by the sense of newness, of new covenant and new creation, and so by the sense of anticipating in worship something that would come completely true when that new creation was finished. To recognize this inaugurated eschatology within the earliest texts may be to alert ourselves once again to this dimension in the later developing liturgies. If the Spirit is the one who brings God's future forward into the present, worshiping in the Spirit the God who raised Jesus from the dead means standing both at the overlap between heaven and earth and also at the place where past, present, and future are mysteriously held together. That, I believe, is the best framework for understanding Christian sacramental theology; but that, too, is a topic for another time.

[17] See, e.g., N. T. Wright, *The New Testament and the People of God* (*Christian Origins and the Question of God*, vol. 1) (London: SPCK; Minneapolis: Fortress Press, 1992), 459–64.

N. T. Wright

Ruth Langer

2. The Presence of God in Jewish Liturgy

Contemporary Jews do speak of "spirituality," and search today
for more "spiritual" forms of worship, but Jews use this word in English, and even translated it into a Hebrew neologism (*ruḥniut*), without thinking about its origins. Judaism, of course, has no trinitarian
understanding of God. When we speak today of "spirituality" we
do not refer to a working of the Holy Spirit, but rather to a general
mood of religious intensity and fervor, ideally generated by a sense
of being in the presence of God. Prayer in the presence of God is a
topic for which there are rich resources in the formative texts that en-
code the shape of rabbinic prayer. Hence that will be the focus of my
contribution to this discussion of "Worship in the Spirit."

The ancient rabbis understood that their innovative liturgical
system had validity, not only because it was oriented to God but
also because it was performed in God's presence. In the wake of the
destruction of the Temple, there were internal Jewish needs to make
this claim. The nature of their arguments, however, suggests the like-
lihood that the rabbis were also responding to Christian polemical
charges, especially the supersessionist assertion that the destruction
of the Temple signaled God's abandonment of the Jews, and the replacement of the Jewish worship system (and its covenant) with the
heavenly high priesthood of Jesus.[1] Thus the challenge of constructing post-Temple liturgical systems played a role in the constructions
of Jewish and Christian identities during the "partings of the ways."

As many now agree, the specific form and content of rabbinic
liturgy developed in response to the destruction of the Jerusalem
Temple in 70 CE. For the rabbis, the question of how to gain access
to the presence of God in the absence of the Temple and its biblically prescribed sacrifices was critical. The rabbis never name this

---

[1] Letter to the Hebrews, chap. 7ff. This becomes a standard trope in *Adversos
Judaios* literature.

liturgical presence of God, whether locally present or not, as *ruah haqodesh*, "holy spirit." They apply this term, which appears only three times in the Hebrew Bible,[2] only to genuine human inspiration from God, generally historic, when describing the inspiration of biblical books[3] or prophecy (t. Sotah 6:2), or as knowledge of correct behavior.[4] In this respect rabbinic usage of the term is consistent with its appearance in the liturgical texts of the Dead Sea Scrolls. There the *ruah haqodesh* is primarily a source of knowledge already conferred, to which the worshiper is responding, not a presence within a liturgical context.[5] The rabbis assert that though prophetic inspiration from the *ruah haqodesh* ceased with Haggai, Zechariah, and Malachi early in the Second Temple period, certain rabbis did merit receiving such inspiration, but their generation was deemed unworthy. In its place some of these rabbis received a lesser form of divine communication, a *bat qol* or heavenly voice.[6] But the rabbis

[2] Isa 63:10, 11; Ps 51:13. Of course, in the Hebrew Bible God's "spirit" (without the specification of its holiness) hovers over the waters in Gen 1:2, and is a source of wisdom (Exod 31:3; 35:31) and of prophecy (see, for instance, Num 24:2, regarding Balaam, and 1 Sam 10, regarding Saul).

[3] Other than the Pentateuch itself, which God revealed directly. See t. Yad. 2:14, b. Meg. 7a.

[4] t. Pes. 4:14, t. Pes. 2:15 (comp. b. Erub. 64b), legitimating rabbinic decisions.

[5] See the "Words of the Luminaries," 4Q504 frag. 4:5, "These things we know because you have favored us with a h[oly] spirit." Compare 1QHᵃ IV:26, 1QHᵃ VI:12-13, 1QHᵃ XV:6-7, 1QHᵃ XX:12, 1QHᵃ VIII:20, and 1QHᵃ XXIII:13, which invoke God's holy spirit for purification and atonement. See Florentino Garcia Martinez, and Eibert J. C. Tigchelaar, eds., *The Dead Sea Scrolls Study Edition* (Leiden: Brill / Grand Rapids, MI: Eerdmans, 1997–98) 1:148–49, 152–53, 156–57, 176–77, 192–93, 198–99; 2:1010–11. My thanks to Esther Chazon for her help with this discussion. See also Alex P. Jassen, "Prophets and Prophecy in the Qumran Community," *AJS Review* 32 , no. 2 (November 2008): 299–334.

[6] t. Sot. 13:3-4, b Sanh. 11a. Note that this tradition is not fully consistent with those that assert that the *ruah haqodesh* inspires correct *halakhic* decisions. For an overview of these issues, see Alan Unterman, Howard Kreisel, and Rivka Horwitz, "Ruᵓah Ha-Kodesh," *Encyclopaedia Judaica*, ed. Michael Berenbaum and Fred Skolnik, 2d ed. (Detroit: Macmillan Reference USA, 2007) 17:506–9 (electronic version). See also Benjamin D. Sommer, "Did Prophecy Cease? Evaluating a Reevaluation," *Journal of Biblical Literature* 115, no. 1 (1996): 31–47, and the earlier discussions he cites that evaluate this rabbinic

Ruth Langer

associate neither the *ruaḥ haqodesh* nor the *bat qol* with the experience of worship.[7]

Indeed, the rabbis were quite nervous about divine interventions in human affairs. Was the rabbinic determination that God had chosen no longer to communicate through the *ruaḥ haqodesh* part of Jewish self-definition in the face of emerging Christian trinitarian theology? The more we look, the more this dynamic emerges. This choice may have responded to Christians understanding the incarnate Jesus as a prophet, as well as to their understanding of the Holy Spirit. Both undermine the unique role of Torah and its rabbinic interpretation as God's guidance, placed physically in human hands on earth.[8]

The rabbis were even willing to contradict the instructions of the *bat qol*, the heavenly voice. Rabbis of the early second century outright rejected, first, the evidence of miracles, and then heavenly voices resolving a practical dispute. They asserted, quoting Torah itself, that Torah is no longer in heaven, but has been given to humans to apply, based on majority rule (Deut 30:12; Exod 23:2). The coda to the story is perhaps most telling. A rabbi asks Elijah what God's response had been to this human decision, and Elijah reports that God laughed and said, "My children have defeated me!" (b. B. Meẓ. 59b). It should come as no surprise, then, that rabbis do not expect that their liturgy will create an experience of ecstasy, or invoke a spirit of prophecy. This is fully coherent with the rabbinic sense that such experiences belong to the esoteric realm, not to the worlds of public prayer and Torah study.

---

claim in the light of historical evidence for a much more complex process extending into the early Christian era.

[7] One possible exception to this is y. Suk. 5:1, 55a's discussion of the Sukkot waterdrawing festival, the *Simḥat Beit HaShoevah*, "Rejoicing of the Place of Waterdrawing." The Talmud explains that the joy derives from the fact that people drew or derived from the festival's rituals *ruaḥ haqodesh*, and the *ruaḥ haqodesh* only dwells with people when they are in a state of joy. But what does this mean? Perhaps being in a state of receiving prophecy.

[8] For nuanced discussions of this, see Michael Wyschogrod, "Incarnation and God's Indwelling in Israel," in *Abraham's Promise: Judaism and Jewish-Christian Relations*, ed. R. Kendall Soulen (Grand Rapids, MI: Eerdmans, 2004), especially 175–78; rpt. from *Incarnation*, ed. Marco M. Olivetti (Padua: CEDAM, 1999), 147–57; and Elliot R. Wolfson, "Embodiment: Judaism and Incarnation, the Imaginal Body of God," in *Christianity in Jewish Terms*, ed. Tikva Frymer-Kensky et. al., 239ff. (Boulder, CO: Westview Press, 2000).

The Presence of God in Jewish Liturgy

This is not to say that rabbinic Judaism lacks a sense of the immanent presence of God, but that the terms employed for this are not cognate to the Christian "Holy Spirit." Early rabbinic texts frequently call God *HaMaqom*, "The Place," referring to God's place of indwelling on earth, the Temple. This term persists even in the absence of the Temple, speaking to God's continuing presence there, but appears more frequently in discussions about liturgy than in prayers themselves, perhaps because most prayers use biblical names for God.[9]

Drawing on the biblical language for God's presence, the rabbis speak most frequently of the Shekhinah, the indwelling presence of God.[10] Pre-rabbinic texts preserve no precedent for this particular Hebrew root as a proper name for God, not a verbal or adjectival description of God's state of being. In rabbinic parlance Shekhinah is simply another name for God, a name that, like so many others, highlights a specific divine quality, here one particularly relevant to prayer, God's indwelling presence. Only in medieval kabbalah does this name become something more discrete, a primary designation of the tenth *sefirah*, the emanation that mediates between heaven and earth.[11]

---

[9] In the Passover Haggadah *HaMaqom* appears in a sort of primitive blessing formula preceding the midrash of the four children. Both the context and the nature of the blessing suggest that this may have originated in conjunction with study, not with prayer. The other obvious exception is the greeting given to mourners, "May God (*HaMaqom*) comfort you among all the mourners for Zion and Jerusalem." This greeting does not appear in classical rabbinic texts, or in premodern texts included on the Bar-Ilan CD ROM, so further research is needed to determine its origin. God's comforting the mourner is an immanent divine function; referring to God as "the Place," while including the mourner with those mourning for Zion, is fully appropriate.

[10] This word appears as a verb describing God's presence on Sinai, in the desert tabernacle (called the *mishkan*, the place of indwelling), and in the Jerusalem Temple. See Exod 24:16; 25:8; 29:45-46; 40:35; Num 35:34; Deut 12:5; 12:11; 14:23; 16:2, 6, 11 (all understood to mean the Jerusalem Temple); Isa 8:18 (with explicit reference to Zion); Ezek 43:7, 9; Joel 4:17; Zech 2:14-15; 8:3, 8; Pss 15:1; 26:8; 43:3; 68:17; 74:2; 87:2; 132:7; 135:21; Ezra 6:12; 7:15; Neh 1:9 (with explicit reference to Jerusalem). The root applies equally to all things that dwell on earth.

[11] See Arthur Green, "Shekhinah, the Virgin Mary and the Song of Songs: Reflections on a Kabbalistic Symbol in Its Historical Context," *Association for Jewish Studies Review* 26, no. 1 (2002): 17ff.

Ruth Langer

To understand the significance of these designations we must first ask what it means for Jews to pray in the presence of God. Lurking in the rabbinic discussions about prayer is the question, "What makes liturgy effective? What is it supposed to achieve, and what mechanisms does it use to ensure this?" The rabbinic question asks, "Does my human action fulfill what God expects of me? Is it pleasing and acceptable to God?"[12] We recite Psalm 19:15 at the end of every *ʿamidah*: "May the words of my mouth and the prayer of my heart be acceptable to You, O Eternal One . . ."

Jewish liturgy asks this question of effectiveness within the context of covenantal responsibility. God has commanded us to worship him in a regular manner. These commandments (*mitzvot*) are explicit in the Torah's expectation of daily communal sacrifices, with additional sacrifices on Sabbaths and holy days (Num 28–29). These communal sacrifices offered in the Jerusalem Temple constituted Israel's ritual response to life in covenant with God.[13] Therefore, these sacrifices had to be pleasing to God; they had to be offered with absolute precision, according to the best human understanding of what God desires (b. Sanh. 49b). After the Romans destroyed the Temple, the only legitimate place for these offerings, Jews sought to compensate for these missing covenantal acts in a manner pleasing to God. Rabbinic liturgy was one answer. Although how quickly their answer received broad acceptance is unclear, it did eventually become normative Judaism.[14]

[12] See the discussions of this in my *To Worship God Properly: Tensions between Liturgical Custom and Halakhah in Judaism* (Cincinnati: Hebrew Union College Press, 1998), chap. 1, "The Creation of a Valid Non-Sacrificial Liturgy."

[13] On the ideological centrality of this Temple worship for Second Temple-period Jews, see Seth Schwartz, *Imperialism and Jewish Society 200 B.C.E. to 640 C.E.* (Princeton, NJ: Princeton University Press, 2001), chap. 2, "Religion and Society before 70 C.E."

[14] See my "Early Rabbinic Liturgy in Its Palestinian Milieu: Did Non-Rabbis Know the 'Amidah?" in *When Judaism and Christianity Began: Essays in Memory of Anthony J. Saldarini*, 2: *Judaism and Christianity in the Beginning*, ed. Daniel Harrington, Alan J. Avery-Peck, and Jacob Neusner, 423–39 (Leiden and Boston: E. J. Brill, 2004). In the early eighth century, Jews of Kairouan (today's Tunisia) were praying the rabbinic liturgy in a way that met rebuke from the Babylonian Pirqoi ben Baboi; see Louis Ginzberg, *Ginzei Schechter* (New York: Jewish Theological Seminary, 1929) 2:504–73 (in Hebrew). In the late ninth century the Jews of Spain requested basic liturgical guidance from the Babylonian

The Presence of God in Jewish Liturgy

Spirituality, in the modern generic sense, played at best a minor role in official discussions of this system. This is not to say that the rabbis did not pray with spiritual intensity. They were, however, cognizant of the fact that individual piety could detract from the successful imposition of a universal obligation of daily communal worship. Thus we hear that the ideal is to spend an hour preparing to pray, an hour praying, and another hour reflecting on that experience of prayer—three times a day. This tradition then wonders how time was left for study of Torah and for earning a living; it acknowledges that such a system is only possible for super-pietists (b. Ber. 32b; compare y. Ber. 5:1, 8d). More graphic is a tradition about the early second-century Rabbi Aqiva, that "when he prayed with the community, he would abbreviate his prayer, but when he prayed alone, one would leave him in one corner and find him [at the end] in another [this during a prayer when one does not move one's feet]. Why? Because of all [his] bowings and prostrations." The Talmud suggests that he abbreviated his public prayer so as not to burden the community (t. Ber. 3:5, b. Ber. 31a). The greatest spiritual intensity demands generous amounts of time, and thus was not a practical norm for universally required communal prayer. However, Rabbi Aqiva himself obviously had a profound sense that he was praying in the presence of the One to whom he was bowing and prostrating himself.

It is to this understanding of the presence of God that we now turn. Until modern times all Jews lived with a profound sense of being in exile from the Temple and from Jerusalem. Themes of exile and redemption are omnipresent in traditional rabbinic liturgy. Central to this is a consciousness of our inability to fulfill the biblical commandments for sacrificial worship, and a profound sense of loss of the sure access to God guaranteed by God's choice to be present in the Jerusalem Temple.

Rabbi Elazar ben Pedat (d. 279, Land of Israel) taught that "ever since the Temple was destroyed, a wall of iron has separated Israel from her Heavenly Father," and "the gates of prayer have been locked" (b. Ber. 32b). It is hard to imagine a more despairing statement about the impact of the destruction; Israel has lost not only the indwelling Divine Presence but even a channel by which to reach the now exclusively transcendent God. Were we to rely entirely on this

---

sages, resulting in our first preserved rabbinic prayer books, the model for most subsequent texts.

Ruth Langer

statement, prayer would appear utterly meaningless. Rabbi Elazar mitigates this only a bit in a third tradition, teaching that "even though the gates of prayer are locked, the gates of tears are not locked." He therefore leaves a small lachrymose window of hope.

However, we err if we read this text in isolation or as an absolute, authoritative theological statement that confirms the Christian accusations of the ongoing worthlessness of Judaism. Within the rabbinic context such statements need to be understood poetically, as statements of grief and uncertainty, rather than as incontrovertible fact. In actuality, this represents a pole tethering one end of the spectrum of rabbinic statements about Divine Presence—one omnipresent lurking element that stands in marked tension with other teachings that are actually more determinative of actual Jewish life and practice.

We read in the Talmud a series of traditions establishing the context in which Israel experiences an ongoing divine presence.

> It is taught: Abba Binyamin (? before 200) says: A person's prayer is only heard [by God] in the synagogue, for it says, "To listen to the cry and to the prayer" (I Kgs 8:28).[15] In a place where there is crying, there should be prayer.

> Rabin bar Rav Ada cited Rabbi Isaac (late 3rd c.): From whence do we know that the Holy One, blessed be He, is found in the synagogue? For it is said, "God stands in the divine assembly" (Ps 82:1a).

> And from whence do we know that when ten pray [together] the Shekhinah is with them? For it is said, "God stands in the divine assembly" (Ps 82:1a).

> And from whence do we know that when three form a law court, the Shekhinah is with them? For it is said, "Among the ʾelohim (here read as "judges") He pronounces judgment" (Ps 82:1b).

> And from whence do we know that if two sit and engage themselves with Torah, the Shekhinah is with them? For it is said, "In this vein have those who revere the Eternal been talking to one another. The Eternal has heard and noted it . . ." (Mal 3:16).

> . . .

---

[15] Bible translations follow or are based upon the New Jewish Publication Society version.

The Presence of God in Jewish Liturgy

And from whence do we know that one person who sits and engages with Torah, the Shekhinah is with him? For it is said, " . . . in every place where I cause My name to be mentioned I will come to you [singular] and bless you" (Exod 20:20b).

(A later, anonymous discussion) And once this happens with only one, why do we need two? With two, their words are written in the Book of Remembrances, but with one, his words are not written in the Book of Remembrances. And once this happens with just two, why do we need three? Lest you say that the judgment of the court is only a way of making peace in the world and does not involve the Shekhinah. Therefore it comes to tell us that a court's judgment is also Torah (i.e., divinely approved law). And once this happens with just three, why do you need ten? With ten, the Shekhinah arrives first; with three, not until they sit down.[16]

The heart of this tradition is attributed to a slightly younger contemporary of Rabbi Elazar. It too concerns itself with questions of access to God, but its answer is radically different. There may be no Temple, but humanly created situations invoke the Divine Presence. That Torah study itself has this effect appears already in an earlier version of this text.[17] In the late third century, exactly when rabbinic leadership was becoming a force in the Jewish community, Christianity was becoming a significant presence,[18] and more Jews were participating in rabbinic prayer, Rabbi Isaac explicitly taught that God is present in the prayer community and in the workings of the rabbinic court system.

[16] b. Ber. 6a. A similar idea appears in y. Ber. 1:5, 8d in a series of traditions encouraging people to pray in the synagogue or study hall because these are the places where God is present. See also b. Sanh. 22a, which teaches that worshipers must consider themselves as if in the presence of the Shekhinah, based on Ps 16:8.

[17] Compare m. Avot 3:2. m. Avot 3:6 (and Avot R. Nat B 18) establishes the presence of God among groups of ten, five, three, two, and one who study Torah. The Talmud's rewriting of this text (while maintaining many of its proof texts) suggests the possibility of the integration of rabbinic prayer into the synagogue's study context.

[18] See Lee I. Levine, *The Rabbinic Class of Roman Palestine in Late Antiquity* (Jerusalem: Yad Izhak Ben-Zvi / The Jewish Theological Seminary of America, 1989); and Schwartz, *Imperialism* (n. 13), chap. 3, "Rabbis and Patriarchs on the Margins."

Ruth Langer

We see in this tradition, then, a companion discussion to Rabbi Elazar's "wall of iron." If indeed we have any right to demand that these two traditions be reconciled (rabbinic tradition finds no reason to insist on this), we may say that human prayer might not penetrate the wall of iron, but certain human actions, most powerfully prayer in community, invoke the Shekhinah. God not only circumvents the wall, but is so eager for human worship as to "arrive" first.[19] Rabbinic tradition had always presumed the efficacy of Torah study, and the ritual reading and study of Torah was apparently the original function of the synagogue in the Second Temple period. Now the systems developed to compensate for the lack of Temple worship make the same claim for efficacy. God is in exile too, but in exile with Israel, present in the gathered prayer quorum, which is itself increasingly located in a dedicated architectural space—the place of Torah reading, the synagogue.

THE TEMPLE IN THE SYNAGOGUE

By no means does this understanding negate the sense of exile, or the sense that this presence of God is less certain than that which existed in the Temple itself. In the resultant tension the Temple continues to play a significant symbolic role in the structuring of rabbinic prayer and of its prayer space.

One of the early rabbinic names for God, *HaMaqom*, the Place, suggests that the Temple is a synecdoche for God. Rabbinic texts characterize human actions of various sorts, including prayer, as occurring *lifnei HaMaqom*, "before the Place," i.e., in God's presence.[20] Obviously this does not mean that all prayer takes place at the Temple, but the sense that prayer, even from afar, relates to that space draws on a precedent derived from Solomon. In his prayer at the dedication of the First Temple, Solomon describes repentant Jews around the world as praying "in the direction of their land which You gave to their fathers, of the city which You have chosen, and of the House which I have built to Your name,"[21] i.e., of Jews directing prayer from afar toward

---

[19] Another reading of these traditions about the importance and efficacy of prayer in the synagogue, or communal context, sees these as rabbinic polemic against those who fail to join the community. On this, see my *To Worship God Properly*, 14ff.

[20] m. Avot 2:13, t. Ber. 3:17 (and its citation in b. Ber. 10b).

[21] 1 Kgs 8:48. We have no evidence for what Solomon means by his people's prayer. We know of no verbal liturgies from the First Temple period, other

The Presence of God in Jewish Liturgy

Jerusalem and the Temple. Based on what the rabbis understand is
the exilic example of Daniel, this remains valid even in the absence
of the Temple. Early rabbinic texts instruct that the physical direction
of prayer is toward the Holy of Holies. This orientation is an absolute
requirement for those who are able.[22] Minimally, one must direct one's
heart there.[23]

Does this orientation to the Temple from afar create a sense of divine absence? Yes, but it also encourages one to imagine oneself in
Jerusalem, and presumes that God does indeed still dwell within the
human realm. We perceive this imaginative move in synagogue archi-
tecture, which shows increasing signs of incorporating rabbinic prayer.
There was an increasing "templization" of the synagogues throughout
the rabbinic period, with symbols of the Temple playing a growing
role in communicating the purpose and meaning of the structure.[24]

---

than perhaps psalms associated with sacrifices.

[22] m. Ber. 4:5-6, t. Ber. 3:15-16, b. Ber. 30a (with an added layer of instruction
what to do if one is actually inside the Holy of Holies), j. Ber. 4:5, 8b-c.

[23] While the Mishnah and the Jerusalem Talmud speak of bodily orientation
when this is possible, the Tosefta and the Babylonian Talmud consistently use
the language of directing the heart, even where one might expect otherwise.
See Saul Lieberman's discussion, *Tosefta Kifeshuta*, 2d ed. (Jerusalem: Jewish
Theological Seminary of America, 1993), *Seder Zeraʾim*, 1:44 (Hebrew). He suggests that the difference is integral to the texts. The medieval explanations
he cites do not explain the difference satisfactorily. See also Uri Ehrlich, "The
Place of the Shekhinah in the Consciousness of the Worshiper," *Tarbiẓ* 65, no.
2 (1996): 315–29, here 316–18 (Hebrew). In his conclusion, p. 329, he suggests
that continued prayer toward the Temple is eschatological in nature, expressing a yearning for its return there, reversing the original sense of the gesture
that derives from before the Temple's destruction. In this he minimizes any
sense of the ongoing presence of God at the Temple, a move supported by
neither archaeological nor textual evidence. Note that in his *The Nonverbal Language of Prayer: A New Approach to Jewish Liturgy*, trans. Dena Ordan (Tübingen:
Mohr Siebeck, 2004), chap. 12, "Directional-Intentional Foci: The Locus of the
Shekhinah" (which substantially reproduces this article in English), Ehrlich
does not include this suggestion.

[24] See Steven Fine, *This Holy Place: On the Sanctity of the Synagogue during the
Greco-Roman Period* (Notre Dame: University of Notre Dame Press, 1997), pas-
sim. The difficulty of doing Jewish archaeology in the Muslim world today
means that we have too little evidence to make reasonable generalizations
about the extent to which this applied to diaspora synagogues in the first mil-
lennium CE.

Ruth Langer

Central to this evolution of the synagogue was the creation of a locus of holiness within the synagogue itself, beginning in the third century, with the placement of a permanent cabinet to house the Torah scrolls on the wall facing Jerusalem. Previously the scrolls had been housed elsewhere in a movable chest, brought in procession for ritual reading. Now the orientation of prayer and the orientation of the synagogue space corresponded. This fixed ark acquired physical characteristics reminiscent of the Temple's Holy of Holies, including a curtain screening it, often pillars on each side, and illumination with candelabra shaped like the Temple's menorah. While the actual shape of the ark was generally not preserved, numerous synagogue floors incorporated mosaic panels directly in front of this ark, mirroring it with a depiction of the Holy of Holies (or perhaps the ark itself) flanked by two menorahs, usually accompanied by additional ritual objects associated with the Temple.[25]

This assimilation of Temple imagery into the synagogue itself, while widespread, was never universal,[26] but it does draw our attention to other elements of the rabbinic liturgical system that deliberately transferred Temple rituals to the synagogue. I refer to those surrounding the blowing of the *shofar* (ram's horn), the processions involving the *lulav* (palm branch), the recitation of *hallel* (Pss 113–18), and the priestly benediction. The rabbis also decreed that the number of services, their names, and their timing would be based on the pattern of regular communal Temple sacrifices. In various contexts biblical and rabbinic texts about the day's sacrifices also entered the liturgy. Thus, rabbinic prayer was construed ever more deeply as being in the presence of God in ways analogous, if not fully equivalent, to the biblically commanded worship in the Temple itself, the locus of God's indwelling on earth.[27]

[25] For images of the mosaic floor from the synagogue in Hammat Tiberias, see http://www.archaeology-classic.com/Israel_E/Hammath_Tiberias.html.

[26] Nor does it persist. However, this sense of parallelism to the Temple, orientation to it, and use of its symbols never disappears entirely. A striking example is the 1970 sanctuary of the Beth El Synagogue Center in New Rochelle, New York, where the grand freestanding ark is a deliberate image of the Holy of Holies of the Temple. The external façade of the sanctuary section of the building, facing the main thoroughfare, also conveys this message. See http://www.bethelnr.org/index.cfm.

[27] See my *To Worship God Properly*, 6–10.

The Presence of God in Jewish Liturgy

For rabbinic liturgy, the prayer space is technically created by the gathering of the community. As we saw above, where the community gathers the Shekhinah eagerly arrives first. But the rabbis also suggest that prayer in a synagogue is more assuredly in the Divine Presence than prayer elsewhere. Exodus 20:20, after commanding that the Israelites erect an earthen altar on which to offer sacrifices, cites God as saying, "In every place where I cause my name to be mentioned, I will come to you and bless you." The Jerusalem Talmud (j. Ber. 4:4, 8b) indicates that this is the reason why one must pray in a place designated for prayer. The verse does not say "wherever you mention My name," but "where I cause My name to be mentioned." Humans do not control, or even invoke, the Divine Presence; they respond to it.

RESPONDING TO GOD'S PRESENCE

How does one respond to the Divine Presence? How does this situation evoke behavior different from the ordinary? In many synagogues today this concern determines the Talmud-inspired inscriptions placed prominently above the Torah ark. We often find the imperative, "Know before Whom you [singular] are standing,"[28] or the Psalm verse, connected with the presence of the Shekhinah already in the Talmud, "I am ever mindful of the Eternal's presence."[29] Human nature is apt to forget the invisible Divine Presence; reminders help.

Judaism rarely relies on abstract or philosophically driven directions to achieve a religious goal, preferring to legislate concretely. For at least the central prayers, the rabbis also direct the postures in which the prayers must be recited. In the case of the most important of these prayers, the *amidah*, the understanding that one is standing before and in the presence of God drives the requirements surrounding its performance. Typical of rabbinic methods, the authority that dictates most decisions here is biblical proof texts, as this is the way to know what

[28] First documented in the ethical will of Rabbi Eliezer (Rabbi Eliezer ben Hyrcanus, d. early second century, or perhaps an eleventh-century European sage), where he writes, "My son, when you enter before your Creator, enter in fear and awe, and when you pray, know before Whom you are standing." See J. D. Eisenstein, ed., *Oẓar Midrashim* 1 (1915; rpt. New York: E. Grossman, 1956), "Eliezer," p. 29, #18. Compare b. Ber. 28b.

[29] Ps 16:8; b. Sanh. 22a. For the combination, see the geonic *Halakhot Gedolot*, Siman 1, *Laws of Blessings* 5. Some synagogues use the verse "Let them make Me a sanctuary that I may dwell among them" (Exod 25:8).

Ruth Langer

36

will be pleasing to God. One of the earliest sources preserved on this issue establishes that this prayer should be recited from a low place, not while standing on a couch, bench, or chair, so that it will be "from the depths" in accordance with Psalm 130:1. The Talmudic version of this tradition explains this, saying, "because there is no self-elevation before *HaMaqom*."[30]

How should one stand? The Talmud cites another early teaching that "the worshiper must straighten his legs" because, according to Ezekiel's description, the angels had legs fused into "a single rigid leg." The Jerusalem Talmud indicates that to stand like the angels is to stand with legs together, placed side to side.[31] Later texts establish that this posture, logically, is also the correct posture for human participation in the angelic liturgy.[32]

Talmudic-era texts choreograph only how to leave this posture, not how to enter it.[33] The instructions appear with a discussion of how the High Priest left the Holy of Holies on Yom Kippur: he left in the way he had entered, i.e., without turning his back to it. This principle extends to all who witness Temple rituals, and their departure from the Temple itself, with only their heads turned to see where they are going, as well as to students leaving their teacher. Consequently, the Talmud teaches that the person concluding the *ʿamidah* "must take three steps backwards and then give [a farewell] greeting . . . if he

[30] t. Ber. 3:17; b. Ber. 10a; j. Ber. 2:3, 4d; j. Meg. 1:9, 72c. This has usually meant that this prayer is led by someone standing at floor level before the ark, but the occasional synagogue, like the Alt-Neu Shul in Prague, built a recessed space for the precentor to stand in. Compare also b. Yev. 105b's instruction that when one prays one's face should be directed to the ground, but one's heart to heaven, presumably also an expression of humility.

[31] Ezek 1:7, b. Ber. 10a, j. Ber. 1:1, 2c. However, see Uri Ehrlich, *Nonverbal Language* (n. 23), chap. 1, "The Standing Posture." He suggests that the discussion of standing derives from the fact that there was no sitting in the Temple, making standing the appropriate posture in the presence of God.

[32] Three loci for the *qedushah* or *sanctus/trishagion* exist in rabbinic liturgy, but only that embedded in the repetition of the *ʿamidah* is understood to be an act of actual participation in the angelic praise of God, not merely a description of it. On the complexities of this, see my *To Worship God Properly* (as in n. 12), chap. 4.

[33] Instructions for the worshiper to walk forward three steps before beginning the prayer appear in texts from the twelfth-century school of Rashi in Northern France. See *Maḥzor Vitry* #21 and *Siddur Rashi* #29.

The Presence of God in Jewish Liturgy

fails to do this, it is as if he has not prayed at all." "Giving a [fare-well] greeting" means bowing to the right and then to the left. Why? Because two verses speak of God's right hand (Deut 33:2; Ps 91:7). Fourth-century sages then discuss whether this means that one should first bow to the left, because that would be God's right.[34]

Numerous aspects of this Talmudic discussion underline our points here. The high priest's experience in the Holy of Holies on Yom Kippur was the single annual entry of any human into the inner sanctum of the Divine Presence. It was understood to be an intense encounter, fraught with danger. Praying the *amidah* is only a shadow of this, but it also occurs in the Divine Presence and requires proper etiquette. The rabbis derive this etiquette both from the Temple and from the patterns of human behavior expected in their world between people of different social ranks. The three steps they require are symbolic, for while one can determine when one has left the presence of another human or the Temple precincts, one never actually leaves the presence of God. However, we humans do need to reenter the profane realm.[35] Nevertheless, the space in which the prayer was recited was holy space in which God was really present, a space the rabbis determine radiates four cubits around the worshiper.[36]

Thus, the rabbis, while never ceasing to mourn for the Temple and to pray for its reconstruction, adamantly reject Christian claims that the Temple's absence deprives Jews of the Divine Presence and cove-

[34] b. Yoma 53b. This question of toward which direction to bow first continues to be an issue. See, for instance, *Halakhot Gedolot 1, Hilkhot Berakhot 5*.

[35] Medieval instructions direct that one reenter this holy space by stepping back into it for the *qedushah*. However, there is not another formal leave-taking. An apparently modern custom observed in Orthodox contexts is that worshipers omit the instruction to remain standing where they complete their steps backwards, but instead immediately return three steps forward and bounce on their toes, usually three times. I have found no adequate explanation for this, nor any instruction to do it, except in a few (but not all) ArtScroll prayer books (without the bounces). Possibly this derives from a popular conflation of the choreography of the *qedushah* with that of the private recitation of the *amidah*.

[36] b. Ber. 31b. See also Ehrlich, *Nonverbal Language*, 17–18, 240–43, and the sources he cites. These discuss the prohibition of praying within four cubits of urine, symbolic of necessary human activities that are incompatible with God's sanctity. For the larger topic discussed in this paragraph, see his chap. 6, "Taking Leave of Prayer."

Ruth Langer

nantal life. It is possible that the polemic that emerged during the "partings of the ways" shaped their teaching about the presence of God in the synagogue and their consequent directions for performance of prayer. God wants Jewish prayer so badly as to arrive first in the synagogue, and humans should behave there accordingly. Of course, God's locus remains primarily on the Temple Mount—even when it serves as the location of a pagan temple, a Christian garbage dump, or, since the seventh century, a Muslim holy place. The synagogue building and the liturgy performed there can and do invoke the Temple, especially as a preferred place to encounter God. The rabbis state with conviction that their liturgy, performed properly, is efficacious and pleasing to God.

Simon Chan

3. The Liturgy as the Work of the Spirit: A Theological Perspective

THE SPIRIT AND THE CHURCH

From ancient times the church has always recognized the intimate connection between pneumatology and ecclesiology. This can be seen, for example, in the third article of the Apostles' Creed where the Spirit and the church occur in close proximity to each other: "I believe in the Holy Spirit, the Holy Catholic Church, the communion of saints . . ." In some early baptismal creeds, the question posed to catechumens was: "Do you believe in the Holy Spirit *in* the holy church?"[1] A comparison between the doxology at the end of the Roman canon and the eucharistic prayer of the so-called *Apostolic Tradition* shows how closely the Holy Spirit is identified with the church in ancient liturgies.

The focus of this paper is on the pneumatological dimension of the church. Nothing is said about the christological dimension that is necessary for a fuller account of the church. When considering the Third Person of the Trinity, the First and Second Persons are presupposed; otherwise there is no coherent trinitarian narrative to speak of.

[1] *Apostolic Tradition* 21.17; see Gregory Dix, *The Treatise on the Apostolic Tradition of St. Hippolytus of Rome* (London: Alban Press, 1937, 1992), 37. For a critical discussion of the difference between the Latin version ("Do you believe in the Holy Spirit and the holy church?") and the others, see Alistair Stewart-Sykes, *On the Apostolic Tradition* (Crestwood, NY: St. Vladimir's Seminary Press, 2001), 115–16. See the critical edition of all versions of the *Apostolic Tradition* in: Paul F. Bradshaw et al., *The Apostolic Tradition: A Commentary*, Hermeneia (Minneapolis: Fortress Press, 2002).

Roman Canon	Apostolic Tradition
Per ipsum et cum ipso et in ipso	*Per quem*
est tibi	*tibi*
Deo Patri omnipotenti	*gloria et honor*
in unitate Spiritus Sancti	*Patri et Filio cum Sancto Spiritu*
omnis honor et gloria	*in sancta Ecclesia tua*
per omnia saecula saeculorum	*et nunc et in saecula saeculorum*

Notice that where the Roman Canon has "in the unity of the Holy Spirit," the *Apostolic Tradition* has "in your holy Church." This has prompted J. A. Jungmann to comment that "the 'unity of the Holy Ghost' in the modern Mass is only another way of saying the 'holy Church'. . . . She *is* the unity of the Holy Ghost."[2] This close relationship between the Spirit and the church is not an invention of the church for its own ulterior purposes, but reflects faithfully the biblical story of the trinitarian economy. To this story we must now turn.

Although there are many ways of conceiving the trinitarian relationship,[3] the "sending" model is probably the most basic. The trinitarian economy can be understood in terms of the story of the sending of Jesus Christ and the Holy Spirit, commonly called the "two sendings." In the unfolding of the trinitarian mission Jesus Christ is the fulcrum. It is through his coming that we are given a fuller knowledge of God. It was Jesus' own self-consciousness of who he was and what he was called to do in relation to YHWY that constitutes the beginnings of a uniquely Christian conception of God. As N. T. Wright observes,

> Jesus of Nazareth was conscious of a vocation: a vocation, given him
> by the one he knew as "father," to enact in himself what, in Israel's
> scriptures, God had promised to accomplish all by himself. He would

---

[2] J. A. Jungmann, *The Mass of the Roman Rite: Its Origin and Development*, trans. Francis A. Brunner (New York: Benziger Bros., 1955) 2:265. Emphasis mine.

[3] Kilian McDonnell identifies four other models: the Effective Act Model, the Kyrios Model, the Historical Model, and the Access Model. See *The Other Hand of God: The Holy Spirit as the Universal Touch and Goal* (Collegeville, MN: Liturgical Press, 2003), 7–8.

Simon Chan

be the pillar of cloud and fire for the people of the new Exodus. He would embody in himself the returning and redeeming action of the covenant God.[4]

The early disciples' understanding of this fact, confirmed by the resurrection of Jesus, led to the radical reordering of their understanding of God. But the recognition of Jesus as standing in the place of YHWY does not in itself establish the trinitarian doctrine. In fact, for a time the early church tended to speak more in binitarian than in trinitarian terms.[5] What led the church eventually to the formulation of the trinitarian dogma?[6]

The answer is to be found in the story of the "second sending." In the second sending Jesus makes known the identity of the Holy Spirit. What is unique about the second sending is the special relationship that the Holy Spirit bears to Jesus. Jesus is the sender of the Spirit; more specifically, he is the Spirit-baptizer. This is the unambiguous testimony of Scripture. Of all the New Testament references to the identity of Jesus, that as Spirit-baptizer is perhaps the most widely attested (Matt 3:11-12; Mark 1:8; Luke 3:6; John 1:26-27, 33; Acts 1:5; 11:16). This fact, more than any other, led the church toward a full-orbed trinitarian doctrine. Its development can be traced briefly as follows. In the Old Testament the outpouring of God's Spirit as the sign of the messianic age is seen as the direct work of YHWY (cf. Acts 2:17 = Joel 2:28). Further, it is generally agreed that the Spirit of YHWY does not refer to a separate identity but to YHWY in action. We have as yet no clear "hypostasis" of the Spirit. In the New Testament Jesus claims to send the Spirit from the Father (Luke 24:49; John 15:26). This claim puts him in the position of YHWY, but, unlike the other claims to divinity, this one requires revising the Old Testament identification of the Spirit with YHWY himself; otherwise Jesus would be "lord" over the Father. This juxtaposing of God and Jesus as Spirit-baptizer makes it

---

[4] N. T. Wright, *The Challenge of Jesus* (London: SPCK, 2000), 91–92.

[5] But this was, as Kilian McDonnell has pointed out, more of a habit of mind than a theology. The Trinity was presupposed but trinitarian theology was not given explicit form until about a quarter century before the Council of Constantinople. See *The Other Hand of God*, 16.

[6] Ibid., 92; cf. N. T. Wright, *The New Testament and the People of God* (Minneapolis: Fortress, 1992), 362, 448.

The Liturgy as the Work of the Spirit

necessary for the Spirit to be differentiated from the Father.[7] In other words, it is primarily in relation to Jesus as Spirit-baptizer that the full trinitarian doctrine is revealed.

The distinct identity of the Spirit is given fuller elaboration in the so-called Farewell Discourse in John 14–16. Raymond Brown in his commentary notes that nowhere else in the New Testament is the person of the Spirit more clearly disclosed.[8] In this Discourse the Spirit is identified as "another" (*allos*) Paraclete, that is, another of the same kind as Jesus. Brown also notes that everything that is said about the Paraclete has been said about Jesus (1140). The Paraclete can be no less a person than Jesus if he is to be an adequate replacement of Jesus after his ascension.

But the Holy Spirit is more than a substitute for the absent Jesus. There is something new in, and unique to, the economy of the Spirit.[9] What the Spirit does goes beyond what Jesus did. His work in relation to Christ is not only to remind the disciples of what they had heard from Christ. The Spirit also shows them "things to come." These are not just events about to happen to Jesus, especially his coming death, resurrection, and glorification. As Max Turner has pointed out, "Jesus does, after all, say the Spirit will announce what he *shall* hear (not what he *has* heard), and it would be difficult to restrict 'all the truth' and 'the things to come' to the significance of Jesus' glorification alone, and absolutely nothing else."[10]

---

[7] Max Turner, *The Holy Spirit and Spiritual Gifts* (Peabody, MA: Hendrickson, 1998), 169–78. See also Frank Macchia, *Baptized in the Spirit: A Global Pentecostal Theology* (Grand Rapids, MI: Zondervan, 2006), 110.

[8] Raymond E. Brown, *The Gospel according to John*, The Anchor Bible (Garden City, NY: Doubleday, 1970) 2:1139.

[9] Some would go further and argue that some aspects of the Spirit's work in the divine economy belong uniquely to the Spirit alone. They are the Spirit's *propria*, rather than being his by appropriation. Yves Congar notes that this is increasingly acknowledged in the Catholic West. See *I Believe in the Holy Spirit* (New York: Seabury, 1983) 2:86–88. Cf. Ralph Del Colle, *Christ and the Spirit: Spirit-Christology in Trinitarian Perspective* (Oxford: Oxford University Press, 1994), 74.

[10] Turner, *The Holy Spirit*, 83–84. Oddly, Turner would not include "the *church's* future" as part of that revelation (84). I would argue that despite his attempt to expand the scope of the Spirit's future revelation, Turner's understanding is still too restrictive.

Simon Chan

44

The uniqueness of the economy of the Spirit becomes clearer in light of the Pentecost event. Just as a story makes full sense only when it reaches its end, the story of the triune God is more fully understood only with the coming of the Spirit at Pentecost. Pentecost may be considered the dénouement of the story of salvation: the "last days" have arrived (Acts 2:17). To be sure, this is not the final End but a provisional End, since the Spirit is the "firstfruits" that anticipates the final harvest at the Parousia.[11] Pentecost, nonetheless, completes the story of the triune God.[12] But what is the story of the Spirit? It is essentially the story of the Spirit's coming to the church and constituting it as the church. The story of the church is so inextricably linked to the story of the Third Person of the Trinity that any attempt to de-link the church from that story simply does not do full justice to the real identity of both the church and the Holy Spirit. If the coming of the Spirit *to the church* is the completion of the trinitarian mission, and the church is the *locus* of the revelation of the Spirit *as* Third Person, then the church must be part of the definition of the Spirit and the Spirit part of the definition of the church. This biblical insight is what the third article of the Creed is about; it has been extensively developed in Orthodox theology and preserved in its liturgy. It is not an overstatement to say that in the Orthodox liturgy we see the full ramifications of the third article of the Creed.

The Protestant tradition, particularly the Reformed variety, on the other hand, tends to distance the Spirit from the church rather than seeing them as mutually constitutive.[13] Karl Barth may be cited as a case in point. Many appreciative critics of Barth's high Christology have also pointed out that Barth's ecclesiology suffers from a serious pneu-

[11] The Spirit himself as Person can be said to be the causation of the divine narrative; he is "the Power of God's *own* and our future" (Robert W. Jenson, *Systematic Theology* [New York: Oxford University Press, 1997] 1:160).

[12] See Del Colle, *Christ and the Spirit*, 25.

[13] This is true of most evangelicals. We already see something of this in Turner. Many others may be cited, such as Donald Bloesch, *The Church: Sacraments, Worship, Ministry, Mission* (Downers Grove, IL: IVP, 2002), 47–48; George Vandervelde, "The Challenge of Evangelical Ecclesiology," *Evangelical Review of Theology* 27 (2003): 4–26; John Webster, "The Church and the Perfection of God," in *The Community of the Word*, ed. Mark Husbands and Daniel J. Treier, 75–95 (Downers Grove, IL: IVP, 2005); Mark Saucy, "Evangelical, Catholic and Orthodox Together: Is the Church the Extension of the Incarnation?" *Journal of the Evangelical Theological Society* 43 (June 2000): 193–212.

matological deficit.[14] According to Barth, the Spirit's work is merely to "realize subjectively" what has been accomplished by God in eternity in Christ.[15] This is due to the fact that Barth, in good Reformed fashion, so stresses the sovereignty of grace, more specifically the totally determinative nature of election in Christ, that it leaves no room for a sacramental theology or for the Spirit's own constitutive work in the church. Part of the reason for this pneumatological reserve is the fear that to identify the Spirit too closely with the church would lead to triumphalism. The consequence is that Protestantism has not developed a fully sacramental and liturgical theology. What I mean by a fully sacramental and liturgical theology is one in which the liturgy, that is, the "work of the people," is simultaneously the work of the Spirit.

The Protestant fear of claims about special possession of the Spirit is understandable in light of the Reformation, which began as a protest against such unwarranted claims from both the medieval church and the enthusiasts. It has often been said that ecclesiology in the Roman

[14] See Robert W. Jenson, "You Wonder Where the Spirit Went," *Pro Ecclesia* 2 (1993): 296–304; Nicholas M. Healy, "The Logic of Karl Barth's Ecclesiology: Analysis, Assessment and Proposed Modifications," *Modern Theology* 10 (1994): 253–70; Stanley Hauerwas, *With the Grain of the Universe: The Church's Witness and Natural Theology* (Grand Rapids, MI: Brazos, 2001), 144–45, 192–95; Reinhard Hütter, *Suffering Divine Things: Theology as Church Practice* (Grand Rapids, MI: Eerdmans, 2000), 105–12; Joseph L. Mangina, "Bearing the Mark of Jesus: The Church in the Economy of Salvation in Barth and Hauerwas," *Scandinavian Journal of the Old Testament* 52 (1999): 269–305; idem, "The Stranger as Sacrament: Karl Barth and the Ethics of Ecclesial Practice," *International Journal of Systematic Theology* 1 (1999): 322–39; James J. Buckley, "Christian Community, Baptism, and Lord's Supper," in *The Cambridge Companion to Karl Barth*, ed. John Webster, 195–211 (Cambridge: Cambridge University Press, 2000). Cf. Kimlyn J. Bender, *Karl Barth's Christological Ecclesiology* (Aldershot, UK: Ashgate, 2005), 280.

[15] What is said about Christ and the church parallels what Barth says about the relationship between Good Friday and Easter. The resurrection bears "witness" to the work of reconciliation that was effectively completed on the cross, which raises the question whether the resurrection adds anything new. See Mangina, "Bearing the Mark of Jesus," 275–77. The church is identified with Christ only at the level of election in eternity, "sheerly as a predicate of divine action," not at the level of its concrete existence (ibid., 278, 280). Consequently, Barth's understanding of Christ and the church tends to vacillate between "complete identity and complete non-identity" (302).

Simon Chan

46

Catholic Church has tended to focus on its institutional life, hierarchically ordered around its single head, the pope. But this cannot be said of the Eastern Church. Far from becoming triumphalistic, its doctrine of the church existing in epicletic relation to the Spirit recognizes the church's total dependence on grace. The church must constantly empty itself in order to be filled with the Spirit. Deep humility is needed if the church is to experience what Nikos Nissiotis calls a "perpetual Pentecost."[16] This is why, according to Nissiotis, the epiclesis is the only point in the Orthodox liturgy when the congregation kneels.[17] Recognizing that the liturgy is "pneumatologically conditioned"[18] keeps us from seeing the church as a dispenser of grace. Rather, the church must place itself always at God's disposal.

Theologically, the Spirit is the gift of love from the Father poured out on the church (Rom 5:5). As gift to the church, the Spirit enables the church to return love to the Father through the Son.[19] The Spirit draws believers into a filial relationship and enables them to cry out, "Abba! Father!" (Rom 8:15; Gal 4:6) This *responsive* love is the foundation of Christian worship. Worship may be defined as the Spirit-inspired response of the church to the revelation of the triune God in which praise is rendered "to the Father, through the Son and in the Spirit." The liturgy schematizes or enacts this dynamic.

THE PARADOXES OF THE LITURGY

Gordon Lathrop notes that the liturgy is characterized by many "juxtapositions."[20] That is to say, the truths that the various liturgical

[16] Nikos A. Nissiotis, "Called to Unity: The Significance of the Invocation of the Spirit for Church Unity," in *Lausanne 77: Fifty Years of Faith and Order*, Faith and Order paper 82 (Geneva: World Council of Churches, 1977), 48–64, here 54.

[17] Ibid., 55. Nissiotis is obviously referring to epicleses in Orthodox liturgies other than the Sunday eucharistic celebration. Canon 20 of the Council of Nicaea explicitly forbids kneeling on Sunday.

[18] John Zizioulas, "The Doctrine of God the Trinity Today: Suggestions for an Ecumenical Study," in *The Forgotten Trinity*, ed. Alasdair Heron, 27–28 (London: British Council of Churches, 1991).

[19] This "return model" of the Trinity has been developed by David Coffey, *Deus Trinitas: The Doctrine of the Triune God* (New York: Oxford University Press, 1999), 38–41.

[20] This interpretive strategy is basic to Gordon W. Lathrop's work; see his book *Holy Things: A Liturgical Theology* (Minneapolis: Fortress, 1993).

The Liturgy as the Work of the Spirit

elements convey are often set in paradoxical relation to one another. Thus Sunday is the first day as well as the eighth day, juxtaposing the old and the new creations respectively; baptism is both burial of the old life and resurrection to new life, etc. These paradoxes reflect the church's eschatological existence created by the coming of the Spirit as the "firstfruits" of the new creation (Rom 8:23). In other words, these paradoxes can only be understood in terms of the special relation between the Spirit and the church. The Spirit coming *from the future* to the church existing *in history* cannot be other than paradoxical. But the paradox runs deeper, and has to do with the way in which the Spirit and church are *mutually* constitutive.

Zizioulas describes the Spirit as the one who comes from "beyond history" to act upon our history rather than to be incarnated in our history like Jesus Christ (only Jesus shares our history). But the coming of the Spirit transfigures history, turning historical events into "charismatic-Pentecostal events." There is a sort of "extrinsicism" in the Spirit's operation, his standing, as it were, over against the church, acting "on" rather than "becoming" part of history.[21] This constant coming *from beyond* history challenges the church and keeps it open to a future that is not within its control.

While the Spirit is not the church's possession to be dispensed at will, yet it is also true to say that the Spirit in coming to indwell the church is ecclesially conditioned, taking on an ecclesial "shape."[22] This is well summed up by Ralph Del Colle:

> The economy of the Holy Spirit follows that of the Son because the Spirit is the image of the Son even as the Son is the image of the Father. The Holy Spirit is the only divine person who does not have an image in another person of the trinity. This is why the Holy Spirit remains hidden even in the work of redemption.[23]

But in coming to the church, Del Colle continues,

---

[21] Zizioulas, *Being as Communion*, 130.

[22] This indwelling is to be distinguished from the hypostatic union that belongs only to the Second Person. The Holy Spirit is not incarnated in the church, so that he can both "be in" and "act on" the church.

[23] Del Colle, *Christ and the Spirit*, 25. The point was made by Vladimir Lossky, who traces it to John of Damascus. See *The Mystical Theology of the Eastern Church* (London: James Clarke, 1957), 160.

Simon Chan

The image of the Holy Spirit, not borne by another divine person, becomes actual in created persons . . . through his deifying work. In this sense the ministry of the Holy Spirit is associated with ecclesiology; some even make the argument that ecclesiology is best understood when it is a branch of pneumatology. (25)

In coming to the church, the Spirit experiences a *kenosis*. He becomes the "localized" Shekinah in the church just as YHWY's Shekinah was localized in the tabernacle.[24] Again, in the words of Del Colle,

The triune economy reaches its goal in the economy of the Holy Spirit, who like the Son undergoes his own kenosis in a temporal mission. Just as the Son emptied himself by becoming flesh through the union of his hypostasis to a human nature, so, too, the Holy Spirit empties himself by indwelling human hypostases through the impartation of uncreated grace. The former unifies common human nature in the one hypostasis of the Son; the latter diversifies God's gifts among many human persons or hypostases.[25]

This does not mean that the Spirit is placed at the beck and call of the church. The Spirit is still "the Lord and Giver of life." As one Orthodox theologian reminds us, "His presence, as the giver of life, is not to be interpreted in terms of an immanent principle by which the Church succeeds to the authority of her Lord. In His sanctifying presence it is the Lord God Himself who exercises His own authority over His chosen and elect people."[26] What this means is that the Spirit bears a special relation to the church such that the purpose of God for the whole

[24] Lossky, *Mystical Theology* 164; cf. 244; see also Boris Bobrinskoy, "The Church and the Holy Spirit in 20th Century Russia," *The Ecumenical Review* (July 2000): 334, citing Lossky and Bulgakov. Jürgen Moltmann, however, sees the Spirit's *kenosis* and Shekinah only in connection with his descent upon Jesus and in his identification with Jesus' suffering. See *The Way of Jesus Christ: Christology in Messianic Dimensions* (London: SCM, 1990), 174; *The Spirit of Life: A Universal Affirmation* (Minneapolis: Fortress, 1993), 62.

[25] *Christ and the Spirit*, 25. The idea that Christ unifies while the Spirit diversifies is also found in Lossky, *Mystical Theology*, 166–68.

[26] Angelos J. Philippou, "The Mystery of Pentecost," in *The Orthodox Ethos*, ed. A. J. Philippou, 91 (Oxford: Holywell, 1964).

The Liturgy as the Work of the Spirit

49

creation finds its actualization only by the Spirit-in-and-through-the-church.[27] The Spirit's relation to the church is characterized by a deep paradox. The Spirit is always over and acting upon the church, yet he is also within, acting alongside of the church both in his work of sanctifying grace and in his own person (uncreated grace).[28] The Spirit both shapes the church and is ecclesially shaped. This mystery of the Spirit in the church—the mystery of the third article of the Creed—is concretely actualized in the liturgy as the work of the Spirit in "the work of the people."

THE WORK OF THE SPIRIT IN THE WORK OF THE PEOPLE

But how is the work of the people the work of the Spirit? To understand this dialectic we can begin with Luther's "marks" of the church as a number of "evangelical-catholic" scholars have done in recent years.[29] Luther identifies seven marks of the church: the preached word, baptism, the Lord's Supper, the keys (church discipline), church offices, worship, and cross-bearing. He understands these marks as the works of the Holy Spirit: "the great holy possession whereby the Holy Spirit effects in us a daily sanctification and vivification in

[27] This thought is captured in the ancient phrase *extra ecclesiam nulla salus* (no salvation outside the church) but goes beyond the matter of salvation. It implies a relation between the church and creation in which the church is the goal of creation rather than the instrument to fulfill God's purpose in creation; that is to say, creation exists for the church rather than vice versa. It is in terms of this special relationship that we can properly understand the doctrine of *Creator Spiritus*. See my *Liturgical Theology: The Church as Worshipping Community* (Downers Grove, IL: IVP, 2006), chap. 1.

[28] Del Colle—citing Matthias J. Scheeben, *The Mysteries of Christianity*, trans. Cyril Vollert (St. Louis, MO / London: Herder, 1946), and Émile Mersch, *The Theology of the Mystical Body*, trans. Cyril Vollert (St. Louis, MO: Herder, 1951)—sees the presence of the Spirit in the church not only as gift of God (*donum Dei*) but also as hypostatic identity (*donum hypostaticum*), i.e., the Spirit is both present as created grace (*sanctifying grace*) and in his own person as uncreated grace (*Christ and the Spirit*, 44).

[29] E.g., Reinhard Hütter, "The Church as Public: Dogma, Practice, and the Holy Spirit," *Pro Ecclesia* 3 (1994): 334–61; idem, *Suffering Divine Things* (Grand Rapids, MI: Eerdmans, 2000); Carl Braaten and Robert W. Jenson, eds., *Marks of the Body of Christ* (Grand Rapids, MI: Eerdmans, 1999); James J. Buckley, and David S. Yeago, eds., *Knowing the Triune God: The Work of the Spirit in the Practices of the Church* (Grand Rapids, MI: Eerdmans, 2001).

Simon Chan

Christ, according to the first table of Moses,"[30] and adds, "I would even call these seven parts the seven sacraments . . ." (LW 165–66). Luther calls them "holy possession" (*Heilthum* or *Heiligthum*) (LW 149). David Yeago notes that in the medieval church *Heilthum* refers to a miracle-working relic, so these marks are a "'miracle working holy thing' through which the Holy Spirit fashions a holy people in the world."[31] These marks also constitute the church as church, as can be seen in a point Luther makes repeatedly, but phrased in various ways when he elaborates on each of them: "Wherever you see this done, be assured that God's people, the holy Christian people, are present" (LW 150, 151, 154). Thus Yeago calls the marks the "core practices" of the church. All these marks are related either directly or indirectly to the worship of the church, thus establishing the inseparable link between the Spirit and the liturgy.[32]

But in what sense are these core practices the works of the Spirit? The point of convergence between the core practices and the work of the Spirit is to be found in their being radically constitutive of the church. In line with the Eastern tradition that we have noted above, Hütter believes that the Spirit's work in the church creates something "completely new," thus indicating a decisive break with world history.[33]

> Creation is redeemed insofar as the triune God draws it into this communion. The eschatological goal is participation in the communion of the Father with the Son in the Holy Spirit. In the incarnation, suffering, death, and resurrection of Jesus Christ, the triune God has begun to draw creation into his communion in a *completely new fashion*

[30] These marks relate principally to God (the first table of the Law) and are therefore the more primary. Luther also recognizes "holy possessions" according to the second table of the Law, but they are secondary and not determinative of the church as church. Martin Luther, "On the Councils and the Church," *Luther's Works*, ed. Eric W. Gritsch (Philadelphia: Fortress, 1966) 41:166. Henceforth LW.

[31] David S. Yeago, "'A Christian, Holy People': Martin Luther on Salvation and the Church," *Modern Theology* 13 (1997): 110.

[32] Ibid.

[33] Hütter notes that it is this break with universal history that Pannenberg could not allow for; he needs to keep the Spirit within world history in order to establish the truth-claims of Christianity on a universally accepted basis (*Suffering Divine Things*, 121).

The Liturgy as the Work of the Spirit

transcending its original state. This end time is already present "in the Spirit" now in the economic mission of Jesus Christ and the Holy Spirit through the communion of the ecclesial body of Christ.[34]

This distinctive work of the Spirit corresponds to the nature of the core practices that are also constitutive of the church as church. If the Spirit is constantly forming the church as the "public of the Spirit," i.e., a community defined by its own distinctive and authoritative (though not coercive) dogmas, the core practices are the "creatures of the Spirit," the means by which this public or *polis* is constantly being shaped.[35] The Spirit creates new things (*poiesis*), but they develop on existing dogma rather than contradict it.[36] The process is implied in Acts 15:28: "For it has seemed good to the Holy Spirit *and to us . . .*" The Spirit's new work of defining the ecclesial *polis* was very much bound up with the decision of a church council!

SYNERGY

In the Orthodox tradition this working of the Spirit in the church is expressed by the term *synergy*.[37] According to Lossky, synergy "admits of two wills and two operations taking place simultaneously: the priest who consecrates the bread and wine upon the altar invokes the Holy Spirit, and the Spirit effects the eucharistic sacrament; the confessor pronounces the words of absolution, and the transgressions are remitted by the will of God."[38] Unlike in the West where grace is seen either as the *cause* of the "meritorious acts" of our free will (Augustine) or as the *effect* of free will (Pelagius), in the East what we do cannot be perceived as some kind of "merit," whether as cause or effect of grace; rather, synergy means that grace and freedom occur "simultaneously." Synergy "expresses the mystery of the coincidence of grace and human freedom in good works, without recourse to positive and rational terms." This refusal to explain rationally the relation of grace and human freedom reflects the "apophatic attitude" characteristic of Orthodoxy.[39]

[34] Hütter, *Suffering Divine Things*, 124. Emphasis mine.
[35] Hütter, "The Church as Public," 358.
[36] Ibid., 359.
[37] For a helpful study of the liturgy as synergy, see Jean Corbon, *Wellspring of Worship*, trans. Matthew J. O'Connell (New York: Paulist Press, 1988).
[38] Lossky, *Mystical Theology*, 187.
[39] Ibid., 196–97, 239.

Simon Chan

52

Synergy must be seen in relation to the distinctively Eastern concept of freedom as part of the *imago Dei*. Freedom is not to be equated with a *superadditum* of grace or an "original righteousness" but is an ontological reality that distinguishes human nature as such. It is, as Nikos Nissiotis puts it, "the essence of the original relationship of love between the Creator and His creature" which "cannot be effaced, because it constitutes the being of man in relation to His Creator." The *imago Dei* "is the very essence of the creation of man."[40] It is what makes a human being human. It is God's gift from God's very own nature. Synergy is simply human beings acting freely as human beings in response to God's initiative in Christ for their redemption. Responsibility is an essential part of human nature before and after the Fall. Thus the Western debate between Pelagians and Augustinians over the nature of grace, or between Arminians and Calvinists over the extent of human depravity, does not come into consideration at all. This Western predilection is also reflected in the question about the nature of the liturgy: whether it is the work of the people or the work of God (*opus Dei*). If the liturgy is a synergy, then it is both truly the work of the people and truly the work of God. It is the work of God in and through the work of the people.

EPICLESIS

The entire liturgy is a synergy; and the supreme synergy is the epiclesis. Nissiotis considers the church as "the permanent *epiclesis* of the Holy Spirit from the Father and in virtue of the salvation of Christ," and goes on to say, "If we absolutely need a definition of the church, this is the best we can give."[41] In other words, the church may be defined by its relation to the Spirit as the one who is regularly invoked in its eucharistic celebration. It is in this sense that the Eucharist *makes* the church. As John Meyendorff puts it, "The epiclesis . . . is the fulfillment of the Eucharistic action, just as Pentecost is the fulfillment of a divine 'economy' of salvation."[42] Orthodoxy reinforces the sense of the Holy Spirit's presence in the Eucharist in a number of distinctive

[40] Nikos A. Nissiotis, "The Importance of the Doctrine of the Trinity for Church Life and Theology" in *The Orthodox Ethos*, ed. A. J. Philippou, 49 (Oxford: Holywell Press, 1964).

[41] Nissiotis, "Called to Unity," 54.

[42] John Meyendorff, *Byzantine Theology: Historical Trends and Doctrinal Themes*, 2d ed. (New York: Fordham University Press, 1979), 207. See also Paul

The Liturgy as the Work of the Spirit

ways, such as the prayer for healing, the use of leavened bread, and the pouring of hot water into the consecrated wine.[43]

The epiclesis that presupposes the dynamic and continuous coming of the Spirit to the church—"a perpetual Pentecost"[44]— is nothing but a faithful enactment of the third article of the Creed. Synergy means that the Spirit comes in response to the church's invocation. The action of the Spirit is no more or less certain than the action of the church. It is significant that in connection with the sending of the Holy Spirit Jesus promises his disciples: "You may ask me for anything in my name, and I will do it" (John 14:14-15); not coincidentally, his teaching on prayer in Luke's gospel encourages his disciples to ask specifically for the Holy Spirit: "If you then, though you are evil, know how to give good gifts to your children, how much more will your Father in heaven give the Holy Spirit to those who ask him!" (Luke 11:13). Prayer for the coming of the Spirit is the one prayer that is certain to be answered because it is grounded in and flows out of the Pentecost event itself.

The epiclesis is addressed to the Father. This is in keeping with the pneumatology mentioned earlier where the Spirit is not imaged in another Person but always remains, in the words of Yves Congar, the Person "without a personal face."[45] This is why there are few liturgical prayers *to* the Spirit.[46] One such prayer is the ancient hymn *Veni Creator Spiritus* ("Come, Creator Spirit") attributed to Rabanus Maurus (776–856). Another example is the opening prayer at Matins in the Orthodox liturgy: "O Heavenly King, Comforter, Spirit of Truth, who art everywhere and fillest all things, the treasury of blessings, and giver of life, come and abide in us. Cleanse us of all impurity, and of thy goodness save our souls."[47] Is this a slipup on the part of the church? If the

---

McPartlan, *The Eucharist Makes the Church: Henri de Lubac and John Zizioulas in Dialogue* (Edinburgh: T&T Clark, 1993).

[43] Yves Congar, "Renewed Actuality of the Holy Spirit," *Lumen Vitae* 28 (1973): 29–30. Congar notes a fourth-century Syriac eucharistic prayer that goes as follows: "The body of Jesus Christ, the Holy Spirit, for the healing of soul and body" (29).

[44] Nikos Nissiotis; see n. 16.

[45] Congar, *I Believe in the Holy Spirit*, 3:5.

[46] J. A. Jungmann notes that prayers to the Spirit are rarely found except in the Armenian church; see *The Place of Christ in Liturgical Prayers*, trans. A. Peeler (London: Geoffrey Chapman, 1965, 1989), 221.

[47] *A Manual of Eastern Orthodox Prayer* (Crestwood, NY: St. Vladimir's Seminary Press, 1983), 2.

Simon Chan

coming of the Spirit to the church is precisely the coming of the Spirit as the Third Person of the Trinity in his own right, then we can understand why the church has allowed some such prayers to the Spirit to slip in. In these prayers the Spirit is being acknowledged as person: he is being prayed *to*. Further, it is an acknowledgment that we need a continuous Pentecost—thus again underscoring the epicletic nature of the church.[48] And because the Spirit has come to the church, the Spirit *and* the church can pray with one voice: "Come!" and "Amen. Come, Lord Jesus" (Rev 22:17, 20). The church's eschatological longing itself is induced by the eschatological Spirit in the church.

ACTIVE PARTICIPATION

If synergy means that both the Holy Spirit and the church are active simultaneously, then the only appropriate stance for worshipers is "active participation."[49] Active participation requires the whole community of the faithful collectively, but also each member personally, to be engaged.[50] Personal active participation, however, does not mean that one engages the liturgy with a view to discovering what might be most beneficial for one's own spiritual formation. Rather, as a member of the Body of Christ who has been incorporated into the Body by baptism, I place myself in the corporate life of the church. Active participation, then, is the actualizing or manifesting of our baptismal faith.[51] One cooperates with others to carry out the "work of the people of God." When I place myself in the liturgy, rather than trying to apply the liturgy to myself, I am gradually formed as a member of the Body of Christ. My own feelings are not the primary consideration.

[48] Congar, *I Believe in the Holy Spirit*, 1:108–10.

[49] See the Constitution on the Sacred Liturgy of Vatican II (*Sacrosanctum Concilium*), no. 30.

[50] This is repeatedly stressed in various post–Vatican II documents, such as *Redemptionis Sacramentum*, nos. 36–42. The caption of this section (II.1) is "Active and Conscious Participation." Similarly, *Sacramentum Caritatis* speaks of "the personal conditions required for fruitful participation on the part of individuals" (no. 55; cf. no. 63). <http://www.vatican.va/roman_curia/congregations/ccdds/documents/rc_con_ccdds_doc_20040423_redemptionis-sacramentum_en.html>; <http://www.vatican.va/holy_father/benedict_xvi/apost_exhortations/documents/hf_ben-xvi_exh_20070222_sacramentum-caritatis_en.html#top>

[51] See *Redemptionis Sacramentum*, no. 37.

The Liturgy as the Work of the Spirit

But this does not mean that the liturgy has no effect on me. As Jardine Grisbrooke puts it, the liturgy "cuts grooves in the mind," such that one begins to engage the liturgy contemplatively and attains a state of active passivity as the liturgy takes a firmer hold of one's life.[52] Active participation, therefore, is not necessarily to be found in the activism that is often associated with the lively "contemporary" service. A close parallel exists between active participation in the liturgy and the teaching on prayer in the mystical tradition of the church. The life of prayer, as Saint Teresa of Avila has taught us, begins with active, vocal prayer and meditation and progresses to contemplative, more passive forms.[53] The same can be said about active participation in the liturgy. The "contemporary" service often captures one's initial attention, but over time one discovers that the constant stirring of emotions may actually prevent one from entering into a deeper level of active participation in the liturgy. This may explain why in recent years a number of Pentecostal-Charismatic Christians are discovering a deeper level of engagement in sacramental theology and liturgical worship.[54]

On the other hand, those who grow up with the liturgy can all too easily fall into a mindless routine. Then the Holy Spirit is no longer experienced as one coming from "beyond history" but as a domesticated spirit. Here is where Pentecostals can make a distinct contribution by a practical pneumatology that creates an expectation of the Holy Spirit's continuing operation in the church in the here and now, as exemplified in one of their popular choruses:

Come, Holy Spirit, I need thee
Come, sweet Spirit, I pray
Come in thy strength and thy power
Come in thy own special way

[52] W. Jardine Grisbrooke, "Towards a Liturgical Spirituality," *Studia Liturgica* 17 (1987): 77–86.

[53] E.g., in *The Interior Castle*. See my discussion in *Pentecostal Theology and the Christian Spiritual Tradition* (Sheffield, UK: Sheffield Academic Press, 2000), 58–60.

[54] E.g., the International Communion of the Charismatic Episcopal Church, the Communion of Evangelical Episcopal Churches, and others. The phenomenon has not gone unnoticed in the Pentecostal-Charismatic world. See Paul Thigpen, "Ancient Altars, Pentecostal Fires," *Ministry Today* (Nov.–Dec. 1992): 43–51.

Simon Chan

We may question whether the song meets the standards of good liturgy, but it has at least the effect of jolting us out of our complacency. The Spirit coming from beyond drives home the point that there is more to the work of the Spirit in the work of the people than just ensuring that the liturgy is carried out in a prim-and-proper manner.

CONCLUSION

In this paper I have tried to show that the affirmation that the liturgy is the work of the Holy Spirit stems from a theological understanding of the Spirit's coming to the church as an extension of the trinitarian economy. The Spirit's coming creates a profound dialectical relationship with the church: the Spirit is "from beyond" and yet is intimately linked to the life and practices of the church; he is both Lord over the church and at the same time he takes shape within the temple as the Shekinah. And yet in his kenosis the Holy Spirit is no less the Lord and giver of life. The church's understanding of this dialectic is encapsulated in the doctrine of synergy which finds its culmination in the epiclesis and calls for the church's active participation. Only when the church takes full cognizance of all these realities is there a living liturgy and a living tradition energized by the Holy Spirit.

Matthew Myer Boulton

4. The Adversary: Agony, Irony, and the Liturgical Role of the Holy Spirit

In the varied corridors of Christian visual art, depictions of Jacob's long night on the shores of the Jabbok (Gen 32:22-32) are typically entitled "Jacob Wrestling with the Angel." On the contrary, however, the unnamed adversary in this story is no angel—and Jacob knows it. After all, angels conventionally come bearing messages (Greek *angelos*, "messenger"), but in the throes of this contest Jacob demands not a message but a blessing, something angels normally announce but rarely bestow. No, this is no angel. At daybreak the stranger gives Jacob a new name: *Israel*, that is, "one who strives with God" (Gen 32:28). In turn, Jacob names the struggle's site after his rival: "So Jacob called the place *Peniel* [the face of God], saying, 'For I have seen God face to face, and yet my life is preserved'" (Gen 32:30).

In other words, Jacob's nocturnal adversary in this story is none other than God. And for Christians reading with the divine Trinity in mind, while it is too much to say that Jacob's adversary here is God the Spirit, the story is strikingly resonant with the various ways Christian biblical texts and interpreters so often figure the Holy Spirit in adversarial terms. Alongside the widely familiar names for the Spirit that emphasize her supportive, assistive role ("Sustainer," "Comforter," "Advocate," and so on), the adversarial dimension of the Spirit's work is a fundamental, indispensable theological theme in Christian thought and life. In this essay I trace this theme in broad outline and then suggest some implications for understanding and practicing Christian worship today.

To anticipate: I argue that the epicletic character of Christian worship—that is, the extent to which it takes the explicit or implicit form of epiclesis, a plea for the Spirit to come and be present to and in the worship service itself—should be conceived and enacted as a recognition of worship's own destitution and malformation, its urgent need for the Spirit's gracious, transformational presence. In other words, worshiping Christians properly call on the Holy Spirit not so that she may come and supplement or enhance their already excellent, beautiful, and just proceedings, but rather so that she may creatively oppose and remake their profoundly destitute, malformed proceedings into something excellent, beautiful, and just. Practitioners properly pray, then, for the arrival of the divine Sustainer, Comforter, and Advocate—but also the divine Adversary. Like Jacob, those embroiled in services of Christian worship require a new blessing and a new name, which is to say, a struggle that will challenge them, change them, strengthen them, and eventually send them out in a genuinely new direction.

In what follows I will first spell out these ideas exegetically, briefly reviewing key biblical loci for Christian theological reflection on the Spirit, including the opening creation narrative in Genesis; the broad witness of the Hebrew prophets; the baptism of Jesus; the day of Pentecost; and Paul's cosmic, liturgical construal of the Spirit in Romans 8. This list is by no means exhaustive, of course, but rather represents the broad range of biblical texts that have been formative for Christian reflection upon and experience of the Holy Spirit. And in each case, as I will show, the agonistic, adversarial dimension of the Spirit's work is a crucial, if often overlooked, part of the picture. Finally, I will briefly point toward how these themes might be developed theologically and liturgically, drawing on Karl Barth's case in *Church Dogmatics*, that a primary and governing mission of the Holy Spirit is no less than "the abolition of religion," which for Barth most fundamentally means the "abolition" (*Aufhebung*) of Christian worship.

Accordingly, I write from a position standing in the broadly Reformed theological tradition, with wide, ecumenical interests in view. Indeed, the theme of this essay is arguably the central theological motif of the sixteenth-century Reformations in Western Europe: that is, the idea that apart from God even the most excellent human resources, even the most prestigious Christian practices, even the very best of Christian liturgical life—even these "holy things"—in themselves only epitomize and perpetuate humanity's fundamental predicament, and therefore are utterly incapable of providing deliverance from it. Only God can do that. And though God may and, Christians confess, does intervene in and through Christian worship, the distinctively (though not exclusively) Protestant task is continually to emphasize that this is always precisely an *intervention*, a divine interruption and

Matthew Myer Boulton

transformation of what is otherwise no "holy thing" at all, but quite the contrary. Put another way, the task is continually to emphasize that Christian worship itself, like the rest of human life, stands in need of divine deliverance—and so Christian worship's epiclesis, the calling on the Holy Spirit to come and be present to and in the worship service, is properly an urgent call, always issued from the depths of what the psalmist styles "the day of trouble" (Ps 50:15).

THE SPIRIT IN SCRIPTURE

To begin, then, at "the beginning": Christian and Jewish exegetes of Genesis 1 have long recognized that the story stands in connection and contrast with other ancient Near Eastern creation narratives, including the *Enuma Elish*, the Babylonian epic in which the god Marduk battles and kills Tiamat, the primeval goddess who is also the primeval saltwater sea. To culminate his victory, Marduk fashions heaven and earth out of Tiamat's oceanic corpse, dividing it in half. On the one hand, then, by contrast, Genesis 1 is a markedly less gruesome affair, with God creating the world not by way of elaborate, deicidal violence, but rather by way of simple, sovereign speech ("Let there be . . .").

On the other hand, however, the basic underlying scenario of divine confrontation with "the sea" is nevertheless discernible in the opening lines of Genesis 1, especially when they are read against the ancient, mythopoetic background found not only in the *Enuma Elish* but also in various places across the Hebrew canon. In Psalm 74, for example, the psalmist invokes a memory of divine victory over "the sea," using images reminiscent of the *Enuma Elish*: "Yet God my King is from of old, / working salvation in the earth. / You divided the sea by your might; / you broke the heads of the dragons in the waters. / You crushed the heads of Leviathan" (Ps 74:12-14). Or again, in Isaiah 51 the prophet calls on God to "Awake, as in days of old, the generations long ago! / Was it not you who cut Rahab [the sea dragon] in pieces, / who pierced the dragon? / Was it not you who dried up the sea, / the waters of the great deep?" (Isa 51:9-10).

With this background in mind, the opening lines of Genesis 1 may be read as a critical variation on this ancient theme. The variation is *critical* inasmuch as divine brutality (whether perpetrated against a goddess or a dragon) is conspicuously absent; and yet the narrative is nevertheless a critical *variation* on the theme inasmuch as here, too, God confronts primeval, oceanic chaos as a creative adversary, working both with it and against it to create the exquisitely ordered world

The Adversary

61

detailed over the course of the story.[1] That is, Genesis 1 begins with God the creator facing not an absolute vacuum but rather *tohu vabohu*, a state often translated into English as "without form and void" (KJV) or "formless void" (NRSV), but which is perhaps more felicitously glossed "chaotic abyss," or better, "wild and waste" (Gen 1:2).[2] And just as the psalmist and Isaiah cast the primeval, chaotic opponent as "the sea" or "the waters of the great deep [*tehom*]," the author of Genesis 1 puts it this way: "and darkness covered the face of the deep [*tehom*], while the spirit of God swept over the face of the waters" (Gen 1:2; my translation). Finally, after creating light (Gen 1:3-5), the

---

[1] For a feminist theological treatment of this material, and an important, provocative attempt to retrieve the categories of "chaos" and "the deep" in more positive ways than typical Christian interpretations of Genesis allow, see Catherine Keller, *The Face of the Deep: A Theology of Becoming* (New York: Rout-ledge, 2003). For my purposes here I take Genesis 1 to represent a theological position by no means simply hostile to chaos, fearful of it, or crudely contrary to it, but rather one that portrays God as complexly working both with it and against it, precisely as a "creative adversary."

[2] "Wild and waste" is from Everett Fox's brilliant translation, *The Five Books of Moses* (New York: Schocken Books, 1995). The term "abyss" may also be especially apt, with its marine etymology (from the Greek, *a-*, "without," and *byssos*, "bottom of the sea," hence "bottomless sea"). In one respect, then, the longstanding Christian (and Jewish) doctrine of *creatio ex nihilo* ("creation out of nothing") may thus be specified: here *nihilo* means not an absolute vacuum but rather a chaotic disorder out of which God makes order, much as a gardener fashions a beautiful and fruitful plot out of "wild and waste." And yet this point should not be overdrawn, for while Genesis 1 does portray God fashioning cosmos out of chaos, in effect using primordial, disordered stuff as a kind of raw material for the new ordered world (as when, for example, the primeval waters are divided), God also apparently creates certain things "out of thin air," as we say (as when, for example, God creates "a dome," uses it to separate the waters, and calls it "sky"). Moreover, in the text's opening sentence the phrase "the heavens and the earth" may well be an all-embracing merism, implying that God originally created the chaotic abyss too. And so in the end, the doctrine of *creatio ex nihilo* may have at least two possible valences: first, a fashioning and ordering of primordial, disordered stuff (*nihilo* in the sense of chaos, i.e., no-thing-ness); and second, a fabricating out of naught (*nihilo* in the sense of vacuum or vacancy, i.e., nothingness). For a Jewish perspective on these issues, see Jon Levenson, *Creation and the Persistence of Evil: The Jewish Drama of Divine Omnipotence* (Princeton, NJ: Princeton University Press, 1988), esp. 3–13.

Matthew Myer Boulton

condition of the intelligibility, duration, and sequence of all subsequent creative acts,[3] God's first illuminated move—again, evoking the mythic choreography represented in the *Enuma Elish*, Psalm 74, and elsewhere—is to divide the waters (Gen 1:6-7).[4]

And precisely here, "in the beginning," as God creatively confronts deep-sea oblivion and begins to make order out of it by dividing it—precisely here, the divine presence moving "over the face of the waters" is identified as *ruah elohim*, a phrase translatable as "the wind of God," "the breath of God," and "the spirit of God" (Gen 1:2).[5] That is, in precisely the place where God the creator is figured as a divine

[3] According to the narrative, when God creates "light" what emerges is not so much the abstract phenomenon or materiality of light but rather light in a particular form, namely, "Day," the periodic time span of worldly illumination: "God called the light Day, and the darkness he called Night. And there was evening, and there was morning, the first day" (Gen 1:5). In other words, God's first creative act, considered as a whole, is not so much to create "light" as to create "Day"—and days, of course, serve as the chronological basis for the rest of the narrative, the temporal units and framework that make possible everything that follows. Thus the initial creation of "light" is also the inauguration of time (itself a form of order), including the possibilities of duration and sequence, all grounded in the rhythm of "Day" and "Night," "evening" and "morning."

[4] It is worth noting that while on the first and third days God creates merely by speaking ("Let there be . . . and there was," and "Let the . . . And it was so"), divine speech is not enough on the second day when God divides the waters: God speaks the "Let there be," but then proceeds to "make the dome," "separate the waters," and so on, modes of action reminiscent of other Near Eastern creation narratives, as if critically trading on their fundamental ideas. And intriguingly, only this second day lacks a version of the refrain, "And God saw that it was good," perhaps another trace of the appropriation's critical character.

[5] Gerhard von Rad goes so far as to interpret Genesis 1:2 in terms of Daniel 7:2 ("the four winds of heaven stirring upon the great sea"), and, accordingly, to recommend rendering *ruah elohim* in Genesis 1:2 as "the storm of God," a reading that could help clarify the text's adversarial aspect. Rather rashly, however, von Rad then goes on to declare that after this verse "this 'spirit of God' takes no more active part in creation"—a view that, at the very least, puts his interpretive approach at some remove from Christian theological interpretation (since the idea of a triune God would mean affirming the Holy Spirit's "active part" all the way along), and in any case is unsupported by the text of Genesis 1. On the interpretive propriety of reading Genesis in light of

The Adversary

wrestler with chaos, dividing and ordering but not eliminating it, God is figured as "spirit"; or, to put the same point conversely, the one whom Christians come to call "the Holy Spirit" is introduced here as a divine adversary, a creative opponent whose work is to bring order out of disorder, cosmos out of chaos, a livable world out of the unfathomable deep.[6]

Or, as the Hebrew prophets would put it: deliverance out of danger, righteousness out of ruin, justice out of what amounts to moral *tohu vabohu*, the abysmal "wild and waste" of injustice, indifference, and contempt for the needs of creation's most vulnerable members. It is a cardinal Christian idea, of course, that the Holy Spirit "spoke through the prophets of old," and speaks through them still, in effect working continually to create and re-create moral order out of various forms of

---

Christian trinitarian doctrine, see below, n. 6. See Gerhard von Rad, *Genesis: A Commentary* (Philadelphia: The Westminster Press, 1972), 49.

[6] It may be objected, of course, that the Christian doctrine of the divine Trinity (including Christian pneumatology) is wholly foreign to the mindset of the author(s) of Genesis 1, and so can only be eisegetically projected or "read into" that text. On the other hand, however, strictly speaking, when it comes to the Christian Bible the doctrine of the divine Trinity is often (and possibly always) eisegetically projected to some degree, since even the New Testament lacks any clear articulation of what comes to be that doctrine's orthodox formulation; in that sense, at least, the doctrine must be "read into" New Testament texts as much as into Genesis. More precisely: insofar as it is grounded in Scripture, trinitarian doctrine is derived from the church's theological reflection on the Christian biblical canon as a whole; then, in turn, precisely on this canonical, theological, and finally ecclesiological basis, trinitarian ideas are applied and attributed to particular texts within that canon, whether the book of Genesis, the Gospel of John, or Paul's Letter to the Romans. Thus, even if historical methods could definitively demonstrate (and please note, since the historical record is so spare and fragmentary, they cannot) that the author(s) of Genesis 1—or for that matter, the author(s) of the Gospel of John, or Paul—did not have in mind ideas parallel or prototypical to what later became orthodox trinitarian doctrine, Christian readers may still legitimately interpret these texts as portraying the triune God on the canonical grounds just described. Indeed, the Christian biblical canon itself, with all its juxtapositions, resonant parallels, and apparent contradictions, produces a whole range of interpretive options of which the individual canonical authors may or may not have been (and in many cases likely were not) aware. Thus canonical (i.e., Christian scriptural) exegesis, by definition, involves moving beyond the field of interpretive possibilities available to individual canonical authors.

Matthew Myer Boulton

moral chaos. And recalling this idea is to recall that the Holy Spirit frequently speaks through the prophets in an adversarial register, railing against the powers that would exploit or ignore the weak and downtrodden. Moreover, though at times the prophetic Spirit speaks as Israel's "Comforter," inspiring consolation and hope for a new future, at least as often (and arguably, more often) she speaks as Israel's adversary, critiquing past and present socioreligious practices in the strongest theological terms. Again, this prophetic criticism often involves advocating for Israel's disinherited, and arraigning the powerful for their apathy, ignorance, or willful abuse. In many signature cases, however, the explicit target of the critique is Israel's worship.

When many Americans hear the line, "let justice roll down like waters, and righteousness like a mighty stream," they may think of the preaching of Martin Luther King, Jr., or indeed any number of historic struggles for justice and equality. But for Amos himself, the line is the culmination of a divine polemic against Israel's liturgical life:

> I hate, I despise your festivals,
> and I take no delight in your solemn assemblies.
> Even though you offer me your burnt offerings and grain offerings,
> I will not accept them;
> and the offerings of well-being of your fatted animals
> I will not look upon.
> Take away from me the noise of your songs;
> I will not listen to the melody of your harps.
> But let justice roll down like waters,
> and righteousness like an everflowing stream. (Amos 5:21-24)

Or again, the well-known sentence in Micah 6:8—"What does the LORD require of you but to do justice, and to love kindness, and to walk humbly with your God?"—concludes another anti-worship tirade, this one rife with prophetic sarcasm: "Will the LORD be pleased with thousands of rams, with ten thousands of rivers of oil?" (Micah 6:7). Parallel ideas appear in Isaiah (1:11ff.), Jeremiah (6:20ff.; 7:21ff.), Hosea (6:6), and the Psalter (Pss 40:6-8; 50:9-15), among other texts.

When they encounter them at all, Christians typically interpret these polemics as intended for somebody else, or, at most, as hyperbolic endorsements of social justice. The texts themselves are uncompromising: they do not characterize God's rejection of worship as contingent on, say, the existence of particular injustices, as if the instant these are rectified God will welcome our offerings and anthems. Nor do they

The Adversary

portray God as opposing some particular set of worship practices (say, non-Christian practices), while approving another (say, modern Christian practices). On the contrary, the prophetic attack poses a clear, sharp disjunction: God says no to supposedly right worship, and yes to genuinely right livelihood. We Christians may flatter ourselves by insisting that *our* worship, as "sacrifices of thanksgiving" (Ps 50:14) or "living sacrifices" (Rom 12:1), are somehow exempt from this critique—but we can only do so at the expense of not taking these prophetic texts seriously, or by dramatically distancing ourselves from them in what amounts to a cryptic neo-Marcionism.[7] For Christians these options are decisively ruled out by the fact that, if the New Testament gospels are any guide, Jesus of Nazareth knew these prophetic texts exceedingly well, valued them highly, and understood himself to stand in their heraldic, adversarial tradition. With respect to liturgy's sacrificial aspects, for example, Jesus speaks plainly, quoting Hosea, quoting God: "I desire mercy, not sacrifice" (Matt 9:13; Hos 6:6).

Indeed, the gospel writers situate Jesus squarely in the Spirit-filled, prophetic tradition, not only in his teaching and preaching (as in his early sermon in Luke, where he applies Isaiah 61:1ff. to himself: "The spirit of the Lord God is upon me, because the LORD has anointed me; he has sent me to bring good news to the poor" [see Luke 4:16-21]), but also in his baptism by John in the Jordan River, the event that inaugurates his public ministry. In the first place, even before the baptism itself, John prophetically describes Jesus as an imminent, apocalyptic, adversarial figure working closely in concert with the Holy Spirit: "He will baptize you with the Holy Spirit and fire. His winnowing fork is in his hand, and he will clear his threshing floor and will gather his wheat into the granary; but the chaff he will burn with unquenchable fire" (Matt 3:11-12; Luke 3:16-17). That is, John portrays Jesus as a farmer poised to purge the fruit of his harvest baptismally, first with wind— the "winnowing fork" being an implement used to throw grain up into the air, so that the wind may sweep away the lighter husks and other unwanted particles ("the chaff")—and second with fire, so that the chaff may be burned away once and for all. It is no accident, of course, that both these images—wind and fire—are the leading Christian biblical images for the Holy Spirit: Jesus is here presented as the purveyor

---

[7] Marcion (ca. 85–160) was an early Christian theologian who advocated expunging Jewish ideas and elements from Christianity as much as possible, including the exclusion of all Hebrew scripture from the Christian canon.

Matthew Myer Boulton

of the sanctifying baptism of the Spirit, the holy "wind" and "fire" who transforms every individual grain of wheat—that is, every Christian—by separating and burning away its husk (see also Mark 1:8 and John 1:33). And it is likewise no accident that both these images are adversarial and creative, or rather, re-creative, by virtue of their purgative, renovative, and therefore transformational associations. In this context, both "wind" and "fire" aim to sweep away and destroy, but not for the sake of death; rather, they aim to purge, refine, and reform—in a word, to sanctify—for the sake of new and thriving life.

From this angle two key pneumatological themes come into view: the irony and the agony of the Holy Spirit's sanctifying work. The irony of the Spirit's work is that she characteristically harnesses conventional forces of destruction—the primeval "sea" in creation, for example, or the "wind" and "fire" in sanctification—and puts them to life-giving use. This harnessing is a form of adversarial opposition, to be sure, but its signature is a creative co-option of apparently death-dealing forces, incorporating them into the service of life, peace, and renewal. Antagonists are thereby recast as protagonists. In a kind of divine judo, the Holy Spirit opposes chaos and destruction not by bluntly attacking them head-on, but rather by ironically undertaking and therefore subsuming them into the divine mission, turning them toward new, constructive purposes.[8] Thus the often ironic character of the Spirit's activity, variously discernible across the traditional topoi by which Christian interpreters typically understand her work: she speaks through, anoints, indwells, and sanctifies precisely those persons and things that are ostensibly unsuitable prophets, apostles, temples, and saints. That is, she sanctifies sinners. She makes "the sea," "wind," and "fire" into instruments of life. She turns "swords into ploughshares" (Isa 2:4; Mic 4:3). She salvages and restores the very stones that "the builders rejected," remaking each one into a "cornerstone" (Ps 118:22; Acts 4:11).[9]

[8] Judo, from the Japanese, *ju*, "gentle," and *do* (from the Chinese, *dao*), "way"—hence, "the gentle way," or, more expansively, the maximally humane, maximally efficient way to counter an aggressive antagonist, strategically blending with the attacker's destructive force as a way of neutralizing and transforming it into its reversal, i.e., into something peaceful and creative.

[9] Examples of the varieties of this pattern abound in Christian Scripture, from Luke's Christmas story, in which the Holy Spirit elects and works in and through Mary, thereby, as she puts it, "lifting up the lowly" (Luke 1:52), to

The Adversary

The second pneumatological theme, the agony of the Spirit's work (Greek *agon*, "struggle," "athletic contest"), is that within the sphere of the church this ironic transformation is typically manifest in terms of struggle, exercise, sanctification, and practical formation, much as an athlete is formed and reformed through training and practice. That is, as the divine wrestler the Holy Spirit means to purge, train, strengthen, and transform, and Israel, the "one who strives with God," is thereby meant to be liberated, blessed, empowered, and remade in and through the struggle. To describe this kind of agonistic renovation early Christians borrowed language from the Greek gymnasium, and developed the so-called "ascetic" traditions of personal and communal practice (Greek *askesis*, "training"). Conceived in this way "ascetic Christianity" is confined to neither the desert nor the monastery: all followers of Jesus Christ, bar none, precisely as recipients of the Holy Spirit, are "ascetics" in the sense that they are embroiled in programs of practical formation and sanctification. In short, by definition, all disciples are in training (Latin *discipulus*, "student"), and as such they engage in disciplines, in practices—including and especially practices of Christian worship. And this formative Christian exercise has its principal theological foundation in Jesus' baptism: both his own baptism in the Jordan, and the baptism of the Spirit he administers at Pentecost.

According to Matthew, Mark, and Luke, when John the Baptizer baptized Jesus in the Jordan, "heaven was opened, and the Holy Spirit descended upon him in bodily form like a dove" (Luke 3:22; cf. Matt 3:16 and Mark 1:10).[10] From this point on, these texts suggest, the

---

John's description of the oracular function of even Caiaphas's scapegoating formula, "it is better for you to have one man die for the people than to have the whole nation destroyed." "He did not say this on his own," John writes, "but being high priest that year he prophesied that Jesus was about to die for the nation, and not for the nation only, but to gather into one the dispersed children of God" (John 11:50-52). That is, as John conceives and presents it, even the very plot to kill Jesus is divinely co-opted into a prophecy announcing the good news of the gospel, in effect rendering the scheme an unwitting sermon ironically delivered by one of Jesus' (ostensibly) leading opponents. Put another way, and borrowing a line from Joseph on the last page of Genesis: "Even though you intended to do harm . . . God intended it for good" (Gen 50:20).

[10] The Gospel of John includes a similar image of the Spirit's descent upon Jesus, though in this case the report is embedded in John the Baptizer's testimony and not in explicit connection to a particular act of baptism. See John 1:29-34.

Matthew Myer Boulton

68

Spirit serves as an indwelling power and guide for Jesus in his public ministry—and in this regard the very first thing the Spirit does is compel Jesus out into the wilderness, precisely so he may undergo an epic, harrowing wrestling match of his own. The celebrated Celtic image of the Holy Spirit as a "wild goose" comes to mind, less a cooing dove from the clouds and more a challenging, earthbound provocateur, nipping at Jesus' heels on the banks of the Jordan. Mark puts it this way: "And the Spirit immediately drove him out into the wilderness. He was in the wilderness forty days, tempted by Satan; and he was with the wild beasts; and the angels waited on him" (Mark 1:12-13).

In other words, the Holy Spirit's inaugural move upon her descent, in effect the ensuing extension of Jesus' baptism, is to drive the Son of God directly into confrontation with Satan—which is to say, the divine Adversary compels Jesus to face the demonic adversary, the personification of resistance to God's purposes (Hebrew *satan*, "adversary"). And though the precise rationale for this turn of events is not elaborated in the gospels, the wilderness sojourn's link to fasting (in Matthew and Luke) and its sequential placement in each overall narrative suggest a primarily preparatory, purgative, ascetic purpose: to test Jesus, to orient him, to cleanse and refine him, to strengthen him, and thereby to send him into his public ministry. In this sense the rationale is fundamentally apostolic (Greek *apostellein*, "send forth"), and so the episode serves both to prepare Jesus for the road ahead, and, at the same time, to initiate the journey. This is all in keeping, of course, with the Spirit's agonistic, ironic modus operandi, and in fact epitomizes it, since here even Satan himself is recast in the constructive role of sparring partner. That is, the Spirit's ascetic regimen creatively incorporates demonic opposition, now rendering it a useful irritant in the oyster around which the messianic pearl will form. Or, to shift to a more "apostolic" metaphor, the Spirit co-opts the leverage of Satan's resistance as an aid to drawing back the divine archer's bow, the better to "send forth" the arrow on its way.

As Luke tells it, the way leads first through Galilee, including a preaching turn for Jesus at the synagogue in Nazareth, his hometown. Jesus is "filled with the power of the Spirit," Luke reports, and, as we have seen, in his sermon he explicitly applies Isaiah's pneumatological, eschatological language to himself: "The Spirit of the Lord is upon me, because he has anointed me to bring good news to the poor . . . to proclaim the year of the Lord's favor" (Luke 4:14, 18, 19). This "good news" and "favor" are by no means received as such by the hometown crowd, however, especially after Jesus goes on to imply that his healing gospel is not intended for them. Predictably, the crowd responds to this adversarial gesture in kind: "When they heard this, all in the synagogue were filled with rage. They got up, drove him out of the town, and led him to the brow of the hill on which their town was built, so that they might hurl him off the cliff" (Luke 4:28-29).

For Luke, this is not Jesus' first sermon, but it is the first one the evangelist decides to describe in detail, as if to emphasize and foreshadow that the Messiah's Spirited, prophetic, adversarial mission will itself meet with violent adversity—and that ultimately Jesus will meet the grim fate reserved for prophetic apostles in Jerusalem, "the city that kills the prophets and stones those that are sent to it" (Luke 13:34). Jesus too will be rejected and killed. But at the very outset of the gospel, in John the Baptizer's preaching, Luke anticipates the divine plan to circumvent even that rejection and death: "He will baptize you with the Holy Spirit and fire" (Luke 3:16). That is, not only will Jesus undergo baptism, he will also administer a baptism of the Holy Spirit, thus creating and empowering the church to carry on his mission even after his death—and he does so, as Luke tells it, on the Jewish festival day of Pentecost (*Shavuot*).

Shavuot commemorates the divine gift of the Torah (Hebrew *torah*, "instruction"), the law that guides, binds, and continually constitutes Israel as a nation in covenant with God. Accordingly, in Acts 2 the festival setting frames the in-breaking Spirit in the same way, that is, as a divine gift that will guide, bind, and continually constitute the Christian community. But again, the Spirit arrives not so much as a "Comforter" as a cause for alarm: "And suddenly from heaven there came a sound like the rush of a violent wind, and it filled the entire house where they were sitting. Divided tongues, as of fire, appeared among them, and a tongue rested on each of them. All of them were filled with the Holy Spirit and began to speak in other languages" (Acts 2:2-4). It is an unsettling scene: the roar of "violent wind," "tongues of fire" riddling the air, and a linguistic riot rising from the assembly. In all three aspects—wind, light, and language—the scene evokes the opening verses of Genesis 1; but as Peter's ensuing Pentecost sermon makes clear, they also evoke the apocalyptic "last days" envisioned by the prophet Joel, when such dramatic signs will herald "the coming of the Lord's great and glorious day": "In the last days it will be, God declares, that I will pour out my Spirit upon all flesh" (Acts 2:17-20; Joel 2:28-32).

Matthew Myer Boulton

70

The universalistic thrust of the whole scene in Acts 2—clear in both the key phrase, "I will pour out my Spirit upon all flesh," and in the consequent miraculous preaching in languages "from every nation under heaven" (Acts 2:5)—amounts to a creative reversal of the ancient Tower of Babel story (Gen 11:1-9). There, in order to foil humanity's prideful attempt to approach God, "the LORD confused the language of all the earth," and thereby "scattered them abroad over the face of all the earth" (Gen 11:9); here in Acts 2 these tables are turned. Now God approaches human beings, making constructive use of their linguistically balkanized condition in order to undo it. That is, the Spirit attracts a crowd "from every nation under heaven" precisely by "amazing and astonishing" them with a linguistic wonder: preaching by Galileans that listeners nevertheless "hear, each of us, in our own native language" (Acts 2:5, 7, 8). The miracle of Pentecost, then, is that the Holy Spirit uses the very thing that divides and scatters humanity in Genesis (God's "confusion" of human language into many mutually unintelligible tongues) in order to bring humanity together anew, or, as the Gospel of John puts it, "to gather into one the dispersed children of God" (John 11:52). Again, the Spirit's modus operandi is clear: out of chaos she fashions community. And she does so, please note, not by simply conquering or eliminating the chaotic, divisive conditions, but rather by making use of them to re-create a new world, and so herald a new life. As we have seen, this kind of creative irony is the Spirit's signature, as is her unsettling, alarming, and in that sense adversarial entrance on Pentecost, complete with "violent wind" and "tongues of fire."

Finally, if the gospel writers liturgically locate the Holy Spirit's work in prophetic preaching, baptism, and the festival of Pentecost, in his letter to the Christian church in Rome Paul highlights the Spirit's role in prayer. In Romans 8 Paul outlines a sharp antithesis between "Spirit" and "flesh," *pneuma* and *sarx*, and assures his readers that "you are not in the flesh; you are in the Spirit, since the Spirit of God dwells in you"—and moreover, that this indwelling "spirit of adoption" renders them "children of God, and if children, then heirs" (Rom 8:9, 15, 17). For Paul, the distinguishing mark of this state of affairs, the consoling evidence of this indwelling and adoption, is found by listening to our own prayers: "When we cry, 'Abba! Father!' it is that very Spirit bearing witness with our spirit that we are children of God" (Rom 8:16). That is, the church's own calling on God may itself serve as the most reassuring testimony addressed to the church, since there

The Adversary

Christians may hear not only their own voices but also the voice of the Holy Spirit—and in particular the Spirit's testimony that she in fact indwells, leads, and adopts the church into the divine family as "heirs of God and joint heirs with Christ" (Rom 8:17).

Moreover, this testimony may be especially reassuring for Christians, Paul suggests, since on their own our prayers themselves demonstrate and epitomize our destitution and malformation—in short, "our weakness": "Likewise the Spirit helps us in our weakness; for we do not know how to pray as we ought, but that very Spirit intercedes with sighs too deep for words" (Rom 8:26). In this way Paul echoes the prophetic attack on Israel's liturgical life, summing up "our weakness" not in terms of moral failing or theological heterodoxy, but rather in terms of worship: "we do not know how to pray as we ought." And in the same breath, both developing and moving beyond the prophets, Paul proclaims the divine remedy to this distinctively liturgical predicament: "but that very Spirit intercedes with sighs too deep for words." That is, the Holy Spirit intervenes in Christian worship, conspiring with it by subsuming our malformed prayers into her own better sighing, lifting up our words into her own wordless breath of life.

This divine conspiracy, subsumption, and transformation may itself be understood as part and parcel of the Spirit's ironic, agonistic, sanctifying work, a working-with Christian worship that is also a working-against it. For with Paul, we may say, "We do not know how to worship—that is, how to live—as we ought." On our own terms and by our own lights, our liturgies and lives only too closely resemble that mythic, presumptuous attempt to "make a name for ourselves" by building "a tower with its top in the heavens" (Gen 11:4). So when the Spirit joins her voice and presence to this insolent work, conspiring with it and incorporating it into her own mission, she thereby simultaneously conspires against it, covers its shamelessness, transforms its pretension, bridges its divisiveness—in short, she "intercedes" in and for Christian worship. She transforms the Christian liturgy of Babel so that it may also and decisively be the genuine liturgy of Jesus Christ, worship that actually takes place not only in our own names but also "in the name of Jesus Christ," and that is actually carried out not only by our own questionable social body, but also by "the Body of Christ." We Christians cannot accomplish this transformation on our own; in every Christian worship service the Spirit must come again and accomplish such transformation afresh. In this sense a primary and governing mission of the Holy Spirit is what the Swiss theologian

Matthew Myer Boulton

Karl Barth calls the "abolition" (*Aufhebung*) of Christian worship. To conclude this essay, I briefly sketch Barth's position, focusing on the section of his *Church Dogmatics* entitled "True Religion."[11]

KARL BARTH AND THE "ABOLITION" OF CHRISTIAN WORSHIP

Over the course of his theological work, from his early *Epistle to the Romans* all the way through to the posthumously published drafts for chapter 17 of his *Church Dogmatics*, Karl Barth develops a broad, ambitious critique of religion, and positions it at the heart of his whole theological program.[12] In the third part of chapter 2 in the *Dogmatics*, "The Outpouring of the Holy Spirit," is a section entitled, "The Revelation of God as the Abolition of Religion." There Barth sketches religion as always and everywhere "unbelief, i.e., opposition to the divine revelation, and therefore active idolatry and self-righteousness"—a critique he applies to religion in general, and especially to Christianity.[13] This view of religion, he contends, is revealed by the outpouring of the Holy Spirit, and as such may be discerned in Christian Scripture: in the prophets' critique of Israel's worship, to be sure, but also in the repeated idolatry, faithlessness, and self-righteousness of Israel, and likewise in the repeated idolatry, faithlessness, and self-righteousness of Jesus' first disciples and the early Christian church.[14] Thus for Barth a governing mission of the Holy Spirit is to expose and oppose religion, and in particular to expose and oppose Christianity. In this sense the Holy Spirit acts as Christianity's divine Adversary. And for Barth, since the epitome and "very best" of Christianity is Christian worship,

[11] Karl Barth, *Church Dogmatics* (Edinburgh: T&T Clark, 1956) 1/2:325–61.

[12] For an overview of this critique, and a constructive systematic theology built up from it, see my *God Against Religion: Rethinking Christian Theology through Worship* (Grand Rapids, MI: Eerdmans, 2008).

[13] Barth, *Church Dogmatics*, 1/2:327. On the critique's special application to Christianity, see, e.g., "It does not affect only other men with their religion. *Above all* it affects ourselves also as adherents of the Christian religion" (300; emphasis added). Again, on 337 Barth claims that though all religions commit the same idolatrous, unbelieving sin, "in the history of Christianity, just because it is the religion of revelation, the sin is, as it were, committed with a high hand."

[14] Ibid., e.g., 328ff.

The Adversary

the Adversary's work is paradigmatically liturgical.[15] In and through Christian worship the Spirit wrestles and struggles and works— toward the "abolition" of Christian worship.

The German term rendered here as "abolition" is *Aufhebung*, translatable as (1) "elevation," (2) "preservation," and (3) "abolition." Barth, following Hegel, employs the term in a way that at once keeps all three meanings in view. The English word "lift" may give some indication of this semantic range, since "to lift" can mean both "to raise up" ("to lift a glass") and "to annul" ("to lift a ban"); holding both ideas simultaneously in mind, we might say that for Barth the Spirit's work is to "lift religion" once and for all. The term "abolition," then, provides only a partial—and therefore a misleading—glimpse of Barth's case. In fact, his argument is that "the outpouring of the Holy Spirit" involves a threefold engagement with religion generally, and above all with Christian worship: the Spirit (1) elevates worship to a new level by participating in it, subsuming or taking it up into the divine mission; (2) preserves and works with worship insofar as it is subsumed and not merely vanquished or eliminated; and (3) ends or abolishes worship insofar as this subsumption radically refigures and transforms it. Analogies to this threefold form of "taking up" abound: in science, for example, when one picture of the world is "taken up" into another (e.g., Newtonian physics taken up into Einsteinian physics), at once incorporating, preserving, and transfiguring the prior picture; or in political life, when an oppressed community "takes up" an object or symbol of their oppression, preserving its significance precisely in order to overturn it (e.g., the Nazi "pink triangle," originally used to identify homosexuals in concentration camps, now recast as a symbol of pride and solidarity in gay and lesbian communities). On the one hand, then, worship is preserved and improved by the Spirit's conspiracy; on the other hand, worship is cancelled, annulled, and ultimately swept away by it. Thus the Spirit's ironic, agonistic work vis-à-vis Christian worship, not opposing it by an assault from above, but rather undertaking it by a conspiracy from below, and a transformation from the inside out.[16]

[15] Ibid., e.g., 304–5.
[16] Barth treats the theme of the Holy Spirit's conspiracy in and through Christian worship most extensively in the late drafts for chapter 17 of the *Dogmatics*, posthumously published under the title *The Christian Life*. There he argues, for example, that the fundamental human act of "invocation" (that

Matthew Myer Boulton

Only on this basis, Barth contends, does Christian worship become "true worship," and Christianity, "true religion." Without divine conspiracy and solidarity, Christian worship is manifestly false. It is only "contradiction against grace."[17] But as freely and unconditionally elected by God, graciously adopted not because of its immanent features but precisely in spite of them, Christian worship becomes "true." That is, its truth depends strictly on the basis of "the outpouring of the Holy Spirit," the Spirit's conspiracy, and, through the Spirit, the Son's solidarity with Christian worship and Christian life.[18]

In this way, for Barth Christianity is "'true' religion only in the sense in which we speak of a 'justified sinner.'"[19] God adopts Christianity as "true" even as it remains, in itself, "idolatry and self-righteousness." Thus God's election of Christianity is utterly unmerited, utterly free, utterly gracious. It is unconditioned by Christian technique, liturgical, creedal, or otherwise, and in fact takes place *over against* such technique. Far from a cause for Christian boasting, then, this election is properly a cause for Christian humility, dumbfounded gratitude, and transformative joy. Likewise, far from a possession already held in Christian hands, the Holy Spirit, free and unfettered, conspires with and against Christian worship wherever and whenever she wills.

------

is, calling upon God), the "form" through which all Christian life is properly lived, is "totally inconceivable" apart from "the fruitful meeting and the living fellowship of the Holy Spirit with them and with their spirits," such that "the Spirit intercedes for us, with his own better sighing, which we can never express." See Barth, *The Christian Life* (Grand Rapids, MI: Eerdmans, 1981), 90, 86. See also my *God Against Religion*, 122ff.

[17] Barth, *Church Dogmatics*, 1/2:339.

[18] The implications of this view for conceiving the status of other religions is a subject for another day, but suffice it to say that the position outlined here—that Christianity is the worst offender against God among religions (see above, n. 13), and is graciously forgiven and "adopted" as such—would seem to point toward an account of universal salvation, on the principle that "if the worst, then also the better." That is, since Christians are by no means the cream but rather the depths and dregs of human religiosity, the fact that God rescues and welcomes the dregs would suggest that God rescues and welcomes the whole barrel. On this view, the Christian gospel may take the form: if God loves and saves Christians, surely God loves and saves everyone! But full development of this argument must await another day.

[19] Ibid., 325.

The Adversary

Christian disciples are not marked by their custody of the Holy Spirit. If anything, they are properly marked by a clear understanding that they have no such custody, and at the same time that they require the Spirit's presence in order to live—for without her, their *leitourgia* ("work of people") can only amount to work unto death. Insofar as we undertake this barren work as Christians, as if we ourselves act over against God; and insofar as we live out our Christianity as if the Holy Spirit is under our power or within our grasp, as if she is an extension of our own religious identity or virtuosity; insofar as we do these things, the Spirit stands against us in judgment as our Adversary. And yet, as we have seen, a signature of the Spirit's adversarial work is that even as she stands against her opponents, she also stands with them, gracefully transforming Christian futility and vanity, and indeed ironically making use of just these unholy things in her holy, transformative work. Thus she mercifully wrestles with Christianity. She cries out in and through Christian prayer. She intercedes in and for Christian worship with sighs too deep for words. And likewise, like a wild goose, she drives Christians to call on her, to worship—that is, to live—in the form of an epiclesis, a concrete and continual call on the Holy Spirit to come, to breathe with us and in us, for us and against us, wrestling us to the ground and bringing us back to life.

In a key passage, Barth puts it this way: "the Christian is justified when he is without God." That is, the Christian is justified when he or she "is like the publican in the temple, the prodigal son, wretched Lazarus, the guilty thief crucified with Jesus Christ"[20]—and to this list we may add: the Canaanite woman at Tyre, and the hemorrhaging woman who touches Jesus' cloak (Mark 7:24ff.; 5:21ff.). Here, then, are the proper role models for Christian discipleship today, and in particular the role models for Christian worship. They by no means claim divine presence or favor as a possession of their own, or as an extension of their own impeccably religious technique. Instead, in their "day of trouble," with or without words, they call on God (Ps 50:15). They reach out to God. They speak and act not from a position of strength and self-sufficiency but rather from a clear-eyed understanding that theirs is a position of weakness and need—in this sense, they are truly strong. They do not rely on the merit or worth of their own resources but rather on the merit and worth of divine resources and grace—in this sense, they are truly faithful. They are "without

---

[20] Barth, *Church Dogmatics*, 1/2:333.

Matthew Myer Boulton

76

God." And yet for just this reason they turn to God, and in that sense truly live "with God," walking humbly at God's side (Micah 6:8). They speak, and ask, and reach. They are humble but also quite beautiful and bold. They call out with the thief, "Remember me," with the publican, "Have mercy," and with Jacob, "I will not let you go, unless you bless me," (Luke 18:13; 23:42; Gen 32:26).

And so I argue that the epicletic character of Christian worship—that is, the extent to which it takes the explicit or implicit form of epiclesis, a plea for the Spirit to come and be present to and in the worship service itself—should be conceived and enacted as a recognition of worship's own destitution and malformation, its urgent need for the Spirit's gracious, transformational presence. Every epiclesis is an urgent call. Even and especially Christian worship requires divine deliverance. Without the *ruah elohim*, notwithstanding our ostensibly well-organized, well-executed liturgical proceedings (whether "low church" or "high church," simple or elaborate, ecstatic or refined), Christian worship is *tohu vabohu*, "wild and waste." Thundering through Amos and Micah and Isaiah, the Holy Spirit can and does condemn it—but she does not merely abandon it to its self-imposed exile. By the grace of God she also "falls afresh" on worship, as the old revival chorus goes, to "melt," "mold," "fill," and "use" it in her own renewing work.[21] That is, she wrestles with Christian worship, ironically and creatively. She "lifts" it, subsumes it into her mission, at once preserving and abolishing it by transposing it into another register. In a word, she joins it: as a Comforter and Sustainer, to be sure, but also as an Adversary, a cunning opponent, a merciful foe, a prophetic challenge, a violent wind, and a purgative fire, blowing and burning away whatever chaff would keep her beloved children from life.

[21] "Spirit of the Living God," by Daniel Iverson, 1926. See, e.g., *Chalice Hymnal* (St. Louis, MO: Chalice Press, 1995), #259.

The Adversary

Paul F. Bradshaw

5. The Rediscovery of the Holy Spirit in Modern Eucharistic Theology and Practice

The title of my paper is to some extent misleading. The Holy Spirit was of course never lost from eucharistic theology and practice in the Christian East, and not even completely in the West. One has only to think of the effect on the Reformed tradition of Calvin's eucharistic theology for one example of this survival. But it would be fair to say that the role of the Holy Spirit, not only with regard to the Eucharist, but also more generally in relation to Christian worship, did suffer a major eclipse in the ecclesiastical traditions of the West in past centuries, and that continued to be the case for a good part of the twentieth century too.[1] For example, it does not occupy a prominent place in Romano Guardini's classic work *The Spirit of the Liturgy*, published in German in 1918 and in an English translation in 1930, nor in *Mediator Dei*, the 1947 encyclical of Pius XII. Similarly, references to the Holy Spirit in connection with worship are few and far between in Odo Casel's work on the mystery of Christian worship. He mentions just once the Body of Christ praying in *pneuma*, alluding to Romans 8:26f., and once the praise offered to the Father through the Son in the Holy Spirit,[2] but otherwise it is the Spirit given in baptism to which he chiefly refers.

Such reticence in speaking about the Holy Spirit was, however, not peculiar to liturgical theology alone. Major works of systematic theology of the period commonly did not contain a distinct section on pneumatology as they did on Christology, but merely included it

---

[1] For an explanation of how this came to be, see Patrick Regan, "Pneumatological and Eschatological Aspects of Liturgical Celebration," *Worship* 51 (1977): 332–50, here at 334–42.

[2] Odo Casel, *Das christliche Kultmysterium* (1932); English translation from the 4th ed., *The Mystery of Christian Worship and Other Writings*, ed. Burkhard Neunheuser (London: DLT / Westminster: Newman Press, 1962), 30, 49.

within their study of the Trinity, and even that section was not often very extensively developed. Indeed, Karl Adam's *Das Wesen des Katholizismus*, a work held in very high regard among Roman Catholics in the first half of the twentieth century, summarized the structure of the Catholic faith as follows: "I come to a living faith in the Triune God through Christ in his Church. I experience the action of the living God through Christ realizing himself in His Church. So we see the certitude of the Catholic faith rests on the sacred triad: God, Christ, Church."[3] Karl Barth's massive multivolume *Church Dogmatics* too lacks a systematic treatment of the Third Person of the Trinity. Even as recently as 1985, Kilian McDonnell was still speaking of pneumatology as the neglected branch of theology, although he rather overstates the case as by then, as we shall see later, greater attention had begun to be paid to the doctrine of the Holy Spirit.[4] Yet, as if to prove his point, a two-volume work entitled *Systematic Theology: Roman Catholic Perspectives*, published in 1991, to which a variety of notable scholars contributed, still lacks a separate treatment of the Spirit.[5]

Nevertheless, although the role of the Spirit may not have featured in discourse about the nature of Christian worship in general for much of the twentieth century, where it did reappear right from the start was in discussions that took place about the character and location of the epiclesis in eucharistic liturgy, and to that we now turn.

THE EUCHARISTIC EPICLESIS AND THE ROMAN CANON

Roman Catholic attitudes toward the role of the Holy Spirit in relation to the Eucharist were generally distorted for much of the century as a result of polemics with the Eastern Orthodox Church. As the latter tended to assert that consecration was brought about by the invocation of the Spirit alone, the Roman Catholic response was to insist that on the contrary it was effected by the recitation of the dominical words alone—a doctrine that had been specifically reaffirmed by Pius X in 1910.[6]

---

[3] (Düsseldorf: Schwann, 1924); English translation from the 4th ed., *The Spirit of Catholicism* (New York: Macmillan, 1929), 51.

[4] Kilian McDonnell, "A Trinitarian Theology of the Holy Spirit?" *Theological Studies* 46 (1985), 191–227, here at 191–93.

[5] Edited by Francis Schüssler Fiorenza and John P. Galvin (Minneapolis: Fortress Press, 1991).

[6] *Acta Apostolicae Sedis* 3 (1911), 118ff.

Paul F. Bradshaw

However, at the beginning of the century many still believed that the eucharistic liturgy in Book 8 of the *Apostolic Constitutions*—with its explicit invocation of the Holy Spirit in its eucharistic prayer—even if not genuinely apostolic, still represented universal Christian practice in the second and third centuries. Hence the issue of the absence of anything comparable from the Roman Canon of the Mass had to be addressed. A number of scholars could see no alternative but to acknowledge that the Roman Rite must originally have included an explicit invocation of the Spirit and that this was subsequently removed, according to one of them, Adrian Fortescue, "apparently deliberately, because of the growing Western insistence on the words of institution as the Consecration form."[7] Such views were opposed by several scholars, including Edmund Bishop, who denied that a developed consecratory epiclesis had emerged anywhere in East or West prior to the end of the fourth century.[8]

The position that Bishop took was strengthened when toward the end of his life the ancient document hitherto known as "The Egyptian Church Order" was identified (or misidentified[9]) as the lost third-century *Apostolic Tradition* of Hippolytus of Rome and the source from which *Apostolic Constitutions* Book 8 had later been derived. While its eucharistic prayer did contain a petition after the institution narrative for God to send the Spirit on "the oblation of your Church," this did not specifically ask for it to be changed into the Body and Blood of Christ. Because of this, and because some scholars regarded that section of the prayer as a later interpolation in any case,[10] pressure was to some extent reduced on the need to explain how the Roman tradition

[7] Adrian Fortescue, *The Mass: A Study of the Roman Liturgy*, 2d ed. (London: Longmans Green & Co., 1913), 402–7. Among others holding similar views were Rudolph Buchwald, *Die Epiklese in der römischen Messe* (Vienna: Verlag der Leo-Gesellschaft, 1907); W. C. Bishop, "The Primitive Form of Consecration of the Holy Eucharist," *Church Quarterly Review* 66 (1908): 385–404.

[8] Edmund Bishop, "The Moment of Consecration," in an appendix to *The Liturgical Homilies of Narsai*, translated by R. H. Connolly, Texts and Studies 8/1 (Cambridge: Cambridge University Press, 1909), 126–63; idem, "Liturgical Comments and Memoranda II," *Journal of Theological Studies* 10 (1909): 592–603. See also George Every, "Edmund Bishop and the Epiclesis," in *Rediscovering Eastern Christendom*, ed. A. H. Armstrong, 77–89 (London: DLT, 1963).

[9] See Paul F. Bradshaw, Maxwell E. Johnson, and L. Edward Phillips, *The Apostolic Tradition: A Commentary* (Minneapolis: Fortress Press, 2002), 1–17.

[10] Ibid., 42.

The Rediscovery of the Holy Spirit

had once had an epiclesis and then lost it, although the theory that a major dislocation of the Canon had taken place after Hippolytus's day lived on for several decades.[11]

Some Roman Catholic scholars even denied that the word *epiclesis* was used by Christian writers in the second and third centuries with the same meaning as in later times. In 1917 the Anglican scholar J. W. Tyrer had argued that in primitive Christianity the word had primarily signified "a solemn appeal to God to intervene."[12] This conclusion was challenged by the noted Roman Catholic Benedictine scholar R. H. Connolly, who asserted: "I do not know of any passage in an ante-Nicene writer which can be held to justify the statement that *epiclesis* signifies a *petition*. . . . It is certain at least that, both in Ante-Nicene times and after, words denoting invocation were freely used with reference to formulae into which petition need not and often did not enter at all."[13] He claimed that its primary reference was to a religious formula involving the use of divine names.

In a subsequent exchange between the two of them, Tyrer continued to maintain that the primary sense was to express the idea of petition, although admitting that the word did come to acquire a wider secondary meaning, while Connolly continued to claim that it was the naming that was fundamental, which might or might not be linked to petition.[14] Odo Casel attempted a mediating position between them, suggesting that the word could have either one or the other meaning, and that Tyrer had overstressed the importance of petition in the epiclesis while Connolly had failed to give it sufficient recognition.[15] One can easily see why the claim that the primitive Christian use of the word epiclesis need not necessarily involve petition would be particularly attractive to Roman Catholics as well as to Anglicans

---

[11] See for example the references in Louis Bouyer, *Eucharistie* (Paris: Desclée, 1966); English translation: *Eucharist* (Notre Dame: University of Notre Dame Press, 1968), 187–88, and his challenge to the theory, 188–91.

[12] J. W. Tyrer, *The Eucharistic Epiclesis* (London: Longmans & Co., 1917), 5–6.

[13] R. H. Connolly, "On the Meaning of 'Epiclesis,'" *Downside Review* 41 (1923): 28–43, here at 29 (italics in original).

[14] See *Journal of Theological Studies* 25 (1923–24): 139–50 and 337–64.

[15] Odo Casel, "Neue Beiträge zur Epiklesenfrage," *Jahrbuch für Liturgiewissenschaft* 4 (1924): 169–78.

Paul F. Bradshaw

of a Catholic disposition,[16] as helping to defend not only the legitimacy of the Roman Canon of the Mass, but also the official teaching of the Roman Catholic Church with regard to eucharistic consecration. Indeed, Casel himself explicitly asserted that the Canon was both Eucharist and epiclesis in the ancient and broad sense of the word: it was a naming in praise of the Trinity.[17]

In spite of such attempts to prove that an invocation of the Holy Spirit was neither primitive nor universal in ancient eucharistic prayers, many Roman Catholic scholars still felt the need to point to parts of the Roman Canon as being the equivalent of the Eastern epiclesis, even though these made no explicit mention of the Spirit. Some opted for the *Supra quae* and/or *Supplices te* section of the prayer as its counterpart, because, as Louis Duchesne argued, both in subject matter and position it occupied the same place in the prayer and was also "a prayer to God for his intervention in the mystery."[18] Still others looked instead to the *Hanc igitur* and/or *Quam oblationem* section prior to the institution narrative. Thus J. A. Jungmann, rejecting the arguments for an older invocation that had disappeared from the rite, claimed that the epiclesis "represents the fourth century custom of only one of the three great patriarchates, namely, that of Antioch, while in the other two, Alexandria and Rome, the traditional practice, going back at least to the same early period, involved an invocation of the divine power *before* the words of institution."[19] In other words, his case was that an invocation without mention of the Holy Spirit was at least as ancient as one with, and its position before the narrative at least as old as the location after it, and in any case was found elsewhere besides Rome. Gradually, a consensus emerged that both parts of the prayer

[16] J. Armitage Robinson, "Invocation in the Holy Eucharist," *Theology* 8 (1924): 89–100, adopted a similar position to Connolly, while F. E. Brightman, in correspondence on the issue in *Theology* 9 (1924): 33–40, held that the word could have both meanings.

[17] Odo Casel, "Zur Epiklese," *Jahrbuch für Liturgiewissenschaft* 3 (1923): 100–102.

[18] Louis Duchesne, *Les origines du culte Chrétien* (Paris: Thorin, 1899), 173; English translation from 3d ed., *Christian Worship: Its Origins and Evolution* (London: SPCK, 1903), 181. See also Maurice de la Taille, *Mysterium fidei*, 3d ed. (Paris: Beauchesne, 1931), 276.

[19] Josef A. Jungman, *The Mass of the Roman Rite* (New York: Benziger Bros., 1951) 2:193 (italics in original).

The Rediscovery of the Holy Spirit

together should be seen as forming the equivalent of the Eastern invocation. The Roman Canon was thus said to have a split epiclesis: a consecratory one, an invocation on the bread and wine before the narrative, and a communion epiclesis, an invocation on the people, after it.[20]

THE EUCHARISTIC EPICLESIS AND THE CHURCH OF ENGLAND

While Roman Catholic scholars were thus engaged in defending the legitimacy of their eucharistic prayer in spite of the absence of an explicit invocation of the Spirit, things were different in the Church of England, where the desirability of incorporating such a petition had been affirmed for a considerable period of time in some quarters, not least because of a longstanding interest in Eastern Christianity. The eucharistic prayer in the first Anglican Prayer Book of 1549 had included the petition "with thy Holy Spirit and word vouchsafe to bless and sanctify these thy gifts and creatures of bread and wine" before the institution narrative, and although this disappeared in subsequent revisions in England, it had reappeared in the Scottish tradition in 1637 and was moved to what might be described as the "Eastern" position after the institution narrative in 1755 under the influence of the research into ancient liturgies that had been undertaken by the English Non-Jurors.[21] From there it was subsequently adopted in the American Prayer Book from 1789 onward.

When the Church of England embarked upon an ill-fated process of revision of its Prayer Book in the early decades of the twentieth century, it was therefore natural that the question was raised as to whether something similar should be introduced into the English rite. The renowned liturgical scholar Walter Frere thought that until the divergence of belief between the Latin West, and what he described as "the more primitive East" as to the doctrine of eucharistic consecration, was nearer a settlement, "it would be inopportune to take any steps towards the reinsertion of the Invocation of the Holy Spirit. . . . When our own mind is clearer, we may be able to go forward; but not

---

[20] See for example Bouyer, *Eucharist*, 145–46.

[21] See W. Jardine Grisbrooke, *Anglican Liturgies of the Seventeenth and Eighteenth Centuries*, Alcuin Club Collections 40 (London: SPCK, 1958).

Paul F. Bradshaw

until then."[22] His judgment was that either the narrative of institution or the epiclesis,

> whether with or without the other, must be held to be adequate to effect the consecration, if the Church uses them with that intention. No other theory is really possible in view of past history or present practice. But a more satisfactory position is that which has both, and recognises the place of each in the act of consecration.
>   This, then, is the conclusion to which the English Church must be advancing; and in due course it will be able to restore the Invocation and give it its right place, and thus, in this respect as in others, stand as a mediator between the East and Rome, comprehending the parts of the truth for which each is contending.[23]

Others, however, were not content to wait. Already in 1911 a proposal that consideration be given to providing a eucharistic prayer along the lines of the 1549 Scottish and American rites was only narrowly defeated in the Convocation of Canterbury,[24] and invocations of the Spirit were included in the several publications that advocated revision of the Prayer Book in the years that followed.[25]

Not surprisingly, therefore, a proposal for the inclusion of an invocation of the Holy Spirit surfaced in the official revision process in 1914 and was given textual form in 1919.[26] Unlike the earlier suggestions, however, which had been looking back to a 1549-style pre-narrative petition, under the expert guidance of Frere this was in the "Eastern" position after the narrative of institution. A revised version of the text found its way into the final proposals submitted for parliamentary approval in 1927, although it was the subject of considerable disagreement with regard to both its necessity and its location in the

---

[22] W. H. Frere, *Some Principles of Liturgical Reform* (London: John Murray, 1911), 188–89.

[23] Ibid., 189–90.

[24] See Donald Gray, *The 1927–28 Prayer Book Crisis* 2, Alcuin/GROW Joint Liturgical Study 61 (Norwich, England: SCM-Canterbury Press, 2006), 19.

[25] Anonymous [actually Percy Dearmer], *A Prayer Book Revised* (London: Mowbray, 1913), 81 (see also its preface, written by Charles Gore, bishop of Oxford, xii); B. W. Randolph, *A Revised Liturgy* (London: Mowbray, 1914), 4; R. J. Edmund Boggis, *Revision of the Book of Common Prayer from the Point of View of a Parish Priest* (Canterbury, England: Cross & Jackman, 1914), 78.

[26] Gray, *The 1927–28 Prayer Book Crisis* 1:43, 46.

The Rediscovery of the Holy Spirit

prayer. Many Anglo-Catholics, including Darwell Stone and F. E. Brightman, opposed its being placed after the institution narrative as undermining the Western Catholic belief in the consecratory power of the dominical words in the narrative. Frere then attempted to secure the option of its being said before the institution narrative in order to pacify the opposition, but he failed to win support.[27] The revision of the Prayer Book was subsequently defeated in Parliament, not least because of the opposition to features such as this from both Anglo-Catholic and Evangelical quarters, although for different reasons: while Anglo-Catholics did not want anything that challenged the role of the institution narrative, Evangelicals did not want anything that implied a change in the bread and wine.

In other parts of the Anglican Communion, however, the English proposals did exercise an influence on liturgical revision, and a eucharistic epiclesis of the same type was adopted in South Africa in 1929, in Ceylon (as it then was) in 1933, and in India in 1960. In Japan in 1953 a 1549-type petition was inserted before the institution narrative instead. Both Canada and the West Indies in 1959 were more cautious, merely adding the words "by the power of the Holy Spirit" to the petition for the communicants toward the end of the prayer. The novelty in Lutheranism of the introduction of a full epiclesis of word and spirit on both the congregation and the eucharistic elements in a post-institution-narrative position in the 1958 *Service Book and Hymnal of the Lutheran Church in America*[28] is probably also to be attributed to the influence of the Episcopal Church there.

AFTER THE SECOND VATICAN COUNCIL

The Constitution on the Sacred Liturgy of Vatican II has only five references in total to the Holy Spirit, and just one of these is in direct relation to worship, when it speaks of the Church celebrating the Eucharist "and at the same time giving thanks 'to God for his unspeakable gift' (2 Cor. 9:15) in Christ Jesus, 'in praise of his glory' (Eph. 1:12), through the power of the Holy Spirit."[29] Nevertheless, as the

---

[27] Gray, *The 1927–28 Prayer Book Crisis* 2:19–20.

[28] (Minneapolis: Augsburg, 1958), 11.

[29] *Sacrosanctum Concilium*, no. 6. For criticism of the lack of reference to the Holy Spirit in this document, see for example Vilmos Vajta, "Renewal of Worship: De Sacra Liturgia," in *Dialogue on the Way*, ed. George A. Lindbeck, 107 (Minneapolis: Augsburg, 1965).

Paul F. Bradshaw

actual work of revising the liturgical texts was undertaken, the desire emerged to add more explicit reference to the operation of the Spirit in the Eucharist. In particular, Cipriano Vagaggini, who was among those still tending to believe that the primitive Roman Rite had originally included an epiclesis[30] and who exercised a major influence on the composition of the new texts,[31] listed among the defects of the Roman Canon "the lack of a theology of the part played by the Holy Spirit in the Eucharist," which he said was of prime importance.

> Today we have quite rightly become aware of this, not only for ecumenical reasons, but also because of the rediscovery of that aspect of the Trinity we call "economic", an aspect underlined by the Second Vatican Council. This means to think of the persons of the Trinity not so much in terms of their unity in their inner nature as in terms of their relative distinction, known to us principally through their manifestation in the history of salvation.[32]

Vagaggini did not think that the addition of an explicit reference to the work of the Spirit would undermine the traditional Western understanding of the christological basis of eucharistic consecration. He wrote:

> The action of Christ and the action of the Holy Spirit are not two diverse actions, but a single action of Christ in the Holy Spirit or through the Holy Spirit. Theoretically speaking, therefore, it is possible to emphasize quite well that which is, so to speak, the role of the Holy Spirit in the Mass without thereby abandoning the idea that Christ, our High Priest, now in heaven at the right of the Father, is the principal minister of the Eucharistic sacrifice.[33]

[30] Cipriano Vagaggini, *Il senso teologico della liturgia* (Rome: Edizioni Paoline, 1958); English translation from the 4th ed., *The Theological Dimensions of the Liturgy* (Collegeville, MN: Liturgical Press, 1976), 228–29.

[31] See Annibale Bugnini, *La riforma liturgica* (1948–1975) (Rome: Edizioni liturgiche, 1983); English translation, *The Reform of the Liturgy, 1948–1975* (Collegeville, MN: Liturgical Press, 1990), 450.

[32] Cipriano Vagaggini, *Il canone della messa e la riforma liturgica* (Turin: Elle Di Ci, 1966); English translation: *The Canon of the Mass and Liturgical Reform* (London: Chapman / Staten Island, NY: Alba House, 1967), 100–101.

[33] Vagaggini, *The Theological Dimensions of the Liturgy*, 263.

The Rediscovery of the Holy Spirit

Thus when the new texts appeared in 1968, although the Roman Canon itself remained unchanged, all the new eucharistic prayers did include a reference to the operation of the Spirit in twofold form: in the petition for the consecration of the elements before the institution narrative, and in a petition for the communicants that came after it. So, for example, in Eucharistic Prayer II, based on that in the *Apostolic Tradition*, God is asked: "Let your Spirit come upon these gifts to make them holy, so that they may become for us the body and blood of our Lord, Jesus Christ." And later: "May all of us who share in the body and blood of Christ be brought together in unity by the Holy Spirit."

Louis Bouyer welcomed the invocation of the Spirit in the new prayers for ecumenical reasons, saying, "undoubtedly, this will contribute toward a rapprochement with the East as well as toward the reunion of the Christian West." While the texts still bore witness to the fact that consecration finds its source in the dominical words, yet "it becomes effective in each celebration within the prayer of the Church in which she uses these words herself in order to invoke their accomplishment from the Father through the sole power of his Spirit." He defended the retention of a split epiclesis as "a recognition of the underlying harmony" of Eastern and Western traditions, "which up to now have seemed separate."[34] Other commentators followed suit. J. D. Crichton thought the second invocation highly appropriate because "the church is the Spirit-filled body of Christ; in that body the Holy Spirit is regarded as the animating principle and it is to him that the fruitfulness of Christ's saving work in the hearts of Christians is attributed. Now that people can *hear* the invocation they become more aware of the work of the Spirit in their midst and the eucharist becomes a more adequate sign of the church."[35]

On the other hand, the retention of the split epiclesis has come in for some criticism on the grounds that it artificially divides the working of the Spirit and destroys its essential unity: the Spirit is invoked on the elements *in order that* all who partake of them may become united in the Body of Christ. It is thus argued these are not two separate requests but two aspects of the same request, and this theology is better articulated when they are conjoined in the prayer. Aidan Kavanagh criticized in particular the inclusion of a pneumatic epiclesis

[34] Bouyer, *Eucharist*, 460–61.
[35] J. D. Crichton, *Christian Celebration: The Mass* (London: Chapman, 1971), 92–93.

Paul F. Bradshaw

just before the narrative because it "not only welds both sections into a unit that is longer and more strongly consecratory than before: it also interrupts the flow of sequence in narrating the divine mercies for which eucharistic prayer is made and sets the institution narrative off from this cursus." [36]

THE EPICLESIS IN OTHER CHURCHES

In the years that followed the publication of the Roman Catholic prayers, eucharistic invocations of the Holy Spirit began to appear in the liturgical texts produced in many other churches. In the Church of England, for instance, the failed attempt of 1928 was remedied in 1973 when a split epiclesis of the Roman Catholic kind was included in several of the prayers in modern language that were then authorized for trial use and later adopted in the 1980 *Alternative Service Book*. The words "by the power of your Spirit" were added to the petition for consecration before the institution narrative and a request for the action of the Spirit on the people inserted later in the prayer. It was not until twenty years later, in the *Common Worship* series of texts, that the Church of England followed the lead given centuries earlier by the Episcopal Churches in Scotland and the U.S.A., and included several eucharistic prayers containing a single epiclesis that came after the institution narrative as well as other prayers that retained the split epiclesis.[37]

In other churches it was a single epiclesis that was generally adopted, and in most cases the Spirit was invoked both on the people and on the eucharistic elements, although with considerable variation as to what it was exactly that the Spirit was expected to do.[38] On the

[36] Aidan Kavanagh, "Thoughts on the New Eucharistic Prayers," *Worship* 43 (1969): 2–12, here at 9. See also John H. McKenna, *Eucharist and Holy Spirit*, Alcuin Club Collections 57 (Great Wakering, Essex: Mayhew McCrimmon, 1975), 206–7; Frank C. Senn, "Towards a Different Anaphoral Structure," *Worship* 58 (1984): 346–58, here at 348.

[37] *Common Worship: Services and Prayers for the Church of England* (London: Church House Publishing, 2000), Order One: Eucharistic Prayers D, F, G, & H have a single epiclesis after the institution narrative, while Prayers A, B, C, & E retain the split epiclesis.

[38] See the detailed study of those in a number of American churches in John H. McKenna, "The Epiclesis Revisited," *Ephemerides Liturgicae* 99 (1985): 314–36; reproduced in *New Eucharistic Prayers*, ed. Frank C. Senn (New York: Paulist Press, 1987), 169–86.

The Rediscovery of the Holy Spirit

other hand, Prayer C in the American Episcopal Church's 1979 Prayer Book mentioned the bread and wine alone; in several other churches prayers were included that referred to the communicants alone;[39] and a few were ambiguous in their intent—probably deliberately so.

Such innovations did not meet with a favorable reaction everywhere. For instance, the leading Lutheran theologian Peter Brunner, while putting forward strong reasons for the appropriateness of a eucharistic epiclesis, had firmly rejected a location after the institution narrative: "a consecration petition following the words of institution is no longer possible for the Occidental churches. Since the work of the Spirit does not complete the work of Christ in consecration, but only accompanies it co-operatively, an epiclesis petitioning for consecration must stand, in our Western tradition, before the words of institution, if it is to be used in any form whatsoever."[40] On the other hand, the Reformed theologian J.-J. von Allmen responded to him and put forward arguments in support of the Eastern position.[41] Later some conservative Lutherans opposed the introduction of a eucharistic prayer at all into their rites, and especially one containing an epiclesis, because they believed that it contradicted Luther's emphasis on the "gift" character of the Eucharist—the action of prayer being from human beings to God, whereas the Eucharist was the gift of God to human beings.[42] Similarly, as early as 1951 the Anglican Evangelical J. E. L. Oulton had

[39] For example, The Evangelical Lutheran Church in America, *The Lutheran Book of Worship* (Minneapolis: Augsburg, 1978), Prayers I & II; The Presbyterian Church (USA), *The Service for the Lord's Day: The Worship of God* (Philadelphia: Westminster Press, 1984), Great Prayers of Thanksgiving A, G, & H.

[40] Peter Brunner, "Zur Lehre vom Gottesdienst der im Namen Jesu versammelten Gemeinde," in *Leiturgia. Handbuch des evangelischen Gottesdienstes* 1, ed. K. F. Müller, and W. Blankenburg (Kassel, Germany: J. Stauda-Verlag, 1954); English translation, *Worship in the Name of Jesus* (St. Louis, MO: Concordia, 1968), 298–307, here at 307.

[41] J.-J. von Allmen, *Worship: Its Theology and Practice* (New York: Oxford University Press, 1965), 28–32. See also idem, *Essai sur le repas du Seigneur* (Neuchâtel: Delachaux & Niestlé, 1966); English translation: *The Lord's Supper* (London: Lutterworth Press / Richmond, VA: John Knox Press, 1969), 30–35.

[42] See for example Charles Evanson, "The Lord's Supper according to the World Council of Churches," *Concordia Theological Quarterly* (1985): 117–34, here at 128; William E. Thompson, "The Epiclesis and Lutheran Theology," *Logia* 4, no.1 (January 1995): 31–35.

Paul F. Bradshaw

been critical of liturgies that invoked the Holy Spirit on the people as well as the elements because this implied that the Spirit was not already abiding in them, a view that was shared by his fellow Anglican and liturgical scholar J. G. Davies, who also echoed Gregory Dix's criticism that the Eastern invocation on the elements made Christ passive rather than active in the Eucharist.[43]

In spite of exceptions like these, the addition of a form of epiclesis to eucharistic prayers was mostly welcomed in many Christian denominations. It would be gratifying to suppose that this positive support arose as a result of a renewed interest in the theology of the Holy Spirit more generally. However, there is very little sign that this was so. Even though, as we saw in the extract from his writings cited earlier, Vagaggini claimed that an interest in the economic Trinity had paved the way for the adoption of the epiclesis in the Roman Catholic Church, such an interest actually seems to feature relatively little in theological writings prior to the composition of the new Roman Catholic prayers, like more specific discussions of the relation of the Holy Spirit to worship in general, or to the Eucharist in particular, in any Christian tradition.[44] Similarly, although these liturgical changes were taking place at the same time as the Charismatic movement was beginning to make itself felt in the mainstream churches, there is no evidence of any direct cross-fertilization between the two. Thus, while ecumenical interest certainly did motivate a minority to press for the adoption of an epiclesis, its introduction into many denominations seems to owe more to the results of the historical scholarship of the time, and especially to the status given to the *Apostolic Tradition* attributed to Hippolytus. At the time this was thought to confirm that some reference to the work of the Spirit had been a standard feature of early eucharistic prayers, and so needed to be replicated in modern revisions that were attempting to get back to the historical roots of Christian liturgy.

[43] J. E. L. Oulton, *Holy Communion and Holy Spirit, A Study in Doctrinal Relationship* (London: SPCK, 1951), 133; J. G. Davies, *The Spirit, the Church and the Sacraments* (London: Faith Press, 1954), 137–38; Gregory Dix, *The Shape of the Liturgy* (Westminster: Dacre, 1945), 278.

[44] See for example the Reformed theologian Hendrikus Berkhof, *The Doctrine of the Holy Spirit* (Richmond, VA: John Knox Press, 1964), who does not mention the Spirit's role in worship.

The Rediscovery of the Holy Spirit

Nevertheless, once the epiclesis did begin to make an appearance in prayer texts, then references to the operation of the Spirit also started to feature more frequently in writings about the Eucharist. While very many of these were expressed only in a quite brief form, a few scholars did develop a more comprehensive theology of the Spirit's relationship to the rite. Among the first of these were Jean Tillard, the Roman Catholic ecumenist; Max Thurian, at that time subprior of the ecumenical Taizé community and a non-Catholic observer at the Second Vatican Council and at the Consilium for implementing its liturgical reforms; and Lukas Vischer, director of the Faith and Order Department of the World Council of Churches, who urged the churches of the Reformation to adopt an epiclesis as a means of fostering unity.[45] Roman Catholic writings were particularly concerned to work out the relationship between the christological and pneumatological dimensions of the Eucharist,[46] and several drew attention to Latin patristic and medieval sources that had acknowledged the part played by the Holy Spirit as well as the institution narrative in eucharistic consecration, in order to demonstrate that this idea was not alien to the Western tradition. This had already been done by Sévérien Salaville in 1913[47] but now greater attention was paid to it, notably by Yves Congar in his three-volume study of the Holy Spirit.[48] Yet even in such a major work as this, the precise role of the Holy Spirit in relation to worship and the Eucharist remains very underdeveloped.

Official denominational statements about the Eucharist and the text of ecumenical agreements on the Eucharist between churches,

[45] Max Thurian, *Le pain unique* (Taizé, France: Les Presses de Taizé, 1967), 47–50; English translation, *The One Bread* (New York: Sheed & Ward, 1969), 28–33; J. M. R. Tillard, "L'eucharistie et le Saint-Esprit," *Nouvelle revue théologique* 90 (1968): 362–87; Lukas Vischer, "The Epiclesis: Sign of Unity and Renewal," *Studia Liturgica* 6 (1969): 30–39.

[46] See for example Edward J. Kilmartin, "The Active Role of Christ and the Holy Spirit in the Sanctification of the Eucharistic Elements," *Theological Studies* 45 (1984): 225–53; McKenna, *Eucharist and Holy Spirit*.

[47] "Epiclèse eucharistique," *Dictionnaire de théologie catholique* (1913) 5:194–300.

[48] Yves Congar, *Je crois en l'Esprit Saint* (Paris: Cerf, 1979–80); English translation: *I Believe in the Holy Spirit* (New York: Seabury / London: Chapman, 1983) 3:250ff.

Paul F. Bradshaw

too, tended to contain only quite brief statements about the role of the Holy Spirit.[49] However, two documents in particular stand out in contrast to this general tendency; they developed the theme of the Spirit's relationship to the Eucharist quite extensively. The first was the 1982 World Council of Churches' *Baptism, Eucharist and Ministry*, which tried to strike a balance between the role of the institution narrative and that of the invocation of the Holy Spirit. It affirmed that "the presence of Christ is clearly the centre of the eucharist, and the promise contained in the words of institution is therefore fundamental to the celebration." But it also insisted:

> The Spirit makes the crucified and risen Christ really present to us in the eucharistic meal, fulfilling the promise contained in the words of institution. . . . The bond between the eucharistic celebration and the mystery of the Triune God reveals the role of the Holy Spirit as that of the One who makes the historical words of Jesus present and alive. Being assured by Jesus' promise in the words of institution that it will be answered, the Church prays to the Father for the gift of the Holy Spirit in order that the eucharistic event may be a reality: the real presence of the crucified and risen Christ giving his life for all humanity.[50]

In the commentary that was attached to this section of the document, it went on to say:

> This is not to spiritualize the eucharistic presence of Christ but to affirm the indissoluble union between the Son and the Spirit. This union makes it clear that the eucharist is not a magical or mechanical action but a prayer addressed to the Father, one which emphasizes the Church's utter dependence. There is an intrinsic relationship between the words of institution, Christ's promise, and the *epiklesis*, the invocation of the Spirit, in the liturgy. The *epiklesis* in relation to the words of institution is located differently in various liturgical traditions. In the early liturgies the whole "prayer action" was thought of as bringing about the reality promised by Christ. The invocation of the Spirit was made both on the community and on the elements of bread and wine.

---

[49] Examples of ecumenical texts can be found in Kilmartin, "The Active Role of Christ and the Holy Spirit in the Sanctification of the Eucharistic Elements," 226–33.

[50] Section 14; *Baptism, Eucharist and Ministry* (Geneva: World Council of Churches, 1982). This and the following quotations are from p. 13.

The Rediscovery of the Holy Spirit

93

Recovery of such an understanding may help us overcome our difficulties concerning a special moment of consecration.

Finally, the document appended a number of further affirmations with regard to the role of the Spirit in the Eucharist:

15. It is in virtue of the living word of Christ and by the power of the Holy Spirit that the bread and wine become the sacramental signs of Christ's body and blood. They remain so for the purpose of communion.

16. The whole action of the eucharist has an "epikletic" character because it depends upon the work of the Holy Spirit. In the words of the liturgy, this aspect of the eucharist finds varied expression.

17. The Church, as the community of the new covenant, confidently invokes the Spirit, in order that it may be sanctified and renewed, led into all justice, truth and unity, and empowered to fulfil its mission in the world.

18. The Holy Spirit through the eucharist gives a fore-taste of the Kingdom of God: the Church receives the life of the new creation and the assurance of the Lord's return.

A second major statement on the Spirit and the Eucharist came in the text on the Holy Spirit produced by the Theological-Historical Commission of the Roman Catholic Church in preparation for the Jubilee Year 2000.[51] Here a whole chapter was given over to the Holy Spirit and the liturgy, and a substantial section of this (106–13 in the English edition) dealt with the Eucharist under such headings as "The Spirit actualizes the Paschal Mystery," "Pentecost is continued in the Eucharist," "The Spirit in the Eucharist gives a foretaste of the Future Kingdom," "In the Eucharist, along with Christ, we receive the Holy Spirit," and "The Holy Spirit incorporates us into the 'total Christ.'" The document was unequivocal in stating that it was the Spirit that made Christ present in the Eucharist by consecrating and converting the holy gifts into his Body and Blood (106–7).

CONCLUSION: UNFINISHED BUSINESS
After a century or more of protracted debate over the nature of the eucharistic epiclesis, of which I have only been able to touch the

---

[51] *Del tuo Spirito, Signore, è piena la terra* (Milan: Edizioni Paoline, 1997); English translation, *The Holy Spirit, Lord and Giver of Life* (New York: Crossroad, 1997).

Paul F. Bradshaw

fringes in this paper, recent decades have generally seen a greater expansion of the theology of the Spirit in relation to the Eucharist, making an appearance in official denominational literature, in ecumenical statements, and in theological writings. However, there appear to be at least two areas of unfinished business.

First, in several ecclesiastical traditions—specifically the Roman Catholic, Anglican, and Lutheran—there still seems to be a lack of agreement over the balance between the christological, pneumatological, and trinitarian dimensions of the Eucharist. For instance, in a recent important article Patrick Regan has drawn attention to the eucharistic theology in the encyclical *Ecclesia de Eucharistia* issued by Pope John Paul II in 2003[52] and to the 2004 *Lineamenta* in preparation for the Synod of Bishops on the Eucharist,[53] in which he asserts that their teaching with regard to the epiclesis is "reductive, regressive, embarrassing ecumenically and confusing" in comparison with official Roman Catholic documents published only a few years earlier—the *Catechism of the Catholic Church* of 1992, the apostolic letter *Dies Domini* of 1998, and the most recent version of the *General Instruction on the Roman Missal* of the year 2000—because they focus on the christological dimensions of the Eucharist to the detriment of trinitarian and pneumatological aspects.[54] Clearly, more theological reflection is needed in this area.

Second, all denominations need to give some further consideration to the precise wording of their epicleses. In the academic world, consensus seems to have been reached that what has been called a "communion epiclesis" is more primitive than what has been called a "consecration epiclesis," but Robert Taft has rightly pointed out that the distinction between the two types should not be pressed too far: "It is clear that *any prayer* for the power of God to come upon something in order that it be unto salvation for those who partake of it or participate in it as God intended necessarily implies that God *do something* by his coming to make that object salvific. . . . It does not imply the more primitive, less explicit epicletic prayer is not implicitly

[52] (Vatican City: Libreria Editrice Vaticana, 2003).

[53] *Eucharistia: Fons et Culmen Vitae et Missionis Ecclesiae. Lineamenta* (Vatican City: Libreria Editrice Vaticana, 2004).

[54] Patrick Regan, "Quenching the Spirit: The Epiclesis in Recent Roman Documents," *Worship* 79 (2005): 386–404, here at 402.

The Rediscovery of the Holy Spirit

consecratory."[55] Yet, even the so-called communion epiclesis does not represent the most ancient form of the invocation. As Gabriele Winkler has shown, its historical roots lie in a simple appeal to the Messiah or his Spirit to be present,[56] and, as Taft has revealed in another article, early epicleses might take quite a variety of forms.[57]

On the one hand, therefore, there is good historical precedent for the great diversity that exists in the wording of epicletic formulae in modern rites. On the other hand, at least some of this diversity seems to stem from a theological uncertainty as to what it is precisely that the Holy Spirit is expected to do in relation to the Eucharist, or alternatively from a fear of saying something that might imply a belief that the framers did not wish to articulate. Thus, the absence of any connection with the bread and wine in some denominations seems to have arisen from a desire to avoid implying that a change was being sought in the elements. Closer examination of ancient examples will reveal that this implication does not necessarily accompany such a reference, and that there are a number of such forms that describe the Spirit's activity in relation to the bread and wine in quite different terms. Similarly, the vagueness encountered in some modern forms seems at least in part to reflect an unnecessary reluctance to invoke the Holy Spirit directly on believers who are thought already to possess that Spirit through their baptism. Above all, too many modern epicleses lack any explicit ecclesiological dimension in their wording that in some way asks for the Spirit to unite all the communicants into the one communion, and as a result they can easily be heard in an individualistic way. Clearly, therefore, greater theological reflection is needed in these areas too.

[55] Robert F. Taft, "The Epiclesis Question in the Light of the Orthodox and Catholic *Lex Orandi* Traditions," in *New Perspectives on Historical Theology*, ed. Bradley Nassif, 210–37 (Grand Rapids, MI: Eerdmans, 1996), here at 214–15 (italics in original).

[56] See for example Gabriele Winkler, "Nochmals zu den Anfängen der Epiklese und des Sanctus im Eucharistischen Hochgebet," *Theologische Quartalschrift* 74 (1994): 214–31, esp. 214ff.

[57] Robert F. Taft, "The Fruits of Communion in the Anaphora of St John Chrysostom," in *Psallendum: Miscellanea di studi in onore del Prof. Jordi Pinell i Pons, OSB*, ed. Ildebrando Scicolone, Studia Anselmiana 115 (Rome: Pontificio Ateneo S. Anselmo, 1992), 275–302, here at 281ff.

Paul F. Bradshaw

Part 2

Historic Trajectories

Simon Jones

6. Wombs of the Spirit: Incarnational Pneumatology in the Syrian Baptismal Tradition

That the Syriac noun *ruḥa*, spirit, is grammatically feminine has attracted more attention than many of the distinctive features of Syriac Christianity. Noting this characteristic, some theologians,[1] including a number of feminists, have identified the Spirit as most frequently representing the feminine dimension in God. Other writers, such as Sarah Coakley, have rejected this feminine ascription to the Third Person of the Trinity alone as artificially restricting the range of the Spirit's activity to traditional "feminine" qualities. Thus, Coakley claims, at worst "feminine Spirit may become nothing more than the soothing but undervalued adjunct to the drama of an all-male household."[2] In this study our concern is not so much the gender of the godhead, whether a grammatically feminine Spirit allows us to locate a feminine Person in God, but rather the relationship between *ruḥa* and the imagery used to describe the activity of the Spirit within the Syrian baptismal tradition.[3]

Sebastian Brock has demonstrated that three periods can be identified in which the gender of *ruḥa* was treated in grammatically different ways. Before 400 CE the Holy Spirit was nearly always treated as a feminine noun. From the beginning of the fifth century some writ-

[1] See, for example, Yves Congar, *I Believe in the Holy Spirit* (London: Chapman, 1983), 3:157.

[2] Sarah Coakley, "'Femininity' and the Holy Spirit," in *Mirror to the Church: Reflections on Sexism*, ed. Monica Furlong, 132 (London: SPCK, 1988).

[3] This article draws upon the writer's doctoral thesis, "Womb of the Spirit: The Liturgical Implications of the Doctrine of the Spirit for the Syrian Baptismal Tradition" (University of Cambridge, 1999); see also Simon Jones, "The Womb and the Spirit in the Baptismal Writings of Ephrem the Syrian," *Studia Liturgica* 33, no. 2 (2003): 175–93.

ers attached to this feminine noun masculine verbal and adjectival forms whenever it referred to the Holy Spirit. From the sixth century onward, with a few exceptions, it became the norm to treat *ruḥa* as if it were a masculine noun.[4] In this essay I will argue that, whereas in its grammatical development *ruḥa* slowly but surely lost its feminine identity, in the language used to describe the activity of the Spirit within the process of Christian initiation feminine images in no way mirrored this decline. Indeed, it is a female image, that of the womb, that remains the principal symbolic focus of the activity of the Holy Spirit within the Syrian baptismal tradition. Within the constraints of this essay it is only possible to consider a relatively limited selection of texts. Taking examples from East and West Syria, I will begin with the primitive *Odes of Solomon*, before moving to Ephrem the Syrian in the fourth century, to the fifth-century bishop Philoxenus of Mabbug, and, finally, to the West Syrian baptismal *ordines* of Severus of Antioch and Jacob of Serugh, for which the earliest textual evidence can be found in the eighth century.

ODES OF SOLOMON

In his 1912 edition of the *Odes of Solomon*, J. H. Bernard considered these primitive poetic texts to have originated as "baptismal hymns."[5] While the majority of scholars has not shared Bernard's confident assertion concerning these hymns' identity, many writers are in agreement with his general conclusion that they are in some sense baptismal.[6]

Ode 19, while not containing any of the *Odes'* more explicit baptismal allusions, is significant because of the feminine imagery used to describe the activity of the Spirit:

[4] Sebastian Brock, "The Holy Spirit as Feminine in Early Syriac Literature," in *After Eve: Women, Theology and the Christian Tradition*, ed. Janet Martin Soskice, 73–88 (London: Marshall Pickering, 1990).

[5] J. H. Bernard, *The Odes of Solomon* (Cambridge: Cambridge University Press, 1912), 42.

[6] For example, Mark Pierce, "Themes in the 'Odes of Solomon' and Early Christian Writings and Their Baptismal Character," *Ephemerides Liturgicae* 98 (1984): 35–39.

Simon Jones

1 A cup of milk was offered to me
  And I drank it with the sweetness of the Lord's kindness.
2 The Son is the cup,
  And he who was milked is the Father;
  And she who milked him is the Holy Spirit;
3 Because his breasts were full,
  And it was undesirable that his milk should be spilt without purpose,
4 The Holy Spirit opened her womb [Syr: ʿuba]
  And mixed the milk of the two breasts of the Father,
5 And gave the mixture to the world without their knowing,
  And those who take (it) are in the perfection of the right hand.
6 The womb [Syr: karsa] of the Virgin caught (it)
  And she received conception and gave birth.
7 And the Virgin became a mother through great mercy.[7]

An initial reading of the text reveals that it is not just the Holy Spirit who attracts feminine attributes but also the Father, who possesses breasts full of milk. Verse two is trinitarian in structure and identifies the Father as the source of grace, the Son as the cup in which the grace is offered to the world, and the Spirit as the agent, the milking maid, who communicates the grace of the Father to the Son. The following verse describes God's breasts as overflowing with grace and needing to be emptied for a particular purpose.

The Syriac noun ʿuba can be translated in a number of ways, including womb, bosom, hollow, and cavity.[8] In verse 4 the "bosom of the Spirit" is favored by several commentators.[9] While this is not out of keeping with the imagery that this Ode has already established, "womb" is surely to be preferred since it allows the image to develop in terms of the milk / grace of the Father being mixed in the womb of

[7] H. J. W. Drijvers, "The 19th Ode of Solomon: Its Interpretation and Place in Syrian Christianity," *Journal of Theological Studies* 31 (1980): 339–40.

[8] J. Payne Smith, ed., *A Compendious Syriac Dictionary* (Oxford: Oxford University Press, 1902), 403.

[9] See, for example, Joseph Chalassery, *The Holy Spirit and Christian Initiation in the East Syrian Tradition* (Rome: Mar Thoma Yogam, 1995), 14; for a discussion of this Ode, see also Bryan D. Spinks, *Early and Medieval Rituals and Theologies of Baptism* (Aldershot / Burlington: Ashgate, 2006), 17–18, and Maxwell E. Johnson, *The Rites of Christian Initiation* (Collegeville, MN: Liturgical Press, 2007), 47–49.

the Spirit, who gives birth to the "mixture" that is communicated to Mary in order that she may conceive.[10]

Also noteworthy are the two Syriac nouns used to describe the womb of the Spirit in verse 4 and the womb of the Virgin in verse 6. The Peshitta renders the Greek κόλπος, "bosom," in John 1:18 as ʿuba. The choice of this word, which has a broader semantic range than the Greek, allows the Johannine Prologue to portray the divine Logos dwelling in the womb of the Father, an idea that we will encounter in the *Ordo* of Severus. The other Syriac noun for womb, *karsa*, is not absent from the gospels. It is used for the womb of the Virgin in Luke 1:42, and, more interestingly, in John 3:4, where, within the Syrian tradition, the context is clearly understood to be baptismal.

H. J. W. Drijvers puts forward an interesting hypothesis for understanding some of this imagery by referring to the Old Syriac version of the Johannine Prologue. This version differs from the *Peshitta* in that Christ, who is full of grace and truth, comes to the world *from* the womb of the Father rather than residing *in* the womb of the Father. Thus, in connection with this Ode Drijvers suggests that:

> The female element of the Father which gives birth to the Son is represented by the (female) Holy Spirit who functions as the womb of the Father, from where His grace and truth, the milk of His two breasts, His only begotten Son, are born. Father, Holy Spirit, and Son are three divine hypostases, who function in a sexually colored interacting process to express the idea that God's grace and truth are given to the world as His only begotten Son, who is from the womb of His Father.[11]

Focusing on the role of the Spirit within this trinitarian process, Ode 36.3 provides further evidence that the Spirit is involved, among other things, in the act of giving birth: "[The Spirit] gave birth to me before the Lord's face, and because I was Son of Man, I was named the light, the Son of God."[12] Noting at this juncture the use of primitive birth im-

---

[10] There is, of course, a biological link between breast and womb; for example, through postnatal contractions brought about from oxytocin released in the initial stages of breast-feeding.

[11] Drijvers, "The 19th Ode of Solomon," 343–44.

[12] James Hamilton Charlesworth, ed. and trans., *The Odes of Solomon* (Missoula, MT: Scholars Press, 1977), 126. Gabriele Winkler's research into the Armenian baptismal tradition has drawn attention to a reference to "birth from the womb of the Spirit" in the *History of Agathangelos*; see her "Zur

Simon Jones

agery associated with the Spirit in the *Odes of Solomon*, let us move on
to consider how this tradition, associated with baptism, is developed
in the writings of the greatest of the Syrian theologians, the fourth-
century deacon known as the "harp of the Spirit," Ephrem of Nisibis.

EPHREM THE SYRIAN

At the heart of Ephrem's theology of baptism lie regeneration and
its associated imagery. In a verse from one of his *Hymns on Virginity*
baptism is described in terms of a pregnant woman giving birth to a
baby, her labor pains being articulated through the cry of a trinitarian
formula:

> A royal portrait is painted with visible colors,
>
> and with oil that all can see
>> is the hidden portrait of our hidden King portrayed
>
> on those who have been signed:
>> on them baptism, that is in travail with them in its womb,
>
> depicts the new portrait, to replace the image of the former Adam
>
> who had become corrupted; it gives birth to them with triple pangs,
>
> accompanied by the three glorious names,
>> of Father, Son and Holy Spirit.[13]

There can be little doubt that this imagery is connected to Nicodemus's question in John 3:4: "Can one enter a second time into the
mother's womb and be born?" The questioner's incomprehension
is the starting point for much of what Ephrem has to say concerning
baptism and the Spirit.

In addition to this text from the Fourth Gospel, mention must also
be made of the variant reading in Luke's account of the baptism of
Jesus: "You are my beloved Son; today I have begotten you" (Luke
3:22). This reading places a birth image at the heart of Jesus' baptism

---

frühchristlichen Tauftradition in Syrien und Armenien unter Einbezug der
Taufe Jesu," *Ostkirchliche Studien* 27, no. 4 (1978): 282.

[13] *De virginitate 7.5. Hymnen de virginitate*, ed. Edmund Beck, Corpus Scriptorum Christianorum Orientalium 223, Scriptores Syri 94 (Louvain: Secrétariat
du Corpus SCO, 1962), 25–26. Sebastian P. Brock, *The Harp of the Spirit: Twelve
Poems of Saint Ephrem*, Studies Supplementary to *Sobornost* 4 (London: Fellowship of St Alban and St Sergius, 1975), 49.

by John, and, according to Kilian McDonnell, may well lie behind Ephrem's description of the Jordan event as a "second birth."[14] Although a possible explanation, this imagery does not require the influence of the Lukan variant to justify its presence. The origin of this birth image, which is so characteristic of the Syrian tradition,[15] is more likely to be located in Jesus' dialogue with Nicodemus, not least since the Syriac noun *karsa*, which is of fundamental importance to the linking together of birth and water, appears in John 3:4 but not in Luke's description of the baptism of Jesus. Moreover, the variant reading "this day I have begotten you" is not found in the *Peshitta*.

In relation to the debate concerning the gender of the Spirit, it is clear that the grammatically feminine *ruḥa*, with its natural propensity for female imagery, has had a considerable effect upon the tradition's understanding both of the action of the Spirit in baptism and, consequently, upon the nature of baptism itself. In a passage where Ephrem juxtaposes the image of the womb with the forgiveness of sins, baptism itself is described as a mother: "Baptism is a mother who gives birth daily to spiritual ones and solemnly raises new children for God. . . . Inside the womb (*ʿuba*) of baptism is the inner debt repaid, mercies wipe away the large bill of Adam in the water and oil of baptism, and it is torn to pieces."[16]

The imagery of new birth is no less present in the teachings of other fourth-century Syrian writers who describe the role of the Spirit in the birth process. Aphrahat, who exhorts unmarried men to love and honor God as their father and the Holy Spirit as their mother,[17] also

---

[14] Kilian McDonnell, *The Baptism of Jesus in the Jordan: The Trinitarian and Cosmic Order of Salvation* (Collegeville, MN: Liturgical Press, 1996), 93.

[15] Since the Syrian church celebrated both the birth and the baptism of Jesus on 6 January, it is likely, as Gabriele Winkler suggests, that the understanding of the baptism of Jesus as a birth event has its origin in Syrian Christianity. Winkler, "Zur frühchristlichen Tauftradition," 299.

[16] *De Epiphania* 13.1-2. *Hymnen de nativitate (Epiphania)*, ed. Edmund Beck, Corpus Scriptorum Christianorum Orientalium 186, Scriptores Syri 82 (Louvain: Secrétariat du Corpus SCO, 1959), 189. Although Beck and others have questioned the authorship of the Epiphany hymns, they are of considerable importance for any study of the baptismal theology of the East Syrian Church in this period. See Edmund Beck, "Le baptême chez Saint Ephrem," *L'Orient Syrien* 1 (1956): 111.

[17] *Demonstration* 18.10. *Aphraatis Sapientis Persae: Demonstrationes*, ed. and trans. J. Parisot, Patrologia Syriaca 1 (Paris: Firmin-Didot, 1894), 840.

Simon Jones

speaks of "our Lord who was born from the Spirit."[18] Theodore of Mopsuestia discusses Jesus' discourse with Nicodemus in which "he tells him about the symbolical birth that takes place at baptism." Later in the same homily Theodore states that Jesus "speaks of the Spirit because this birth is due to the Spirit's operation."[19]

Returning to Ephrem, in one of his *Hymns on the Church* a comparison is drawn between the activity of the Spirit upon the womb of Mary, the Mother of Jesus, and upon the womb of the Jordan:

> As though on an eye
> the Light settled on Mary.
> It polished her mind,
> made bright her thought
> and pure her understanding,
> causing her virginity to shine.
>
> The river in which he was baptized
> conceived him again mystically;
> the moist womb [Syr: ʿuba] of the water
> conceived him in purity,
> bore him in chastity,
> made him ascend in glory.[20]

In another verse of the same hymn, Christ's conception, birth, and ascension, events both past and future from the perspective of his baptism, come together and are focused upon the Jordan event:

> As the Daystar in the river,
> the Bright One in the tomb,
> he shone forth on the mountain top
> and gave brightness too in the womb;
> he dazzled as he went up from the river,
> gave illumination at his ascension.

---

[18] *Demonstration* 6.17. *Aphraatis Sapientis Persae*, ed. Parisot, 301.

[19] *Baptismal Homily* 3.3. See Edward Yarnold, *The Awe-Inspiring Rites of Initiation: The Origins of the RCIA*, 2d ed. (Edinburgh: T&T Clark, 1994), 182.

[20] *De ecclesia* 36. *Hymnen de ecclesia*, ed. Edmund Beck, Corpus Scriptorum Christianorum Orientalium 198, Scriptores Syri 84 (Louvain: Secrétariat du Corpus SCO, 1960), 90; Sebastian P. Brock, "St Ephrem on Christ as Light in Mary and in the Jordan: Hymni De Ecclesia 36," *Eastern Churches Review* 7 (1975): 138.

Wombs of the Spirit

As Brock points out, the whole of Christ's incarnate life is gathered up together at his baptism.[21] This corresponds with the Eastern Orthodox distinction between sacred time and ordinary time (καιρός and χρόνος). Behind the former is the understanding that the significant staging-posts in Christ's incarnate life may be present in sacred time at one moment. Thus Christ's baptism can be spoken of as the "fountain-head" of Christian baptism even though in historical time Christ's baptism takes place before his crucifixion and resurrection, since all three events are present at one moment in sacred time and may, therefore, be experienced together at Christian baptism.[22]

Alongside this womb imagery, it is important to note that Ephrem's baptismal theology is not lacking in references to the paschal mystery. In one of his *Epiphany Hymns* he makes clear that participation in the baptism of Christ also signifies a participation in his death and resurrection: "His Birth flowed on and was joined to His baptism;—and His Baptism again flowed on even to His Death;—his Death led and reached to His Resurrection,—a fourfold bridge unto His Kingdom; and lo! His sheep pass over in His footsteps."[23] Elsewhere, it is the image of the womb that Ephrem uses to link together Christ's birth, baptism, and the paschal mystery. For example, in one of his *Songs of Nisibis*: "Behold the virgin brought him forth, and Sheol the barren brought him forth; two wombs that contrary to nature have been changed by him; the virgin and Sheol both of them. The virgin in her bringing forth he made glad; but Sheol he grieved and made sad by his resurrection."[24]

---

[21] Brock, "St Ephrem on Christ as Light," 140.

[22] Sebastian P. Brock, *The Luminous Eye: The Spiritual World Vision of St Ephrem*, Cistercian Studies Series 124 (Kalamazoo, MI: Cistercian Publications, 1992), 29–30.

[23] *De epiphania* 10.9; *Hymnen de nativitate*, ed. Beck, 182; "Selections Translated into English from the Hymns and Homilies of Ephraim the Syrian and from the Demonstrations of Aphrahat the Persian Sage," in *A Select Library of Nicene and Post-Nicene Fathers*, ed. Henry Wace and Philip Schaff, Second Series 13 (Oxford: James Parker & Co., 1898), 280.

[24] *Carmina Nisibis* 37.4; *Sancti Ephraem Carmina Nisibis*, ed. Edmund Beck, Corpus Scriptorum Christianorum Orientalium 240, Scriptores Syri 102 (Louvain: Secrétariat du Corpus SCO, 1963), 16. J. E. Richardson, "Feminine Imagery of the Holy Spirit in the Hymns of St Ephrem the Syrian," (PhD diss., University of Edinburgh 1990), 189.

Simon Jones

The link between Christ's birth and death is also expressed in *De Domino nostro* 2, where Ephrem maintains that Christ's "death on the cross witnesses to his birth from the woman" and, later, that "his conception in the womb is bound up with his death on the cross."[25] The same homily also mentions both events as two links in a chain of four births:[26]

> The Father gave birth to him and through him created the creatures;
> Flesh gave birth to him and through him killed lusts;
> Baptism gave birth to him, that through him it might wash away stains;
> Sheol gave birth to him, that through him its treasures might be
>   emptied out.[27]

Thus the whole economy of salvation, from creation to redemption, is expressed in terms of a series of births of Christ that bring about the redemption of humanity, united and brought to fruition by the activity of the Spirit.

PHILOXENUS OF MABBUG

In considering the West Syrian Philoxenus, who was bishop of Mabbug from 485 until he was exiled in 519, we need to recall that, according to Brock, by the time we reach the sixth century *ruḥa* was normally treated as if it were a masculine noun. That being the case, it is all the more striking that Philoxenus's writings reveal no lack of female images associated with the activity of the Spirit. A passage from his *Commentary on the Gospels of Matthew and Luke* has a distinctly liturgical feel to it, including one section that takes the form of an epicletic prayer placed on the lips of Jesus directly after his baptism:

> I indeed, O Father, according to your will have become man. . . .
> And now I have been baptized and have prepared baptism that it

---

[25] *Sermo de Domino nostro* ed. Edmund Beck, Corpus Scriptorum Christianorum Orientalium 270, Scriptores Syri 116 (Louvain: Secrétariat du Corpus SCO 1966), 2.

[26] Although the three births most commonly articulated are from Mary, the Jordan, and Sheol, this passage makes reference to the Son's birth from the Father and his agency in the work of creation. A further chain, from the Godhead, from humanity, and from baptism, is also expressed at the beginning of this homily.

[27] *Sermo de Domino nostro*, ed. Beck, 2.

may become the spiritual womb [Syr: *karsa*] which gives birth to men anew. . . . But you, O Father, through my prayer, open heaven and send your Holy Spirit upon this new womb of baptism! And as he dwelt in the womb of the virgin and embodied me from her, so may he dwell in this womb of baptism and sanctify it, and form men, and cause them to be born of it new sons, and make them your sons, my brothers and inheritors of the kingdom.[28]

Here is a prayer constructed upon the firm theological foundation that, according to the Father's will, the Word became flesh in Jesus Christ. The importance that Philoxenus places upon the doctrine of the incarnation within his theology of baptism speaks for itself. Beginning with this reference to the incarnation, the prayer goes on to describe the spiritual birth that, as a result of Jesus' own descent into the Jordan, will now be effected through baptism. For humankind, this will be a second birth in which men and women will be born anew. Here we encounter another resonance with John 3:3. Jesus himself is born again in order that his followers may also become children of God with Jesus through their participation in his second birth.

This central tenant of Philoxenus's teaching is expressed most clearly with reference to the Prologue of the Fourth Gospel in his commentary on Luke 3:23: "And they may receive the Holy Spirit and become the sons of God because the Word became flesh. . . . And as flesh when it receives a soul becomes a man, so a man when he receives the Holy Spirit is known as a son of God. And whereas flesh receives a soul within the womb, in baptism the Holy Spirit is given to a man, which first, as the first-fruits, (Christ) received . . ."[29] The indwelling of the Holy Spirit, given in baptism, makes the Christian a child of God.[30] The connection between this text and John 3 cannot be overemphasized. The latter is so clearly interpreted by Philoxenus within the context both of the Jordan event and Christian baptism that certain

---

[28] *Fragments of the Commentary on Matthew and Luke*, ed. and trans. J. W. Watt, Corpus Scriptorum Christianorum Orientalium 392/3, Scriptores Syri 171/2 (Louvain: Secrétariat du Corpus SCO, 1978), 69/59.

[29] Ibid., 83/71.

[30] A further example can be found in Philoxenus's *Commentary on the Johannine Prologue*: "Each one of us becomes in power a son of God in the womb of baptism," in *Commentaire du prologue johannique*, ed. and trans. André de Halleux, Corpus Scriptorum Christianorum Orientalium 380, Scriptores Syri 165 (Louvain: Secrétariat du Corpus SCO, 1977), 16.

Simon Jones

phrases from Philoxenus could easily be inserted into the dialogue as answers to the Pharisee's question. The relationship between Jesus' incarnation and baptism holds the key to regeneration.

Considering further Philoxenus's use of birth imagery, in the course of an argument in which he states how necessary it was for the Word to become flesh in order for the church to be united with God, the bishop states: "Now it is first necessary for the Word to become flesh as it is written; and because of this he was also born according to the flesh; and after this birth, spiritually from baptism."[31] Philoxenus's writings reveal three births that Jesus undergoes: his birth from the essence of the Father in eternity, his birth from the Virgin in time, and his new birth that takes place in the Jordan. The excerpt cited above makes reference to the second and third of these. The first two are mentioned in chapter 14 of his *Commentary on the Johannine Prologue*. Dominated by a discussion on how the divine Logos could retain his divinity after the incarnation, Philoxenus talks of the two wombs through which the Christian passes, "the two wombs of woman and of baptism." The bishop then goes on to compare these with the two births of the Logos, the births "from the essence and from the Virgin."[32] In a not too dissimilar way we have already seen how the primitive imagery of Ode 19 describes a chain of birth and rebirth from the Father through to Mary in which the uniting agent is the Spirit.

Returning to the prayer placed on the lips of Jesus, it is clear that, although the Jordan event is for Philoxenus Jesus' third birth, the primary motivation for this episode is that Jesus might "prepare baptism that it may become the spiritual womb." Indeed, this action performed by John, which is both the preparation for and the institution of Christian baptism, is defined more clearly as the prayer progresses. Significantly, it is Jesus who, after his immersion in the Jordan, calls upon the Father to send the Spirit to dwell in the womb of baptism just as the Spirit dwelt in the womb of Mary, thus setting the waters apart for a particular purpose. Philoxenus prefers this interpretation to that of the Father sending the Spirit upon Jesus after his baptism, as recorded in the gospels, or, as is found in Ephrem, the waters of the Jordan being consecrated by Jesus' descent into them.[33]

---

[31] *Commentaire*, ed. Halleux, 215.
[32] Ibid., 35.
[33] For a discussion of this see Brock, "St Ephrem on Christ as Light," 140.

Wombs of the Spirit

With the Father petitioned to send the Spirit, the next sentence expresses very concisely the incarnational heart of Philoxenus's theology of initiation. The pneumatic process by which the divine Logos became flesh in the womb of Mary and was born as Jesus, the Son of God, is replicated in the womb of baptism: by the power of the same Spirit the candidate is "formed" in the water in order to emerge as a child of God, a brother or sister of Christ, and an inheritor of the kingdom.

BAPTISMAL *ORDINES*

In the West Syrian baptismal *ordines* it is clear that a central element within the rite of initiation is the transformation of the font into a womb of new birth through the activity of the Holy Spirit. In the *Ordo* of Severus the second part of the liturgy opens with a prayer for the font to be "mixed with the power and operation of your Holy Spirit, that it may become a spiritual womb [Syr: *karsa*] and a furnace which pours forth incorruptibility."[34] That it is the activity of the Spirit upon the waters that effects this transformation is again articulated in the prayer before the Lord's Prayer: You, O God, "have blessed these waters by the descent of your Holy Spirit that they may become a womb [Syr: *karsa*] of the Spirit for the regeneration of the new man from the old order."[35]

The same image is used to great effect in the prayer of invocation of the Spirit in the Maronite *Ordo*. Here a parallelism is set up between Eve and the font, as well as the Spirit's hovering over the waters of creation and baptism:

> As the womb of our mother, Eve, gave birth to mortal and corruptible children, so may the womb of this baptismal font give birth to heavenly and incorruptible children. And as the Holy Spirit hovered over the waters at the work of creation, and gave birth to living creatures and animals of all kinds, may he hover over this baptismal font which is a spiritual womb. May he dwell in it and sanctify it. Instead of an earthly Adam, may it give birth to a heavenly Adam. May those who enter it to be baptized be permanently changed and receive a spiritual nature, instead of a corporal one, a participation in the invisible reality,

[34] *The Sacrament of Holy Baptism according to the Ancient Rite of the Syrian Orthodox Church of Antioch*, ed. Athanasius Y. Samuel (Hackensack: A. Y. Samuel, 1974), 47.

[35] Ibid., 79.

Simon Jones

instead of the visible one, and instead of the weakness of their spirit, may the Holy Spirit abide in them.[36]

Returning to the Severan prayer, in language that resonates with the *Peshitta's* use of ʿuba in the Johannine Prologue, God himself is described as having a womb from which he is asked to send the Spirit: "Have mercy on us, O God the Father almighty, and send upon us and upon this water that is being consecrated, from your dwelling that is prepared, from your infinite womb (ʿuba), the Paraclete, your Holy Spirit."[37] Here God sends the Spirit from his womb down to the water of baptism, to transform it into another womb and to abide there, "so that it might bring forth spiritual sons."

With some of the womb imagery present in the *ordines* highlighted, we should note that the symbolic depiction of baptismal regeneration is not limited to this image, and that other female images are also used. For example, in the Maronite Diaconal Proclamation following the Liturgy of the Word, baptism is described as a mother:

> O Christ our God,
> you came into this world
> and made baptism to be like
> a mother who brings forth spiritual children unto life eternal.[38]

In the same *Ordo*, baptism is described as a princess, "the daughter of the King," and the church as the "faithful queen."[39] Both Syrian Orthodox and Maronite *ordines* describe the font and the church as two sisters united in the mystery of baptism. The same reference is made in the *Ordo* of Severus just before the consecration of the font: "Who has ever seen two noble sisters such as the pure baptism and the Holy

---

[36] Maronite Antiochene Church, *Mysteries of Initiation: Baptism, Confirmation, Communion* (Washington, DC: Diocese of St Maron, 1987), 34.

[37] This paragraph, labeled *i* by Brock, is not particularly well supported in the manuscripts and editions. See Sebastian P. Brock, "The Consecration of the Water in the Oldest Manuscripts of the Syrian Orthodox Baptismal Liturgy," *OCP* 37 (1971): 329–30. The paragraph does not appear in Samuel's edition or in the French translation of G. Khouri-Sarkis, "Prières et cérémonies du baptême selon le rite de l'Église syrienne d'Antioche," *L'Orient Syrien* 1 (1956): 156–84.

[38] *Mysteries of Initiation*, 21.

[39] Ibid., 22.

Church; the one gives birth to the new and spiritual children and the other nurtures them; whomsoever baptism bears from the water, the Holy Church receives and presents to the altar, alleluia, alleluia."[40]

CONCLUSION

Now that we have considered this limited selection of texts, what conclusions can be drawn? First, that the Johannine language of rebirth, focused on the image of the womb, is a central and constantly recurring theme within the Syrian baptismal tradition. The womb, whether it be the womb of the Father, of Mary, of the Jordan, of Sheol, or of the font, and other associated female imagery, continues to occupy a significant, even an increasingly significant place within the Syrian tradition as it develops. At the same time the noun *ruḥa* is, with few exceptions, treated grammatically as a masculine rather than a feminine noun.

Why should this be? Why continue to associate such strong female imagery with the activity of the Spirit once, as Brock puts it, a "revulsion against the idea of the Holy Spirit as mother" sets in?[41] Surely the most likely explanation is that the tradition's strong incarnational pneumatology was of such fundamental importance to the understanding of baptism that it outweighed concerns over some groups' misuse of female imagery, or the previous experience of some pagan converts of a divine triad of Father, Mother, and Son.[42]

This is not to say that womb imagery and the language of rebirth are absent from other Christian traditions: far from it. For example, the prayer for the blessing of the font in the Gelasian Sacramentary, quoting Romans 8:2, asks God to "send down the Spirit of adoption." Later in the same prayer this invocation is developed:

> Let your Holy Spirit, by the secret admixture of his light, give fruitfulness to this water prepared for human regeneration, so that, sanctification being conceived therein, there may come forth from the unspotted womb of the divine font a heavenly offspring, reborn unto a new creature: that grace may be a mother to people of every age and sex, who are brought forth to a common infancy.[43]

[40] Samuel, *The Sacrament of Holy Baptism*, 54–55.
[41] Brock, "The Holy Spirit as Feminine," 81.
[42] Ibid., 82.
[43] E. C. Whitaker, *Documents of the Baptismal Liturgy*, ed. Maxwell E. Johnson, 3d ed. (London: SPCK, 2003), 233–34. For more on this, see Teresa Berger's essay in this volume.

Simon Jones

Womb imagery and the language of regeneration are by no means lacking in the baptismal theology and liturgies of other churches, but they do not occupy the same central position that they enjoy in the Syrian tradition.

With the centrality of this image established, a second concluding point follows: that the womb is the principal focus for the activity of the Spirit in the Syrian baptismal tradition. If this is the case, then Gabriele Winkler's influential theory about the development of Syrian baptismal rites is called into question. Winkler, while acknowledging that regeneration is one of the central themes of the primitive Syrian baptismal tradition, believes that by the end of the fourth century a significant shift took place: the font became associated more with the tomb than the womb as the Pauline notion of baptism as participation in the death and resurrection of Christ became more prominent than the Johannine language of rebirth.[44]

The evidence presented in this essay suggests that no clearly identifiable shift from Johannine to Pauline imagery took place. We have encountered womb imagery and the language of rebirth in the baptismal *ordines* as well as the *Odes of Solomon*. There are passages in the *Odes* that reveal an embryonic baptismal theology of death and new life[45] as well as more explicit references to participation in the paschal mystery in later writings. This is not to deny that, at different times and in different places, particular images were emphasized more than others, but rather to suggest that the theological driving force that animates the theologians of East and West Syria, and to which their baptismal rites and writings bear witness, is an incarnational pneumatology.

"Can one enter a second time into the mother's womb and be born?" In the Syrian baptismal tradition the answer is unequivocal, and the womb of rebirth is, first and foremost, a womb of the Spirit.

---

[44] Gabriele Winkler, "The Original Meaning of the Pre-Baptismal Anointing and its Implications," *Worship* 52 (1978): 24–45. For an explicitly gender-attentive reading of the Syrian tradition, see Winkler's essay "Überlegungen zum Gottesgeist als mütterlichem Prinzip und zur Bedeutung der Androgynie in einigen frühchristlichen Quellen," in *Liturgie und Frauenfrage: Ein Beitrag zur Frauenforschung aus liturgiewissenschaftlicher Sicht*, ed. Teresa Berger and Albert Gerhards, Pietas liturgica 7 (St. Ottilien: EOS-Verlag, 1990), 7–29.

[45] For example, Ode 24, where the baptism of Jesus is juxtaposed with the harrowing of hell. See McDonnell, *The Baptism of Jesus*, 151.

Wombs of the Spirit

Peter Galadza

7. The Holy Spirit in Eastern Orthodox Worship: Historical Enfleshments and Contemporary Queries

Western theological literature has highlighted the perdurability of pneumatology in Eastern Orthodoxy.[1] Nonetheless, a substantial book-length study of the Holy Spirit in Orthodox worship has yet to be written. As I proceed, it should become apparent that the author of that future book will have a pleasant yet difficult task: pleasant because not only the Orthodox liturgical tradition and luminaries such as Pavel Florensky (†1937), Sergius Bulgakov (†1944), and John Zizioulas (b. 1936), explicate "teachings strange and new,"[2] but difficult because a great deal of patristic theology and liturgical history has yet to be assimilated by Orthodox scholarship. In addition, the strong confessionality of Orthodox theology, while facilitating a holistic integrity, also prevents the kind of conceptual and analytic probing so necessary for discerning the "really real."

By way of introduction, I should note that Boris Bobrinskoy,[3] Paul Evdokimov,[4] and Ioannes Fountoules[5] are among the Orthodox

---

[1] See, for example, Yves Congar, *I Believe in the Holy Spirit*, trans. David Smith (New York: Crossroad, 2006) 3:72–78; and Veli-Matti Kärkkäinen, *Pneumatology: The Holy Spirit in Ecumenical, International, and Contextual Perspective* (Grand Rapids, MI: Baker Academic, 2002), 68. In this paper the terms "Eastern Orthodox" and "Byzantine Christian" will be used interchangeably. Eastern Orthodoxy is not to be confused with Oriental Orthodoxy; I will not be treating Coptic, Armenian, and other non-Chalcedonian traditions.

[2] First *Sticheron* (Tone 4) at "Lord, I have cried" (Pentecost Sunday Evening). *The Pentecostarion* (Brookline, MA: Holy Transfiguration Monastery, 1990), 418.

[3] *Communion du Saint-Esprit* (Bellefontaine: Abbaye de Bellefontaine, 1992).

[4] "L'Esprit saint et l'Église d'après la tradition liturgique," in *L'Esprit Saint et l'Eglise. Catholiques, orthodoxes et protestants de divers pays confrontent leur science, leur foi et leur tradition: l'Avenir de l'Eglise et de l'oecuménisme*, ed. Académie internationale des sciences religieuses (Paris: Fayard, 1969), 85–123; *La prière de l'Église d'Orient* (Paris: Desclée de Brouwer, 1985).

[5] Owing to the language barrier and the inaccessibility of his study for most Westerners, allow me to summarize Fountoules's well-crafted synthetic

who have produced solid building blocks for that future monograph on pneumatology and Orthodox worship; even more solid historical foundations have been laid by philo-Orthodox such as Miguel Arranz,[6] Stefano Parenti,[7] and Sebastian Brock.[8]

The present paper is organized according to a convention that I find helpful, though not without its pitfalls, that is, the categories of (1) theology (in this case, pneumatology) as applied *to* worship, (2) theology (pneumatology) derived *from* worship, and (3) worship itself as

---

overview entitled "The Holy Spirit in the Liturgical Life of the Church." The late Greek liturgist outlines how Orthodox worship manifests worship (a) "in the Spirit," (b) "enlightened by the Spirit," and (c) "maintained by a fullness of faith concerning the Spirit" (97). He highlights the prominence in Orthodox worship of (1) Psalm 50 (51) with its references to the Spirit, (2) the invocation, "*Vasileu ouranie*," and (3) Luke's "The Holy Spirit will overshadow you" (98). He then lists a string of orations that includes requests for the "enabling and instructing Spirit" (99–100). Fountoules notes the importance of early patristic references to the "Holy Spirit in the Holy Church" and how the gathering (the *ekklesia*) is a privileged locus of the Spirit's activity (101–2). Finally, he reviews the epicletic dimension of each of the seven sacraments (102–9). I. Φουντούλης, "Τὸ ἅγιον Πνεῦμα ἐν τῃ λειτουργικῃ ζωῃ τῆς ἐκκλησίας" in *Τὸ ἅγιον Πνεῦμα*, ed. Ioannes Anastasios (Thessalonike: Seminarion Theologôn Thessalonikês, 1971), 97–109.

[6] "Évolution des rites d'incorporation et de réadmission dans l'Église selon l'Euchologe byzantin," in *Gestes et paroles dans les diverses familles liturgiques: Conférences Saint-Serge XXIVe semaine d'études liturgiques*, ed. Institut Saint-Serge (Rome: Centro Liturgico Vincenziano, 1978), 31–75; "Les Sacrements de l'ancien Euchologe constantinopolitain (3): II-me partie—Admission dans l'Église des enfants des familles chrétiennes (premier catéchumenat)," *OCP* 49 (1983): 284–302; *Избранные Сочинения по Литургике: Таинства Византийского Евхология*, том 1 (Москва: Институт философии, теологии и истории св. Фомы, 2003), 318–414.

[7] Stefano Parenti and Elena Velkovska, "'Re celeste, Paraclito, Spirito di Verita': Il *Veni Creator Spiritus* della Liturgia Bizantina," in *Spiritus spiritalia nobis dona potenter infundit: A proposito di tematiche liturgico-pneumatologiche*, Studia Anselmiana 139, Analecta Liturgica 25 (Rome: Pontificio Ateneo Sant'Anselmo, 2005), 387–404. My thanks to Prof. Parenti for providing me with a prepublication copy of the article.

[8] Sebastian P. Brock, "The Transition to a Post-Baptismal Anointing in the Antiochene Rite," in *The Sacrifice of Praise*, ed. Bryan D. Spinks, 215–25 (Rome: Edizioni Liturgiche, 1981). Of course, outstanding specialists in early Christian and patristic liturgy such as Paul Bradshaw, Maxwell Johnson, and Gabriele Winkler, to name just a few, have also provided important building blocks.

Peter Galadza

theology (pneumatology), or to use the phrase popularized by David Fagerberg, the liturgical act itself as a "stab at meaning."[9] Owing to limitations of space, category one will receive the greatest attention, though, as will become apparent, categories two and three could be developed quite extensively. In the interest of breaking new ground and focusing on neglected issues I will not be discussing the careworn epiclesis.

PNEUMATOLOGY APPLIED *TO* ORTHODOX WORSHIP

The Problem of Initiation and the Bestowal of the Spirit

Certainly among the most contentious and convoluted issues concerning pneumatology as applied to Byzantine Christian worship is the question of the bestowal of the Spirit vis-à-vis initiation rites. As will become apparent, the description of confirmation as "a sacrament in search of a theology"[10] also applies to Byzantine chrismation. Among the Orthodox it is even permissible to gainsay the status of chrismation as the "second sacrament." (More on this below.) There is certainly no need here to review the debates that have occupied theologians and liturgists—most of them Western, but also, as we shall see, some Eastern—regarding whether or not the giving of the Spirit is to be identified with a postbaptismal rite, and the allied question of the necessity of practicing such a rite.[11] For our purposes, it suffices, at this point, to note the following:

[9] *Theologia Prima: What Is Liturgical Theology?* (Chicago: Liturgy Training Publications, 2004), 81.

[10] I had always presumed that the phrase was Aidan Kavanagh's, but a computer search yields "William J. Bausch." However, the same search provides so many citations of the phrase—without attribution—that the question of attribution may be almost irresolvable.

[11] For a concise, albeit confessionally skewed, summary of the debates from 1836 to 1954, see Bernard Leeming, s.j., *Principles of Sacramental Theology* (London: Longmans, 1960), 184–88. The debates generally involved Anglican scholars, with the two most noteworthy protagonists being Dom Gregory Dix (who insisted on the need for the second sacrament as the moment of pneumatic bestowal) and G. W. H. Lampe, who, in his famous study, *The Seal of the Spirit: A Study in the Doctrine of Baptism and Confirmation in the New Testament and the Fathers*, 2d ed. (London: SPCK, 1967), argued that the New Testament and early Christian writings associate this sealing with baptism itself. In *Dogmatique de l'Église orthodoxe catholique*, trans. Pierre Dumont

The Holy Spirit in Eastern Orthodox Worship

1. Key New Testament passages clearly associate Christian life, that is, becoming and remaining a Christian, with bearing the Spirit.[12] In other words, to be a Christian means to have become a pneumatophor.

2. At the same time, the early church knew various liturgical traditions that evidenced no discrete rite or gesture—apart from water baptism itself—for epiphanizing this pneumatic dimension of Christian initiation.[13]

3. Nonetheless, prominent Orthodox theologians, liturgists, and ecumenical commissions not only insist that a postbaptismal donation of the Spirit and/or pneumatic gifts have been "joined indissolubly to baptism from the beginning"[14] but that this postbaptismal rite is the unique moment of the Spirit's bestowal during Christian initiation.[15]

(Chevetogne: Editions de Chevetogne, 1961) 3:130–40, Panagiotis Trembelas relies on Leeming for his review of the debates, and, not surprisingly, culls material from the "pro-confirmation" camp. Fortunately, the 1960s brought a diminution of tendentious scholarship among Western Christians, with researchers less inclined to "squeeze" history into doctrinal categories. Material cited below takes us, of course, beyond the studies summarized by Leeming. As will be obvious, Orthodox scholars have not always matched their Western counterparts as regards objectivity.

[12] Rom 8:9; 1 Cor 12:13; Acts 2:38; 10:48; 19:1-6; Titus 3:5.

[13] The most significant example is John Chrysostom's own rite described in his baptismal catecheses; see *Huit catéchèses*, ed. A. Wenger, SC 50bis (Paris: Cerf, 1970), 87. There Chrysostom states that after the prebaptismal anointing "by the words of the priest and by his hand, the presence of the Holy Spirit flies down upon [the candidate] and another man comes up out of the font . . ."

[14] Trembelas, *Dogmatique de l'Église*, 3:131, contrivedly hypothesizes that such rites are not always mentioned during the New Testament and subapostolic period because "when local Churches were less numerous, all of the sacraments were conferred by the local bishops, and chrism was administered by them immediately after baptism." According to Trembelas, only the subsequent devolution of chrismation to presbyters made references to this anointing necessary.

[15] This problem, incidentally, possesses not only ecumenical significance but intra-Orthodox implications as well. Once it is admitted—as it should be—that becoming a Christian involves receiving the Spirit, an Orthodox insistence that chrismation alone confers the Spirit will not only question the status of Christians who do not practice such a postbaptismal rite, but will also question the

Peter Galadza

Before elaborating these three summary statements, note that even among the Orthodox themselves the issue of chrismation as the second sacrament would never have developed as it did had not a self-standing chrismation rite with *myron* and the accompanying formula "the seal of the gift of the Holy Spirit" begun to be used in the fifth century for the reconciliation of heretics in the Byzantine realm.[16] As Boris Bobrinskoy has hinted, prior to this period the relation between water baptism and the post-immersion chrismation would, no doubt, have evoked little debate.[17] Early Byzantine prayers, for example, use the single term "baptism" even when referring to a rite that includes a post-immersion chrismation.[18]

Let us now return to the three summary statements made above in order to flesh out their contents and amplify their significance. Among the more recent, and certainly most authoritative and concise, summaries of New Testament theology regarding the necessary link between Christian initiation and reception of the Spirit is a study by George T. Montague in which we read: "The gift of the Spirit was such an expectation [in the New Testament period] that without the Holy Spirit one could not be considered a Christian." Turning more specifically to Pauline texts, Montague states: "For Paul, to be a Christian is to have the Holy Spirit" (Rom 8:9).[19] This, of course, is not news, and for Eastern Orthodox such statements will appropriately confirm the validity

---

status of millions of Orthodox baptized clandestinely during the Soviet era by pious grandmothers, but never chrismated.

[16] See Bernard Botte, "Postbaptismal Anointing in the Ancient Patriarchate of Antioch," in *Studies on Syrian Baptismal Rites*, ed. Jacob Vellian, 71 (Kerala, India: Kottayam, 1973).

[17] Bobrinskoy, *Communion du Saint-Esprit* (n. 3), 191. In general, within Orthodox scholarship Bobrinskoy's analysis of initiation rites in chapter 6 of the above-cited work is the most nuanced and accurate in its historical and theological conclusions. Even though it was first delivered as a public lecture in 1968, it did not influence the work of Argenti, Schmemann, and other Orthodox theologians. Apparently, its contents were not disseminated until 1992.

[18] The following excerpt from the post-ambo prayer of Theophany is typical: τὸ πανάγιόν σου Πνεῦμα δοξάζωμεν τὸ καταβὰν ἐπ᾽ αὐτὸν καὶ φανερῶσαν αὐτὸν τῷ βαπτίζοντι, ἐν ᾧ καὶ ἡμᾶς σφραγίσας καὶ χρίσας διὰ τοῦ βαπτίσματος μετόχους ἐποίησας τοῦ Χριστοῦ σου. Ἱερατικόν (Rome: Sacred Congregation for the Eastern Churches, 1950), 300.

[19] George T. Montague, "The Fire in the World: The Holy Spirit in Scripture," in *Advents of the Spirit: An Introduction to the Current Study of Pneumatology*,

of Orthodoxy's pneumatic accents. But a problem does arise the moment one identifies the bestowal of the Spirit with a post-immersion chrismation or an analogous rite so univocally that the absence of such a rite requires the denial of Christian identity to an otherwise properly baptized individual. Such an approach—with implications, incidentally, for Orthodoxy's own theology of chrismation (more on this below)—is particularly problematic in view of what was stated above in summary statement number 2. Most Orthodox will be surprised to learn that John Chrysostom himself not only initiated neophytes without a post-immersion chrismation or hand-laying, but associated the bestowal of the Spirit with the immersion itself[20]—an approach which is certainly defensible, especially on scriptural grounds.[21] In view of this, as well as a plethora of other examples from liturgical history, the following assertions by an Orthodox theologian require correction:

1. Chrismation was a universal practice of the Christian Church of the second to the fifth centuries.

2. Everywhere in that period chrismation was celebrated immediately on coming up out of the water, and consequently constituted an anamnesis of the anointing of the Lord Jesus.

3. Chrismation was everywhere understood to confer the gift of the Holy Spirit as a logical consequence of baptism and its necessary complement.[22]

Such historically erroneous assertions would not warrant repetition or deserve comment were it not for the authoritative nature of the volume in which they appear, as well as the fact that they find sup-

---

ed. Bradford E. Hinze and D. Lyle Dabney, 35, 51 (Milwaukee: Marquette University Press, 2001).

[20] See n. 13 above.

[21] All of Lampe's *Seal of the Spirit* is a defense of this approach; one need not accept some of Lampe's more polemically motivated assertions in order to accept the validity of the association: baptism (itself) and Spirit.

[22] Cyrille Argenti, "Chrismation," in *Ecumenical Perspectives on Baptism, Eucharist and Ministry*, ed. Max Thurian, 61 (Geneva: World Council of Churches, 1983).

Peter Galadza

port in other works.[23] The author of these statements was able to arrive at such conclusions by an extremely selective use of sources. He excluded, for example, all the evidence from early "East Syrian" practice[24] in addition to the aforementioned material from Chrysostom.

Owing to the less historical nature of his study, Alexander Schmemann, in his book *Of Water and the Spirit*,[25] avoids some of the gaffes of other Orthodox scholars writing on this topic. However, Schmemann remains adamant about the strict identification between chrismation and the bestowal of the Spirit, with baptism being associated strictly with dying and rising (74–75). He stresses the nature of chrismation as a "personal Pentecost" (79) and insists that "in the sacrament of anointment [*sic*] we receive the Holy Spirit Himself, and not merely 'grace': such has always been the teaching of the Church" (104). To argue his case, Schmemann quite appropriately insists that scholars avoid the method of those who "simply do not hear what the Church says, [and] do not see what she does" (78). In other words, they should "receive the meaning of the sacraments from liturgical tradition" instead of creating "their own definitions of sacraments and then, in the light of such definitions . . . interpret the liturgy of the Church, to 'squeeze' it into their own *a priori* approach" (76–77). But while Schmemann is absolutely right about methodology, as we now analyze what the Orthodox Church actually does when she initiates neophytes, it will become clear that his own categorization of immersion as dying and rising on the one hand, and chrismation as unique bestowal of the Spirit on the other hand, requires revision.

If we look at the prayer recited immediately before the chrismation we note that it states that the neophyte has (already) been regenerated by water and the Spirit.[26] Some English translations of the prayer, no

---

[23] See, for example, the response of the Finnish Orthodox Church to the document "Baptism, Eucharist and Ministry" in *Churches Respond to BEM*, ed. Max Thurian (Geneva: World Council of Churches, 1986) 2:26.

[24] For a convenient summary of this evidence see Brock, "The Transition" (n. 8), 215–25.

[25] Alexander Schmemann, *Of Water and the Spirit* (Crestwood, NY: St. Vladimir's Seminary Press, 1974).

[26] ὁ καὶ νῦν εὐδοκήσας ἀναγεννῆσαι τὸν δοῦλον σου τὸν νεοφώτιστον δι᾽ ὕδατος καὶ πνεύματος ["You have now been graciously pleased to regenerate this Your neophyte servant by water and the Spirit . . ."], *Sacraments and Services: Book One*, trans. Spencer T. Kezios and Leonidas Contos (Northridge, CA: Narthex Press, 1995), 28.

The Holy Spirit in Eastern Orthodox Worship

doubt under the influence of the aforementioned categorization, do violence to the Greek original (and Slavonic) by turning the aorists and their aorist participles into progressive indicatives and present participles.[27] Then there is the actual "form" of the sacrament itself, the famous "Seal of the gift of the Holy Spirit." One need not know the history of the interpretation of this phrase to suspect that it need not be interpreted as *the* "moment of the bestowal of the Spirit." Certainly, as Miguel Arranz has suggested, it can refer to the sealing of the rite as a whole, or more specifically, to the conviction that initiation as a whole involves the bestowal of the Spirit. Arranz writes: "The 'seal' is God's concluding gesture by which is completed and established the gift which is gradually received during the entire process of enlightenment."[28] As regards the history of this sealing in relation to sacramentology, Boris Bobrinskoy is among the few Orthodox who correctly view the development of this rite as an organic attempt by the church to draw out symbolically and rehearse the pneumatic dimension of initiation.[29] Ioannes Fountoules also seems to echo such an approach. Fountoules cites patristic sources that correlate baptism and the Spirit, and then develops an interpretation of chrismation that does not make it the sole sacramental locus of pneumatic bestowal.[30]

Of course, no reasonable scholar would ever suggest that the Orthodox change their practice. But Orthodox theologians must correct the faulty readings of history that have led them to sequentialize, dogmatize, and fragment this di-une mystery of initiation in a way reminiscent of the old debates regarding the "moment" of eucharistic consecration. Ironically, the same Schmemann who, following his teachers, Nicholas Afanasiev and Kiprian Kern, championed a more integrative approach to the entire anaphora (and even the Divine Liturgy as a whole) as consecratory, reverted to a segmented approach to initiation. Schmemann and others did, of course, have the mystagogy of Cyril of Jerusalem to support their approach,[31] but one Father (or

---

[27] See, for example, *The Great Book of Needs: Expanded and Supplemented—The Holy Mysteries*, trans. St. Tikhon's Monastery (South Canaan, PA: St. Tikhon's Seminary Press, 2000) 1:39.

[28] Арранц, *Избранные Сочинения* (n. 6) 1:358.

[29] Bobrinskoy, *Communion du Saint-Esprit*, 191.

[30] Ι. Φουντούλης, "Τὸ ἅγιον Πνεῦμα" (n. 5), 105–6.

[31] As Juliette Day has pointed out in her recent study, "The allocation of the different effects of initiation to separate rituals . . . is a feature of MC [the

Peter Galadza

even several) do not a *consensus patrum* make, especially when other sources—in particular, the liturgy itself—mitigate against such a consensus.

Let me now turn to the more strictly theological defects of the segmented approach to Byzantine-Rite initiation. What is at stake when one bifurcates the realities of Christic dying and rising on the one hand and pneumatic donation on the other? At the risk of sounding facetious, I would say: the economy of salvation and possibly the unity of the Godhead itself. The Gospel according to John, for example, is very explicit about linking Christ's passion and the giving of the Spirit.[32] From the perspective of practical spirituality, the importance of the Spirit's presence in relation to dying and rising cannot be overstated. Among other things, it helps overcome the perception of *pneumatophoria* as either an otherworldly guru-like state on the one hand, or a sensational charismatic enthusiasm on the other. In a properly balanced sacramentology, bearing, or possessing, the Spirit should be inextricably bound up with self-sacrifice and cruciform *martyria*. Put most simply, a neophyte's dying and rising is hardly imaginable without the bestowal of the Holy Spirit.

Boris Bobrinskoy amplifies one of the reasons for this when he writes: "Any and every dissociation between Christ and the Spirit, between Christology and Pneumatology, is contrary to the most profound and most authentic theological vision and spiritual experience of the Syrian tradition."[33] As the context of Bobrinskoy's statement demonstrates, the "Syrian tradition" is intended to apply to Orthodoxy as a whole.

To conclude this section regarding the relation between baptism, chrismation, and the giving of the Spirit, on the basis of what I have argued above I would hope that Orthodox theologians could settle for asserting that the bestowal of the Spirit is certainly an inextricable part of their church's initiation rites—and leave it at that. Many of the debates that have exercised scholars regarding the "second sacrament" could then be avoided by the Orthodox for the simple reason

---

Mystagogical Catecheses]." *The Baptismal Liturgy of Jerusalem: Fourth- and Fifth-Century Evidence from Palestine, Syria and Egypt* (Aldershot: Ashgate, 2007), 109.

[32] On this, see, for example, Montague, "Fire in the World," 49–50.

[33] Bobrinskoy, *Communion du Saint-Esprit*, 189.

The Holy Spirit in Eastern Orthodox Worship

that under normal circumstances the two rites are always joined.[34] As regards the question of how to view those non-Orthodox who do not celebrate a post-immersion (or infusion) rite, it would seem that ecumenical wisdom, not to mention intellectual honesty, would require Orthodox simply to assert that as long as these non-Orthodox do not deny that their initiation rite actualizes a giving of the Spirit, the Orthodox have no reason to object to the absence of the "second sacrament." For the Orthodox, this should be even less problematic, for, as hinted above, they are not burdened by the septinarium. Granted, various Orthodox authorities have for centuries asserted the sevenfold nature of the sacramental economy,[35] but this assertion has never received the kind of dogmatic privileging proclaimed at Trent. Thus, it is common even among those Orthodox who insist on a postbaptismal anointing to suggest that one need not view chrismation as a separate sacrament.[36]

By way of historical footnote, I should mention that in the seventeenth century Catholic detractors of Orthodox sacramental practice were able to convince the Latin-trained Orthodox metropolitan of Kiev, Peter Mohyla, to make conspicuous the distinction between baptism and chrismation by inserting a second opening litany immediately preceding the chrismation prayer.[37] Fortunately, this innovation did not survive in subsequent editions of the Slav euchology, and

[34] J. D. C. Fisher has written: "The Western Church is faced with a dilemma. The more one links the gift of the Holy Spirit with confirmation, the more one seems to detract from baptism; and conversely, the more one associates the gift of the Spirit with baptism, the more one seems to detract from confirmation." *Confirmation: Then and Now* (London: SPCK, 1978), 140. Obviously when the two are joined the problem can easily be obviated.

[35] For Orthodox affirmations of the septinarium—most of them in post-Byzantine catechisms and "Symbolic Books"—see Trembelas, *Dogmatique de l'Église*, 3:74–75. Note, incidentally, that according to East-Slavic usage, retained by certain circles within the Orthodox Church of America (OCA), those being received into Orthodoxy from the Lutheran and Reformed traditions are required to assert their belief in the usual seven, enumerated individually. See St. Tikhon's Monastery, *The Great Book of Needs*, 83.

[36] Alexander Schmemann, *For the Life of the World: Sacraments and Orthodoxy* (Crestwood, NY: St. Vladimir's Seminary Press, 1973), 91.

[37] Arkady Joukovsky, ed., *Требник Петра Могили—Київ 1646* (Canberra, Australia: Ukrainian Autocephalous Orthodox Church, 1988), 62–64.

Peter Galadza

it remains a historical oddity. However, it does illustrate again how forcefully new *leges credendi* can alter older *leges orandi*.

"Gifts" and "Gift": Several Overlooked Sources

Before concluding this section on chrismation, one last issue deserves comment. Alexander Schmemann, in arguing that chrismation actualizes the bestowal of the Spirit per se, and not pneumatic gifts (as the formula is "The seal of the gift [singular] of the Holy Spirit") overlooked some important—and fascinating—historical facts. Note that I am not countering Schmemann's argument by arguing that it is *gifts* rather than *the gift* of the Spirit per se that is granted, but rather that the Byzantine historical sources do not require us to resolve this question univocally. In fact, the materials below demonstrate—again—the danger of constructing overly kataphatic delineations, especially when speaking of what the Byzantine tradition calls (sacramental) *mysteries*. The three schemata below outline chrismation formulae found in scores of Byzantine euchologies that are fuller than the *textus receptus*. Upon review of these now-defunct formulae it becomes evident that any contrasting of "gift" and "gifts" is inadmissible and that a both/and approach is called for.[38]

Historically most intriguing is the fact that the seventeenth-century Moscow euchology—apparently alone among the sources I have discovered—includes quotations from the fourth-century catechesis of Cyril of Jerusalem.[39] One must presume that—as frequently happens—the Slavonic text is simply reproducing older Greek usage

---

[38] It cannot be accidental that Panagiotis Trembelas, who researched and gathered these manuscripts with their fuller chrismation formulae, takes the approach that chrismation "bestows the power of the Spirit and his manifold *gifts*" [emphasis added]. *Dogmatique de l'Église*, 130. Schmemann, of course, did far less historical research.

[39] " . . . upon the forehead, in order that you may be delivered from the disgrace which the first man, a transgressor, carried everywhere, and so that you might reflect the glory of the Lord, by the uncovering of your face. Then upon the ears, so that you might receive ears to hear the divine mysteries, about which Isaiah said 'and the Lord has given me ears to hear,' and the Lord Jesus in the Gospels, 'Whoever has ears to hear, let him hear.' Then upon the nose so that having received the fragrant oil of God, you may say to God, 'We are to God a fragrance of Christ in those being saved.' After this upon the breast, in order that having put on the breastplate of righteousness you may face the works of the devil." See Day, *Baptismal Liturgy*, 111.

The Holy Spirit in Eastern Orthodox Worship

gone defunct. (I am sure that further research will uncover the Greek source.)

> *Forehead:* The seal of the gift of the Holy Spirit. Amen.
> *Eyes:* For the enlightenment of knowledge. Amen.
> *Nostrils:* For a sweet-swelling fragrance. Amen.
> *Mouth:* For [speaking] the word of truth. Amen.
> *Ears:* For the hearing of faith. Amen.
> *Hands:* For [bearing] the yoke of righteousness. Amen.
> *Heart:* For steadfastness of heart. Amen.
> *Feet:* For [walking on] the path of the statutes. Amen.
>
> *Ms. Π, (Mt. Athos) Panteleimon 162; 11th–12th c.*[40]

> *Forehead:* The seal of the gift of the Holy Spirit.
> *Eyes:* The chrism of the gift of the Holy Spirit.
> *Nostrils:* The chrism of the pledge of the Holy Spirit.
> *Ears:* The chrism of participation in life eternal.
> *Hands:* The chrism of the Holy Anointed One of God and the unassailable seal.
> *Heart:* The fullness of the gift of the Holy Spirit and breastplate of faith and truth.
>
> *Ms. M, (Athens) National Library 696, 15th c.*[41]

Anointing

The forehead: The seal of the gift of the Holy Spirit. Amen.
That he/she might be released from the disgrace which the first human, having transgressed [the command] carried everywhere.

The cheeks: The seal of the gift of the Holy Spirit. Amen.
That with uncovered face he/she may see the glory of the Lord.

The eyes: That with his/her eyes he/she may see the light of the Holy Trinity, the image of the first [original] beauty [or, goodness].

The ears: The seal of the gift of the Holy Spirit. Amen.
That he/she might accept with his/her ears the hearing [teaching, proclamation] of the spiritual mystery, the gospel of Christ, as Christ says: "Whoever has ears to hear let them hear"; that evil teaching might not be given [added unto] him/her.

The nostrils: The seal of the gift of the Holy Spirit. Amen.

[40] Π. Ν. Τρεμπελας, *Μικρον Εὐχολόγιον* (Ἀθῆναι, 1950), 364.
[41] Ibid., 363.

Peter Galadza

That he/she also might be filled with the scent of Christ's myrrh of fragrance and the sweet smell of those who are being saved and who no longer smell of the odor of the original deceit.

The mouth: The seal of the gift of the Holy Spirit. Amen.
That the first taste [of the forbidden fruit] might be obstructed by the second, that is, by the Body and Blood of Christ.

The chest: The seal of the gift of the Holy Spirit. Amen.
That having put on the breastplate of righteousness, he/she might confront as an invincible conqueror the works of the enemy.

The hands: The seal of the gift of the Holy Spirit. Amen.
That they [the hands] might be ready to be opened [extended] for good works and the rejection of all evil.

The *Potrebnik* (Euchology) of Patriarch Filaret (Romanov),
Moscow, 1623–25[42]

Symeon the New Theologian

This approach to charismata brings us to the pneumatology of Saint Symeon the New Theologian. Among the many issues that made Symeon so controversial in his day—and a historical oddity to later researchers—was his insistence that true Christians *consciously* experience the Spirit's presence and gifts. To cite just one example, in a discourse entitled "On Those Who Say That They Possess the Holy Spirit Unconsciously," Symeon states:

> Here I am, writing against those who say they have the Spirit of God
> unconsciously, who think that they have Him in themselves as a result
> of divine Baptism, and who, while they believe they have this treasure,
> yet recognize themselves as deaf to Him. I am writing against those who,
> even while confessing they felt nothing whatever in their baptism, still
> imagine that the gift of God has indwelt and existed within their soul,
> unconsciously and insensibly, from that moment up to the present time.
> Nor are they the only ones, but I am also against those who say they have
> never had any perception of that gift in contemplation or in revelation,
> but that they shall receive it by faith and thought alone, not by experi-
> ence, and hold it within themselves as a result of hearing the scriptures.[43]

---

[42] Арранц, *Таинства Византийского Евхология*, 359–60.
[43] *On the Mystical Life: The Ethical Discourses—On Virtue and Christian Life*, trans. Alexander Golitzin (Crestwood, NY: St. Vladimir's Seminary Press, 1996), 44.

The Holy Spirit in Eastern Orthodox Worship

Regardless of how one evaluates such exhortations from the perspective of a "fundamental sacramentology," what is fascinating is that recent research seems to indicate that from a historical perspective Symeon was hardly a maverick. In their study *Christian Initiation and Baptism in the Holy Spirit*, Kilian McDonnell and George T. Montague cite fathers from Tertullian to Cyril of Jerusalem, to the Cappadocians and Chrysostom, to Theodoret of Cyrrhus—and beyond—and summarize their thought with the words: "All of them testify that the charisms were sought, or expected, and received within the rites of initiation or in relation to them."[44] If anything, such an assertion indicates that Symeon was actually quite restrained in his insistence that Christians experience the Spirit, as he tends to associate this experience more frequently with personal prayer than with liturgical worship, and the liturgical experience of the Spirit's activity is not as variegated as that described in the aforementioned patristic writings.

The "Permanent Pentecost" and the Liturgy of the Word

Let us now turn to several other correlations of pneumatology and worship. In the homilies of Chrysostom we encounter references to the church as a permanent or ongoing Pentecost.[45] As a model for ecclesial life, the image is certainly pregnant with innumerable possibilities. When we apply it, however, to Orthodox worship, that professedly privileged icon of *ecclesia*, we discover several surprises as well as disappointments. Among the surprises: canonical Orthodox iconography depicts the event of Pentecost as a Liturgy of the Word. The apostles are seated on a liturgical *synthronon*, proclaiming—if I may be allowed to meld iconography and hymnography—"Christ, the immortal Word and God."[46] The question then arises: If church is Pentecost, and Pentecost is depicted as a Liturgy of the Word, how does one explain the relative absence of Orthodox theologies of preaching, not to mention the virtual neglect of disciplined and well-crafted preaching itself in

[44] *Christian Initiation and Baptism in the Holy Spirit: Evidence from the First Eight Centuries* (Wilmington, DE: Michael Glazier Books, 1990), 314.

[45] *De s. Pentecoste*, PG 50:454D and 459A, cited in Bobrinskoy, *Communion du Saint-Esprit*, 329.

[46] Second sticheron (Tone 1) at "Lord, I have cried," Pentecost Sunday (Holy Transfiguration Monastery, *Pentecostarion*, 404). An example of the icon can be found in Leonid Ouspensky and Vladimir Lossky, *The Meaning of Icons* (Crestwood, NY: St. Vladimir's Seminary Press, 1989), 206.

Peter Galadza

so many Eastern Christian communities?[47] Most Orthodox liturgical reflection, in fact, seems to presume that the homily is not even part of the Eucharist. Certainly regaining "the patristic mind" would require Eastern Christians to revitalize what in Chrysostom's day was among the most prominent parts of the liturgy.

Pavel Florensky and the "Unrepeatable" in Worship

Another aspect of Orthodox pneumatology that can be applied to the Liturgy of the Word is Pavel Florensky's insight regarding unrepeatability as a characteristic of the Spirit. In his seminal *The Pillar and Ground of the Truth*, Florensky reflects on the fact that theological descriptions of the third hypostasis are rare precisely because the Spirit's activities and qualities eschew the formulaic: a certain unrepeatability characterizes the Spirit's work.[48] Again, one is compelled to ask how the Spirit is revealed in worship if the only unrepeatable element of Orthodox worship, the homily, is neglected? Presumably, the *lex orandi* was never intended to be only a *lex repetendi*.

Sergius Bulgakov and the "Conditions for the Possibility" of Cosmic Deification

Turning to the brilliant pneumatology of Sergius Bulgakov, we find an articulation of creation's receptivity to the Spirit that provides an engaging and cogent apologia for the continued prominence of euchological blessings in Orthodox practice.

As is well known, especially in traditionally Eastern Christian lands, large numbers of faithful regularly participate in the blessing of everything from poppies to grapes. Such practices, long derided as quasi-superstitious, take on new significance during the present ecological crisis. As is often noted, the "disenchantment of nature" has not only led to an inability to appreciate the sacramentality of the world; it has also led to environmental degradation. Bulgakov formulates his "creation spirituality" thus:

> How can things and matter be sanctified? . . . It is usually thought that only the spiritual can receive the spiritual, whereas here, things

[47] My assertion regarding such neglect is based on participation in worship in churches from Moscow to Athos, Kiev to Athens, Istanbul to Etna.

[48] Pavel Florensky, *The Pillar and Ground of the Truth*, trans. Boris Jakim (Princeton, NJ: Princeton University Press, 1997), 89.

The Holy Spirit in Eastern Orthodox Worship

and matter absorb the invisibly descending grace of the Holy Spirit the way the earth absorbs moisture. Matter's receptivity to spirit has as its precondition the creaturely descent of the Spirit, His *kenosis* in creation . . . And in virtue of this natural or, more precisely, *sophianic* spirit-bearingness, creation is capable of receiving spirit through sanctification. *The similar receives the similar*, and without this similarity, the very concept of sanctification becomes incomprehensible and contradictory . . . In sanctification we have a descent of the Holy Spirit and a communication of His force to natural and spirit-bearing creation . . . There occurs a mysterious, i.e. invisible, transfiguration of creation, in which the latter, while ontologically remaining itself, becomes transparent for the Spirit, receives the faculty of communion with God, is deified.[49]

Many Westerners will be surprised, if not alienated, by reference to a "deification of creation." But the notion does resonate—albeit faintly—with Scripture (Rom 8:21; Col 1:15) and becomes less incongruous if we recall that in Orthodox theology the key cosmo-theological dichotomy is not matter/spirit, but created/uncreated. The incarnation joins matter to divinity, generating practices such as the veneration of icons.

John Zizioulas and the "Conditions for the Possibility" of Liturgy Itself
Turning to John Zizioulas, the third luminary of modern Orthodox theology, we find, *inter alia*, a coupling of pneumatology and eschatology that grounds the "conditions" for the very possibility of liturgy, at least as the latter has been understood by patristically oriented authors. After outlining some of the limitations of a purely historical approach to apostolic continuity and everything bound up with it, Zizioulas writes the following:

In the eschatological approach, however, things are again different. Here the Spirit is the one who brings the *eschata* into history [Acts 2:17 is cited in a footnote]. He [the Holy Spirit] confronts the process of history with its consummation, with its transformation and transfiguration. By bringing the *eschata* into history, the Spirit does not vivify a pre-existing structure; He *creates* one; He changes linear historicity into a *presence*. It is no longer possible to understand history simply as "past," i.e. to apply to it the psychological and experiential notion of

[49] Sergius Bulgakov, *The Comforter*, trans. Boris Jakim (Grand Rapids, MI: Eerdmans, 2004), 221.

Peter Galadza

anamnesis in the sense of the retrospective faculty of the human soul. When the *eschata* visit us, the Church's *anamnesis* acquires the Eucharistic paradox which no historical consciousness can ever comprehend i.e. the *memory of the future* as we find it in the anaphora of the Liturgy of St. John Chrysostom: "Remembering the cross, the tomb, the resurrection, the ascension, *and the second coming*, Thine own of Thine own we offer Thee." Unless the Church lets Pneumatology so condition Christology that the sequence of "yesterday-today-tomorrow" is transcended, she will not do full justice to Pneumatology; she will enslave the Spirit in a linear *Heilsgeschichte*. Yet the Spirit is "the Lord" who transcends linear history and turns historical continuity into a presence.[50]

Zizioulas's insights ground the reasonableness of the liturgical "today" (*sêmeron, hodie*) as well as experiences of the real presence and the actuality of the paschal mystery.

PNEUMATOLOGY *FROM* WORSHIP

Praying to the Holy Spirit

The question of praying to the Spirit serves as an appropriate interface between sections 1 and 2 of this essay. Prayers and hymns *to* the Holy Spirit constitute an example of both pneumatology as applied *to* worship as well as pneumatology *from* worship. The Orthodox insistence on Spirit as hypostasis requires that one be able to address this personal "agent"; these addresses in turn define teaching about the Spirit's nature and "identity."

Interestingly enough, the Byzantine tradition does not include as many prayers to the Spirit as someone ill-acquainted with the tradition might expect. In addition to the ubiquitous "*Vasileu ouranie*," ("Heavenly King"),[51] one finds only a handful of such compositions, and most of these are sung at Pentecost and during its octave.[52]

---

[50] John D. Zizioulas, *Being as Communion: Studies in Personhood and the Church*, Contemporary Greek Theologians (Crestwood, NY: St. Vladimir's Seminary Press, 1985) 4:180.

[51] Excepting funeral rites, hardly a category of Byzantine services does not include this prayer.

[52] Holy Transfiguration Monastery, *Pentecostarion*, Pentecost Matins, Ode 6, Second Canon, Second Troparion ("As for the apostles"), 412; Pentecost Matins Exaposteilarion ("O Thou, all-holy Spirit"), 415; Divine Liturgy Refrain of Third Antiphon ("Save us, O good Advocate"), 417; Tuesday after Pentecost

The Holy Spirit in Eastern Orthodox Worship

Thanks to the recent work of Stefano Parenti and Elena Velkovska, we now have a much better idea of the history of the *"Vasileu ouranie."*[53] Challenged by Emmanuel Lanne's unconvincing hypothesis that the prayer can be traced to Basil the Great,[54] Parenti and Velkovska sketched the history of the text in liturgical sources rather than simply relying on intertextuality with Basil's works. The two scholars have demonstrated that the prayer derives from eleventh-century Studite circles and began circulating under the influence of Symeon the New Theologian's strong pneumatology. Initially a hymn of the Pentecostarion (as evidenced by an eleventh-century codex), the text becomes a "devotional prayer" intended for the monastic cell. Soon it is appended to the beginning of Prime whence it migrates to other offices. By the twelfth century the prayer has entered the eucharistic liturgy. Certainly its position at the beginning of Offices and as a private clerical prayer immediately preceding the opening exclamation of the Divine Liturgy justifies Evdokimov's reference to it as a "general epiclesis at the threshold of each mystery."[55] A curious feature of *"Vasileu ouranie"* is the fact that it applies a Byzantine christological title, "Heavenly King,"[56] to the Holy Spirit. Of itself, this need not be problematic—except perhaps for neurotic systematizers—but it does raise the question of whether the prayer's author was attempting to say more than is immediately apparent.

The Anabathmoi, *Byzantine Rite Songs of Ascent*

Turning to another example of pneumatology *from* worship, one of the most intriguing yet neglected examples in Byzantine worship is the *anabathmoi*, hymnography partially inspired by the gradual psalms and originally used as refrains for the latter. The last verse of

---

Matins, Aposticha, Third sticheron ("Come to us from on high"), 439; Wednesday after Pentecost Vespers Second Sticheron at "Lord, I have cried" ("God's rhetoricians"), and Third Sticheron of the Aposticha ("O eternal unceasing spring"), 442.

[53] See n. 7.

[54] E. Lanne, "La prière au Saint-Esprit en Orient et en Occident," in *La prière liturgique: Conférences Saint-Serge XLVIIe semaine d'études liturgiques*, ed. A. M. Triacca, 273 (Rome: Edizioni Liturgiche, 2001).

[55] Cited by Parenti and Velkovska, "Re celeste," 388.

[56] For example, the title refers to Christ in the Dogmaticon of the Eighth Tone, *The Great Octoechos—Tones Seven and Eight*, Service Books of the Byzantine Churches (Boston: Sophia Press, 2000), 163.

Peter Galadza

each antiphon is a theology of the Spirit in doxological form with no parallel in Byzantine worship save several *stichera* sung at Pentecost. A succinct—albeit general—description of their theology is available elsewhere;[57] thus, I turn here to several unresolved questions.

Authorship of the *anabathmoi* is usually attributed to Theodore Studites and sometimes to John of Damascus.[58] Unfortunately, a search of the *Thesaurus Linguae Grecae* does not yield the kind of intertextual relations that would enable us to confirm either attribution. In fact, the search provides no direct leads to any patristic author. Lexemes such as *monokratoria* (from Tone 1, antiphon 1) and *palindromousa* (from Tone 1, antiphon 2), and phrases such as *to Pneuma symmorfon* (from Tone 8, antiphon 3), which owing to their rarity might lead us to the writings of a particular father, never appear in any patristic work in connection with the Holy Spirit, or, for that matter, in connection with anything that might bear on the *anabathmoi*.

Notwithstanding the frustration of not being able to situate this hymnography historically, I would like to propose a hypothesis that might help explain an aspect of its inspiration. My hypothesis is probably impossible to verify with the historical sources presently available to us, but is worth proposing not only because of its cogency, but also because it has the potential to become the kind of hermeneutical interpretation that retains validity even when "exegesis" or other forms of historical research remain inconclusive.

What I mean is the following: Anyone reading the *anabathmoi* is eventually led to ask, why this particular *déroulement* of themes? The *anabathmoi* are unique in Byzantine hymnography in that they proceed

[57] V. Palachkovsky, "Les 'Pneumatica' des antiphones graduelles," in *Le Saint-Esprit dans la liturgie: Conférences Saint-Serge, XVIe semaine d'études liturgiques*, 141–48 (Rome: Edizioni Liturgiche, 1969). Palachkovsky deals with some of the aspects of the structure and gives a general account of their contents. Except for the musicological study cited below, to date only this seven-page article—without references—has been written on the pneumatic section of the *Anabathmoi*.

[58] Oliver Strunk, "The Antiphons of the Octoechos," in *Essays on Music in the Byzantine World*, 165 (New York: W. W. Norton and Co., 1977). Incidentally, the commentary on the *Anabathmoi* by Nicephorus Callistus referred to by Strunk (on the basis of a reference in Trembelas's *Eklogê*, Athens, 1949) is not available in Western libraries. My thanks to Christian Hannick who is familiar with the commentary and informed me that it is a rather superficial work undeserving of greater attention.

The Holy Spirit in Eastern Orthodox Worship

from (1) a close paraphrase of the psalm, to (2) a remoter evocation of the psalm, but with christological elements, to (3) a doxological "verbal epiphany" of the Spirit. This *déroulement* is also noteworthy because in standard late-Byzantine hymnography, the chant following the *nun kai aei* ("both now and for ever . . . ") is almost always a *theotokion*. In fact, the *anabathmoi* represent the only instance, except for Pentecost and its octave, when liturgical units conclude with a *pneumatikon*.

If we keep in mind the name of these hymns (the *anabathmoi*), and also remember how important the writings of Gregory Nazianzen remained throughout the middle- and late-Byzantine periods, the following passage from Gregory's "Oration on the Holy Spirit" of his *Fifth Theological Oration* may give us a vital clue regarding the *anabathmoi*'s construction.

> The old covenant made clear proclamation of the Father, a less definite one of the Son. The new covenant made the Son manifest and gave us a glimpse of the Spirit's Godhead. At the present time, the Spirit resides amongst us, giving us a clearer manifestation of himself than before. It was dangerous for the Son to be preached openly when the Godhead of the Father was still unacknowledged. It was dangerous, too, for the Holy Spirit to be made (and here I use a rather rash expression) an extra burden, when the Son had not been received. It could mean men jeopardizing what did lie within their powers, as happens to those encumbered with a diet too strong for them or who gaze at sunlight with eyes as yet too feeble for it. No, God meant it to be by piecemeal additions, "ascents" as David called them, by progress and advance from glory to glory that the light of the Trinity should shine upon more illustrious souls [ὡς εἶπε Δαβίδ, ἀναβάσεσι, καὶ ἐκ δόξης εἰς δόξαν προόδοις καὶ προκοπαῖς, τὸ τῆς τριάδος φῶς ἐκλάμψη τοῖς λαμπροτέροις]. This was, I believe, the motive for the Spirit's making his home in the disciples in gradual stages proportionate to their capacity to receive him—at the outset of the gospel when he performs miracles, after the Passion when he is breathed into the disciples, after the Ascension when he appears in fiery tongues. He was gradually revealed by Jesus also, as you too can substantiate by a more careful reading.[59]

---

[59] St. Gregory of Nazianzus, *On God and Christ: The Five Theological Orations and Two Letters to Cledonius*, trans. Frederick Williams and Lionel Wickham (Crestwood, NY: St. Vladimir's Seminary Press, 2002), 137.

Peter Galadza

In sum, I am arguing that the author of the *anabathmoi* may have hoped to convey the sense of the Father's revelation in the Old Testament by a close paraphrase of the Old Testament text, then proceeded to a "disclosure" of Christ in the next verse, and then completed the ascent with a thoroughly articulated theology of the Spirit. An additionally significant element may be the fact that the *anabathmoi* are sung almost immediately before the Matins gospel, that is, as the summit of the first half of Byzantine orthros.

PNEUMATOLOGIA PRIMA: LITURGICAL PNEUMATOLOGY

Let us now proceed to a liturgical pneumatology à la David Fagerberg. In this all-too-brief section I will focus on the gestural, musical, and physical. Notwithstanding the aforementioned marginalization of preaching in modern Orthodoxy, Orthodoxy's liturgical genius lies in its ability to enflesh the word via a dynamic aesthetic that genuinely turns liturgy into "revelation in action."[60] In particular, the canonically prescribed environment of Orthodox worship helps generate an efficacious image of "the holy city Jerusalem coming down out of heaven," a sight to which one is led "in the Spirit" (Rev 21:10, RSV).

Liturgical Environment

Let us begin with the absence of pews. Several years ago, in an article entitled "Anathema 'sit,'" Andriy Chirovsky noted how the absence of pews facilitates a freedom during worship redolent of the Spirit's unpredictable and unrestrainable promptings. "In an Eastern church, one is free to light a candle, kiss an icon, or greet a friend, as the Spirit moves one. . . . The price to pay for 'organization' is a loss of spontaneity and a severe limitation in options for activity, resulting in passivity on the part of the faithful."[61]

Singing and "Breathing Divinely"

Then there is the stress on singing. As is well known, essentially every word of an Orthodox service is chanted or otherwise sung. In addition to a myriad of other theologically significant reasons for stressing this form of vocality, there is the fact that prolonged, disciplined breathing—which is what singing is very much

[60] Fagerberg, *Theologia Prima* (n. 9), 3.
[61] Andriy Chirovsky, "Anathema 'Sit': Some Reflections on Pews in Eastern Christian Churches and Their Effects on Worshippers," *Diakonia* 15 (1980): 171.

The Holy Spirit in Eastern Orthodox Worship

about—potentially effects communion with God's Holy Breath in a manner that we moderns, possibly owing to a kind of Gnostic, Docetic, or even crypto-Manichean pneumatology usually overlook. Imagine the sacramental power of acknowledging and enacting one's inhalation and exhalation as a means of communing with the Spirit. Nonetheless, when we look to the Eastern Christian tradition we notice a dearth of substantive theological reflection on liturgical singing as an act. Thus, the one contemporary work devoted to this topic merits attention. In a delightful essay, Nicholas Lossky plants several seeds for the development of an acknowledgment of breathing's sacramental power. Nonetheless, Lossky fails to nurture these seeds adequately owing to what I believe are several conceptual restraints imposed by his restricted liturgical theology. But let us first take note of these seeds:

> One could say that the liturgy is the way the Church breathes. There is then an obvious connection with the act of breathing. We all know that in Greek the word for breath is *pneuma*, which means both "breath" and "spirit" (or "Spirit"). Lancelot Andrewes, the Anglican theologian and bishop—after having recalled that the Holy Spirit is the "Heart of the Church" with Christ being the "Head" of the Body—speaks of liturgical time not only in terms of respiration but also of a succession of "systoles" and "diastoles."[62]

Unfortunately, after announcing this theme, Lossky virtually ignores it. The failure, I would argue, is the result of a limited notion of liturgical theology.

Throughout his essay Lossky tends to dwell on the textual, verbal, proclamatory, instructional, and communal aspects of liturgical music, without developing with equal force its thoroughly corporeal dimension, that is, the full-bodied nature of liturgical experience. Thus, in my opinion Lossky loses the opportunity to proclaim how flesh can become word when breath joins Breath. Among the symptoms of Lossky's "spiritualization" of singing is his approach to the Orthodox requirement that all services, in their entirety, be sung. Lossky believes that the main reason for doing so is that it prevents a disruptive individualism in the assembly: discrete members of the congregation

---

[62] Nicolas Lossky, *Essai sur une théologie de la musique liturgique: Perspective orthodoxe* (Paris: Cerf, 2003), 35.

Peter Galadza

are inhibited from interjecting idiosyncratic stresses into the liturgical text. But as anyone who has ever attended Orthodox worship knows, protodeacons, cantors, conductors, and lectors are certainly capable of distracting from the text through idiosyncratic chanting thereof. Consequently, I would insist that a far more important reason for chanting the entire service lies in the physical commitment required to do so. Cantors understand in a unique way the force of Romans 12:1: "I appeal to you therefore, brethren, by the mercies of God, to present your bodies as a living sacrifice, holy and acceptable to God, which is your spiritual worship" (RSV). Singing involves physical sacrifice; ideally, in keeping with the Pauline exhortation, this sacrificial spirit extends into daily life.

Kalophonic Cacophony

We should also note a peculiarity of Russian and East Ukrainian liturgical music. In a hierarchical divine liturgy, as the clergy bow toward the gospel and melismatically chant the conclusion of the Third Antiphon, "Come, let us bow in worship and fall down before Christ. O Son of God, risen from the dead, save us who sing to you. Alleluia," they are "violently" (cf. Acts 2:2 NJB) interrupted by a fortissimo tetrachord recitativo of the above-cited words "O Son of God, risen from the dead . . ." The recitative is chanted in an entirely different key from the clergy's melismatic chant and overlaps their singing, creating a disorientingly beautiful cacophony. An intriguing rubrical detail is that the choir must wait until the hierarch has reached the ambo to begin its kalophonic cacophony. A medieval-minded allegorizer would, no doubt, relish the possibility of associating it with the "perplexity" experienced when the first "hierarchs" proclaimed "God's deeds of power" at Pentecost (Acts 2). Allegorizing aside, even anti-Platonic moderns are brought to an experience of Pentecostal-like energy and constructive chaos as they hear this clash of chants.

The Spirit Embodied during Liturgical Fasting

Finally, there is the actual physical state of those gathered for the Eucharist. Among traditional Orthodox it is common to fast from midnight—that is, to avoid all food and drink—even when one is not receiving the Eucharist that day. Eugene F. Rogers begins his superb work *After the Spirit* with the statement: "[One of the initial insights for this book] was that the Spirit had grown dull because unembodied,

The Holy Spirit in Eastern Orthodox Worship

and bodily experience unpersuasive because un-Spirited."[63] Orthodox theology stresses the connection between Spirit and ascesis, and
ascesis and liturgy, in a way that most Western theology and liturgical
study do not. In fact, prescriptions regarding the type of fast to be
observed are an inseparable part of the Orthodox liturgical *ordo*. In an
age when we appropriately focus on "the construction of self" as an
intellectual paradigm, it seems that we might want to ask ourselves
what kind of self—at the most concrete level of appetite and desire—
arrives at church?

CONCLUSION

Allow me to conclude with a quotation that sums up several of the
themes treated in this paper and grounds the last theme, ascesis, in
Christ's *martyria*. This moving passage is from a letter written by an
anonymous Soviet-era Christian cited by Bobrinskoy:

> The unique and common path of the saints to the mystery of the
> Spirit, of the Church and of Christ, proceeds by ascesis—by partici-
> pation in the Son's Golgotha. St. Symeon the New Theologian calls
> the Holy Spirit the royal purple of our great God and Savior, that is,
> Christ's tunic before the crucifixion. In the Eucharistic prayer of the
> ancient liturgy of Saint Clement [*sic*] the Holy Spirit is called "the wit-
> ness of the sufferings of the Lord Jesus." It is only by the sufferings
> of Christ, by ascesis, that one enters into the communion of the Holy
> Spirit.
>
> But if the way to the Holy Spirit proceeds through the Son and His
> cross, the Son for His part can only be recognized through the grace
> of the Spirit, for "no one can confess Jesus as Savior, except by the
> Holy Spirit" (1 Cor. 12:3), and because "the Holy Spirit proceeds from
> the Father and rests on the Son" (Pentecost propers). This intimate
> connection in knowledge between the Spirit and the Son is not a
> dogmatic confession, but an organic and living reciprocal love which
> strikes us when we read the liturgical texts and the writings of the
> saints . . .
>
> Those Christians who separate themselves from the Son's Golgotha,
> imagining that they have no need of Him in order to possess the res-
> urrection in the Holy Spirit, fall into delusion—pseudo-spiritualism

[63] Eugene F. Rogers Jr., *After the Spirit: A Constructive Pneumatology from Resources outside the Modern West* (Grand Rapids, MI: Eerdmans, 2005), 3.

Peter Galadza

and self-exaltation. These people reject the straight path and in one way or another follow the world which lies in evil (1 John). On the other hand, those who, while fully accepting the straight path of Golgotha forget the Resurrection and forget the Kingdom of the Holy Spirit which is already revealed on earth, render their Christianity dead, or according to Saint Paul [sic] tasteless salt and faded light.[64]

[64] B. Bobrinskoy, "Quelques réflexions sur la pneumatologie du culte," in *Mélanges liturgiques offerts au R. P. Dom Bernard Botte, O.S.B.*, ed. Ambroise Verheul, 28–29 (Louvain: Abbaye de Bellefontaine, 1972).

Teresa Berger

8. *Veni Creator Spiritus*: The Elusive Real Presence of the Spirit in the Catholic Tradition

The Latin invocation in this essay's title—*Come, Creator Spirit*—opens one of the most prominent prayers to the Holy Spirit in the Catholic tradition. The text probably dates from the ninth century and possibly was written by Rabanus Maurus in support of the then-disputed insertion of the *filioque* into the Creed. Whatever its exact origin and purpose, this hymn to the Holy Spirit has played a vital role in the Catholic Church for well over a thousand years. Sung at Pentecost, as well as in ordinations and the dedications of churches and altars, *Veni Creator Spiritus* also opens all important synodal liturgies and conciliar assemblies. The Second Vatican Council (1962–65) was solemnly begun with this pleading for the coming of the Holy Spirit. This ninth-century hymn is not only alive and well in the life of the Roman Catholic Church but also has made its way into new domains. For example, several versions of *Veni Creator Spiritus* appear on *YouTube*, the Google-owned video-sharing website where people can upload, view, share, and discuss video clips. Well over one hundred million videos are watched every day, and one version of *Veni Creator Spiritus* alone has had close to twelve thousand viewers on *YouTube*.[1]

If one looks back at the ninth-century prayer itself,[2] one can see how the Spirit is imaged in this text. Without entering into a detailed analysis, the sense of vibrant movement connected with the Holy

---

[1] http://www.youtube.com/watch?v=7cuOFKwp2Vg&feature=related. Accessed March 4, 2008.

[2] The text (whose wording, punctuation, accents, and even position of words can differ from one Latin text to another) is easily accessible, for example, in Raniero Cantalamessa, *Come, Creator Spirit: Meditations on the Veni Creator* (Collegeville, MN: Liturgical Press, 2003), 5. An English translation of the hymn introduces each of the sections of this book.

Spirit stands out. The actions attributed to the Spirit bear ample witness to this: coming, creating, visiting, comforting, empowering, setting ablaze, pouring out love, strengthening, repelling evil, guiding, granting peace as well as knowledge and faith, and leading to life. One might ask whether there is anything good in the life of the church that does not originate with the Holy Spirit! *Veni Creator Spiritus*, moreover, is not only a spoken but an embodied prayer, traditionally begun on one's knees—a gesture of intense pleading.

The hymn's moving witness to the Holy Spirit counters the commonly held notion that the Western tradition is forgetful of the Third Person of the Trinity. In this paper I will argue that much in this commonly held notion depends on what one allows to count as evidence for the Spirit's presence or absence. If, for example, the evidence comes to be narrowly confined to the question of a consecratory Spirit-epiclesis in the eucharistic prayer, then the Catholic tradition will in fact seem inattentive to the Holy Spirit. Such a focus on a eucharistic Spirit-epiclesis is encouraged of course by comparison with Eastern eucharistic prayers, which make their Latin counterpart look deficient. Or, to use a very different example, most Catholic liturgies will seem lacking if the crucial marker for the Spirit's presence is the charism of speaking in tongues. However, if in order to chart the Spirit's presence one begins with the *Veni Creator Spiritus*, or the ancient Blessing of Baptismal Water, or the liturgical exposition of Rupert von Deutz (†1129/30), then a significantly different picture emerges. This is what I propose to develop.

I myself ponder the tension between a perceived absence and a believed presence of the Holy Spirit as a Roman Catholic who owes much to the charismatic movement both within and beyond the Catholic Church. I will thus begin with reflections on the presence of the Spirit. The *Catechism of the Catholic Church* also encourages this starting point. In a chapter devoted to worship as the "Work of the Holy Trinity" there is a remarkable section on "The Holy Spirit and the Church in the Liturgy."[3] I quote the opening paragraph, which

---

[3] For background to this section of the *Catechism* (namely in the writings of Jean Corbon), see Cassian Folsom, "The Holy Spirit and the Church in the Liturgy: *CCC* 1091–1109 and the Influence of Fr. Jean Corbon," in *Spiritus spiritalia nobis dona potenter infundit: A proposito di tematiche liturgico-pneumatologiche* (Festschrift Achille M. Triacca), ed. Ephrem Carr, Studia Anselmiana 139, Analecta Liturgica 25 (Rome: Pontificio Ateneo S. Anselmo, 2005), 231–41.

Teresa Berger

describes the relationship between the Spirit, the church, and worship, and the concluding paragraph, which summarizes what the Spirit's presence brings about in the liturgical assembly:

> In the liturgy the Holy Spirit is teacher of the faith of the People of God and artisan of "God's masterpieces," the sacraments of the New Covenant. The desire and work of the Spirit in the heart of the Church is that we may live from the life of the risen Christ. When the Spirit encounters in us the response of faith which he has aroused in us, he brings about genuine cooperation. Through it, the liturgy becomes the common work of the Holy Spirit and the Church.
>
> The mission of the Holy Spirit in the liturgy of the Church is to prepare the assembly to encounter Christ; to recall and manifest Christ to the faith of the assembly; to make the saving work of Christ present and active by his transforming power; and to make the gift of communion bear fruit in the Church.[4]

The four dimensions of the Spirit's work in worship mentioned here—preparing the assembly, recalling and manifesting Christ, rendering salvation present, and making communion bear fruit—are each given sustained attention in the *Catechism*. Again one may ask: Does anything good in the life of the church not originate with the Holy Spirit? Or, to sharpen the focus: Does anything good in the life of the church not originate with the "genuine cooperation" the Spirit brings about in the liturgy, which is understood as the "common work of the Holy Spirit and the Church"?

THE REAL PRESENCE OF THE HOLY SPIRIT

Endeavoring to sketch the presence of the Spirit in the Catholic liturgical tradition, I will start with the sacrament of baptism. This is an appropriate starting point not least of all because the baptismal liturgy seems to have been the locus of the earliest Spirit-epicleses, predating those in eucharistic prayers.[5] Looking at how the Spirit

---

[4] *Catechism of the Catholic Church*, 2d rev. ed. (Vatican City: Libreria Editrice Vaticana/Washington, DC: United States Catholic Conference, 2000), nos. 1091, 1112.

[5] Gabriele Winkler has argued that the earliest Spirit-epicleses appear in connection with the prebaptismal anointing in the Syrian tradition, and the blessing of baptismal waters; see, for example, her "Nochmals zu den Anfängen

Veni Creator Spiritus

143

is inscribed into the baptismal liturgy, one cannot help but notice a strong resemblance to *Veni Creator Spiritus*. Both plead for the Spirit's life-giving movement, especially for the gift of the Spirit's descent and coming. It is worth taking a closer look at individual elements of how the Spirit is inscribed into the baptismal liturgy.

Pleading for the Spirit, in Prayer

Based on the baptismal liturgy, one could say the fundamental speech-act of worship is to plead for the coming of the Holy Spirit and for her life-giving presence.[6] This posture of pleading is very clear in the Blessing of Baptismal Water that precedes the act of baptism. One of the earliest extant Latin texts for such a blessing dates from the eighth century and is found in the Gelasian Sacramentary (*Sacramentarium Gelasianum Vetus*),[7] which predates the *Veni Creator Spiritus* by roughly one hundred years. The liturgical texts collected in this sacramentary continued to be in use in the Roman Catholic Church for well over a thousand years. The Blessing of Baptismal Water in the Gelasian Sacramentary is a fascinating (and complicated) text. I wish to highlight just two features in connection with our theme.[8]

First, the Gelasian Blessing clearly focuses on baptism as birth "by water and the Holy Spirit" (John 3:5). The baptismal font is imaged as a womb; the baptismal waters are consequently understood as amniotic fluid. It is Mother Church and the grace present within her that give birth to the catechumen. The Holy Spirit renders fruitful the

---

der Epiklese und des Sanctus im Eucharistischen Hochgebet," *Theologische Quartalschrift* 174 (1994): 214–31.

[6] In the problematic choice (especially in the English language, which lacks grammatical gender) of masculine or feminine pronouns for the Holy Spirit, I will here privilege the feminine in cases where it is linguistically impossible or truly cumbersome to avoid personal pronouns for the Divine.

[7] Text in *Liber Sacramentorum Romanae Aeclesiae ordinis anni circuli*, ed. Leo Cunibert Mohlberg et al., Rerum Ecclesiasticarum Documenta, 2d rev. ed. (Rome: Herder, 1968), 72–74.

[8] Following Gerard Rouwhorst, I consider it wise not to speculate about what in this text might be "really Roman" and what might be later Gallican additions. See Gerard Rouwhorst, "Baumstark's Methodology in Practice: Historical Research on the Blessing of Baptismal Water in the Roman Liturgy," in *Comparative Liturgy Fifty Years After Anton Baumstark (1872–1948)*, ed. Robert F. Taft and Gabriele Winkler, Orientalia Christiana Analecta 265 (Rome: Pontificio Istituto Orientale, 2001), 963–77.

Teresa Berger

womb of the baptismal font, thus enabling it to bring forth new life. To quote but the clearest expression of this theme in the Blessing:

> [L]ook down, O Lord, upon your Church and multiply in her your generations, . . . let your Holy Spirit by the secret admixture of his light give fruitfulness to this water prepared for human regeneration, so that, sanctification being conceived therein, there may come forth from the unspotted womb of the divine font [*ab immaculate divini fontis utero*] a heavenly offspring, reborn unto a new creature: that grace may be a mother to people of every age and sex, who are brought forth into a common infancy.[9]

The image of Spirit-induced fecundity and birthing obviously is sexual, or better, erotic. (The contemporary postmodern fascination with "desire" may help us to appreciate this again.) Absent from this text is the image of baptism as dying and rising with Christ as in Romans 6. The post–Vatican II reform, in its reworking of the Gelasian Blessing of Baptismal Water, stressed this christological motif of Romans 6, thereby eclipsing the image central to the ancient blessing itself, namely that of fecundity and rebirth.[10] I note that in thus reworking the text the post–Vatican II reform also pressed the primary role of the Holy Spirit, so clearly expressed in the ancient Roman blessing, into the background.

Second, the Gelasian Blessing of Baptismal Water is important for our theme not only because of its image of baptism as Spirit-induced conception and birth, but also because the text already gives evidence of fundamental patterns of liturgical prayer to or for the Holy Spirit that mark the Roman Catholic tradition throughout. To highlight the most important elements:

In Anamnesis: The Spirit's redemptive presence in history is recalled. In the Gelasian Blessing of Baptismal Water this is especially evident in the allusions to the biblical creation story, as seen in the invocation of God as the One "whose Spirit at the beginning of the world was

---

[9] I use the English translation in E. C. Whitaker's *Documents of the Baptismal Liturgy*, rev. and expanded ed., ed. Maxwell E. Johnson, Alcuin Club Collections 79 (London: SPCK, 2003), 233f.

[10] Dominic E. Serra has convincingly argued this; see most recently, "The Blessing of Baptismal Water at the Paschal Vigil: Ancient Texts and Modern Revisions," *Worship* 64 (1990): 142–56.

Veni Creator Spiritus

borne upon the waters [Gen. 1.2], that even the nature of water might conceive the power of sanctification."[11]

In Epiclesis: The Holy Spirit is invoked as gift, and called upon to descend, especially in consecratory prayers. In the Gelasian text are a couple of such epicletic invocations: "Almighty everlasting God, . . . send down the Spirit of adoption," and, "May the power of your Holy Spirit descend into all the water of this font and make the whole substance of this water fruitful with regenerating power."

In Doxology: In the Gelasian text, a clear trinitarian doxology appears in the prayer at the episcopal consignation that follows the post-baptismal presbyteral anointing. The prayer asks "God, the Father of our Lord Jesus Christ" to send upon the baptized "your Holy Spirit the Paraclete"; it concludes "in the name of our Lord Jesus Christ with whom you live and reign ever God with the Holy Spirit, throughout all ages of ages."

In Confession of Faith: A fourth fundamental speech-act embedded in the sacrament of baptism is the confession of faith. The Holy Spirit is always an integral part of the baptismal confession of faith in the tri-une God. In the Gelasian text the baptizand confesses her faith in the Spirit in answer to this question: "Do you believe in the Holy Spirit; the holy Church; the remission of sins; the resurrection of the flesh?" Upon this confession, she is baptized.

So much for four fundamental liturgical speech-acts related to the Holy Spirit that are embedded in the baptismal liturgy. Texts of course are only a small part of liturgical life and traditioning. We must not forget the rich heritage of symbols and ritual actions in the Catholic Church that also relate to the Spirit's presence and power.

The Gift of the Spirit in Symbols and Ritual Actions

The first ritual symbolic actions to examine are the laying on of hands and anointing. For Roman Catholics these immediately conjure up memories of confirmation, and in the popular Catholic imagination this indeed is *the* sacrament of the Holy Spirit. Historically, confirmation is merely a concluding piece of the ancient Roman baptismal liturgy, namely the episcopal consignation. The rubrics of the Gelasian Sacramentary explicate consignation thus: "Then the seven-fold Spirit is given to [the baptized] by the bishop. To seal them [*ad*

---

[11] The quotations are taken from Gelasian Sacramentary XLIV, in *Documents of the Baptismal Liturgy*, 233.

Teresa Berger

146

consignandum], he lays his hand upon them with these words . . ."[12] The prayer of consignation follows. This consignation became separated from baptism when infant baptism became the norm and the scope of episcopal oversight changed in the early Middle Ages. Liturgical scholars love to hate the sacrament of confirmation, and with reason: confirmation presents an unsolvable problem, namely, how to give theological meaning to a sacrament that locates the giving of the Spirit separately from, and outside of, baptism. None of the possible theological gymnastics around this issue are elegant, to say the least. Suffice it here to note that the gift of the Spirit is expressed liturgically in particular symbols and ritual actions such as the laying on of hands and anointing.[13]

Second, and simply for the record, I stress that there are other symbols, now lost, associated with the gift of the Holy Spirit, such as the ancient water, honey, and milk chalice for the baptized. The Verona [Leonine] Sacramentary explicitly links the Holy Spirit to the blessing and drinking from this chalice.[14]

A third set of symbolic actions that invoke the Holy Spirit (even if used infrequently today in the West) are exorcistic rites, especially the rite of exorcism itself. The prebaptismal rites traditionally also contain exorcistic elements, their theme being the expulsion of evil spirits so that the Holy Spirit may find room. The Gelasian Sacramentary, for example, includes the following exorcism over men (different words are used for women): "Listen, accursed Satan, adjured by the name of the eternal God . . . Give honor [therefore] to the Holy Spirit as he approaches, descending from the highest place of heaven."[15] Such prebaptismal exorcisms are performed both on human beings and on natural elements, e.g., salt, oil, and water. The Gelasian Sacramentary

---

[12] Ibid.

[13] There are other liturgical occasions than consignation/confirmation where these occur, such as ordination. For more on this subject see Virgil E. Fiala, "L'imposition des mains comme signe de la communication de l'Esprit-Saint dans les rites latins," in *Le Saint-Esprit dans la Liturgie: Conférences Saint-Serge*, BELS, 87–103 (Rome: Edizioni Liturgiche, 1977).

[14] English text in *Documents of the Baptismal Liturgy*, 207. For background on this rite, see Johannes Betz's important essay, "Die Eucharistie als Gottes Milch in frühchristlicher Sicht," *Zeitschrift für Katholische Theologie* 106 (1984): 1–26, 167–85.

[15] Gelasian Sacramentary XXXIII, in *Documents of the Baptismal Liturgy*, 217.

Veni Creator Spiritus

contains one such exorcistic Blessing of Baptismal Water that begins
with the water itself being addressed: "I exorcise you, creature of
water."[16] Similarly, a Blessing of the Oil begins: "I exorcise you, creature of oil."[17] Gestures that accompany these exorcistic words are the
sign of the cross, *sufflatio* (in the double sense of blowing out the devil
and breathing in the Spirit), and anointing.

A host of other symbols and ritual actions that invoke the Holy
Spirit could be named, from making the sign of the cross when praying "In the name of the Father . . . ," or kneeling when intoning the
Veni Creator Spiritus, to votive Masses to the Holy Spirit and novenas
before Pentecost. Further areas to explore would be the visual arts
and the traditions associated with Pentecost in popular Catholic religiosity. I will have to leave all these aside; they would, however,
need attention for a comprehensive picture of the presence of the
Spirit in the Catholic tradition. Instead, I will highlight one other area,
namely, the Holy Spirit in the thoughts of those who have pondered
and interpreted Catholic liturgy throughout the centuries. I focus on
Rupert von Deutz, an early twelfth-century monastic theologian, as an
example.

The Holy Spirit in the Liturgical Commentary of Rupert von Deutz

Rupert von Deutz (1075/76–1129/30) is best known as the author of
one of the medieval allegorical expositions of the liturgy. His *Liber de
divinis officiis*, written between 1108 and 1111/1112,[18] is of interest for
our theme especially for its chapter dedicated to the feast of Pentecost.
Rupert, moreover, attributes his own calling to a vision of the Holy
Spirit. He speaks of this vision in his commentary on Pentecost in
the *Liber*. Rupert's description of the Holy Spirit entering and filling the
human soul is startling. Not only is the text moving in its sense of the
vibrancy and sweetness of the encounter, but it is also stunning in its
powerfully erotic imagery. Rupert writes:

[16] Gelasian Sacramentary LXXIII, in *Documents of the Baptismal Liturgy*, 241.
[17] Gelasian Sacramentary LXXVI, in *Documents of the Baptismal Liturgy*, 243.
[18] To date, no English translation is available of Rupert's work. I use the
critical edition of the *Liber de divinis officiis* edited by Helmut and Ilse Deutz in
the series "Fontes Christiani: Zweisprachige Neuausgabe christlicher Quellen-
texte" (Freiburg i.B.: Herder, 1999) 33:1–4.

Teresa Berger

Suddenly, without anyone's being aware of it, the Holy Spirit springs close, and as through an opening glides into the secret enclosure of the soul. Immediately on the Spirit's entrance the human spirit in its weakness begins to tremble on account of the unusual vigor, which it feels, and the weight. First, the One who entered comforts the quaking soul with the familiar caress of his sweetness as with a kiss. Then, . . . rising up, he moves about in the womb of the soul, and by moving about he enlarges what was previously small and straitened, indicating by the wonderful increase of his circlings [the soul's] own coming growth in divine knowledge, sometimes overwhelming her with such vastness as if one of the rivers of paradise was flowing through the widened pelvis of that soul. . . . When the soul is at length filled with the measure this Spirit wishes to give her . . . the wonderful happening quietens, and the soul returns to herself.[19]

Three themes stand out in Rupert's descriptions of the Holy Spirit.

First, there is the strong sense of unfettered movement that Rupert associates with the Holy Spirit, witnessed by the verbs used for the Spirit's coming. This image of movement is both biblically based and also rooted in Rupert's own mystical experience, which he describes as a quite sudden *visitatio*. Rupert sees this sense of vibrant movement substantiated in the liturgy: Pentecost, he insists, is the feast of the *coming* of the Holy Spirit (*solemnitas de adventu sancti Spiritus*[20]). Indeed, Rupert will argue that, while Christ came once, the Spirit comes again and again.[21]

Second, there is the tenderness of devotion Rupert expresses toward the Spirit. This tenderness is evident, for example, in his interpretation of the baptismal liturgy. In a moving passage this Benedictine monk describes the Spirit who hovers over the baptismal waters like a mother bird brooding and giving life through her own warmth, and then spreading her wings over her young and carrying them up. More compelling yet than this quintessentially feminine image is Rupert's further claim that the Holy Spirit, the "mother," will descend and spread her wings even over those "outside of the nest of baptismal waters," if only they so desire![22]

---

[19] Rupert von Deutz, *Liber de divinis officiis*, 10, 11. Translation mine; I gratefully acknowledge the expert advice of John Leinenweber.

[20] Ibid., 11, 1.

[21] Ibid., 10, 9.

[22] Ibid., 7, 4. Translation mine. I note the gender-bending that occurs in this passage.

Veni Creator Spiritus

Third, it is important to note that Rupert also covers the basic doctrines, such as the divinity of the Holy Spirit, in considerable depth.[23] Clearly, this twelfth-century liturgical commentator does not suffer from Spirit-obliviousness. But is Rupert an exception? Not everyone, after all, encounters the Holy Spirit as intensely and erotically charged as Rupert. Yet there were others, even in Rupert's own time, who, like him, evidenced a deep devotion to the Holy Spirit. Hildegard von Bingen (†1179), in her eucharistic theology (especially *Scivias* 6, 2), expresses a profound sense of the Spirit's agency in liturgy. Like Rupert, she wrote hymns to the Holy Spirit; and also Abelard, including one addressed to the Spirit as divine lover.[24] Last, but not least, is the famous so-called Golden Sequence, *Veni, Sancte Spiritus*, written around 1200, and attributed to Stephen Langton of Canterbury (†1228), which continues to be used in the Roman Catholic Church to this day as a sequence for Pentecost. If we take all these witnesses together, Rupert von Deutz and his deep devotion to the Holy Spirit are not so much exceptions as part of a larger picture of the Spirit's real presence in the Catholic tradition.

Given this fact, what then does one make of the claim that the Western tradition is deeply forgetful of the Holy Spirit? In order to assess the validity of this claim, I turn to an analysis of the evidence that typically is invoked to substantiate the claim.

THE REAL ABSENCE OF THE HOLY SPIRIT

Four elements are routinely invoked as evidence of the Catholic liturgy's forgetfulness of the Holy Spirit.

First, it is generally held that the Roman tradition knows no public liturgical prayer addressed to the Holy Spirit. In other words, the Third Person of the Trinity is said never to be directly invoked in

[23] See especially the long and detailed book 19 of the *Liber de divinis officiis*, but also book 11.

[24] For more, see Elizabeth A. Dreyer, "An Advent of the Spirit: Medieval Mystics and Saints," and Wanda Zemler-Cizewski's response to this essay, both in *Advents of the Spirit: An Introduction to the Current Study of Pneumatology*, ed. Bradford E. Hinze and D. Lyle Dabney, Marquette Studies in Theology 30 (Milwaukee: Marquette University Press, 2001), 123–62, 163–72. Zemler-Cizewski rightly notes that the liturgical books are an understudied source for the pneumatology of the Latin church; see 170. For more on medieval metaphors for the Spirit, see Elizabeth A. Dreyer's important book *Holy Power, Holy Presence: Rediscovering Medieval Metaphors for the Holy Spirit* (New York: Paulist Press, 2007).

Teresa Berger

Catholic worship. What can one say about this claim and its meaning? The following important factors need to be borne in mind when interpreting the evidence.

1. Liturgical prayer in the Western tradition may not be governed by Spirit-forgetfulness as much as by faithful adherence to a maxim that first surfaces in late fourth-century North African councils (Hippo Regius, 393 CE; Carthage, 397 CE). This maxim, repeated throughout the Middle Ages, insisted that "when standing at the altar, prayer should always be directed to the Father" (*cum altari adsistitur, semper ad Patrem dirigatur oratio*).[25] Even if liturgical rules reveal as much about contestations as about actual practices, this one did govern public prayer in the West for centuries and prevented not only a proliferation of prayers addressed to the Holy Spirit but also to Christ.

2. The fact that the Western tradition lacks prayers addressed to the Holy Spirit does not mean that the Third Person of the Trinity is not invoked in prayers, only that no prayer is addressed to the Spirit. In fact a good number of prayers in which the Holy Spirit is named exist—albeit not as the one addressed. Moreover, the Holy Spirit is addressed in prayers other than those of the presider, e.g., in hymns, sequences, acclamations, antiphons, and responsories.

3. Finally, the claim that the Roman tradition knows no (presider's) prayer addressed to the Holy Spirit is actually only a half-truth (and even less than half true if one considers the Gallican and Mozarabic parts of the Catholic tradition). Scholars have repeatedly noted presidential prayers addressed to the Spirit, from epicletic prayers added to Mass texts including those of the Roman Canon, and invocations of the Spirit in confession and absolution, to the Spirit being directly addressed in devotional prayers of the presider.[26] The Catholic tradition also knows a number of Votive Masses to the Holy Spirit, two of which

---

[25] For more on this Canon, see Burkhard Neunheuser, "*Cum altari adsistitur semper ad patrem dirigatur oratio*: Der Canon 21 des Konzils von Hippo 393. Seine Bedeutung und Nachwirkung," *Augustinianum* 25 (1985): 105–19.

[26] See especially Joaquim O. Bragança "L'Esprit Saint dans l'Euchologie médiévale," in *Le Saint-Esprit dans la Liturgie: Conférences Saint-Serge*, BELS 8, 39–53 (Rome: Edizioni Liturgiche, 1977); and Aimé-Georges Martimort, "L'Esprit Saint dans la liturgie," in *Mirabile laudis canticum: Mélanges liturgiques*, BELS 60, 47–74 (Rome: Edizioni Liturgiche, 1991).

Veni Creator Spiritus

are ascribed to Alcuin (†804), possibly the author of the *Veni Creator Spiritus*, with whom Rabanus Maurus studied.[27]

A second element routinely invoked as evidence of the Catholic liturgy's forgetfulness of the Holy Spirit is the fact that the Roman Canon has no consecratory Spirit-epiclesis. The crucial question is how to interpret this simple fact. The absence of such an epiclesis could be evidence of the sheer antiquity of the Roman Canon, as it predates the fourth-century trinitarian debates on the heels of which consecratory Spirit-epicleses flourished.[28] As Robert Taft has shown, such epicleses were unknown before Cyril/John of Jerusalem, that is, before the end of the fourth century.[29] The Roman tradition's lacuna, in comparison with the Eastern tradition, might thus simply be evidence of the greater antiquity of its eucharistic prayer rather than proof of Spirit-forgetfulness.

A third element routinely invoked as evidence of the Catholic liturgy's forgetfulness of the Holy Spirit is the sense of "lack" or "absence" of the Spirit across a broad range of liturgical realities. Think only of the following: most sacred images of the Holy Spirit are impersonal. No popular pilgrimage sites are linked to the Holy Spirit, as many are, for example, to Mary. The Holy Spirit has not generated the kind of intense devotional practices characteristic of, say, the passion of Christ or those surrounding Christmas. This lack or absence of course is shared with almost all other ecclesial communities in both West and East.

Finally, it is true that *Sacrosanctum Concilium*, Vatican II's Constitution on the Sacred Liturgy, initially made no reference to the Holy Spirit. The Holy Spirit came to be mentioned in the text only after Eastern Catholic bishops criticized this omission in the initial document. This fact must simply be acknowledged.

---

[27] The collect of one of these Votive Masses became known to Anglicans in its English translation as the Collect for Purity. Text in PL 101:446: "Missa de gratia Sancti Spiritus postulanda."

[28] I follow Bragança here; see "L'Esprit Saint dans l'Euchologie médiévale," 40. Klaus Gamber, however, argues that the Roman Canon originally knew an epiclesis; see his "Die Christus- und Geist-Epiklese in der frühen abendländischen Liturgie," in *Praesentia Christi* (Festschrift Johannes Betz), ed. Lothar Lies, 131–50 (Düsseldorf: Patmos, 1984).

[29] See Robert Taft, "From Logos to Spirit: On the Early History of the Epiclesis," in *Gratias agamus: Studien zum eucharistischen Hochgebet* (Festschrift Balthasar Fischer), ed. Andreas Heinz and Heinrich Rennings, 489–502 (Freiburg i.B.: Herder, 1992).

Teresa Berger

So much for the reasons why the Western tradition has seemed Spirit-forgetful. For two of the four reasons, the evidence for Spirit-forgetfulness is much less clear than has generally been assumed. Based on that insight, I offer the following revision of the traditional image of the Catholic tradition as Spirit-forgetful.

RECONFIGURING AN APPARENT ABSENCE: THE HOLY SPIRIT'S ELUSIVE REAL PRESENCE

As we have seen, much hinges on what counts as evidence for the Holy Spirit's presence or absence. The standard places in which liturgical scholars are prone to look for substantiating evidence, namely texts, and especially presidential prayer texts, are important, but they are not everything that matters in liturgy and devotion.

Think only of holy silence (*sacrum silentium*).[30] How do we interpret such silence, which is supposed to be an important part of liturgical celebration? Can such silence be seen as a placeholder, an indication of the truly un-speakable depth of yearning for the coming of the Holy Spirit?[31] In the *Traditio apostolica*, for example, the imposition of hands at ordination is followed by silence, a silence in which all pray in their hearts for the descent of the Spirit (2:4). As liturgical scholars, are we able to read silence as a pointer to the presence of the Spirit?

Harkening back to *Catechism of the Catholic Church* and the four dimensions of the Spirit's work in worship mentioned there (preparing the assembly, recalling and manifesting Christ, rendering salvation present, and making communion bear fruit): if the Holy Spirit gathers the church in worship, this reality is constituted prior to any liturgical texts being prayed. May we not count as evidence of the Spirit's presence the sheer gathering of a community for worship?[32] Maybe the fact that Roman Catholic Christians—more than half of Christians world-

---

[30] See *Sacrosanctum Concilium*, the Constitution on the Sacred Liturgy of Vatican II, no. 30.

[31] I owe this thought to Achille M. Triacca, "Spirito Santo e Liturgia: Linee metodologiche per un approfondimento," in *Lex orandi, lex credendi* (Festschrift C. Vagaggini), ed. Gerardo J. Békés and Giustino Farnedi, Studia Anselmiana 79 (Rome: Editrice Anselmiana, 1980), 133–64, here 157f.

[32] Philipp Harnoncourt argues this beautifully in his "Vom Beten im Heiligen Geist," in *Gott feiern: Theologische Anregung und geistliche Vertiefung zur Feier von Messe und Stundengebet*, ed. Josef G. Plöger, 2d ed. (Freiburg i.B.: Herder, 1980), 100–15, here 108.

Veni Creator Spiritus

wide—have continued to gather to share bread and wine, Sunday after Sunday, for two thousand years, is the most basic and most important witness to the Holy Spirit's presence.[33]

Given such a line of argument, liturgical scholars may have to interrogate their own interpretive lenses. How do we discern the Spirit's liturgical presence *in actu*? Are our categories open and flexible enough to attend to this vibrant, strong, wonderful, fiery, startling holy presence, a presence who "causes holy mischief" (in the words of Amy Laura Hall) in the womb of a young Jewish girl in Nazareth, in the lives of scared disciples at Pentecost, and with the elements of bread and wine whenever we gather for Eucharist? What on earth makes us think that she will not also cause mischief in our scholarly labors, and especially in our feeble attempts to categorize her untamable presence?

One point is essential here: An elusive real presence is something very different from a real absence, even if both such presence and absence render their subject difficult to capture. Can this elusiveness of the possibility of capturing the Spirit be precisely the marker for her presence? The real presence of the Holy Spirit, after all, can only be traced by marking this presence as ultimately unsayable and utterly unrepresentable because it is the presence of the One who ruptures all that can ever be captured in human categories. What the Catholic tradition does affirm, in the face of such an elusive unsayable presence, is that she responds with overwhelming grace to the pleading for her coming. This affirmation brings us back to where we started, namely to the ancient prayer to the Holy Spirit, *Veni Creator Spiritus*. Going back to praying these words may just be the best we can do when pondering the Spirit's elusive real presence in the church.

---

[33] Martimort suggests at the end of his sustained essay that the clearest evidence of the Spirit's presence might after all not be found in liturgical texts but in the continued faithful celebration of the sacraments in the life of the church; see "L'Esprit Saint dans la Liturgie" (n. 26), 74.

Teresa Berger

9. The Holy Spirit and Lutheran Liturgical-Sacramental Worship

Lutheran theology has always rightly placed a central emphasis on the role of the Holy Spirit in the gracious and saving gifts of Word and Sacrament. It is "through the Word and the sacraments, as through instruments," says Article V of the Augsburg Confession, that "the Holy Spirit is given, and the Holy Spirit produces faith, where and when it pleases God, in those who hear the Gospel."[1] Similarly, notes Luther in his Small Catechism, it is the Holy Spirit who "calls, gathers, enlightens, and sanctifies the whole Christian Church on earth" (ibid., 345). Lutherans have always looked to Word and Sacrament as the vehicles by which the Spirit does this.

As is well known among liturgical scholars, throughout the history of Christian worship this role of the Holy Spirit has most often been expressed in the prayer of blessing or sanctification of water in the rite of baptism and in the anaphora, eucharistic prayer, and Great Thanksgiving, either by an invocation (epiclesis) of the Spirit to "come," or by asking the Father to "let come," or "send" the Holy Spirit upon the baptismal waters and upon the bread and wine of the Eucharist and the assembled community itself.[2] With regard to the Eucharist, traditional scholarship has argued that such epicleses have tended to be of two general types: either "consecratory," in

---

ABBREVIATIONS: ELCA, Evangelical Lutheran Church in America; ELW, *Evangelical Lutheran Worship*; ILCW, Inter-Lutheran Commission on Worship; LBW, *Lutheran Book of Worship*; LCMS, Lutheran Church, Missouri Synod; LSB, *Lutheran Service Book*; LW, *Lutheran Worship*; *Prex* and PEER, see n. 5 below.

[1] Theodore Tappert, ed., *The Book of Concord: The Confessions of the Evangelical Lutheran Church* (Philadelphia: Fortress Press, 1959), 31.

[2] See Sebastian Brock, "The Epiklesis in the Antiochene Baptismal Ordines," in *Symposium Syriacum 1972*, OCA 197 (Rome: Pontificio Istituto Orientalia, 1974), 183–218.

The Holy Spirit and Lutheran Liturgical-Sacramental Worship

that they request the Spirit to make, change, show, declare, bless, or sanctify the bread and wine as Christ's Body and Blood; or a "communion" type, in that they ask that the assembled community itself might receive various fruits of Holy Communion by the Spirit's activity.[3] Often they combine both forms. However, as Robert Taft has demonstrated, "originally . . . the epiclesis was primarily a prayer for communion, not for consecration; it was directed at the sanctification of the communicants, not of the gifts. Or, to put it better, perhaps, it was a prayer for the sanctification of the ecclesial communion, not for the sanctification of its sacramental sign, the Holy Communion."[4]

So also the location of such epicleses in the anaphora has varied within the different liturgical traditions of the church. In the West Syrian and Byzantine East the epiclesis was located after the Words of Institution and anamnesis in the prayer. In the Egyptian (or Alexandrian) Eastern tradition two epicleses of the Spirit developed: one before and one after the Words of Institution and anamnesis. While in the non-Roman West, Spirit-epicleses could and did appear in either location, in the Roman West—that is, in the *canon missae* as it evolved in the Roman tradition—no epiclesis of the Spirit was contained whatsoever. Even so, some form of invocation, or epiclesis-type petition, was still present in that God himself (in the *Quam oblationem*) was asked before the Institution Narrative to "bless and approve" the offering and to "let it become" Christ's Body and Blood, and, at a point after the Narrative (in the *Supplices te rogamus*), the fruits of communion were also requested: "We humbly beseech you, almighty God, bid these things be borne by the hands of your angel to your altar on high, in the sight of your divine majesty, that all of us who have received the most holy body and blood of your

---

[3] Gabriele Winkler has argued that there are actually more than these two types, especially when the earliest form seems to be a direct address to the Holy Spirit to come, without specifying either the eucharistic gifts or the fruits of communion reception. See Gabriele Winkler, "Nochmals zu den Anfängen der Epiklese und des Sanctus im Eucharistischen Hochgebet," *Theologische Quartalschrift* 74 (1994): 214–31.

[4] Robert Taft, "From Logos to Spirit: On the Early History of the Epiclesis," in *Gratias agamus: Studien zum eucharistischen Hochgebet* (Festschrift Balthasar Fischer), ed. Andreas Heinz and Heinrich Rennings, 492–93 (Freiburg i.B.: Herder, 1992).

Maxwell E. Johnson

Son by partaking at this altar may be filled with all heavenly blessing and grace."[5]

EPICLESES OF THE HOLY SPIRIT IN LUTHERAN WORSHIP IN NORTH AMERICA

The Holy Spirit has not always been very obvious in Lutheran worship, but has tended to function behind the scene. In the words of Frederick Dale Bruner and William Hordern, the Spirit is "the shy member of the Trinity,"[6] always directing attention to Christ. Lutheran baptismal and eucharistic liturgies have traditionally not tended to use epicleses of the Holy Spirit in their liturgical prayers. Luther's own reforms of the Roman Rite of baptism in 1523 and 1526, and his similar reforms of the Mass in the same years, the *Formula Missae* and *Deutsche Messe*, did not introduce an epiclesis of the Holy Spirit either over the baptismal waters in his famous *Sindflutgebet* or in the consecration of the bread and wine. With the notable exception of the Paul Zellar Strodach and Luther Reed Eucharistic Prayer in the 1958 *Service Book and Hymnal*, which invoked both the Word and Holy Spirit, in the West Syrian position, "to bless us, thy servants, and these thy own gifts of bread and wine, so that we and all who partake thereof may be filled with heavenly benediction and grace,"[7] explicit epicleses of the Holy Spirit in the trial liturgical booklets leading to the publication of the 1978 *Lutheran Book of Worship* were rather new to United States Lutheranism. In *Contemporary Worship 7: Holy Baptism*, the prayer over the baptismal waters read:

> Pour out your Holy Spirit, gracious Father, to make this a water of cleansing. Wash away the sins of all those who enter it, and bring them forth as inheritors of your glorious kingdom.[8]

[5] *Prayers of the Eucharist: Early and Reformed* (= PEER), ed. R. C. D. Jasper and G. J. Cuming, 3d ed. (Collegeville, MN: Liturgical Press, 1987), 165; *Prex eucharistica: Textus e variis liturgiis antiquioribus selecti* (= *Prex*), ed. Anton Hänggi and Irmgard Pahl. Spicilegium friburgense 12 (Fribourg: Éditions universitaires, 1968), 435.

[6] *The Holy Spirit—Shy Member of the Trinity* (Minneapolis: Augsburg, 1984).

[7] *Service Book and Hymnal* (Minneapolis: Augsburg, 1958), 11.

[8] ILCW, *Contemporary Worship 7: Holy Baptism* (Minneapolis: Augsburg, 1974), 27.

The Holy Spirit and Lutheran Liturgical-Sacramental Worship

The eucharistic epiclesis in the West Syrian or Syro-Byzantine position in *Contemporary Worship 2: The Holy Communion* was equally direct:

> Send the power of your Holy Spirit upon us and upon this bread and wine, that we who receive the body and blood of Christ may be his body in the world, living according to his example to bring peace and healing to all [hu]mankind.[9]

So new, in fact, were these baptismal and eucharistic epicleses of the Holy Spirit for some contemporary Lutherans that the work of the ILCW itself was criticized for having departed from traditional Lutheran doctrinal and sacramental theology. Oliver K. Olson, one of the most outspoken critics of both *Holy Baptism* and *The Holy Communion*, wrote:

> The problem of the epiclesis confronts us in two ways. Not only is the ILCW proposing the epiclesis of the Holy Spirit in the communion order, but also an epiclesis of the baptismal water. To begin with the latter, we should be aware that the answer to the catechism question, "How can water produce such great effects," is a re-statement of the resistance of the Western church to the practice of epiclesis. Luther, in re-stating the position of Augustine that it is the Word of God that is the means of grace, not the water, can be said to speak for the Western church. . . . Restoration of the baptismal epiclesis, as planned, will produce an order at odds with Lutheran doctrine on baptism.[10]

Olson continued: "The Eucharistic epiclesis as at baptism corresponds to a Hellenistic personification of the Spirit . . . , detracts from the actual import of the celebration and . . . runs into contradiction with the apostolic Gospel" (ibid., 141). Another critic argued similarly that:

> Repeated use of Spirit prayers displays a failure to take the Risen Lord at his Word. . . . [T]he approach of the gracious God . . . has been liturgically blunted . . . liturgical gears have been shifted and direction reversed (man to God instead of God to man) at the crucial place in the service where God's sacramental initiative ought to be under-

---

[9] ILCW, *Contemporary Worship 2: The Holy Communion* (Minneapolis: Augsburg, 1970), 35.

[10] Oliver K. Olson, "Contemporary Trends in Liturgy Viewed from the Perspective of Classic Lutheran Theology," *Lutheran Quarterly* 26 (1974): 140.

Maxwell E. Johnson

scored. . . . [T[he focus of the [baptismal] prayer . . . is the water rather than the initiate. . . . Is there a parallel here to the ILCW insistence upon making the bread and wine rather than the communicant the chief focus of its Eucharistic epiclesis?[11]

That these critics were heard, at least in part, was reflected in the final shape of the baptismal and eucharistic epicleses in the 1978 *Lutheran Book of Worship*. The baptismal invocation now simply reads:

Pour out your Holy Spirit, so that *those* who *are* baptized may be given new life. Wash away the sin of *all those* who *are* cleansed by this water and bring *them* forth as *inheritors* of your glorious kingdom.[12]

And the epiclesis in the first optional eucharistic prayer reads:

Send now, we pray, your Holy Spirit, the spirit of our Lord and of his resurrection, that we who receive the Lord's body and blood may live to the praise of your glory and receive our inheritance with all your saints in light. Amen. Come, Holy Spirit. (Ibid., 223)

The second option merely recasts this as:

Send now, we pray, your Holy Spirit, that we and all who share in this bread and cup may be united in the fellowship of the Holy Spirit, may enter the fullness of the kingdom of heaven, and may receive our inheritance with all your saints in light. Amen. Come, Holy Spirit. (Ibid.)

Eucharistic Prayer III is a modern reworking of the Strodach-Reed prayer noted above ("with your Word and Holy Spirit to bless us, your servants, and these your own gifts of bread and wine") and Eucharistic Prayer IV is based on the anaphora in the so-called *Apostolic Tradition*, the epiclesis of which is translated as: "Send your Spirit upon these gifts of your Church; gather into one all who share this bread and wine; fill us with your Holy Spirit to establish our faith in truth . . ." (ibid., 226).

[11] Robert Hughes, "CW 7: A Critique," *The Mount Airy Parish Practice Notebook* 10 (June 1976), 2. I owe this reference to Jeffrey Truscott, *The Reform of Baptism and Confirmation in American Lutheranism* (Lanham, MD: The Scarecrow Press, 2003), 78.

[12] LBW, Ministers' Edition (Minneapolis: Augsburg, 1978), 309.

The Holy Spirit and Lutheran Liturgical-Sacramental Worship

Apart from the possibility of using the Institution Narrative by itself after the *Sanctus*, the other option in LBW was a short pre-Institution Narrative prayer, based on a Church of Sweden model, which contains the following invocation: "Send now your Holy Spirit into our hearts, that we may receive our Lord with a living faith as he comes to us in his holy supper. Amen. Come, Lord Jesus."[13] Along similar lines, the 1982 Lutheran Church, Missouri Synod worship book, *Lutheran Worship*, also included this type of "Swedish prayer" before the Lord's Prayer and Words of Institution in the two settings of Divine Service II, asking God to "send your Holy Spirit into our hearts that he may establish in us a living faith and prepare us joyfully to remember our Redeemer and receive him who comes to us in his body and blood."[14]

The state of Spirit epicleses in baptismal and eucharistic liturgies is little different in the more recent Lutheran liturgical resources, the 2006 *Evangelical Lutheran Worship* of the Evangelical Lutheran Church in America and the 2006 *Lutheran Service Book* of the Lutheran Church, Missouri Synod. The only real difference, in fact, is that the former provides several more examples of basically the same approach.

The baptismal texts in LSB can be dispensed with rather quickly here. No epiclesis of the Holy Spirit appears in the baptismal rites, though in the second option, based directly on Luther's 1523 *Betbüchlein*, a version of his *Sintflutgebet* is employed. This does ask that those to be baptized would be blessed "with true faith by the Holy Spirit."[15]

With regard to a Spirit-epiclesis in the Eucharist, however, LSB is even less explicit than was LW:

---

[13] Ibid., 70. What is most interesting is that the Swedish prayer upon which this was based says explicitly: "Send your Spirit in our hearts that he might work in us a living faith. Sanctify also through your Spirit this bread and wine, fruits of the earth and the toil of people which we bear unto you, so that we, through them, partake of the true body and blood of our Lord Jesus Christ." The text is in *Baptism and Eucharist: Ecumenical Convergence in Celebration*, ed. M. Thurian and G. Wainwright (Grand Rapids, MI: Eerdmans, 1983), 141. The prayer continues after the Institution Narrative with an anamnesis and concluding doxology.

[14] LCMS, *Lutheran Worship* (St. Louis, MO: Concordia, 1982), 171.

[15] LCMS, LSB, *Agenda* (St. Louis, MO: Concordia, 2006), 14.

Maxwell E. Johnson

Divine Service, Settings 1–2: Gathered in his name and the remembrance of Jesus, we beg You, O Lord, to forgive, renew, and strengthen us with Your Word and Holy Spirit.[16]

Divine Service, Setting 4 (Pentecost only): Pour out your Holy Spirit upon your gathered people, that, faithfully eating and drinking the body and blood of Your Son, we may go forth to proclaim his salvation to the ends of the earth. (Ibid., 268)

The Spirit-epicleses in the prayers from all of the modern Lutheran books above, with some exceptions here and there, are ambiguous both liturgically and theologically. In many it is not clear what role, if any, the epiclesis actually plays in the particular sacramental event in question, or even upon what or whom the Holy Spirit is being invoked. In the majority of cases the baptismal epiclesis seems to be for the baptized, not the water, and in the various eucharistic prayers, for the communicants and the fruits of communion, not the bread and wine. It could be argued that with phrases like "Come, Holy Spirit," without specifying any place, person, or thing, Lutherans are in touch with a very archaic epicletic theology such as we see in the classic New Testament invocation *Mara natha!* and in the baptismal and eucharistic epicleses in the third-century Syrian Acts of the Apostles, though it is doubtful that the work of Sebastian Brock and Gabriele Winkler on the early Syrian epicleses played much role in the formulation of these texts.[17] Nevertheless, there is something rather primitive about the formulation of these various texts—either as invoking the Holy Spirit for the baptized or for the communicants—corresponding to Robert Taft's comment above that "originally . . . the epiclesis was primarily a prayer for communion, not for consecration." At the same time, in light of contemporary ecumenical liturgical scholarship, one must ask whether Lutheran theology and liturgy might not be in a position today to embrace a more explicit consecratory form of epiclesis as well.

RETHINKING SPIRIT EPICLESES IN A LUTHERAN CONTEXT

Oliver K. Olson claimed that Luther's liturgical reform testified to "the resistance of the Western church to the practice of epiclesis. Luther, in restating the position of Augustine that it is the Word of

---

[16] LCMS, LSB, *Altar Edition* (St. Louis, MO: Concordia, 2006), 165.
[17] See nn. 2 and 3 above.

The Holy Spirit and Lutheran Liturgical-Sacramental Worship

God that is the means of grace, not the water, can be said to speak for the Western church." But, of course, such a statement is not borne out by any evidence whatsoever, and Olson's position is hopelessly misleading and ultimately deceptive. Only if one takes the Roman *canon missae* as the sole witness to eucharistic praying in the West can one perhaps make the claim that the "West" resists a Spirit epiclesis in the eucharistic liturgy. Even so, as we have seen, the Roman Canon itself has two paragraphs that are clearly petitionary, invocative, and hence epicletic in nature. Also, some of the numerous non-Roman Western Gallican and Mozarabic eucharistic prayers do in fact have explicit epicleses of the Holy Spirit (see *Prex*, 498; PEER, 153). Thus the thesis that the West is against any kind of epiclesis is simply wrong. One prayer from the Roman tradition is hardly the totality of the West, and even that prayer has what might be called an epicletic structure. With regard to baptismal liturgy, Spirit epicleses on the baptismal waters are as old as Tertullian's *De baptismo*, and their existence should be obvious from the multiple liturgical witnesses of both East and West through the Middle Ages and into the present.[18] Luther, in not providing Spirit epicleses in his baptismal and eucharistic reforms, did not simply restate some kind of Western resistance, since no obvious Western resistance existed to begin with.

In 1989 Bryan Spinks published a significant essay entitled "Berakah, Anaphoral Theory, and Luther." One part of this study was a critique of the overreliance on, and dominance of, the West Syrian or Syro-Byzantine pattern of eucharistic praying in contemporary ecumenical liturgical reform and renewal. As Spinks rightly noted, this particular anaphoral structure has been viewed "not only [as] the perfect and only paradigm for authentic Eucharistic prayers," but also that it "can be traced back directly to the Jewish euchology used by Jesus at the Last Supper, and implied by him in the words 'Do this in remembrance of me.'"[19] I will come back to this below. Another part of Spinks's short study has to do precisely with the question of the epiclesis in Lutheran liturgy. Although, as noted, Luther's liturgical reforms of the Roman Rite did not introduce an epiclesis of the Holy

---

[18] Tertullian, *De baptismo*, 4. Compare the blessing of water in the Gelasian Sacramentary in *Documents of the Baptismal Liturgy*, ed. E. C. Whitaker and Maxwell E. Johnson, 3d ed. (London: SPCK, 2003), 233–34.

[19] Bryan D. Spinks, "Berakah, Anaphoral Theory, and Luther," *Lutheran Quarterly* 3 (1989): 267–80, here 279.

Maxwell E. Johnson

Spirit, Luther did relate the Holy Spirit theologically to baptism and Eucharist. In his 1526 *Sermon against the Fanatics* he wrote: "For as soon as Christ says 'This is My Body,' it is his body through the word and power of the Holy Spirit."[20] Regarding this, Spinks argued that "an epiklesis may not be so difficult for Lutheran theology as some have maintained" (ibid.). Similarly, Regin Prenter, in his classic study of the role of the Holy Spirit in Luther's theology, writes that "the Holy Spirit makes the crucified and risen Christ such a present and redeeming reality to us that faith in Christ and conformity to Christ spring directly from this reality."[21] According to Prenter, the Holy Spirit, for Luther, "takes the crucified and risen Christ out of the remoteness of history and heavenly glory and places him as a living and redeeming reality in the midst of our life with its suffering, inner conflict, and death" (53–54). Indeed, if in Lutheran theology the Holy Spirit does all this, then, grounded as Lutheran theology is in Word and Sacrament as the very "means of grace" by which the Spirit works, it would seem that the church's liturgical rites cry out for such an explicit liturgical textual acknowledgment of the Spirit's role and work.

In relationship to the Lutheran epicletic texts we looked at above, it is certainly clear that Lutheran liturgy in the United States has witnessed a more explicit recovery of the role and work of the Holy Spirit in its baptismal and eucharistic rites. But must Lutheran liturgy be characterized by epicletic texts that remain theologically and liturgically somewhat ambiguous? If, in the words of Prenter, it is "the Holy Spirit [who] makes the crucified and risen Christ . . . a present and redeeming reality to us," then why not say so liturgically by petitioning the Spirit to do that sacramentally?

Other Lutherans throughout history have not been as reluctant as have the framers of LBW, ELW, and LSB to embrace a more consecratory-type epiclesis within, at least, the eucharistic liturgy. Taking its structural cue from the *Quam oblationem* of the Roman *Canon missae*, for example, the Pfalz-Neuburg Church Order of 1543 contained the following consecratory petition immediately before the Institution Narrative:

> O Lord Jesus Christ, Thou only true Son of the Living God, who hast given Thy body unto bitter death for us all, and hast shed Thy blood

---

[20] As cited in ibid., 277.
[21] Regin Prenter, *Spiritus Creator* (Philadelphia: Fortress, 1953), 52–53.

The Holy Spirit and Lutheran Liturgical-Sacramental Worship

for the forgiveness of our sins, and hast bidden all Thy disciples to eat Thy Body and to drink Thy Blood in remembrance of Thy death; we bring before Thy Divine Majesty these Thy gifts of bread and wine and beseech thee to hallow and bless them by Thy divine grace, goodness and power and ordain (*schaffen*) that this bread and wine may be (*sei*) Thy Body and Blood, even unto eternal life to all who eat and drink thereof.[22]

Influenced by this, the *Kassel Agenda* of 1896 contained a similar petition, but addressed God the Father rather than directly petitioning Christ:

Almighty God, heavenly Father, who hast delivered Thy Son, our Lord Jesus Christ, into death, and hast ordained that His body and blood be our food unto eternal life, we bring these Thy gifts before Thy divine Majesty, Thy own from Thine own, and pray Thee to hallow and bless them through Thy divine mercy and power, that this bread and this cup may be the body and blood of our Lord Jesus Christ for all who eat and drink of the same, and that Thou wouldst let them be blessings unto eternal life for them. . . . [23]

Prior to the wider "recovery" of the eucharistic prayer among North American Lutherans from the 1958 *Service Book and Hymnal* (the Zeller Strodach-Reed prayer) and into the 1978 LBW and 2006 ELW, what Lutheran attempts at eucharistic praying there were placed an epiclesis of various constructions *before* the Institution Narrative.

Here I find Spinks's critique of the overreliance on, and dominance of, the West Syrian or Syro-Byzantine pattern of eucharistic praying in contemporary ecumenical liturgical reform and renewal compelling and important. With the exception of the eucharistic prayers, in addition to the *canon missae*, in the *Missale Romanum* of Paul VI, and Eucharistic Prayer C in the 1979 Episcopal Book of Common Prayer, one

[22] Luther Reed, *The Lutheran Liturgy* (Philadelphia: Muhlenberg, 1947), 635; German text in Peter Brunner, "Zur Lehre vom Gottesdienst der im Namen Jesu versammelten Gemeinde," in *Leiturgia. Handbuch des evangelischen Gottesdienstes*, ed. Karl Ferdinand Müller and Walter Blankenburg (Kassel, Germany: Johannes Stauda Verlag, 1954) 1:351–52.

[23] Text cited in Peter Brunner, *Worship in the Name of Jesus*, trans. M. H. Bertram (St. Louis, MO: Concordia, 1968), 301; German text in Brunner, "Zur Lehre," 1:351–52.

Maxwell E. Johnson

looks in vain for contemporary eucharistic prayers in North America that follow an alternative anaphoral pattern. Of course, even classic alternatives exist, most notably the one reflecting what has come to be called the Alexandrian or Egyptian anaphoral structure. While the current texts of that tradition, reflected in the Greek and Coptic anaphoras of St. Mark,[24] contain double epicleses (one before and one after the Institution Narrative), many scholars agree that the original Egyptian epiclesis, based on the "full is heaven and earth" in the Sanctus, was a short invocation of the Holy Spirit to "fill" the eucharistic gifts, immediately before the Institution Narrative, which is attached by the Greek word *hoti* ("for" or "because"). As this tradition developed, however, the anaphora came to include either a single expanded epiclesis prior to the Institution Narrative, or, through Syrian influence, the addition of a second epiclesis following the Institution Narrative and anamnesis, with the explicit consecratory focus now located in the second.[25] It is this second epiclesis, in the location of the single epiclesis in the West Syrian or Syro-Byzantine anaphora, that Hans Lietzmann referred to as a "Fremdkörper,"[26] a "foreign body," in the prayer. Two fourth-century Egyptian or Alexandrian anaphoral fragments—the *Dêr Balyzeh Papyrus* and the *Louvain Coptic Papyrus*—provide examples of the single expanded epiclesis of the Holy Spirit before the Institution Narrative.

> *The Dêr Balyzeh Papyrus*: Fill also with the glory from (you), and vouchsafe to send down your Holy Spirit upon these creatures (and) make the bread the body of our (Lord and) Savior Jesus Christ, and the cup the blood . . . of our Lord and . . . (PEER, 80; *Prex*, 125)

[24] *Prex*, 101–15; for an English text see PEER, 59–66.

[25] See R.-G. Coquin, "L'Anaphore alexandrine de saint Marc," *Le Muséon* 82 (1969): 329ff.; C. H. Roberts, and B. Capelle, *An Early Euchologium: The Deir-Balyzeh Papyrus Enlarged and Re-edited* (Louvain: Bureaux de Muséon, 1949), 52; J. van Haelst, "Une nouvelle reconstitution du papyrus liturgique de Deir Balyzeh," *Ephemerides theologicae lovanienses* 45 (1969): 210; A. Baumstark, "Die Anaphora von Tmuis und ihre Bearbeitung durch den hl. Serapion," *Römische Quartalschrift* 18 (1904): 132–34; and Maxwell E. Johnson, *The Prayers of Sarapion of Thmuis: A Literary, Liturgical and Theological Analysis*, OCA 249 (Rome: Pontificio Istituto Orientale, 1995), 270–71.

[26] Hans Lietzmann, *Mass and Lord's Supper: A Study in the History of the Liturgy* (Leiden: Brill, 1979), 63.

The Holy Spirit and Lutheran Liturgical-Sacramental Worship

The *Louvain Coptic Papyrus* even weaves an anamnesis into this pre-Institution position:

> Heaven and earth are full of that glory wherewith you glorified us through your only-begotten Son Jesus Christ, the first-born of all creation, sitting at the right hand of your majesty in heaven, who will come to judge the living and the dead. We make the remembrance of his death, offering to you your creatures, this bread and cup. We pray and beseech you to send out over them your Holy Spirit, the Paraclete, from heaven . . . to make (?) the bread the body of Christ and the cup the blood of Christ of the new covenant. (PEER, 81; *Prex*, 140)

One is struck here by how closely parallel the epicleses in the Pfalz-Neuburg Church Order of 1543 and the *Kassel Agenda* of 1896 are to the formulation of the *Louvain Coptic Papyrus*, including both anamnetic and offering language, even without any possible access to such a text at the time of their compilation. Indeed, the Egyptian anaphoral structure as a pattern for Lutheran eucharistic praying has been appealed to before. In 1947, for example, Arthur Carl Piepkorn composed a eucharistic prayer with the following petition before the Institution Narrative:

> Send down upon us the grace of Thy Holy Spirit, and through Thy Holy Word vouchsafe to bless and sanctify these thy gifts and creatures of bread and wine, that they may be unto us the Body and the Blood of the same Thy most dearly beloved Son, our Lord Jesus Christ, Who, the same night . . . [27]

The real proponent of what we might call the "Egyptian connection," however, was Peter Brunner in his classic study *Worship in the Name of Jesus*, which appeared in German in 1954, but not in English until fourteen years later. For Brunner, while he clearly respected the Syro-Byzantine anaphoral pattern, especially because of its creedal and overall historical plan of salvation structure, the ideal place for a Western epiclesis is before the Words of Christ.[28] Brunner concludes

[27] A. C. Piepkorn, "The Eucharistic Prayer," *Una Sancta* 7, no. 3 (1947): 10–12.
[28] Peter Brunner, *Worship in the Name of Jesus*, trans. M. H. Bertram (St. Louis, MO: Concordia, 1968), 306: "We recognize . . . that the words of institution spoken in Christ's stead are, by the power of Christ, the means of consecration in Holy Communion, in the entire act commanded by Christ. The work of the

Maxwell E. Johnson

that "since the work of the Spirit does not complete the work of Christ in the consecration but only accompanies it cooperatively, an epiclesis petitioning for consecration must stand, in our Western tradition, before the words of institution, if it is to be used in any form whatsoever" (ibid., 307). And Brunner himself provided the following as an appropriate epicletic text:

> Assembled in His name and in His memory, we pray Thee for His saving presence in this sacred Meal. We place this bread and this wine, Thy gifts, before Thy countenance, heavenly Father, and pray Thee to consecrate and to bless them through the power of the Holy Spirit, that this bread be the body of our Lord Jesus Christ and this wine be His blood, as we now administer His own Testament according to His command. (Ibid., 310)

While Brunner's approach may not be above criticism, especially in light of contemporary scholarship on the earliest anaphoral texts,[29] he did provide a way for Lutheran eucharistic worship both to respect its Augustinian-Western heritage of the central importance of the Word

---

Spirit on bread and wine takes place simultaneously with this event, in which bread and wine, by virtue of Christ's institution, become bearers of His body and blood. Here the work of the Spirit enters the work of Christ, ministering and mediating. May this simultaneousness and this cooperation of the Spirit's work, dependent on Christ's institution, be expressed by the position of the epiclesis in the liturgy? The simultaneousness cannot be expressed. Our language is bound to the before and the after. The liturgical language, too, must express simultaneous events in a succession of sentences. Only the proximity of the epiclesis to the words of institution can intimate that both the implored work of the Spirit and the real presence of Christ take place in one pneumatic 'now.'" Note the similarities between Brunner's theological approach and that of Cipriano Vagaggini, who was himself responsible for the three additional eucharistic prayers of the *Missale Romanum* of Pope Paul VI. I owe this reference to Paul Bradshaw's essay elsewhere in this volume.

[29] See Bryan D. Spinks, *Addai and Mari—The Anaphora of the Apostles: A Text for Students*, Grove Liturgical Study 24 (Cambridge: Grove Books, 1980); Gabriele Winkler, "A New Witness to the Missing Institution Narrative," in *Studia liturgica diversa: Essays in Honor of Paul F. Bradshaw*, ed. L. E. Phillips and M. E. Johnson, 117–28 (Portland, OR: Pastoral Press, 2004); and Robert Taft, "Mass Without Consecration? The Historic Agreement on the Eucharist between the Catholic Church and the Assyrian Church of the East Promulgated 26 October 2001," *Worship* 77 (2003): 482–509.

The Holy Spirit and Lutheran Liturgical-Sacramental Worship

in sacramental theology, so strongly emphasized by critics of North American Lutheran liturgical materials like Oliver K. Olson, and to consider an alternative pattern by which Lutherans might embrace other eucharistic prayer structures from the wider liturgical tradition, including that of the West, as well as patterns in its own limited tradition. Indeed, if, as Luther said, "as soon as Christ says 'This is My Body,' it is his body through the word and power of the Holy Spirit," the Lutheran position for a Spirit-epiclesis may well be, as Brunner claims, before and not after the Institution Narrative. In this way the power of the Holy Spirit through which Christ speaks the Word, and by which the bread and wine are his Body and Blood, is given clear liturgical acknowledgment and expression. But such invocation—though not the Holy Spirit, of course—is subordinated and, hence, bound to the *verba Christi* themselves, which remain the vehicle of the Holy Spirit's work of uniting and joining together both bread and cup with Christ's Body and Blood, and the communicants themselves with Christ and one another through them.

Apart from Piepkorn's 1947 version of a Lutheran eucharistic prayer with a pre-Institution epiclesis, the only other North American Lutheran attempt at a eucharistic prayer with a similar pattern was that of Robert Jenson in a volume of *Lutheran Quarterly* entirely dedicated to providing a commentary and critique of then-current experimental Lutheran liturgical resources.[30] Such an attempt must have died the death of neglect among those eventually producing LBW, though Jenson's first model, of the Syro-Byzantine type, became Eucharistic Prayer 2 there. What I have always found fascinating, however, is that then as now the liturgical tradition of the Church of Sweden has a euchological heritage that appears to be quite consistent with what we have seen in the Pfalz-Neuburg Church Order of 1543, the *Kassel Agenda* of 1896, the 1879 *Agenda* of the Lutheran Church in Bavaria, and the work of Brunner and others. While, unlike their North American counterparts, the eucharistic prayers of the Lutheran Church of Sweden[31] are not limited to one anaphoral structure, five of its seven alternative texts have a pre-Institution epiclesis, some of which (like Prayer G) are clearly "consecratory" in content, and two

[30] Robert Jenson, "Liturgy of the Spirit," *Lutheran Quarterly* 26 (1974): 189–203.

[31] http://www.svenskakyrkan.se/gudstjanstbanken/service_book /14gudstjanstens_alternativamoment.htm.

Maxwell E. Johnson

of which even have offering language (Prayers A and D) akin to the prayers for the Preparation of the Gifts in the Missal of Paul VI:

> *Eucharistic Prayer A*: Let Your Holy Spirit come into our hearts to en-lighten us with a living faith. Sanctify by your Spirit this bread and wine, which earth has given and human hands have made. Here we offer them to you, that through them we may partake of the true body and blood of our Lord Jesus Christ.

> *Eucharistic Prayer D*: Send your holy Spirit into our hearts that he may in us kindle a living faith. By your Holy Spirit, bless these gifts of bread and wine and make them holy, fruits of the world and work of human hands that we offer to you. We thank you that through them you give us a sharing in the body and blood of Christ. . . . *After the Institution Narrative and Anamnesis*: Unite us all, by the power of the Holy Spirit, into one body, and make us a perfect and living sacrifice through Christ. Through him and with him and in him, all glory and honour belong to you, God, the Father Almighty in the unity of the Holy Spirit, forever and ever.

> *Eucharistic Prayer E*: Send your Holy Spirit and bless these gifts of bread and wine and make them holy. We thank you that through them you give us a share in the body and blood of Christ.

> *Eucharistic Prayer F*: Send your Spirit on us and on these gifts that we may come to share in the heavenly bread and the cup of salvation that is the body and blood of Christ.

> *Eucharistic Prayer G*: Send your Spirit on us and on these gifts of bread and wine that they may be for us the body and blood of Christ.

The only other place in contemporary liturgical materials I am aware of where a similar anaphoral structure is present is in the liturgical book *Common Worship* (2000) of the Church of England. There, out of its own eight eucharistic prayers in what is called "Use One," a total of four fall in this category (prayers A, B, C, and E).[32] What is intriguing about these Church of Sweden and Church of England eucharistic prayers, together with the theological position of Brunner and the small but significant Lutheran heritage in this context, is how close all of this is to the often maligned structure of the eucharistic prayers

---

[32] *Common Worship: Services and Prayers for the Church of England* (London: Church House Publishing, 2000), 184–93, 196–97.

The Holy Spirit and Lutheran Liturgical-Sacramental Worship

of the Missal of Paul VI, where the emphasis on a pre-Institution epiclesis is so strong that it influenced the way texts like the anaphora from *Apostolic Tradition* 4 and the anaphora called "Egyptian Basil" were used to compose Eucharistic Prayers 2 and 4, respectively. One may certainly criticize changing the structure of classic liturgical texts like these in order to conform to a particular structure and theology (which, by the way, all our liturgical traditions have done in one way or another), yet I suspect that the reason why this aspect of the Roman eucharistic prayers has often been criticized is because it does not correspond to the contemporary hegemony of the Syro-Byzantine anaphoral pattern. This pattern is viewed as "the perfect and only paradigm for authentic Eucharistic prayers . . . traced back directly to the Jewish euchology used by Jesus at the Last Supper, and implied by him in the words 'Do this in remembrance of me.'"[33] And yet this structure, with some obvious affinity to the early Alexandrian liturgical tradition, is itself also clearly a legitimate and self-consciously Western liturgical structure with a legitimate and orthodox theology of the Holy Spirit, which should be ecumenically fruitful in the West for Lutherans, Anglicans, and Roman Catholics. How surprising and lamentable, especially in light of developments in *Common Worship* and in contemporary Swedish eucharistic euchology, that not one example of such a prayer exists in something like ELW.

THE RITUALIZATION OF THE GIFT OF THE HOLY SPIRIT IN BAPTISM AND RITES OF CONFIRMATION

The epiclesis in Lutheran baptismal and eucharistic worship is not the only place to look for a relationship between the Holy Spirit and Lutheran worship. The postbaptismal rites in LBW, ELW, and LSB provide a fascinating look at what we might call a contemporary migration of the Spirit among Lutherans. Before the process of producing those worship books began, almost all Lutheran baptismal rites concluded with a blessing prayer with laying on of hands based on the traditional Western postbaptismal anointing prayer. This was first attested by Ambrose of Milan and revised by Luther in his 1526 *Taufbüchlein* to accompany the giving of the garment: "The almighty God and Father of our Lord Jesus Christ, who hath regenerated thee through water and the Holy Ghost and hath forgiven thee all thy sin,

---

[33] Spinks, "Berakah, Anaphoral Theory, and Luther," 279.

Maxwell E. Johnson

strengthen thee with his grace to life everlasting. Amen. Peace be with thee. *Answer*. Amen."[34]

Often defended by appeal to Luther's 1523 *Taufbüchlein*,[35] the rite called "Holy Baptism" in the LBW restored for the majority of Lutherans in North America many of the traditional rites and ceremonies of the classic Western baptismal rite omitted in the later stages of liturgical revision during the Protestant Reformation. What is by far the most notable distinction between this rite and Luther's 1523 rite, however, was the addition of the following postbaptismal rite at the very place where Luther had originally retained the traditional Western postbaptismal prayer and anointing:

> *The minister lays both hands on the head of each of the baptized and prays for the Holy Spirit*:
>
> P. God, the Father of our Lord Jesus Christ, we give you thanks for freeing your sons and daughters from the power of sin and for raising them up to a new life through this holy sacrament. Pour your Holy Spirit upon ___name___: the spirit of wisdom and understanding, the spirit of counsel and might, the spirit of knowledge and the fear of the Lord, the spirit of joy in your presence.
>
> C. Amen.
>
> The minister marks the sign of the cross on the forehead of each of the baptized. Oil prepared for this purpose may be used. As the sign of the cross is made, the minister says:
>
> P. ___name___, child of God, you have been sealed by the Holy Spirit and marked with the cross of Christ forever.
>
> The sponsor or the baptized responds: "Amen."[36]

Here in the LBW baptismal rite, the traditional Roman confirmation prayer for the sevenfold gift of the Spirit and the chrismation from the

---

[34] Martin Luther, *The Order of Baptism Newly Revised, 1526*, in *Luther's Works* 53, ed. U. Leupold (Philadelphia: Fortress, 1965), 109.

[35] For a comprehensive and detailed account of the modern development and revision of the rites of Christian initiation in North American Lutheranism see Jeffrey Truscott, *The Reform of Baptism and Confirmation in American Lutheranism*, foreword by Maxwell E. Johnson (Lanham, MD: Scarecrow Press, 2003).

[36] LBW, Minister's Edition, 311.

The Holy Spirit and Lutheran Liturgical-Sacramental Worship

Gelasian Sacramentary—reformulated, as in the current Roman rite of confirmation itself, in language more akin to the single postbaptismal chrismation of the Byzantine Rite to refer to being "sealed by the Holy Spirit"—is rather obvious. Similarly, the rite appears to express an explicit conferral of the Holy Spirit in asking for a postbaptismal "pouring of the Holy Spirit" upon the newly baptized. The language of the formula for the signing and optional anointing in the LBW is rather unclear and suggests several possible interpretations. Because the prayer refers to the sealing of the Holy Spirit in the perfect tense (i.e., "you have been sealed . . ."), for example, whether baptism or the hand-laying prayer has supposedly constituted this "sealing" is not certain.

Since Lutheran theology has always been adamant in its assertion that baptism in the trinitarian name, with or without additional rites and gestures, constitutes full Christian initiation in water and the Holy Spirit, the theological question is what LBW intended by a postbaptismal rite such as this. In fact, it is precisely this postbaptismal rite that was cited as problematic for the official adoption of the LBW baptismal rite within the LCMS. In the LCMS "Report and Recommendations of the Special Hymnal Review Committee," the following critical note appeared in relationship to this unit: "Both the rubric and the prayer imply that the Spirit comes after (apart from?) the new life through this sacrament. One wonders why the traditional prayer with its clear connection of water and the Spirit was dropped for this doubtful one."[37]

Questioning even an optional postbaptismal anointing, the LCMS prepared and accepted a final rite, appearing in LW, containing a postbaptismal section that consisted of Luther's own 1526 revision of the anointing prayer with hand-laying followed by the giving of the baptismal garment and a lighted candle. What LW did, therefore, was to restore partially the postbaptismal rites and formulas of Luther's 1523 *Taufbüchlein*, without, however, the anointing. Only then does the baptismal group assemble before the altar for a concluding prayer and welcome (LW, 203–4).[38]

[37] LCMS, "Report and Recommendations of the Special Hymnal Review Committee" (December 1977), 27.

[38] It is instructive at this point to note what happened to this rite in ELW (590–91).

Maxwell E. Johnson

The hand-laying prayer is clearly distinct from the one that appeared at this place in LBW. While the LBW prayer made no reference to John 3:5 or Titus 3:5, and in asking for a postbaptismal "pouring of the Holy Spirit" upon the newly baptized could be interpreted as asking for a postbaptismal conferral of the Holy Spirit, the version of the prayer in ELW is perfectly clear. For ELW baptism and Holy Spirit go together, and the prayer not only acknowledges that but asks simply that the newly baptized might now be "sustained" with that gift already received. Similarly, because the formula for consignation or anointing still refers to the sealing of the Holy Spirit in the perfect tense ("you have been sealed . . ."), the particular wording of the hand-laying prayer in ELW now makes clear that what has constituted this "sealing" of the Holy Spirit is baptism itself. Hence this unit, together with the giving of the garment and candle, is best interpreted as constituting what the current Roman Catholic initiation rites call "explanatory rites," or what the ELCA statement on the practice of Word and Sacrament calls "symbolic acts,"[39] that is, acts or rites that merely explain, underscore, or symbolically express further what the church believes happens and is given in baptism itself.

One might conclude reasonably that in the particular revision of the LBW hand-laying prayer in ELW the theological concerns expressed by the LCMS have now been adequately addressed. Instead, the LCMS has again produced its own liturgical resources, with the LSB and *Agenda* also appearing in 2006. Since the LCMS and the ELCA had both been involved with *Welcome to Christ*, a series of study and ritual books for the adult catechumenate, and with the 1999 African American Lutheran liturgical resource *This Far by Faith*, in which the baptismal rite, while containing some culturally specific adaptations, was essentially that of LBW, this development is to be viewed as most unfortunate.[40] And while the baptismal rite in the *Agenda*—now with prebaptismal exorcism, Luther's Flood Prayer, optional anointing, garment, and candle—more closely resembles Luther's 1523 *Taufbüchlein*

---

[39] *The Use of the Means of Grace: A Statement on the Practice of Word and Sacrament* (Minneapolis: Augsburg Fortress Press, 1997), 33.

[40] *Welcome to Christ: A Lutheran Catechetical; Welcome to Christ: A Lutheran Introduction to the Catechumenate;* and *Welcome to Christ: Lutheran Rites for the Catechumenate* (all Minneapolis: Augsburg Fortress Press, 1997). *This Far by Faith* (Minneapolis: Augsburg Fortress Press, 1999), 64–68.

The Holy Spirit and Lutheran Liturgical-Sacramental Worship

than did LW, we can lament that the two major Lutheran bodies in the United States cannot even share the same baptismal rite!

Some mention must be made here of the question of confirmation in Lutheran worship, especially because of its traditional associations with both baptism and the Holy Spirit. ELW, in a rite entitled "Affirmation of Baptism," provides several different options for its use (1) in confirmation; (2) at the beginning of one's participation in a community of faith, i.e., reception into membership; (3) in renewed participation in a faith community; and (4) at a time of a significant life passage (ELW, 234). In all these options the rite contains a presentation of the candidate(s), the renunciation of evil, and the profession of faith from the baptismal rite, followed by prayers of intercession, a short address to those making the affirmation and their response, and a blessing with a laying on of hands. This consists of a version of the postbaptismal hand-laying prayer with the phrase "sustain <u>name</u> with the gift of your Holy Spirit" replaced by "stir up in <u>name</u> the gift of your Holy Spirit." The following prayer with hand-laying, reserved to confirmation alone in LBW, is provided in ELW as an option to the above prayer:

> Father in heaven, for Jesus' sake, stir up in <u>   name   </u> the gift of your Holy Spirit; confirm *his/her* faith, guide *his/her* life, empower *him/her* in *his/her* serving, give *him/her* patience in suffering, and bring *him/her* to everlasting life. (ELW, 236)

Lutherans and Episcopalians alike have viewed such "affirmation of baptism" rites as repeatable rites adaptable to a variety of circumstances marking significant transition moments in life. They do this "by connecting these significant transitions with the baptismal understanding of our dying and rising with Christ. These rites mark moments when the faith given in Baptism finds new expression, and the spiritual gifts given in Baptism are stirred up to meet new challenges" (LBW, Minister's Edition, 9). As such, "confirmation" is only one of many possible applications.

Theologically speaking, in the ELW confirmation is not understood to be part of the rites of Christian initiation per se but as a rite in which, after a period of catechetical instruction, the "confirmands" publicly affirm God's past baptismal action on their behalf. Among Lutherans, even the term "confirmation" tends not to be interpreted in a liturgical or ritual manner but, consistent with classic Lutheran theology, in catechetical ways. That is, confirmation is seen less as a

Maxwell E. Johnson

particular rite than—as current ELCA policy states—"a pastoral and educational *ministry* of the church that helps the baptized through Word and Sacrament to identify more deeply with the Christian community and participate more fully in its mission." Or, as the introduction to the rite in LBW said, "confirmation marks the completion of the congregation's program of confirmation ministry, a period of instruction in the Christian faith as confessed in the teachings of the Lutheran Church."[41] Seen in this way, the ELW rite of confirmation, while including hand-laying and prayer for the stirring up of the gift of the Holy Spirit, is to be interpreted not as an initiatory rite completing baptism, "for Baptism is already complete through God's work of joining us to Christ and his body, the Church."[42]

The LCMS, as noted above, rejected the baptismal rite of LBW partly because its postbaptismal rites supposedly separated the gift of the Holy Spirit from the water bath of baptism itself. It is thus surprising that the confirmation rite of LW had what could be interpreted as an explicit conferral of the Holy Spirit to those being confirmed. What was referred to as the "blessing" in this rite read: "<u>name</u>, God, the Father of our Lord Jesus Christ, *give* you his Holy Spirit, the Spirit of wisdom and knowledge, of grace and prayer, of power and strength, of sanctification and the fear of God" (LW, 206–7, emphasis added).

This apparent inconsistency between the baptismal and confirmation rites in LW presents a serious theological problem about the gift of the Holy Spirit in baptism and in the life of the baptized. When this conferral of the Holy Spirit at confirmation is related to the specific questions addressed to those being confirmed—inexplicably called "catechumens"—even greater problems arise. Not only do these "catechumens" acknowledge the gifts they received in baptism by reciting a renunciation of evil and a profession of faith, they are also asked specific questions about their acceptance of doctrine (biblical interpretation and Lutheran confessional doctrine) and their desire for church membership (both in the Evangelical Lutheran Church and in this particular congregation), and are subsequently invited and welcomed to "share . . . in all the gifts our Lord has for his Church and to live them out continually in his worship and service" (ibid.). In other

---

[41] ELCA, *The Confirmation Ministry Task Force Report* (September 1993), 1; LBW, Minister's Edition, 324.

[42] ELCA, *The Confirmation Ministry Task Force Report*, 4.

The Holy Spirit and Lutheran Liturgical-Sacramental Worship

words, the confirmation rite in LW can be interpreted less as a rite of baptismal affirmation than as a rite of reception or initiation into the LCMS and one of its congregations. When combined with the explicit language about the gift of the Holy Spirit in this context, one can wonder whether this rite is not the real rite of initiation, with the gift of the Holy Spirit related explicitly to Lutheran Church membership.

How refreshing, then, that the compilers of the confirmation rite in the 2006 LSB and *Agenda* have faced this problem squarely. While it remains unfortunate that the term "catechumen" is still applied to the baptized in this rite, the confirmation blessing with the laying on of hands and signing of the forehead is now the following, adapted from the classic Western postbaptismal anointing prayer: "<u>Name</u>, the almighty God and Father of our Lord Jesus Christ, who has given you the new birth of water and the Holy Spirit and has forgiven you all your sins, strengthen you with His grace to life + everlasting. Amen" (*Agenda*, 30). While one might criticize the use of this particular prayer for a confirmation formula—including the specific use of "strengthen"—this prayer is much more in line with the classic Lutheran theology of confirmation, and, thankfully, has avoided the theological ambiguity of "*give* you His Holy Spirit." But again, with the changes to the LBW rite of baptism represented by ELW, one wonders what objections can possibly exist on the part of the LCMS to either "Baptism" or "Affirmation of Baptism" in ELW.

CONCLUSION

From the 1960s until the present, Lutheran worship, like most other contemporary forms of Christian worship, is characterized by an increasing emphasis upon and recovery of the role of the Holy Spirit, at least in its baptismal and eucharistic rites. Like most other contemporary forms of Christian worship, this emphasis and recovery have been one with a decidedly Eastern Christian, most notably Byzantine, flavor. The current Roman rite of confirmation, for example, especially in the RCIA—where the confirmation chrismation with the formula "N. be sealed with the gift of the Holy Spirit" has replaced the traditional Western postbaptismal anointing—has created an unprecedented connection between Western confirmation and Byzantine postbaptismal chrismation. As is well known, Aidan Kavanagh referred to this as the "Byzantinization of western confirmation."[43]

[43] Aidan Kavanagh, *Confirmation: Origins and Reform* (New York: Pueblo, 1988), 92.

Maxwell E. Johnson

176

Modern Protestant rites have done essentially the same thing. By omitting the traditional Western postbaptismal anointing prayer from the rites altogether, and by similarly placing a version of this Eastern formula for the "seal of the Holy Spirit" in its place, Lutheran baptismal rites may surely be subject to the same criticism.

Further, as we have seen, the charge of "Byzantinization" may also be a fitting way to characterize how and where the Holy Spirit has been recovered in the eucharistic prayer. Here Bryan Spinks's critique of the overreliance on, and dominance of, the West Syrian or Syro-Byzantine pattern of eucharistic praying in contemporary ecumenical liturgical reform and renewal is especially appropriate with regard to the eucharistic prayers in LBW and ELW, where all eucharistic epicleses appear in the West Syrian or Syro-Byzantine post-anamnesis location.

While I have nothing but respect for the Byzantine Rite, Lutherans need not borrow Byzantine liturgical patterns outright in order to give liturgical expression to the role of the Holy Spirit in worship. Critiques like those of Spinks remind us that liturgical alternatives exist. Even from within the liturgical traditions of Western Christianity, as I have attempted to demonstrate above, alternatives for contemporary consideration and use exist. Spinks is correct to assert that "an epiklesis may not be so difficult for Lutheran theology as some have maintained." Prior to LBW and ELW a strong theological position was developing in favor of a pre-Institution Narrative location for such a Spirit invocation, a location obviously characteristic of Swedish Lutheran eucharistic praying as well. Similarly, while I have nothing against being "sealed with the Holy Spirit" in Lutheran baptismal rites, I too lament the loss of the classic Western-Ambrosian-Roman postbaptismal anointing prayer, a prayer that unmistakably relates baptism and Holy Spirit, indeed the entire trinitarian act of baptism, so clearly and closely together: "The Almighty God, the Father of our Lord Jesus Christ, who has made you to be regenerated *of water and the Holy Spirit* [John 3.5], and has given you remission of all your sins, himself anoints you with the chrism of salvation in Christ Jesus unto eternal life. R. Amen."[44]

---

[44] *Documents of the Baptismal Liturgy* (n. 18), 235.

Habtemichael Kidane

10. The Holy Spirit in the Ethiopian Orthodox *Täwaḥədo* Church Tradition

My intention in this article is to reveal the richness of the spirituality of this church, which has been nourished in Ethiopia for centuries. My

The author is grateful to Father Ugo Zanetti of Chevetogne for reading this manuscript and for his valuable suggestions and comments, as well as to Teklu Fessehazion and Aida Habtemariam, to whom he dedicates this work, for introducing him to the American lifestyle.

ABBREVIATIONS: Ethiopian anaphoras are referred to by the initial(s) of the person(s) to whom they are attributed: C, Cyril; D, Dioscorus; E, Epiphanius; G, Gregory I, II; JC, John Chrysostom; JE, John the Evangelist; JS, James of Sarug; MC, Mary, composed by Cyriacus of Bəhənsa; O, the Orthodox Fathers.

AMQ = Ethiopian Missal with *Andəmta*-Commentary (Addis Ababa: Tənśa'e Printing Press, 1988 EC [1995/96]).

EAE 1–3 = *Encyclopaedia Aethiopica*, ed. Siegbert Uhlig (Wiesbaden: Harrassowitz, 2003, 2005, 2007).

EMML 1763 = unpublished manuscript described by Getatchew Haile in *A Catalogue of Ethiopian Manuscripts Microfilmed for the Ethiopian Manuscript Microfilm Library, Addis-Ababa, and for the Monastic Manuscript Library, Collegeville 5* (Collegeville, MN: Hill Monastic Manuscript Microfilm Library, St. John's Abbey and University, 1981), 218–30.

MD = *The Liturgy of the Ethiopian Church* [English-Arabic], trans. Marcos Daoud, rev. Mersie Hazen (Cairo 1959); reprinted June 1991 by the Ethiopian Orthodox Church, Kingston, Jamaica, with an introduction by Abuna Yesehaq. Reedited March 22, 2006. <www.ethiopianorthodox.org>; [English only], trans. Marcos Daoud (London: Kegan Paul, 2005).

MM + page number = *Giyorgis di Saglā: Il libro del mistero (Mäṣaḥafä Məsṭir)*, ed. Yaqob Beyene, Corpus Scriptorum Christianorum Orientalium, 4 vols. (Louvain: E. Peeters, 1990–1993) Part 2: text, 532 = Sc. Aeth. 97, pp. 70–99; trans., 533 = Sc. Aeth. 98, pp. 43–60; text, 532 = Sc. Aeth. 97, pp. 243–86; trans., 533 = Sc. Aeth. 98, pp. 136–59.

MP = *Mälk'a Paraqliṭos*, a hymn for the Holy Spirit (see n. 69 below).

ŚQ = *Śərə'atä Qəddase (Ordo Communis)*.

DATES: EC = Ethiopian calendar (followed by the year AD/CE in parentheses or brackets).

The Holy Spirit in the Ethiopian Orthodox *Täwaḥədo* Church Tradition

analysis is based especially on sources from the fourteenth century and later—homilies, hymns, anaphoras—composed by Ethiopian scholars. Despite the existence of a growing body of literature on the Holy Spirit by these scholars, no proper study of the Third Person of the Trinity exists, as we will see. A doctoral thesis, published only in part, is concerned mainly with the theological meaning of the Office of the feast of Pentecost.[1] In all the liturgical books of the Ethiopian Orthodox *Täwaḥədo*[2] Church the Holy Spirit completes the beginning (the Father), and the continuation (Christ's salvific work), and is equal to the Father and to the Son.

In order to understand the richness of Ethiopian writings on the Holy Spirit let us first look at the titles given the Spirit in Ethiopian liturgical texts. Various names and adjectives indicate the nature and the role of the Holy Spirit, for example, *ḥəyaw wa-qəddus* (living holy: JE 14: MD. n°. 14, p. 65)[;] *maḥəyäwi* (ŠQ 122: MD, n°. 122, p. 29)[3] or *maḥəyäwe* (life-giver) (G 13: MD, n°. 13, p. 165); *wähabe ḥəywät* (giver of life); *Mäṣənə'e* (giver of strength, or, the one who fortifies); *mänṣəhe* (purifier); *mänfäsä ṣədəq* (Spirit of Truth); *mänfäsä ḥəyəwät* (Spirit of life; AMQ 105). In some prayers and epiclesis the Holy Spirit is invoked as fire,[4] which bakes bread,[5] which boils water, and as "consuming

---

[1] Habtemicael Bahlebbi, *The Biblical-Liturgical Theology of the Pentecostal Office of "Gheez,"* diss. Urbaniana University (Rome), 1978; *The Biblical-Liturgical Theology of the Pentecostal Office of Gheez* (Rome: Pontificia Universitas Urbiana, 1989).

[2] *Täwaḥədo* (union), part of the official title of the Church, "is the best expression conveying the faith of the Church, since it emphasises the inseparable unity of the Godhead and Manhood in the Person of Christ" (C. Chaillot and A. Belopopsky, *Towards Unity* [Geneva: "Inter-Orthodox Dialogue," 1998], 82). See also José L. Bandrés and Ugo Zanetti, "Christology," EAE 1:728–32; Getatchew Haile, "Ethiopian Orthodox (*Täwaḥədo*) Church," EAE 2:415–20.

[3] This attribute is present in the short formula of the threefold creedal profession said after the renunciation of Satan. See M. Chaîne, "Le rituel éthiopien: Rituel du baptême," *Bessarione* 17, no. 1 (1913): 52–53; E. Fritsch, *The Ritual of Baptism of the Ethiopian Church* (Arba-Minch: [pro manuscripto], 1990 EC [1998], 12).

[4] Probably connected with Acts 2:3.

[5] Ezra Gebremedhin, "The Anaphora of St. Cyril of Alexandria in the Liturgical Practice of the Ethiopian Orthodox Church: Observations on the Text and the Interpretation of the Ge'ez Version," in *On Both Sides of Al-Mandab: Ethiopia, South-Arabic and Islamic Studies Presented to Oscar Löfgren on His*

Habtemichael Kidane

fire . . . which burns up sins" (ŚQ 33: MD, n°. 33, p. 14). *Melos*[6] is the epithet of the Holy Spirit: "*Melos säyfä 'əsat*" (*Melos*, the sword of fire); "*Melos zä'əsat yənäddəd*" (*Melos*, the burning fire).[7] Two different assignments are given to *Melos*: to fulfil or complete the offering,[8] and to scatter the devils.[9] For a fifteenth-century author, Giyorgis Säglawi, the Holy Spirit "is he that abolishes [the power of the evil] spirits" with his sword.[10]

In the *Andəmta*-Commentary to the *Qəddase*, the Trisagion is given a trinitarian sense, distributing the three adjectives to the persons of the Trinity: "Holy God, the Father; Holy strong, the Son; Holy living, the Spirit,"[11] or, inverting it: "Holy God, the Father; Holy living[12] the Son;

Ninetieth Birthday (Stockholm: Svenska Forskningsinstitutet i Istanbul, 1989), 7–11, here 9.

[6] "In Melos your name, I put myself under your protection." See Déborah Lifchitz, *Textes éthiopiens magico-religieux*, Travaux et mémoires de l'Institut d'ethnologie 38 (Paris: l'Institut d'ethnologie, 1940), 96–97. For an explanation of the meaning of *Melos* and its christological reference see Ernst Hammerschmidt, *Studies in the Ethiopic Anaphoras*, 2d rev. ed., Äthiopistische Forschungen 25 (Stuttgart: F. Steiner Verlag Wiesbaden, 1987), 161–62, and the studies referred to there.

[7] This "burning fire" may be connected with the "burning sword" of Gen 3:24. See Hammerschmidt, *Studies*, 162. C 70: MD, n°. 70, p. 147. See also MD, p. 14, and Gebremedhin, "The Anaphora," 8.

[8] "Let 'Melos', the fearful sword of fire be sent and appear over this bread and cup: to fulfill this offering" (JS 53, MD, n°. 53, p. 154).

[9] "*Melos*, the terrifying sword, is sent to scatter the assemblies of devils" (Lifchitz, *Textes*, 92–93).

[10] Getatchew Haile, "Fəkkare Haymanot or the Faith of Abba Giyorgis Säglawi," *Le Muséon* 94 (1981): 235–58, here 249.

[11] See my *L'ufficio divino della chiesa etiopica: Studio storico-critico con particolare riferimento alle ore cattedrali*, OCA 257 (Rome: Pontificio Istituto Orientale, 1998): 139.

[12] I.e., immortal: *motä zä-'iyəmäwət*, "the immortal died" (JC 58: MD, n°. 58, p. 139; D 35: MD, n°. 35, p. 160; [Abba Emmanuel Fritsch CSSp and Abba Brendan Cogavin CSSp], *The Ethiopian Rite Missal. English Language Edition. For Weekday Celebrations of the Eucharist with Seven Anaphoras. Ad Experimentum.* [Addis Ababa: Abba Emmanuel Fritsch & Abba Brendan Cogavin, 2002], 151). Both anaphoras JC and D continue, saying "he died to destroy death, died to give life to the dead."

The Holy Spirit in the Ethiopian Orthodox *Täwaḥədo* Church Tradition

Holy strong, the Spirit."[13] Very often the adjective "strong" is given to the Son in connection with his sufferings on the cross.

Though few, some Ethiopian churches are dedicated to the Holy Spirit. For example, in a village called Da'əro Täkli, in Təgray (Northern Ethiopia), a church called Maryam-Paraqliṭos is dedicated to Saint Mary and the Holy Spirit. The feast of the church is celebrated on Pentecost day. A village called Ta'osa (Gondär) also has a church dedicated to the Holy Spirit. Abba Iyasu, a saintly monk of the sixteenth century, built a church with the name of the Paraclete on a far precipice. In honor of the Paraclete he instituted a feast to be celebrated annually and on the fifth day of each month (probably because he knew that the fifth day of each month was dedicated to a popular saint named Gäbrä Mänfäs Qəddus, which means "Servant of the Holy Spirit"). Abba Iyasu called this place *Mäkanä Paraqliṭos Amlakənä*, "the Place of the Paraclete, our God,"[14] to indicate that it is reserved only to the Holy Spirit. The *Gädl* (life) of Abba Iyasu goes on to say that he acquired what is necessary for the liturgical services, and appointed deacons and priests to serve that church.[15]

At their baptism Ethiopian infants may be given names with a compound of the Holy Spirit (*Mänfäs Qəddus*), for example *Gäbrä Mänfäs Qəddus* (servant of the Holy Spirit), *Gäbrä Ḥaywät* (the servant of the Life [Holy Spirit]), *Täsfa Ḥaywät* (Hope of the Life), *Zä-mänfäs Qəddus* (or simply *Zä-mänfäs*) (belonging to or of the Holy Spirit), *Zena Mänfäs Qəddus*, or in its short form *Zenawi* (messenger of the Holy Spirit), *Maḥədärä Mänfäs Qəddus*, or in its short form *Maḥədärä*[16] (dwelling place of the Holy Spirit).

[13] Introduction to AMQ, 25. In the Ethiopian tradition the Trisagion makes clear reference to the important moments of Christ's life, giving it a strong christological sense.

[14] "He is our God" occurs in the writings of Giyorgis referring to the Holy Spirit; see Getatchew Haile, "Fəkkare," 248–49.

[15] Osvaldo Raineri, *Atti di Habta Māryām (†1497) e di Iyāsu (†1508), santi monaci etiopici*, OCA 235 (Rome: Pontificio Istituto Orientale, 1990): 212–13, 244–45.

[16] AMQ 94; Chaîne, "Rituel du baptême," *Bessarione* 17, no. 1:54–55 (*fac eos templum Spiritui Sancto*).

Habtemichael Kidane

The Mass[17]

Mäṣəḥafä Qəddase,[18] the "Book of the Hallowing," exactly corresponds to the Western missal. It contains the ordinary part of the Mass and fourteen *Ak^watetä q^wərban* (anaphoras). Today's standard missal was first published in full, with a literal translation into Amharic, in 1918 EC (1925/26).[19] Another important book, *Andəmta Qəddase*, contains liturgical commentaries on the Ethiopian missal, with extensive doctrinal teaching as explained and clarified by Ethiopian scholars. Its compilation is attributed to Kəfle-Gärima Wäldä-Kidan (*Mämhər*), a well known liturgical scholar (EAE 3:954b-955b).[20] The *Andəmta*-Commentary on the *Qəddase* was also published for the first time in 1918 EC.

In the first part of the Mass some preparatory prayers recall the attitude of Moses—who rejected the task given to him by God (Exod 4:10-15)—not because the celebrating priest is a stammerer, but because he feels sinful and seeks the forgiveness of his sins in order to stand in front of the altar and present the sacrifice of thanksgiving (*Q^wərban*).[21] The celebrant in the preparatory section of the Mass asks continuously to be assisted by the power of the Holy Spirit during the Hallowing, saying: "Send your Holy Spirit on us and on this sacrifice," "the grace of the Holy Spirit" (MD, n°. 13-14, p. 13); "send me Thy power from on high that I may be worthy to accomplish Thy

[17] For a brief introduction to the distinctive features of Ethiopian Orthodox eucharistic liturgy see Phillip Tovey, *Inculturation of Christian Worship: Exploring the Eucharist, Liturgy, Worship, and Society* (Burlington, VT: Ashgate, 2004), chap. 4, "The Ethiopian Orthodox Church."

[18] A literal translation of the word *Qəddase* is " hallowing" or "sanctifying."

[19] This edition can be considered the *editio typica* of the Ethiopian Orthodox *Täwaḥədo* Church.

[20] See also my *Bibliografia della liturgia etiopica*, OCA 280 (Rome: Pontificio Istituto Orientale, 2008): 10ff.

[21] The author of the *Mälk'a Gäbrə'el* (Effigy for Saint Gabriel) (on the *Mälk'* see below) felt unable to begin to extol the archangel Gabriel, and likened himself to Moses who was unable to speak (stammer), saying: "If Moses my mouth is to be a stammerer, let the paraclete Aaron be my mouth" (the text in gə'əz: "Afuyä Muse lä'əmmä konä ṣäyyafä, Päraqliṭos Aron yəkunänni afä"). Even if he is unable (like Moses) to do anything, the Paraclete (the advocate) is there to speak and act for him.

The Holy Spirit in the Ethiopian Orthodox *Täwaḥədo* Church Tradition

holy ministry according to Thy will and Thy good pleasure, and that this incense may be a sweet smelling savour" (MD, n°. 55, p. 16). Again, the main celebrant continues: "Yea, Lord, cast me not away, nor let me be put to shame in my hope, but rather send down upon me the grace of the Holy Spirit, and make me worthy to stand in Thy sanctuary, and to offer unto Thee a pure sacrifice with simple heart for the forgiveness of my sins and trespasses" (MD, n°. 20, p. 13). At the end the celebrant agrees to approach the altar and to offer only when he is sure that God is assisting him throughout the *Qəddase* by sending him the Holy Spirit and making him fit to accomplish this service of worship (ŚQ 58: MD, n°. 58, p. 16). The Celebrant again asks, saying "send Thy Holy Spirit on us and upon our offering to glorify it" (ŚQ 27: MD, n°. 27, p. 14).[22]

The deacon, subdeacon, and assistant celebrant, carrying the eucharistic elements, perform a procession from *Betä Ləhem*[23] toward the church. At the same time the main celebrant of the *Mäqdäs* approaches the door through which the bread and the wine enter. After washing his hands[24] he recites an opening exhortation, known by its initial words as *Mi-mäṭän*:[25] "How wondrous is this day and how marvellous this hour in which the Holy Spirit comes down from the highest and hovers over this offering and sanctifies it. In quietness and in fear, stand up and pray that the peace of God may be with me and with all of you."[26]

---

[22] In the "Mälkə'a Iyyäsus" Jesus, who sits at the right of his Father, is asked to send his Paraclete Spirit ("Päraqliṭos Mänfäsəkä fännu") upon those who trust in him (Jesus) to sanctify and purify them. See Tedros Abraha, *Il Mälkə'a Iyyäsus (Effigie di Gesù)*, OCP 71 (2005): 97–120.

[23] A small house annexed to the church on its northeast corner, where the deacon bakes the bread and prepares the wine for each *Qəddase* (Mass).

[24] The celebrating priest does not dry his hands because he is supposed to clean the bread with wet hands at the moment of choosing as he says Psalm 26:8-9 (ŚQ 9: MD, n°. 9, p. 19).

[25] ŚQ 1: MD, n°. 1, p. 19 (Fritsch, *Ethiopian Rite Missal*, 25). For a commentary see AMQ 41.

[26] In the Marian anaphora of Cyriacus there is a peculiar note about Stephen, the first martyr, who "was astonished and whistled through the descent of the Holy Spirit" (MC 116: MD, n°. 116, p. 81; AMQ 258). It is said that when Stephen saw the Holy Spirit he made a whistle of admiration. It seems logical that the celebrating deacon too, a companion of the service, has to whistle, as Stephen did, at the moment of the invocation of the Holy Spirit. In fact,

Habtemichael Kidane

This is the first text that the main celebrant says as he stands before the assembly and waits for the other ministers who are coming from *Betä Ləhem*. All the prayers so far said by him were said privately as his preparation before or behind the curtain that separates the *Mäqdäs* (sanctuary, the central part of the building where the *Tabot* is kept)[27] from the rest of the church, in order to prepare himself to celebrate the *Qəddase*.

Everything is included in this text of *Mi-mäṭän* of wonder and exhortation: the gathering of the faithful, and all the main moments of the *Qəddase* until the last. The faithful are invited, during the whole *Qəddase*, to pray in silence and reverence. This exhortation is unknown to the Coptic liturgical tradition; it comes from the Syrian/Chaldean tradition. In fact, in the Syrian/Chaldean church it is said by the deacon after the epiclesis,[28] which marks the coming of the Holy Spirit on the bread and wine to change them into Christ's Body and Blood. In the Ethiopian liturgy the *Mi-mäṭän* has been placed at the very beginning of the Mass to stress that the role of the Holy Spirit begins there. While in the Syrian/Chaldean liturgy it is said by the deacon, in the Ethiopian liturgy it is said by the presiding priest standing in front of the people. Some Ethiopian scholars claim

----

in some ancient manuscripts of the Ethiopian missal the following rubric is written: "bäzəyä yətəfaṣäy diyaqon" (here the deacon whistles). See Sebastian Euringer, "Die Äthiopischen Anaphoren des Hl. Evangelisten Johannes des Donnersohnes und des Hl. Jacobus von Sarug," *Orientalia Christiana* 33, no. 90 (1934): 74f. Among the teachers of *Qəddase* this fact created a useless debate about the kind of whistle that the deacon has to make during the Mass in order to imitate what Stephen did when he saw the Holy Spirit descending. No doubt the whistle must be one of admiration. See Kidanä Wäldä Kəfle, *Mäṣəhafä Säwasəw wä-gəs wämäzgäbä qalat ḥaddis* [A Book of the Grammar and Verbs, and a New Dictionary. Gə'əz Entries, Amharic Definitions] (Addis Ababa: Artistic Printing Press, 1948 EC [1955/56]), 729.

[27] The *Tabot* "is a sacrosanct object that constitutes the heart of any Ethiopian Orthodox church." It is on the *Tabot* that the body of Christ is broken and his blood poured. It has been always venerated because it is consecrated by the bishop, anointed with *Myron*, and on it is written the name of God. See E. Fritsch, CSSp, *The Liturgical Year and the Lectionary of the Ethiopian Church. The Temporal: Seasons and Sundays* (Addis Abäba: *Ethiopian Review of Cultures*, Special Issue 9–10 [2001]: 385–88 and bibliography.

[28] William Macomber, "Ethiopian Liturgy," in *Coptic Encyclopedia*, ed. Aziz S. Atiya (New York: Macmillan, 1991) 3:987–90.

The Holy Spirit in the Ethiopian Orthodox *Täwaḥədo* Church Tradition

that the consecration of the church's elements takes place during the *Qəddase*, beginning with the following profession of faith: "One is the holy Father, One is the holy Son, and One is the Holy Spirit" said by the celebrant at the beginning of the Mass. Doubtless this unreasonable position reveals the rather naïve view of a few teachers. The baptismal water that becomes the equal of the pure water that flowed from Christ's side (John 19:35) is also blessed by the singing of the words mentioned.[29]

The role of the Holy Spirit in the liturgy is clearer in the anaphoras. The explicit epiclesis is not a prayer only to the Father, asking him for the coming of the Holy Spirit, but is also a prayer to the Son to ask him to send the Holy Spirit and power (Acts 2:4; 1 Cor 2:4). The priest prays that the Son may change the bread and wine into his Body and Blood,[30] and that these consecrated elements may bear fruit as those who receive them enter into communion. In the invocation the Holy Spirit is asked to descend on the gifts, and on the communicants to create a union among themselves. The Holy Spirit is the source of the unity of believers.[31] In the Ethiopian *Qəddase* the celebrant, breaking the bread at the fraction rite, says alternatively with the people the following *Ecphonesis*:

> Grant us the communion (union) of the Holy Spirit (1). And heal us by this-prosphora-offering (2). So that we may live in you (3). Throughout all time (4). For ever and ever (5). Blessed is the Name of the Lord (6). And blessed is He who comes in the Name of the Lord (7). And blessed

---

[29] See Semharay Selim Tekle-Mariam, "La messe éthiopienne," *Revue de l'Orient Chrétien*, 3d ser. 9 (XXIX, 425–44, here 443); Habtemicael Bahlebbi, *The Biblical-Liturgical Theology* (n. 1), 272.

[30] M. Chaîne, "La consécration et l'épiclèse dans le missel éthiopien," *Bessarione* 14 (1909–1910): 188–209, here 199; August Dillmann, *Chrestomathia Aethiopica* (Leipzig: T. O. Weigel, 1866), 55; Hammerschmidt, *Studies* (n. 6), 163.

[31] The second anaphora of Mary, attributed to Giyorgis zä-Gassičča/zä-Sägla (fifteenth century), and known also by its initial *Mä'aza Qəddase* (A pleasant perfume of sanctity), reads: "We pray he may send the union of the Holy Spirit." See *Mäṣaḥafä Qəddase*, ed. Täsfa Gäbrä Śällasse (Addis Ababa: Täsfa Printing Press, 1967 EC [1974/75]), 306; S. Strelcyn, "L'Action de grâce de N.-D. Marie dite Mä'azâ Qeddâse dans la liturgie éthiopenne," *Journal of Semitic Studies* 24 (1979): 241–49.

Habtemichael Kidane

be the name of His Glory (8). So be it (9). So be it (10). So, blessed be it (11). Send the grace of the Holy Spirit upon us (12).[32]

As José Bandrés Urdániz says, "This petition loudly proclaims that the Eucharist is not just a private affair, but the sacrament signifying and effecting the unity of the Church as Body of Christ."[33]

This prayer is taken from the *Testamentum Domini*. It is addressed to God the Father (1), who is the beginning of life; to God the Son (2), as the one who shows us the Father; and to the Holy Spirit, who leads and unites every one of us (Christians) to Jesus (3). The second part of the prayer starts with the Father (7), moves to the Son (8), and at the end the Holy Spirit is invoked (12).

In contrast to the main anaphoras translated into *Gə'əz* (ancient Ethiopic), those anaphoras composed by Ethiopian scholars have the epiclesis for the descent of the Holy Spirit addressed to the Son (JE 100, E 68, JC 70, C 70, D 39). All these anaphoras, however, attribute the consecration of the bread and wine exclusively to the Holy Spirit (EMML 1763–77, ff. 253b).[34] These latter epicleses addressed to Christ have either the imperative form, "Send . . ." (JC 70, D 39) or nonimperative forms such as "May he come . . . ," "May you send him . . . ," "May he descend . . ." (JE 100, C 70). To the question when the bread and the wine become the Body and Blood of our Lord, some Ethiopian theologians answer that it is when the priest recites both the words of institution and the epiclesis.[35]

In the anaphoras the verbs of the epiclesis that express the coming of the Holy Spirit on the priestly table (*mä'ddä kəhənät*) are the following: (may he) come (*yəməṣa'*), descend (*yəräd*), stay (*yənbär*), abide

---

[32] Robert Beylot, ed. and trans., *Testamentum Domini éthiopien* (Louvain: Editions Peeters, 1984), 40. Fritsch, *Ethiopian Rite Missal*, 60. For commentaries see AMQ 126–27.

[33] José L. Bandrés Urdániz, *A Glance behind the Veil: Reflections on the Ethiopian Eucharist* (forthcoming), chap. 6. I am grateful to Father Bandrés Urdániz for allowing me to use his manuscript.

[34] EMML 1763 (76) (Homily for Pentecost). "Glory be to the Father who has been pleased that the pure fatted calf may be killed. Glory be to the Son who is the pure fatted calf. Glory be to the Holy Spirit Who has made this bread the flesh of the pure fatted calf" (C 87: MD, n°. 87, p. 148).

[35] See Abunä Gäbrə'el, *Ortodoks Haymanot* [The Orthodox Faith, Catechism in Amharic language] (Aśmära: Francescana Printing Press, 1983), 43.

The Holy Spirit in the Ethiopian Orthodox *Täwaḥədo* Church Tradition

(*yəḥadər*), stay longer (*yanuḫ*), shine (*yanəṣäbərəq*, rest (*ya'ərf*), manifest (*yastär'i*) on the bread and cup in order to bless and sanctify (*yəbarək wäyəqäddəs*)³⁶ them and to become a perfect (*yəfeṣṣəm*)³⁷ sharing with (*sutafe*) Christ's flesh and blood.³⁸

In some epicleses the Holy Spirit is invoked not only to change the bread and the wine into the Body and Blood of Christ, but to change the taste of the wine³⁹ and to make it equal (*sutafe* = communion) to the blood that Christ shed from his side.⁴⁰ The Holy Spirit is also invoked

---

³⁶ These two *gə'əz* verb-pairs, *baräkä* and *qäddäsä*, are equivalents of the Greek verbs *eulogesai* and *agiyasai* (see Gebremedhin, "The Anaphora," 8). They are "the older nucleus of the Epiclesis of the anaphora of Basil," and are "typical of East-Syrian tradition" (Gabriele Winkler, "The Christology of the Anaphora of Basil in Its Various Redactions, with Some Remarks Concerning the Authorship of Basil," in *The Place of Christ in Liturgical Prayer: Trinity, Christ, and Liturgical Theology*, ed. Bryan D. Spinks, 123 [Collegeville, MN: Liturgical Press, 2008]).

³⁷ JS 53: MD, n°. 53, p. 154. See Gebremedhin, "The Anaphora," 8.

³⁸ M. Chaîne, "La consécration," 199. MD, n°. 101, p. 71; JC 72: MD, n°. 72, p. 140; C 70: MD, n°. 70, p. 147. See J. M. Hanssens, "Une formule énigmatique des anaphores éthiopiennes," *OCP* 7 (1941): 206–23; Samuel A. B. Mercer, "The Epiclesis in the Ethiopic Liturgy," in *Oriental Studies Published in Commemoration . . . of Paul Haupt*, ed. C. Adler and A. Ember, 446–53 (Baltimore, MD: Johns Hopkins Press, 1926).

³⁹ O 114 (MD, n°. 114, p. 93, renders "the nature of this cup"). On the other hand, Giyorgis clearly states that the bread and wine on which the divine force (Holy Spirit) comes remain unchangeable in their aspect (MM, p. 88 tx). "Let the Door of Light be revealed and let the Gates of Glory be opened, and let the Holy Spirit be sent from the place of Thy hidden essence, let Him descend [. . .] and that the taste of this cup may be changed and may become the Blood of Christ our God" (O 113: MD, n°. 113, p. 93; see also D 39: MD, n°. 39, p. 161; E 68: MD, n°. 68, p. 163; O. H. E. Burmester, "A Comparative Study of the Form of the Words of Institution and the Epiclesis in the Anaphoras of the Ethiopic Church," *Eastern Churches Quarterly* 13 [1959/60]: 13–42, here 38).

⁴⁰ John 19:35. D 39; E 68: MD, n°. 68. p. 163 renders "Make this wine the blood of your messiah life-giving," while another edition of the same anaphora (E 68) has: "the blood from your side which speaks" MD, n°. 68, p. 163. "We also believe that this cup is the blood of the Deity shed from the side of God's Lamb" (C 101: MD, n°. 101, p. 149). See also *Zəmmare zädäräsä Qəddus Yared 'ityopəyawi* [Zəmmare composed by Saint Yared the Ethiopian], ed. Täsfa Gäbrä Śəllasse (Addis Ababa: Täsfa Printing Press, 1976 EC [1983/84]), 122.

Habtemichael Kidane

to make this bread the communion (participation) of his life-giving flesh and this cup the communion of his blood.

As Mary conceived the Son of God by the power of the Holy Spirit at the moment of her acceptance of Gabriel's message, so likewise the bread and the wine are changed into the Body and the Blood of Christ through the coming of the Holy Spirit, which happens when the celebrant says the epiclesis (MM 88 tx.).

The doubtful position of the dissident Zä-mika'el (fifteenth century) and his followers regarding the activity of the Holy Spirit and change in the eucharistic elements should be mentioned here. Zä-mika'el says that, because perceiving the appearance of God is impossible, the Holy Spirit cannot come down on the church, and on the church's gift, to change them into the Body and Blood of Christ: God cannot be represented by any kind of creature.[41] The position of Zä-mika'el and his followers was condemned by the established church.

Baptism

Giyorgis of Sägla in his MM strongly disagreed with those who deny the coming of the Holy Spirit on the church. He affirms that without the coming of the Holy Spirit the consecration of the water of baptism, ordination to the priesthood, the celebration of the Mystery (Eucharist), the consecration of the altar, and the casting out of impure spirits could not come about (MM 142, tx.). In fact, every sacrament (initiation, orders, the sacrament of the sick [Book of the Light], etc.), contains a proper epiclesis, implicitly or explicitly expressed. The union of water and the *Myron* is the sign of the presence of the life-giving Holy Spirit. The celebrant who administers the sacrament of baptism invokes the Holy Spirit on the baptistery saying: "Send your Holy Spirit, and may he dwell on this baptistery,"[42] in order that those who come to be baptized can be regenerated to new life. The priest prays that the catechumens become worthy to be the dwelling place (*maḥədär*) of the Holy Spirit.[43] Evidently this is taken from the New Testament (1 Cor

---

[41] E. Cerulli, *Il libro etiopico dei Miracoli di Maria* (Rome: G. Bardo, 1943), 112f.; MM 43 (tr.).

[42] The church, on the feast of the baptism of Our Lord sings: "Greetings to you, O Jordan, for you have been consecrated by the descent of the Holy Spirit" (*Zəkrä Qal*, 125).

[43] Chaîne, "Rituel de baptemê," 52–53; Fritsch, *Ritual of Baptism*, 7, 8, 10, 35; AMQ 94.

The Holy Spirit in the Ethiopian Orthodox *Täwaḥədo* Church Tradition

6:19; see also Eph 2:22; 2 Tim 1:14). At present in the Ethiopian tradition the priest blesses the baptismal font by pouring the *Myron* (the oil of chrism) and by singing *Aḥadu Ab Qəddus* ("One is the Holy Father, One is the Holy Son, and One is the Holy Spirit"), the profession of the holiness of the Trinity.[44] The book of baptism says that the priest pours some of the holy chrism (the sign of the invisible Holy Spirit) into the baptismal font, making a triple sign of the cross, and saying a doxology: "Blessed be God the Father," etc.[45] After that it cannot be said to be ordinary water; it is pure because it is blessed by the action or power of the Holy Spirit (*bägəbrä Mänfäs Qəddus*) and is likened to the pure water that came from Christ's side on the cross (John 19:35): water for baptism, blood for Communion. So we have the sign of the elevation of human nature through baptism. The presiding priest, at the end of the baptismal rite, recites a prayer deconsecrating the water in order that the blessed baptismal water may return to its original state:

> We pray and supplicate you, O good One and lover of men, change this water into its former nature; that it may return to the earth again as before. As for us, let it be a help and a liberation, that we may glorify you at all times, Father, Son and Holy Spirit, and address unto you up to the heights glory and honour now and forever and world without end Amen.[46]

This is to avoid having the water consecrated by the power of the Holy Spirit used for other purposes.[47] Both the eucharistic elements and the baptismal water are blessed by the action of the Holy Spirit, but while the blessed water is deconsecrated, the leftover elements of the holy Body and Blood of Christ (*täräfä śəga wädäm*, "the rest of the

[44] ṢQ 26: MD, n°. 26, p. 21. During the singing of the *Aḥadu Ab Qəddus* all the attendants at the *Qəddase* must stand with reverence and join spiritually the angels in heaven who praise God ceaselessly. Some theologians think that the eucharistic bread and wine are already consecrated at the beginning of the eucharistic liturgy by the singing of the same *Aḥadu Ab Qəddus*. See Abba Mälkä Ṣedeq, *Təmhərta krəstənna*, book 2, "The Christian Teaching" (Addis Ababa: Tənśa'e Publishing House, 1984 EC [1991/92]), 140.

[45] O. H. E. Burmester, *The Egyptian or Coptic Church: A Detailed Description of Her Liturgical Services and the Rites and Ceremonies Observed in the Administration of Her Sacraments*, Publications de la Société d'archéologie copte, textes et documents 9 (Cairo: Société d'archéologie copte, 1967), 119f.

[46] Fritsch, *Ritual of Baptism*, #275, p. 27.

[47] This is taken from the Coptic church use. Ibid., 122.

Habtemichael Kidane

Body and Blood"[48]) cannot be either changed into the bread and wine (*iyyətəwällät ḥabä käwinä ḥəbəst wäwäyən*; AMQ 349) or reserved; both elements are consumed by the celebrants soon after the communion of the faithful inside the *Mäqdäs*.

THE LITURGY OF THE HOURS

Books

Not only most Ethiopian anaphoras, but all the hymnaries for the Liturgy of the Hours (*Dəggʷa, Ṣomä Dəggʷa, Zəmmare, Mäwaśə'ət, Ziq*) as well,[49] state that Jesus sends the Holy Spirit from the Father. The reference to John 16:30 and Luke 24:49 is clear enough. The living and holy Spirit will lead us to the entire truth (John 16:13) and teach and remind us of all that Jesus said (John 14:26):

> 1. Your living Holy Spirit knows the depth of your Godhead. He has declared to us your existence, and told us of your oneness. He taught us your unity, and enabled us to know your Trinity. 2. He has spoken to us about your incorruptible equality and your inseparable unity, and about your immutable nature. 3. The Father is the witness of the Son and the Holy Spirit. And the Son proclaims the Father and the Holy Spirit. And the Holy Spirit teaches about the Father and the Son, in order that the three may be worshipped in one Name. (JE 14-15: MD, n°. 14-15, p. 65)

The *Dəggʷa*,[50] a hymnary for the whole liturgical year, contains a complete Office for the feast of Pentecost. This Office is used, except in churches dedicated to the Holy Spirit, during the seven days of the feast of Pentecost.[51]

---

[48] It is also called *täräfä mäśəwa'ət*, or *täräfä qʷərban*, the "leftover of the sacrifice."

[49] See my *Ufficio*, 45–116.

[50] For the *Dəggʷa* and *Ṣomä Dəggʷa* see my "Il «Deggwa»: libro liturgico della Chiesa etiopica," in *The Christian East*, ed. Robert F. Taft, OCA 251 (Rome: Pontificio Istituto Orientale, 1996): 353–88; "La celebrazione della settimana santa nella Chiesa etiopica," in *Hebdomadae sanctae celebratio*, ed. Antoniius Georgius Kollamparampil, BELS 93 (Rome: C.L.V.–Edizioni Liturgiche, 1997), 93–134; and *Ufficio*, 45ff.

[51] Ethiopian scholars disagree on the starting point of the seven days of Pentecost: some start to count from nine in the morning on Pentecost day to Saturday, and others from Monday after Pentecost to the following Sunday. The week after Pentecost Sunday is called *Wärädä Mänfäs Qəddus* (The Holy Spirit Descended) from the initial words of the hymn of Pentecost.

The Holy Spirit in the Ethiopian Orthodox *Täwaḥədo* Church Tradition

On Pentecost everything is like Easter Sunday. The whole Office tells of the coming of the Holy Spirit. The *Mälṭan* (refrain) of the day announces joyfully the feast of Pentecost: "Hallelujah, today is a great joy [feast] because of the descent of the Holy Spirit from heaven to the earth [lit. to the dry]; the disciples of Jesus have drunk him [the Paraclete] as beer; truly, truly the Paraclete is the giver of grace."

The *Dɔggʷa* gives three *Mäzɔmurat* (pl. of *Mäzɔmur*, hymn) of the Holy Spirit to be sung during the *Mäwäddɔs* (Sunday morning Office).[52] These three hymns are based on Acts 2, John 14, and John 16. The theme of the feast is contained in these hymns. The liturgical books do not indicate clearly which school uses which *Mäzɔmur*, although some modern editions of liturgical books give vague indications. Evidently each traditional school has its own tradition.

The theme of sending the Holy Spirit also appears in the antiphons given in the *Dɔggʷa* of Pentecost day: "He (Jesus) promised them great hope, saying: 'Peace be with you, I shall send you the Paraclete, the Spirit of truth, who will remain with you for ever.'" Again: "I will send you the Paraclete which will be with you for ever."[53] The disciples of Christ become his witnesses "through the Holy Spirit, and bear witness that Christ ascended to heaven,"[54] because "the one who came down from the Father, He will be my witness that I am coming from the Father. Again I will go back to my Father who sent me."[55] To receive the Holy Spirit is to take on a great commitment to announce the resurrection of Christ: "Receive the Spirit, my Spirit and proclaim my resurrection."[56]

Liturgical Readings

Although the Office and readings of Easter are used on Pentecost, we will give the biblical and nonbiblical readings that refer to Pentecost:

1. Biblical Readings

1 Cor 12:1-13; 14:1-5; 1 John 4:1-9; Acts 2:1-18; *Mɔsbak*: Psalm 50:11; John 14:12-18; 16:7-16 (Anaphora of Dioscorus).

---

[52] On the way of executing the *Mäzɔmur*, see my *Ufficio*, 193–94.

[53] Henok Wäldä-Mika'el, *Zɔkrä Qal za-wé'étu Mäúüäfä Zig wä-Mäzmur* ("Aide-Memoire" that is the Book of *Ziq* and *Mäzmur* [Addis Ababa], 1996 EC [2004/05], 350.

[54] Habtemicael Bahlebbi, *Biblical-Liturgical Theology*, 72.

[55] *Zɔmmare*, ed. Täsfa Gäbrä Śɔllasse (n. 40), 122.

[56] Henok Wäldä-Mika'el, *Zɔkrä Qal*, 350.

Habtemichael Kidane

192

2. Nonbiblical Readings

(a) The Ethiopian church during her liturgical service includes appropriate readings taken from the most important service books, which are called *Sənkəssar* (*Synaxarion*).[57] One passage taken from this book, about the descent of the Holy Spirit on the day of Pentecost,[58] concludes with a *Sälam* (short hymn) which can be seen as a summary of the passage read.

(b) Another service book of the Ethiopian Orthodox Church from which readings on Pentecost are taken is *Haymanotä Abäw* (The Faith of the Fathers),[59] a collection of important theological writings from church fathers who wrote in Greek, Coptic, Syriac, and even Arabic.[60] Certain patristic writings, such as those of Cyril, became the foundation, along with the Bible, of all subsequent christological debates. The *Haymanotä Abäw* was translated into *Gə'əz* from Arabic in the sixteenth century. I quote what it says about the procession of the Holy Spirit: "He sent us the Paraclete, the Holy Spirit, which proceeds from the Father, and he is coeternal with the Father and the Son and he redeemed the whole world."[61] The Holy Spirit, with his knowledge, and because he is the revealer of truth, redeems or purifies the world from ignorance and gives strength. He is the cause of our joy (AMQ 105).

(c) Two *Dərsanat* (pl. of *Dərsan*, homiliaries)[62] of various authors and periods are to be read on the feast of Pentecost. These collections of homilies are considered treasures of Ethiopian spiritual literature, and are useful for the study of the Holy Spirit in the Ethiopian liturgical tradition. They allow us to understand the *Gə'əz* liturgy in its general form—anaphoras, baptismal rite, etc. Moreover, these two homiliaries are important because they are written by Ethiopian scholars. Both *Dərsanat* are full of biblical texts, mainly quoted by heart by the

---

[57] On the *Sənkəssar* see Gérard Colin, "Le synaxaire éthiopien: État actuel de la question," *Analecta Bollandiana* 106 (1988): 173–217.

[58] E. A. Wallis Budge, *The Book of the Saints of the Ethiopian Church: A Translation of the Ethiopic Synaxarium Made from Manuscripts Oriental 660 and 661 in the British Museum* (New York: Cambridge University Press, 1976), 900–903.

[59] Haylä Mäsqäl Gäbrä Mädəḫən, ed., *Haymanotä Abäw, Bäga'əzənna bä'amarəña* (Addis Ababa: Tənsa'e Zäguba'e Printing Press, 1955 EC [1962–63]), 114–16.

[60] See G. Graf, *Zwei dogmatische Florilegien de Kopten, OCP* 3 (1937): 345–402.

[61] Kirsten Stoffregen-Pedersen, *Les Ethiopiens* (Turnhout: Brepols, 1990), 51.

[62] G. Lusini, "Dərsan," EAE 2:136–37.

The Holy Spirit in the Ethiopian Orthodox *Täwaḥədo* Church Tradition

authors. These authors also quote the fathers of the church, including the fathers of the Ethiopian church, who were mostly anonymous.

EMML 1763–76 ff. 247–253 gives a homily attributed to Rətu'a Haymanot, "the Orthodox," to be read on the feast of Pentecost.[63] The author of this homily, a theologian of the fifteenth century, out of modesty—or probably because he was considered heretical by the established church—did not want to reveal his name. Many homilies are attributed to him.[64] This homily, and other writings, give reason enough to think that he was a person of high caliber in the Ethiopian church of his time.[65] Rətu'a Haymanot's homily for Pentecost is addressed to the "rətu'anä haymanot ḥəzb" (Orthodox people) to confirm and strengthen them, and to make them aware of heretics who, ignoring the greatness of the Holy Spirit, consider him a servant or messenger (la'k). These heretics, according to the author, do not make the Holy Spirit equal to the Father and the Son (EMML 1763, f. 247b).

Similarly, in the so-called *Mäṣḥafä Məṣṭir* (MM) or "Book of the Mystery," which was "composed in the form of a homily to be read on the great feasts,"[66] is found another *Dərsan* or treatise that aims at explaining the nature of the Holy Spirit and his role in the liturgy. This homily is to be read on the feast of Pentecost (EMML 1763, f. 247a). The author is not anonymous, like the author (Rətu'a Haymanot) of the previous homily and many other Ethiopian authors. His name is Giyorgis.[67] The homily in MM was probably not written for pastoral

---

[63] *Dərsanä Bä'alä* 50: the Homily of/for Pentecost. This *Dərsan* for Pentecost has a continuation (EMML 1763–77 ff. 253b–258a) to be read on the Sunday after Pentecost [bä-sänbät dəḥrä bä'alä 50]. See Getatchew Haile, EMML 5:1763, 77, p. 229.

[64] In EMML 1:12, p. 14, is a list of homilies for different occasions by Rətu'a Haymanot.

[65] See G. Bausi, "L'Omelia etiopica 'sui sabati' di 'Retu'a Haymanot,'" *Egitto e Vicino Oriente* 11 (1988): 205–35, here 208–9. To him is ascribed a homiliary for Great Feasts (*Bä'alat Abäyt*). See Getatchew Haile, "Religious Controversies and the Growth of Ethiopian Literature in the Fourteenth and Fifteenth Centuries," *Oriens christianus* 65 (1981): 102–36, here 109ff.; EMML 1:12, p. 14; EMML 6:2375, p. 451; EMML 7:2584, p. 38.

[66] The same can be said of the homily found in EMML 1763.

[67] See Marie-Laure Derat, *Le domaine des rois éthiopiens* (1270–1527): *Espace, pouvoir et monachisme* (Paris: Publications de la Sorbonne, 2003). The MM is considered the "summa theologiae" of the Ethiopian Orthodox *Täwaḥədo* Church (Yaqob Beyene, "La dottrina della Chiesa etiopica e il 'Libro del

Habtemichael Kidane

reasons but for apologetic or defensive ones, to fight the "ancient heresies." The heretics arriving in Ethiopia had supporters among the monks of the country.[68] Giyorgis composed this huge work to defend the official Ethiopian Orthodox doctrines he adhered to.

In these two important homilies are found important theological statements that reflect traditional Ethiopian teaching on the role and action of the Holy Spirit. Giyorgis, in his *Dərsan* for Pentecost, teaches the godhead of the Holy Spirit and his equal place in the Trinity, stressing the absence of hierarchy among the Divine Persons.

A Hymn to the Paraclete

Mälk'a Paraqliṭos (= MP) (effigy for the Holy Spirit), is a hymn addressed to the Holy Spirit. The *Mälk'* is a poetic composition praising different parts of the body of a saint or of a member of the Trinity.[69] This composition is peculiar to Ethiopian spiritual poetry (hymns),

---

Mistero' di Giyorgis di Saglā," *Rassegna di Studi Etiopici* 33 [1989]: 35–88, here 48). Giyorgis is probably the only local author who signed his name. He is a prolific author, with various books and hymns ascribed to him. See Colin Gérard, "Giyorgis of Sägla," EAE 2:812.

[68] These teachers are called by Giyorgis "false teachers" (see Yaqob Beyene, "La dottrina della Chiesa etiopica e il 'Libro del Mistero' di Giyorgis di Saglā," *Rassegna di Studi Etiopici* 33 [1989]: 35–88, here 40–41), or *'alwan* (heretics) (EMML 1763 f.247b; Getatchew Haile, "Religious Controversies," 107).

[69] *Mälk'* is a Gə'əz term meaning "form, figure," and by extension "image, icon, effigy, portrait, blazon, likeness." See Kidanä Wäldä Kəfle, *Mäṣḥafä Säwasəw wä-gəs wämäzgäbä qalat ḥaddis* [A Book of the Grammar and Verbs, and a New Dictionary. Gə'əz Entries, Amharic Definitions'] (Addis Ababa: Artistic Printing Press, 1948 EC [1955/56]), 566a; Wolf Leslau, *Comparative Dictionary of Gə'əz (Classical Ethiopic): Gə'əz-English. English-Gə'əz, with an Index of the Semitic Roots* (Wiesbaden: O. Harrassovitz, 1987), 313a. Neither the term nor the genre *Mälk'* is new to Western scholars. Regarding the origin of the *Mälk'* see U. Zanetti, "Parallèles antiques au *malke'e* éthiopien," in *Comparative Liturgy Fifty Years after Anton Baumstark (1872–1948)*, ed. Robert F. Taft and Gabriele Winkler, OCA 265 (Rome: Pontificio Istituto Orientale, 2001): 1005–20; Basil Lourié, "S. Alypius Stylite, S. Marc de Tharmaqa et l'Origine des *Malka'* Ethiopiennes," *Scrinium* 1, *Varia Aethiopica*, ed. D. Nosnitsin (Saint Petersburg: Byzantinorossica, 2005), 148–60; and my *Mälkə'*, EAE 3:704–6. On a *Mälk'* for the Eucharist to be sung during communion see Osvaldo Raineri, "L'Inno etiopico 'Malke'a Querban' o 'Effigie dell'Eucarestia,'" *Ephemerides Liturgicae* 98 (1984): 81–87; Emmanuel Fritsch, "Une hymne eucharistique éthiopienne: le *Malk'a Qʷerbān* ou 'Portrait de l'Eucharistie,'" *Irénikon* 75 (2002): 195–229.

The Holy Spirit in the Ethiopian Orthodox *Täwaḥədo* Church Tradition

and an original genre of Ethiopian hagiographic literature; it extols the whole person, from the hair of the head to the nails of the toes, including the inner parts of the body. The MP has thirty strophes of five rhymed verses each.[70] The anatomic parts hailed in the MP are more than the number of the strophes.[71] The parts and the actions of the Holy Spirit praised in the MP are the following: the memory of his name, the hairs of his head (which are not hairs of man), his face ("fearful and terrifying"), his eyelids, eyes, two ears, nostrils, lips, jaw, mouth, teeth, voice, breath, tongue, shoulders, breast, hands, arms, forearms, elbows, palms, fingers (of the hands: "I hail one by one"), loins, stomach (treasure of treasures), conscience, back, knees, umbilicus, existence, proceedings (ṣäʾatəkä), revelation,[72] dwelling/living in the soul and body of the Virgin, descent, and manifestation/second appearance in the temple of Zion.[73] In other words, the Holy Spirit is extolled "from head to foot" because he is an *akal* (a technical word equivalent to *persona*).

In these outstanding compositions the Holy Spirit is greeted and adored as the sun that continuously gives his light (26—the numbers refer to strophes), the highest of high mountains (22), a richness that nourishes the poor (25) and never impoverishes (16), light that sends away the darkness (24); the creator (9), living (23), wisdom and doctor of patients (7), healer (7), patient (7), hope of the hopeless (14), fire that purifies (30), deep from the Ocean and Jericho (3).[74] The Holy Spirit is qualified as the salt (1), the light and ardent coal (5, 22), and a drink that refreshes (12).

---

[70] According to Abba Yonas, a Cistercian monk and my former teacher of *zema*/song and commentary on the *Qəddase*, the *Mälk'* has five metrical lines or verses to remind us that Eve saw with her eyes (1), heard with her ears (2), touched with her hands (3), walked with her feet (4), and tasted with her mouth (5)—the apple?

[71] See M. Chaîne, "Répertoire des Salam et Malk'e," *Revue de l'Orient chrétien* 18 (1913): 183–203, here 185–86.

[72] On the shore of the Jordan, later on Mount Tabor, and finally in the temple of Zion.

[73] Habtemicael Bahlebbi, *Biblical-Liturgical Theology*, 252–62.

[74] Täsfa Gäbrä Səllase, *Mälk'a Guba'e* (Addis Ababa: Täsfa Printing Press, 1959 EC) n° 9; Habtemicael Bahlebbi, *Biblical-Liturgical Theology*, 66ff. The MM 269 (tx.) says that the Holy Spirit is profounder than the abyss of abysses, and is elevated above the heights.

Habtemichael Kidane

When this genre of literature (*Mälk'*) first developed is not known, though it seems plausible that it flourished during the Gondär period (seventeenth–eighteenth centuries). We have no knowledge of the author, or the place and period of the composition of the MP, although among Ethiopian scholars there is a tendency to ascribe it to Abba Səbəhat Lä-'ab, the author of *Mälk'a Śəllasse*. The manuscripts that contain the MP are very few, probably owing to its limited liturgical usage, and the small number of churches and feasts dedicated to the Holy Spirit. We cannot be sure how widely the MP is used in the liturgy because we have no clear references regarding its liturgical use[75] even though its use in churches and on feasts dedicated to the Holy Spirit, and during the days after the Pentecost, is unquestionable. The MP is also intended to be the object of private prayer, and to be sung on the feast of Pentecost and on the fifth day of each month, which in some places is devoted to the Holy Spirit. Moreover, the students (future *Däbtäras*), who have to memorize and master liturgical music (most parts of the hymnary, *Dəggʷa*) and are ambitious, are to wash themselves for seven days or more,[76] reciting the MP over the water, and drink some of it.[77] The water over which the MP is recited is believed to become, by the power of the Holy Spirit, hot water that purifies and gives the gift of knowledge. A student who drinks some of this hot water, and listens to what his teacher tells him, acquires insight from the Holy Spirit (EMML 1763, f. 247b) and obtains the fruits of the Holy Spirit, "wisdom, knowledge, faith, healing, power, interpretation" (EMML 1763, f. 250). Preferably students do this ritual during the days called *rəhəwätä sämay* (opening of heaven), "days on which heaven is open to receive prayer,"[78] desires, fasts, and other spiritual deeds done during that day and year. A *rəhəwätä sämay* occurs

[75] The Cistercian fathers of Eritrea and Ethiopia, at the solemn profession of a member, insert some parts of the MP into the Latin profession rite, replacing the *Veni Creator Spiritus*, perhaps because they see in the MP a prayer addressed to the Holy Spirit like the *Veni Creator Spiritus*.

[76] The use of washing for seven days is taken from 2 Kings 5:14. According to the *Sənkəssar* [Synaxarion], during the days of *Pagʷəmen*, and on the Ethiopian New Year's Day as well, Christians go to nearby rivers early in the morning to have a bath, dipping themselves in the new water. See E. A. Wallis Budge, *The Book of the Saints of the Ethiopian Church*, 1:2.

[77] Sometimes it is preferable to have the water blessed by a *Bahətawi* (hermit).

[78] Leslau, *Comparative Dictionary*, 468b.

The Holy Spirit in the Ethiopian Orthodox *Täwahədo* Church Tradition

every forty-nine days, counting from the feast of Saint Raphael, which occurs on 3 Pag\"amen[79] (26 August).[80] The day of "rəḥəwätä sämay" must occur the same day during the whole year.[81]

EQUALITY OF THE FATHER, SON, AND HOLY SPIRIT

The pneumatology of the liturgical texts of the Ethiopian church cannot properly be understood without taking into consideration the theological controversies that divided this church. The struggle over the Neomacedonian and Zemikalite positions was to ensure that the honor and adoration paid to the Holy Spirit was equal to that given to the other two persons of the Trinity. "The Father, the Son, the Holy Spirit: are one God, one kingdom, one power, one government," three names and one God.[82] This equality is clearly expressed in the anaphora attributed to the 318 Orthodox Nicene Fathers, where Christ himself says: "We have neither 'first' nor 'last,' we have neither 'right' nor 'left,' we have neither 'firmament' nor 'foundation,' we are the 'firmament' and we are the 'foundation.'"[83] The Andəmta-Commentary explains: "Among the three persons of the Holy Trinity there is no inferior, neither stronger nor weaker. Among them, there is no imperfection and addition" (AMQ 288). A Marian anaphora of Cyriacus of Bəhənsa (Oxyrhynchus, Upper Egypt) asserts that the Father, the Son, and the Holy Spirit are equal because they do everything together.[84]

---

[79] This is the thirteenth month, which contains five or (in leap years) six days.

[80] See Peter Jeffery, "The Liturgical Year in the Ethiopian Degg\"â (Chantbook)," in *Eulogema: Studies in Honor of Robert Taft, S.J.*, ed. Ephrem Carr et al., Studia Anselmiana 110 = Analecta Liturgica 17 (Rome: Pontificio Ateneo S. Anselmo, 1993): 199–234, here 234.

[81] I am grateful to Mäggabe Mə́səṭir Mäbərahətu Mäba' for valuable information. One can also find *mälk'at* of various saints used as amulets and charms (Lifchitz, *Textes*, 92–93, 13).

[82] MC 57-66: MD, n°. 57-66, p. 78; (AMQ 246–47; EMML 1763 f. 247b).

[83] O 42: MD, n°. 42, p. 159 (AMQ 288). See also MC 51: MD, n°. 51, p. 77.

[84] They think (they said: "Let us create the word"; AMQ 247), speak ("He spoke and it was done"; Ps 33:9), approve ("And God saw everything that he had made, and behold, it was very good"; Gen 1:31), take counsel (they [the Father, the Son, the Holy Spirit] took counsel to create the world [Gen 1:1] and man as their image [Gen 1:26]; AMQ 247), utter a word (Ps 148:5-6: the Father, the Son and the Holy Spirit create saying "Fiat"; AMQ 247); complete (the creation of the world: MD p 138, n°. 5), make (they from nothing create

Habtemichael Kidane

The same Marian anaphora affirms the distribution of the actions of the Father, the Son, the Holy Spirit,[85] while in other manuscripts these actions are separately attributed to each person of the Trinity.[86] "The activities of the three Divine Persons are conceived as distributed in such a manner that the beginning is ascribed to the Father, the continuation to the Son, and the completion to the Holy Spirit."[87] The Father thinks, the Son speaks, and the Holy Spirit completes. The work of redemption is begun by the Father, continued by the Son, and perfected by the Holy Spirit. What was plural is now singular. References that show the activities of the Holy Spirit alone include: he likes, completes, puts in good order, bears witness, exhorts, sanctifies, teaches, thanks, and asks.[88] In the first Marian anaphora we have the Father, the Son, and Holy Spirit working each on his own. To express the equality of the Trinity Ethiopian scholars use various metaphors. The Father, the Son, and the Holy Spirit are sun, fire, etc.,[89] as the apostles taught (AMQ 249): "The Father (is) the sun, the Son (is) the sun, the Holy Spirit (is) the sun."[90] The anaphora continues: "The Father is fire, the Son is fire, the Holy Spirit is fire, but is one fire of life in the highest heaven."[91] The *Andəmta*-Commentary explains, while not rejecting what is said previously, that "the sun is the symbol of the

---

the world: AMQ 246), unite (they unite the four elements found in the world: earth, water, fire, and wind: AMQ 247), create well (they saw that everything was well done: MD p 138, n°. 8; AMQ 247), send, give authority, bear witness, accustom, advise, purify, cleanse, hallow, strengthen, encourage, teach, crown, clothe, grant grace, sit, judge, examine. This is said in the first anaphora of Mary. See Hammerschmidt, *Studies*, 76. For a German version of the *Andəmta*-Commentary of the Marian anaphoras see Verena Böll, *"Unsere Herrin Maria"*: *Die traditionelle äthiopische Exegese der Marienanaphora des Cyriacus von Behnesa*, Ätiopistische Forschungen 48 (Wiesbaden: Harrassowitz, 1998).

[85] The three Persons of the Holy Trinity work together (MM 249, tx); see Getatchew Haile, "Religious Controversies," 119.

[86] The Father commands, the Son operates, and the Holy Spirit puts in good order (MM 139 tr.).

[87] Hammerschmidt, *Studies*, 76.

[88] MC 66-67: MD, n°. 66-67, p. 78; (AMQ 247).

[89] MC 74-77: MD, n°. 74-77, p. 79.

[90] MC 73: MD, n°. 73, p. 79.

[91] "The Father is the dawn, the Son is the dawn, the Holy Spirit is the dawn: but it is one eastern dawn through which, by the ray of its light, the darkness was destroyed. The Father is the vine, the Son is the vine, the Holy Spirit is the

Trinity; the Father is the sun, the Son is the light; and the Holy Spirit is the heat; the sun of righteousness is one." The Father is fire; the Son is the flame, and the Holy Spirit is the red-hot coal.[92] In the anaphora of the 318 Orthodox Fathers we find a similar affirmation: "My Father and I and the Holy Spirit are the gate, the door, and the dwelling-place. My Father and I and the Holy Spirit are might, grace, and favour. My Father and I and the Holy Spirit are sun, light and heat. My Father and I and the Holy Spirit are fire, flame, and the (burning) coal [respectively]."[93]

Giyorgis strongly rejects this kind of metaphor. He says that "if somebody says: 'the Father is like the sun, the Son like its light, and the Holy Spirit like its heat,' may he be excommunicated because he is introducing two conditions: one is of mixture and the other one is of division" (MM 79–81, tx.) among the persons of the Trinity. The Holy Spirit is real God; he is equal to the Father and the Son (EMML 1763, f. 249). In another quotation it is said: "the Holy Spirit is not alien and a creature, but he is equal to the two persons of the Trinity" (EMML 1763, f. 248). The Holy Spirit is from eternity. This is how Giyorgis expresses it in his *Fəkkare Haymanot*: "If there is anyone who says that the existence of the Holy Spirit is from the baptism of Christ, let him be anathema."[94] This conviction is even clearer in the following passage:

> The one who was sent to the prophets was not a mere creature, but from the Trinity; the one who was sent to the Jordan [baptistery], on the Sacrifice is not a creature but one of the Trinity. All these things [the bread and the wine] cannot be changed into the Body of Christ, and those who are baptized will be not sons of God but of the [evil] spirits (*Mänafəst*). The Apostles thought that the Holy Spirit is from Trinity and by his power the Sacrifice (*Qʷərban*) is changed.[95]

---

vine: but it is one vine of life of which all the world tasted" (MC 76: MD, n°. 76, p. 79).

[92] Getatchew Haile, "Religious Controversies," 118; AMQ 249.

[93] O 45-48: MD, n°. 45-48, p. 89; (AMQ 289); Getatchew Haile, "Religious Controversies," 117 adds "respectively").

[94] Getatchew Haile, "Fəkkare," 250. The second strophe of the *Mälk'a Paraqliṭos* starts as follows: "I adore the memory of your name, which existed before the world" (MG n° 9).

[95] EMML 1763 f. 253b. Giyorgis has a similar statement: "If there is anyone who says that the Holy Spirit is created, let him be anathema like Macedonius" (Getatchew Haile, "Fəkkare," 250; MM 249, tx).

Habtemichael Kidane

THE SYMBOLISM OF THE HOLY SPIRIT

In the Ethiopian liturgical tradition many images are employed as symbols of the Holy Spirit. I mention a few:

1. In the MP the Holy Spirit is greeted as the sun that doesn't set, as salt, fresh water, and burning coal. He is also symbolized by the fire that purifies, as light that sends away the darkness, as the column of cloud that led the Israelites in the desert, as richness that nourishes the poor. His depth is profounder than the ocean's. Other symbols are like those in the anaphoras: fire, sun, milk, dawn. In the *Sälam*, a short hymn that concludes the reading of the *Synaxarion*, the Holy Spirit is represented as a breeze.[96]

2. The liturgical *zema* (plainchant) of the Ethiopian Church has three modes: *gə'əz*, *əzəl*, and *araray*. They are attributed to Yared the musician. Each is consecrated to one of the three persons of the Holy Trinity: the *gə'əz* mode, which is simple, "strong," "dry," symbolizes the Father. The *əzəl* mode, unlike the *gə'əz*, is very delicate. It is commonly known as the symbol of the strong Son who bore the suffering of the cross. The Holy Spirit is symbolized by the third mode, *araray*, which is lighter, gayer. It is sweet in memory of the love of which the Holy Spirit is the symbol.[97] These three modes are distinct one from another by their tonality, their duration of time, and their use in the liturgy. They are also distinguished by the ink in which the musical signs are written on the liturgical texts. The Ethiopian system of liturgical music has its own system of notation (*Mələkkət*), and while the *gə'əz* and *araray* are written in black ink, the *əzəl* is written in red in order to remind us of the blood of Christ. This is how the *Liqawənt* (scholars) explain their meaning (see my *Ufficio*, 244–51). The first part of the Mass is sung in the *gə'əz* and *araray* mode, while the second part (anaphora) is sung in the *gə'əz* or *əzəl* mode, according to the liturgical year.

---

[96] "Sälam lärədätəkä aməsalä nəfas räqiq" (Hail to your descent, like the subtle wind). *Mäṣəḥafä Sənkəssar* [*Synaxarion*] (Aśmära: Kokäbä Ṣəbbaḥ Printing Press, 1991 EC [1998/99], 719).

[97] J. Baeteman, *Dictionnaire amarigna-français* (Dire-Daoua, Ethiopia: Imprimerie Saint Lazare des rr. pp. Capucins, 1929) col. 247a; Abba Tito Lepisa, "The Three Modes and the Signs of the Songs in the Ethiopian Liturgy," in *Proceedings of the Third International Conference of Ethiopian Studies* (1966) (Addis Ababa: Institute of Ethiopian Studies, Haile Selassie University, 1969), 2:162–87; Michael Powne, *Ethiopian Music: An Introduction* (London: Oxford University Press, 1969), 96–97.

The Holy Spirit in the Ethiopian Orthodox *Täwaḥədo* Church Tradition

The *gə'əz* and *əzəl* modes have particular periods during the liturgical year when they are used, while the *araray* does not. The *əzəl* "is used on Good Friday, on funeral days, on great feast days and on certain days of the year."[98] Interestingly, the formula of profession solemnly sung at the beginning of the *Śər'atä Qəddase*[99] is sung in all three modes, as follows: "One is the holy Father" in *gə'əz* mode, "One is the holy Son" in *əzəl*, and "One is the holy Spirit" in the *araray* mode. The faithful answer, stressing the holiness of the three persons: "Truly the Father is Holy; truly the Son is Holy, truly the Spirit is Holy." This expresses and praises at the same time not only the holiness, but also the unity and trinity, with one song expressed in three modes united in one *ḥabärätä zema* (melody).[100]

The Holy Spirit is also symbolized by the three birds that taught Yared the *zema* (chant) when he was taken in ecstasy. The three birds are in fact the three modes, *gə'əz, əzəl, araray*.

3. The ancient iconography of the Descent of the Holy Spirit is known by only one example (Coptic, twelfth century) on a mural at Yəmrəḥannä Krəstos (near Lalibäla). It is the last of a series of icons to be read from left to right, including the entry into the Temple, the ascension, and pentecost. The Holy Spirit is evoked by a large dove descending from a golden heaven on the apostles who are gathered in a room. This is filled with a jovial sun face, which corresponds to all the solar symbols in the Lalibäla area. Rays issuing from the beak of the dove reach each of the apostles.[101] Material later imported or produced by Westerners triggered later representations. But, as Ewa

[98] Lepisa, "The Three Modes," 164.

[99] Dietmar Lenfers, "Ahadu Ab Qudus," *Adveniat Regnum Tuum* (Asmara) 67–68 (1998): 29–32.

[100] Ləssanä Wärq Gäbrä Giyorgis (Märigeta), *Ṭənətawi śər'atä mahlet zä-abunä Yared liq* ["The Ancient Order of Singing of our Father Yared, the Master"], preface by Jacques Bureau, introduction by Hailu Habtu, Bulletin n° 7 de la Maison des Études Éthiopiennes, Maison des Études Éthiopiennes / Tigrai Institute of Languages (Addis Abeba: Makalé, 1997), 53.

[101] On this mural see Ewa Balicka-Witakowska and Michael Gervers, "The Church of Yəmrəḥannä Krəstos and Its Wall-Paintings: A Preliminary Report," *Africana Bulletin* (Warsaw) 49 (2001): 9–47 + 15 plates; Girmah Elias, Claude Lepage, and Jacques Mercier, "Peintures murales du XIIe siècle découvertes dans l'église Yemrehana Krestos en Éthiopie," *Communication. Comptes-rendus de l'Académie des Inscriptions et Belles-Lettres* (Janvier–Mars 2001): 311–34. Agostino Colli, "Dall'Occidente all'Etiopia: cenni di iconografia della Trinità

Balicka-Witakowska says, in some Ethiopian churches at least "the fish in the basin and the large dove of the Holy Spirit appear in Ethiopian representation."[102]

4. The Holy Trinity is usually represented by three identical elderly men, probably alluding to the hospitality of Abraham (Gen 18:1-15).[103] They are always represented sitting or standing, blessing with their right hands; sometimes each of them holds in his left hand a book or a globe (overlapped or not by the cross).[104] Sometimes the three equal Divine Persons are represented holding the same book, or the same globe to express the unity of God, and also the equality of the Holy Spirit. Although this kind of representation of the three Persons of the Trinity can be influenced by European painters, it is deeply rooted in faith in the one (unique) God in three Persons (*Aḥadu Amalak*) characteristic of the Eastern symbols of faith.

5. The anaphora attributed to Cyriacus speaks of Mary's participation in the mystery of the incarnation. Mary, to be the Mother of God, has first been purified and sanctified by the Holy Spirit. The union (*Täwaḥado*) of the natures of Christ in one hypostasis that took place in Mary's womb is the result of the work of the Holy Spirit. Here we have a beautiful image that explains the role of the Holy Spirit in the incarnation: the image of a weaver (MC 29: MD, n°. 29, p 76), who makes a perfect garment, as the Holy Spirit accomplished the incarnation perfectly in Mary's womb. This is why Mary is called the *Tabotä Mänfäs qəddus* (the dwelling of the Holy Spirit).[105] Both Mary and the *Tabot* (the altar) are equally the dwelling place of the Holy Spirit. Both are recipients of the power of the Holy Spirit. As the Word was conceived in the womb of the Virgin by the power of the Holy Spirit, so

---

dal XVI al XVII secolo" (forthcoming). I am grateful to Father Emmanuel Fritsch for this valuable information.

[102] Ewa Balicka-Witakowska, "The Wall Painting in the Church of Mädhane Aläm near Lalibäla," *Africana Bulletin* (Warsaw) 52 (2004): 9–29, 20.

[103] "Il est vrai qu'en Ethiopie la Sainte Trinité est couramment représentée sous forme de trois vieillards aux traits identiques, par allusion à l'Hospitalité d'Abraham" (Zanetti, "Parallèles," 1009).

[104] On its meaning and historical development see Claire Bosc-Tiessé and Anaïs Wion, *Peintures sacrées d'Éthiopie: Collection de la Mission Dakar-Djibouti* (St.-Maur-des-Fossés, France: Sépia, 2005), 46, 95, 111. See also the forthcoming study by Agostino Colli (n. 101).

[105] Luke 1:35. See Enrico Cerulli, *L'Etiopia del secolo XV in minori documenti etiopici*, Estratto da *Africa Italiana* (1933), 105.

The Holy Spirit in the Ethiopian Orthodox *Täwaḥado* Church Tradition

on the *Tabot* the Holy Spirit changes the bread and the wine into the holy Body and Blood of Christ. The *Tabot* is the figure of the Virgin's womb and Christ's throne.[106]

6. Christians are united through communion to the holy Body of Christ, which is transformed by the Holy Spirit, and healed by him. The celebrant, before the Fraction, prays, asking to be united through the Holy Spirit. The second Marian anaphora, known as *Mä'aza Qəddase* and attributed to Giyorgis, says: "We pray He may send the union of the Holy Spirit."[107] The *Səbḥatä Nägh* (antiphon) of Pentecost Sunday echoes this: "We are one flesh, [because we are] baptized in the same Spirit, the Holy Spirit"; for this reason "let us celebrate this feast."[108]

CONCLUSION

From its very beginning the *Qəddase* ensures the unlimited activity of the Holy Spirit, not only in the liturgy but also in the daily life of Christians. Why limit the powerful operation of the Holy Spirit in the *Qəddase* solely to the epiclesis? The Ethiopian Church believes and teaches the constant action of the Holy Spirit in the *Qəddase*. Mary, the mother of the church, was assisted always and everywhere by the Holy Spirit, from her very conception, as is stated in the following important passage of the homily for the archangel Gabriel:

> The Holy Spirit has (already) sanctified and purified Mary in her mother's womb in the sanctification and purity that cannot be told. At the time of the Incarnation of the Son of God, however, the Holy Spirit came upon her in order that her conception would be from the Holy Spirit without the seed of man. And that Holy Spirit has not separated from her even for a moment or a blink of the eye from world to world; it will live with her without separation. And the power of the Most High overshadowed (her) in order that she might be the mother of God.[109]

[106] See Bandrés, *Glance*, chap. 2, "A House Built for Worship: The Distinctive Character of the Ethiopian Liturgy."

[107] Täsfa Gäbrä Śəllasse, ed., *Mäṣəḥafä Qədasse* (Addis Ababa: Täsfa Printing Press, 1967 EC [1974/75]), 306.

[108] Partial translation of *Mäṣəḥafä Dəggwa* [pro manuscripto] by Sr. Begoña Iñarra (ca. 1980–86), 8.

[109] Getatchew Haile, *The Mariology of Emperor Zar'a Ya'eqob of Ethiopia: Texts and Translations*, OCA 242 (Rome: Pontificio Istituto Orientale, 1992): 40–43; MM 87–88 tx.

Habtemichael Kidane

The Holy Spirit is not only present in the everyday life of Christians but he is also the means of reconciliation. "May He (God) give you (*'ərəqä mänfäs qəddus*) the peace (reconciliation) of the Holy Spirit." This is the blessing or wish that a priest or elder delivers at the beginning of a meeting aimed at reconciling two persons or groups after an estrangement. The Holy Spirit's peace is invoked because, as a traditional scholar explained to me, when the Word became flesh in the womb of Mary in order to reconcile God and humankind, Christ became man by the power of the Holy Spirit. The basis of this claim is that "the fruit of the Spirit is love joy, peace, patience, kindness, generosity, faithfulness, gentleness, and self-control" (Gal 5:22).

Formative for this liturgical development we have described were the various heresies that tended to minimize the personality of the Holy Spirit, his actions in the church, and the church's gifts. Thus various liturgical texts, homilies, hymns, and trinitarian icons were developed in reaction to heretical beliefs like those of the Neo-Macedonians and Zemikaelites, teachings that reduced the activity of the Holy Spirit in the liturgy.

I am deliberately refraining from any attempt to make a comparison with the liturgical texts of other churches to which our liturgical tradition is related.

I would not wish to admit that currently the Ethiopian Orthodox *Täwaḥədo* Church is detaching itself from what has been the root of her characteristics and identity. Surely these that I have mentioned are the sources that help the pure water of the Holy Spirit to gush forth. The church must return to her spiritual heritage, reading and teaching it, or she will inevitably create an interruption of her rich tradition.

Melva Wilson Costen

11. The Spirit and African American Worship Traditions

For the purpose of this study the terms *African American* and *Black American* will be used interchangeably to identify two categories of persons to whom the following descriptions apply: first, the descendants of enslaved Africans in the American diaspora who experienced and survived slavery; second, descendants of "free" Black Africans in the American diaspora who might have arrived as free persons and served initially as indentured servants, or simply arrived as free persons and were never subjected to life as slaves. These distinctions are provided because of the gradual influx of "newly arriving" Africans and their descendants who immigrated to America after the abolition of slavery (at least by law!) until the present, regardless of their purpose. These "new immigrants" rightfully prefer to identify themselves with their African country of origin. The current trend for those who become citizens is to identify their countries of origin and then to add American; for example, Kenyan Americans, Ghanaian Americans, Liberian Americans.[1]

Black religion can be described as a Spirit-led belief system inherited from Black cultural interaction while the skills necessary to survive in a society that denied the humanity of people whose skin happens to be black were developed. The term was honed by Black scholars during what Gayraud Wilmore describes as the "apogee of black consciousness and the rise of the black studies movement in the 1960s and 1970s."[2] Wilmore's purpose was to interpret the ways that African American religion illustrates the continuities and discontinuities that

---

[1] This information is provided as a courtesy to Africans who acknowledge the importance of this distinction.

[2] Gayraud S. Wilmore, *Black Religion and Black Radicalism: An Interpretation of the Religious History of African Americans*, 3d rev. ed. (Maryknoll, NY: Orbis, 1998), 3.

influence and reshape the worship styles, spirituality, and belief structures of Black Christians in America.

Black Africans in the early North American diaspora, slave and free, are often acknowledged as pilgrims in search of meaning in a strange and alien land. According to extant evidence, Africans survived slavery mainly because of an internalized religious belief system that allowed them to find meaning amid the confusions of forced slavery and the development of racism. Methods of improvising and adapting to life in a new and strange environment prepared Africans to incorporate Christian concepts into a basic belief system that existed for centuries. Black religion can be described as a religion of survival.

No one knows for sure the extent to which the Black sacred cosmos, and aspects of African traditional religion, continued in the American diaspora. This writer agrees with scholars who contend that enslaved Africans did not arrive on American soil as *tabulae rasae*. This is not a continuation of an ongoing discussion about how much of the African religious heritage survived. Rather, this claim is an affirmation of the freedom of God to empower communities to adapt to new situations. The universality and strength of core beliefs transcend religious definitions and distinctions. This writer is among those who believe that the Holy Spirit freely enabled the foundation upon which the Black church was built, and continues to sustain it in the twenty-first century.

Because of the ubiquitous nature of African traditional religion on the African continent, the supreme God, considered the High Spirit, could function beyond the assumptions of those who doubt the importance of the centrality of Africa in the shaping of the Christian faith. It is believable that the Holy Spirit, African traditional religion, slavery, and the subsequent exposure to—and finally an introduction to—Christianity are the vital forces that merged to shape religious beliefs that allowed African slaves to survive the possibility of extinction in America. Thus, from the perspective of this researcher and writer, traditional African religious beliefs and practices provided the grist—the potential source—for the establishing of the Black church, as well as Black congregations in Euro-American denominations.

AFRICAN ORIGINS

Scholars of African traditional religion say that the profound aspect of African spirituality that pervades that continent is often not captured in approaches to the study of African religions. Dominique

Melva Wilson Costen

Zahan expresses this concern in his observation that "spirituality is the very soul of African religion. It is found principally in the mystical emotion provided by an African's faith, and can also be seen in the meaning he gives to the dialogue between [humankind] and the Invisible."[3] Owing to a lack of knowledge about the depth and essence of African religious rites and practices, earlier researchers grouped all the elements unfamiliar to non-Africans into categories like magic and sorcery. The conclusion, formed by many researchers after a few months, that multiple religions were operative among the "un-informed" Black Africans led to a stigma that still exists. This originated in a lack of awareness of the African spirituality that now permeates religious conversation among African Americans.

With the flood of interest in the origin and status of the many parameters of the Black heritage and Black life engendered in the 1950s by the civil rights movement, the increasing number of African graduate students enrolled especially in African American theological seminaries, and greater potential for African American and African scholars to exchange ideas, research on the African continent has been accelerated. Liturgical renewal movements, combined with openness to learning more about indigenous African religions and practices, excited African American liturgical scholars and musicians. We are also indebted to ongoing efforts to promote intra- and interreligious dialogue and harmony among world religions, led by a number of groups, including the Council for World Religions. These bring together scholars, leaders, and practitioners of African traditional religion to engage in discussions on common concerns. A conference held in Nairobi, Kenya, 19–24 September 1987, included researchers, practitioners, and leaders from a variety of cultures, as well as anthropologists, sociologists, theologians, musicians, linguists, and literary scholars. Once relegated to the realm of the "primitive," and stigmatized as "pagan," African traditional religion is now recognized by academicians and practitioners outside of Africa as central to authentic black African cultures.[4]

[3] Dominique Zahan, *The Religion, Spirituality and Thought of Traditional Africa*, trans. Kate Ezra Martin and Lawrence M. Martin (Chicago: University of Chicago Press, 1979), 1.

[4] Papers from this conference are collected in *African Traditional Religions in Contemporary Society*, ed. Jacob K. Olupona (St. Paul, MN: Paragon House, 1991).

The Spirit and African American Worship Traditions

Research has recognized certain essential elements of traditional African beliefs that may not have occurred across the whole of the continent but include:

(1) Belief in one supreme, all-powerful, and transcendent God or Supreme Being, called by a variety of names in different African societies or cultures, who has the following attributes: the supreme God is spirit, holy and unique, transcendent and omnipresent, all-knowing, almighty, everlasting, merciful, and good. God protects and saves, but is basically understood as far removed from community life. Divinities—lesser gods, as well as spirits—are invoked to attend to the everyday concerns in communities.[5] Although considered as a father in most cultures, the supreme God also appears as mother in some matriarchal societies. For the Dogon of Mali, the supreme God, Amma, is believed to possess both male and female characteristics.[6]

(2) The existence of an invisible, ever-present world of spirits whose intentions can be ascertained, and to whom sacrifices may be offered when protection is needed, through prayer and the pouring of libations.

(3) The invisible as an ever-present world of ancestors who may function as spirits, and who may serve as mediators between God and humankind.

(4) The unity of the sacred and the secular, with no dichotomy between life and religion.

(5) The efficacy of intercessory prayer.

(6) A sense of the sacred and of the sacredness of human life, with special respect for children, acknowledging that the community or village participates in the raising of each child; with special respect for the aged and the elders; and with a sense of mystery, especially regarding the deceased, who pass through stages, including the living dead.

(7) Belief that God created an orderly world and remains present and involved in ongoing creation; that humans are part of God's creation, and are divinely related to, and also involved in, ongoing creation; that "beingness" (ontology) is vertical, directly related to God, and because of this relationship is also communal; that communal

---

[5] See Richard J. Gehman, *African Traditional Religion in Biblical Perspective* (Kijabe, Kenya: Kijabe Printing Press, 1989), 189–91.

[6] See Benjamin C. Ray, *African Religions* (Englewood Cliffs, NJ: Prentice-Hall, 1976).

Melva Wilson Costen

solidarity is expressed in terms of kinship and extended family, both vertically and horizontally; that any harm done to an individual may affect the community, thus requiring rites of purification in order to restore the community and promote healing and health; and that rituals and myths are essential to life.

SPIRITS IN AFRICAN TRADITIONAL RELIGION

Without attempting to specify particularities about traditional African religious beliefs regarding spirits and how this might affect a communal understanding of spirit or Spirit in worship, here we intentionally focus on beliefs as understood on the African continent. Two types of spirits are recognized: the ghosts (or spirits) of those born as humans, and spirits that are created by the community.[7] The majority of "recognized" spirits are those of departed humans, traditionally understood to be ancestral spirits, or spirits of the ancestors. These spirits return or are invoked if they have lived a good life in their interaction with the family and community. Their presence as spirits provides comfort and protection as a service to the community of the living. They are also a source of comfort to those on earth who are conscious of their presence. The spirits of the deceased last in the memory of the community from three to five hundred years; this requires some ritual form to keep them alive and memorable.

The use of the terms "ancestor" and "ancestral" is problematic since all who die young or without descendants are slighted. A more appropriate term is the "living dead," which affirms the ongoing life of people of all ages. An additional service that the "living dead" render is to act as intermediaries between humankind and the supreme God. (Although this possibility exists, there is some indication that it was not a universal practice.)

Both ancestors and the living dead are included in traditional vocabularies, with interpretations that expand the living dead to legendary heroes. Spirits in this group are conceptualized as having merged with nature and with natural phenomena.

Many people throughout sub-Saharan Africa believe in spirits that are not the ghosts of former human beings. These may be spirits that bring diseases and plagues, or spirits that "dwell in trees, forests, mountains, rivers, and/or mighty forces of nature." There are also wandering spirits that find their way into the wombs of women; their

[7] See Zahan, *The Religion, Spirituality and Thought of Traditional Africa*, 138.

The Spirit and African American Worship Traditions

only role is "to be born in order to die."[8] The ancestors are able to "possess" individuals at will. Such possession by a spirit or a lesser god generally takes place within a religious setting, or as a form of therapy. The intervention of skilled persons such as mediums or diviners is required to assure that the spirit is properly removed (or excised). The term "exorcism" does not occur in the oral presentation of practitioners of African traditional religion, but the process appears to be similar.

On the African continent, and in the West Indies where drums were not forbidden, instruments were prepared and seasoned for rituals. Certain instruments and vocal emissions, and the resulting sounds, are described by performers as evidence of good spirits. Some sounds represent a combination of the human and divine spirit empowered by the Spirit of the supreme God. This writer has observed drummers remove their watches before a performance so that the rhythm established (based in the heartbeat) does not interfere with rhythmic patterns.

AFRICANS IN AMERICA, 1565–1693

According to Cyprian Davis, a colony of Spanish-speaking black Catholics was established in what is now northern Florida in 1565. This is significant for a number of reasons: it recalls Roman Catholic missionary involvement in sub-Saharan West Africa, confirms the presence and involvement of Blacks in the founding of St. Augustine (the oldest non-Native American township in North America), and identifies a place of safety for slaves escaping from Georgia and South Carolina.[9]

In 1619 the unexpected arrival of twenty Blacks on a ship that landed in the port at Jamestown, Virginia, was the first exposure of the English colonies to Africans. This landing, which occurred before the arrival of the *Mayflower* and before slavery was legalized, provided a period of freedom for Blacks in early colonial America. A record exists of the birth of William, a child born of African parentage in 1624, and of his baptism by the Anglican Church. His parents,

---

[8] Gehman, *African Traditional Religion*, 138.
[9] Cyprian Davis, *The History of Black Catholics in the United States* (New York: Crossroad, 1993), 30.

Melva Wilson Costen

Antoney and Isabella, along with the others, found a system of indentured servitude.[10]

In the 1620s the first slave ship arrived in Massachusetts from the
West Indies, and in 1641 Massachusetts became the first colony to
recognize legally the institution of slavery. White northern colonists
were negligent about introducing Christianity to slaves. The work of
Cotton Mather (1662–1727), a Congregationalist minister, provides
evidence that a few Blacks, baptized in Massachusetts, were motivated to ask for help in forming their own separate religious meetings. Mather responded to their request and assisted the leaders of
this group in the writing of *"Rules for The Society of Negroes. 1693."*
This is the earliest recorded account of a group of Blacks organizing
for religious meeting.[11]

Conspicuously absent is any reference to the Holy Spirit or the
Scriptures other than the Psalms. Persons were to monitor their gath-
erings, which included a call to worship, opening and closing prayers,
the singing of psalms, a sermon recited, and learning and reciting The
New English Catechism or the Assemblies Catechism in *"The Negro
Christianized"* (ibid.).

According to the documented testimonies of former slaves, corporate worship was both visible, taking place in a public space such as
a church sanctuary, and invisible, meaning that it happened in secret,
away from the sight and sound of the slaveholder and missionaries.
It was in the privacy of invisible worship (later named *The Invisible
Institution*) that Black religion and the Black church were born. In this
religious milieu African spirits and divinities, as contextualized and
understood in diverse cultures of Africa, were transformed into Christian concepts.

No doubt in the privacy of the Invisible Institution the first priority
among slaves was to re-envision themselves as a community formed
by the power of the supreme God of African traditional religion. In
time the one supreme God, no longer totally beyond the immediate
environment, would be conceptualized as the Third Person of the
Christian understanding of the Trinity, and would be called the Holy

[10] Lerone Bennett Jr., *Before the Mayflower: A History of Black America*, 7th ed.
(Chicago: Johnson Publishing Company, 2003), 28 and 459.

[11] See Edward D. Smith, *Climbing Jacob's Ladder: The Rise of Black Churches in
Eastern American Cities, 1740–1877* (Washington, DC: Smithsonian Institution
Press, 1988), 26–27.

The Spirit and African American Worship Traditions

Spirit. In the communal privacy of invisible worship, the One Supreme God, once distanced, was now both immanent and available, wholly One and Holy Other.

The exact moment when this transition occurred is unknown, largely because of the language differences within the slave communities. The communal acceptance of Christian religion was not documented firsthand and published from inside slave communities. Very little is documented about the ways that the conception of the Holy Spirit was taught beyond a few isolated and inconsequential references to the Holy Spirit, and a vague connection to baptism and the Lord's Supper.

A principal reason for the refusal of English planters to allow their slaves to receive religious instruction was the fear that baptism would emancipate the slaves.[12] The notion that if slaves were baptized they should, according to the law of the British nation and the canons of the church, be freed, was legally vague but widely believed. Many Africans became new Christians without totally abandoning traditional beliefs and practices.[13]

Albert Raboteau observes that "a basic Christian doctrine which would not have seemed foreign to most Africans was belief in God, the Father, Supreme Creator of the world and all within it. The divine sonship of Jesus, and the divinity of the third person of the Trinity, the Holy Spirit, would have also seemed intelligible to many Africans accustomed to a plurality of divinities" (ibid., 127).

One proof of the Spirit's presence in slave worship was a form of spirit possession expressed in ecstatic behavior similar to, but different from, the spirit possession that had been central to worship in West Africa. Slaves in American environments and their descendants were not "possessed" by African spirits, but some engaged in ecstatic behavior identified as a form of shouting. Ecstatic behavior during camp meetings sought and welcomed the presence of the Spirit, especially during revivals. Many spirit possession beliefs existed then and exist

[12] See Albert Raboteau, *Slave Religion: The "Invisible Institution in the Antebellum South"* (New York: Oxford University Press, 1978), 98.

[13] For a look at women's practices in particular, see Sharla Fett, "'It's a Spirit in Me': Spiritual Power and the Healing Work of African American Women in Slavery,' in *A Mighty Baptism: Race, Gender, and the Creation of American Protestantism*, ed. Susan Juster and Lisa MacFarlane, 189–207 (Ithaca, NY: Cornell University Press, 1996).

Melva Wilson Costen

now, but a discontinuity exists between the African heritage of spirit possession and the ecstatic responses in Black shouting traditions in America. The Holy Spirit fills converted sinners with the happiness and power that provide the impetus for believers to shout and sing, with an occasional dance (ibid., 54).

The best descriptions of the worship of Africans in the early American diaspora are provided by African Americans. The following description with commentary of a revival service is by W. E. B. Du Bois, and affirms the continuation of African traditional religion in America.

> The people moaned and fluttered, and then the gaunt-cheeked brown woman beside me suddenly leaped straight into the air and shrieked like a lost soul, while round about came wail and groan and outcry, and a scene of human passion such as I had never conceived before.
>
> Those who have not yet thus witnessed the frenzy of a Negro revival in the untouched backwoods of the South can but dimly realize the religious feeling of the slave; as described, such scenes appear grotesque and funny. . . . Three things characterize this religion of the slave,—the Preacher, the Music, and the Frenzy . . .
>
> The Music of Negro religion is that plaintive rhythmic melody, with its touching minor cadences, which . . . still remain the most original and most beautiful expression of human life and longing yet born on American soil. Sprung from the African forests, where its counterpart can still be heard, it was adapted, changed, and intensified by the tragic soul-life of the slave, until, under the stress of law and whip, it became the one true expression of a people's sorrow, despair, and hope. . . .
>
> Finally the Frenzy of "Shouting," when the Spirit of the Lord passed by, and, seizing the devotee, made him mad with supernatural joy, was the last essential of Negro religion and the one more devoutly believed in than all the rest.[14]

Joy and excitement are present in this "unveiling" of what can be considered evidence of the Holy Spirit at work in and through worship. Although Black theologians have not yet focused on detailed discussions or publications on the Trinity, there are what may be called

---

[14] W. E. B. Du Bois, *Souls of Black Folk: Essays and Sketches* (Charlottesville: University of Virginia Library, 1996), 134–35.

The Spirit and African American Worship Traditions

"seams of evidence" of the role of the Spirit in African American life.[15] James Cone, the founder of Black theology, asserts with emphasis: "There is no understanding of Black worship apart from the presence of the Spirit."[16] The Holy Spirit gathers and empowers the worshiping community to function as one body of responsive believers in and through Jesus the Christ. Under the power of the Spirit the community offers praise, adoration, and thanksgiving in response to all that God has done throughout salvation history, and then listens through God's word to what the Spirit has to say to the church.

With a continual struggle for justice and freedom, and concerns not just for ourselves but for humankind wherever injustices occur, we are empowered by the Spirit to affirm our communal bonding as part of the whole Body of Christ, gathered and scattered. Martin Luther King, Jr., acknowledged that "the God that we worship is an ever living God who forever works through history for the establishment of his kingdom . . . the cross is the eternal expression of the length to which God will go in order to restore the broken community. The Holy Spirit is the continuing of creative reality that moves through history."[17]

Perhaps the most frequently cited evidence of the Spirit in African American worship is contained in the history and origin of American Pentecostalism during the familiarly known "Azusa Street Revivals."[18] This series of energetic worship services was inspired by the preaching of a humble African American pastor in a small house on Bonnie Brae Street in Los Angeles, California, where his congregation worshiped. William J. Seymour, thirty-five years old in 1906, and without a seminary degree, was inspired to preach on the doctrinal theme, "Baptism in the Holy Spirit, a belief that Christians can receive empowerment beyond their baptism in water, so that they can heal, prophesy and speak in a God-given spiritual language called tongues." In April 1906 the first person did indeed speak in tongues, and then another, until

[15] See *African American Religious Thought: An Anthology*, ed. Cornel West and Eddie S. Glaude Jr. (Louisville: Westminster John Knox Press, 2003).

[16] James Cone, "Sanctification and Liberation in the Black Religious Tradition," in *Sanctification and Liberation*, ed. Theodore Runyon (Nashville: Abingdon Press, 1981), 174–92, here 175.

[17] Martin Luther King, Jr., "Prayer Pilgrimage to Freedom," from an address delivered 17 May 1957.

[18] See Cecil M. Robeck Jr., *The Azusa Street Mission and Revival: The Birth of the Global Pentecostal Movement* (Nashville: Nelson, 2006).

Melva Wilson Costen

the evidence of empowerment through the baptism of the Holy Spirit abounded. Word spread, and crowds became so large that services were expanded outside the house on Brae Street, with Seymour using the porch as the sanctuary chancel. By then the outdoor sanctuary was filled with noisy manifestations, shouts, moaning, speaking in tongues, and singing in tongues with such fervor that the sudden bursts of sound frightened persons and animals within audible range. The pastor moved the congregation from Bonnie Brae Street to Azusa Street, into a dilapidated building that had been used as a livestock shelter. There, on the sawdust-covered dirt floor of the Apostolic Faith Mission (popularly known as the Azusa Street Mission), thousands of people, an interracial worshiping community of African Americans, Euro-Americans, Asians, and Hispanics, gathered to worship at three services, seven days a week, for nearly three years.

William Seymour facilitated this interactive gathering from the center of the room and the center of the congregation. Worship practices revealed a continuation of the ritual expressions found in a large number of African American congregations across denominations since the nineteenth century: hand-clapping, foot stomping, and shouting. Other bodily movements included holy dancing, holy jumping, head banging, all while speaking in tongues.

There is more than ecstasy in this example of the Spirit in African American worship traditions. A message is embedded in the Spirit's choice of William Seymour, an African American, to serve as "senior pastor" when he was obedient to the Third Person of the Holy Trinity at such a crucial time in American history. Worship services were interracial as well as inclusive of persons of varying educational backgrounds, unlike so many of the religious worshiping communities of the day. Under the leadership of Seymour and others the Azusa Revivals were fulfilling the New Testament reminder of inclusivity. Vinson Synan, a leading authority on Pentecostal movements, attributes the success and spread of the Black Pentecostal movement to the leadership of African American Pentecostals.[19]

CONCLUSION

The experience of teaching in a seminary during the 1960s civil rights movement, the vision of Vatican II, and monumental liturgical

---

[19] See Vinson Synan, *The Century of the Holy Spirit: 100 Years of Pentecostal and Charismatic Renewal, 1901–2001* (Nashville: Thomas Nelson, 2001), 266–91.

The Spirit and African American Worship Traditions

reforms have brought new forms of worship to African Americans. This has been a period when congregations have had to adjust to rapidly changing liturgical expressions. We are faced with "Emerging Worship" and "Alternative Worship Expressions" with emphases on postmodern theology. We are now into the fourth or fifth level of "Emerging Worship" questions, with attempts to balance the "Alternative Worship" concerns with emerging concerns about the theology of the text of some of the hip-hop presentations. Dialogue on postmodern concerns abounds, and enthusiasm about interacting continues.[20]

Theologically speaking, the Holy Spirit assumes the fundamental role in Christian worship as the sign of God's work through Jesus the Christ, while the presence of the Spirit confirms or substantiates God's covenant relationship, which is required in acceptable worship (in spirit and in truth). The Holy Spirit makes it possible for humans to offer themselves to God without reserve. Under the new covenant, the presence of the Holy Spirit identifies those who have chosen God's way through faith in Christ in order for true worship to happen. The Holy Spirit inspired the Word of God and illumines the Word to guide the work of the sacraments. The Spirit breaks into worship with freedom to refresh our messages without changing forms of history or culture.

The Holy Spirit in African American worship creates, shapes, sustains, and unifies the communal nature of the congregation. This is a role that appears to have been a prerequisite in establishing and sustaining the Black church over the centuries. A sense of collective cohesiveness for worship abounds and is made possible only through the Holy Spirit. The Spirit shapes, affirms, and empowers the corporate community in ways that seem to bond and empower the community. This theological reminder is pivotal to the Hebrew covenantal response of obedience. The Spirit creates an environment of freedom in the place of worship so that worshipers can experience an affirmation, an assurance of their humanity. In the Spirit-empowered community they can worship as they please. Such Spirit-inspired and -empowered space will even free them to express this empowerment by shouting, screaming, running or dancing, singing, rolling on the floor, or

[20] See Melva Wilson Costen, and Darius Leander Swann, eds., *The Black Christian Worship Experience* (Atlanta: ITC Press, 1992), and Melva Wilson Costen, *In Spirit and in Truth: The Music of African American Worship* (Louisville: Westminster John Knox Press, 2004).

Melva Wilson Costen

218

merely sitting quietly. Their responses in offering praise to God are Spirit-filled, often with "ecstatic" movement into the community to do justice, love mercy, and walk humbly in service to almighty God, with the empowerment received in the preaching of the Word. The Spirit empowers the communal gathering to pray without ceasing both as a community of faith and as individuals. The Spirit directly influences worshipers' inner lives at the seat of their emotions. Out of the depths of our emotions comes the Spirit's unleashing of our minds and our imaginations. The worshipers sing with gusto the words of William Foulkes:

> Take thou our minds, dear, Lord, we humbly pray.
> Give us the mind of Christ, each passing day.
> Teach us to know the truth that sets us free.
> Teach us in all our ways to honor thee.[21]

Another beloved hymn includes the lines:

> Some times I feel discouraged, and think my work's in vain.
> But then the *Holy Spirit* revives my soul again.

In the light of the biblical witness, historical declarations, present-day affirmations, and newly formulated creeds, the Holy Spirit is:

(1) the living and indwelling presence of God in the church and the world, God actively related to and immanent in creation;

(2) the Spirit who moved and moves over the waters to create the world, who descended on Jesus in his baptism and empowered him throughout his ministry, who at Pentecost initiated the Christian community by transforming fearful disciples into confident witnesses, and who has worked ever since within and outside the church to recreate and renew human life;

(3) God continuing the saving actions fashioned through Jesus Christ, seeking to fulfill God's creative purpose by bringing to reality a new creation;

(4) and more specifically the Spirit is the life-giver who seeks constantly to lead persons from fragmentation to inner harmony and fullness of life, the Spirit of truth who guides persons into a deeper understanding of the God disclosed in Jesus the Christ, and of God's

---

[21] *The Presbyterian Hymnal* (Louisville: Westminster/John Knox, 1990), 392.

The Spirit and African American Worship Traditions

meaning for their lives; the Spirit who, like fire, acts to cleanse, heal, and purify; the Spirit of power, giving courage, victory over temptation, and strength for service in fulfillment of the divine will; and the Spirit of love and unity, forming people of faith into a covenant community marked by love to God and one another, solidarity with persons of all races, nationalities, and languages, and responsibility toward the whole created order.[22]

---

[22] Adapted from S. Paul Schilling, *The Faith We Sing: How the Message of Hymns Can Enhance Christian Belief* (Philadelphia: Westminster Press, 1983), 111.

Melva Wilson Costen

Part 3

Newer Ecclesial Movements

Daniel E. Albrecht

12. Worshiping and the Spirit: Transmuting Liturgy Pentecostally

The twentieth century was marked by an unexpected spread of enthusiastic religion. A young African American pastor led his tiny congregation from a cottage prayer meeting to a rustic building at 312 Azusa Street, Los Angeles, that had previously housed a Methodist chapel, and more recently functioned as a livery stable. William Seymour and his newly formed congregation cleaned and aired out the church/stable. But neither the new congregants nor the surrounding citizens of Los Angles could have foreseen the "fire from heaven" that would soon fall, igniting and transmuting their "tarrying" into Pentecostal praise and worship. Nor did either group expect the winds that would blow through the renovated building on Azusa Street.

Contemporary Pentecostals, who often worship nearer "Main Street" than Azusa Street, agree with Pentecostals of a century ago that worshiping in the Spirit is central to a Pentecostal understanding of liturgy, and to worship itself. Both groups agree that the Holy Spirit makes true worship possible. Any liturgy minus the Spirit, or minus the people's engagement in the work of the worship (liturgy), is in danger of being the mere work of humans, not the work of God in and through and with humans. Today's Pentecostal tradition represents broad and varied theological and "liturgical" currents. Pentecostal diversity results in part from its worldwide expressions emerging within a variety of local cultures, ecclesiologies, and pastoral traditions. No denomination or ecclesiastical organization can claim the Pentecostal tradition as its own. The tradition—or the "movement" as Pentecostals often prefer to call it—moves in and through a host of networks, groups, fellowships, and even independent churches locally and globally. Consequently, Pentecostal liturgies can differ from group to group, region to region, and culture to culture. However, while variety marks the Pentecostal movement and its several liturgical expressions, there is a certain commonality—clustering central expressions, traits, and emphases—that can be recognized.

When one speaks to Pentecostals about their worship, they generally avoid the language of "liturgy."[1] This could be because they know little of the historic idioms of liturgy, and/or they see their worship-forms and the drama of their worship services as quite distinct from so-called liturgical worship. Perhaps an even more fundamental reason they avoid the terminology of liturgy lies in the fact that Pentecostals have produced very little *written* liturgy.

Oral liturgy dominates. Orality in general continues as a highly held value among Pentecostals. Pentecostal liturgies and their spirituality in general move in and through a kind of oral subculture. The virtual absence of written liturgies among Pentecostals around the world should not lead one to conclude that "Pentecostal liturgy" is an oxymoron. While Pentecostals often fail to recognize their practices of ritual as being such, nonetheless their worship rites subsist while being shaped, performed, and transmitted orally.[2]

This paper seeks to sketch a portrait of "worship in the Spirit and the Spirit in worship" within a few categories as they apply to Pentecostal worship. First, I look to a historic, original/foundational ex-

---

[1] Rarely do Pentecostals refer to their worship services as liturgy. However, in this paper I will use the word often to speak of Pentecostal worship practices, and the entire Pentecostal worship service, as the experience and understanding of worshiping God in, with, and through Pentecostal rites and sensibilities.

[2] Scholars of Pentecostalism see orality (or "narrativity" as Steven Land calls it) as integral to its worship, tradition, and spirituality. See, for example, the works of Walter Hollenweger including "Pentecostals and the Charismatic Movement," in *The Study of Spirituality*, ed. Cheslyn Jones et al., 549–54 (Oxford: Oxford University Press, 1986), and the articles in Allan Anderson and Walter Hollenweger, *Pentecostals after a Century: Global Perspectives on a Movement in Transition* (Sheffield, UK: Sheffield Academic Press, 1999). See also Steven Land, *Pentecostal Spirituality: A Passion for the Kingdom*, JPT Supplement Series 1 (Sheffield, UK: Sheffield Academic Press / T&T Clark International, 1993); Russell Spittler, "Spirituality, Pentecostal and Charismatic" in *The New International Dictionary of Pentecostal and Charismatic Movements*, ed. Stanley Burgess et al. (Grand Rapids, MI: Zondervan, 2002), 1096–1102. On a complementary concept see Harvey Cox's description of "primal language" in his *Fire from Heaven: The Rise of Pentecostal Spirituality and the Reshaping of Religion in the 21st Century* (Cambridge, MA: Da Capo, 2001), 81–97.

Daniel E. Albrecht

224

perience of Pentecostal worship and present this as a combining and transmuting of previous worship traditions. Second, I outline a Pentecostal "liturgical vision," an understanding of worship in the Spirit through Pentecostal eyes.

A HISTORICAL PERSPECTIVE OF PENTECOSTAL WORSHIP

I begin with a retrospective to note the rich variety of sources that early twentieth-century Pentecostal worship drew upon, streams of traditions and movements that flowed into, interacted, combined, and were transmuted within the context of a revival of charismatic worship.

The first decade or two of the movement reveals the heart of Pentecostal worship, sensibilities, practices, and spirituality. While a natural evolution, as well as a particular reconfiguration, has occurred over the subsequent decades of Pentecostalism's first century, the initial years of the movement are still instructive to anyone pursuing an understanding of Pentecostal worship.[3] The Azusa Street revival gives us a particular glimpse into the heart of Pentecostal worship. By itself Azusa Street cannot account for the masses that make up the modern Pentecostal movement, nor all of its forms and sensibilities of worship,[4] yet it can, for the purposes of this essay, function as a representative symbol of early Pentecostal worship.

Old Wine in New Wineskins: Sources and Traditions Merging

Pentecostal scholars concede that there are few new elements in the modern Pentecostal movement, its expressions of worship, and its theological concepts.[5] Pentecostal worship emerged at the turn of the twentieth century as a fresh combination of previously practiced

---

[3] Hollenweger and Land, among others, argue that the first decade of Pentecostal history represents the heart of Pentecostalism; its spirituality was formed in the first ten years. Hollenweger, "Pentecostals," 551; Land, *Pentecostal Spirituality*, 26.

[4] Pentecostal "outpourings" were reported in various settings and countries in the first decade of the twentieth century.

[5] For an example of the insight that Pentecostal spirituality and worship have few novel elements, see the Introduction in *Dictionary of Pentecostal and Charismatic Movements*, ed. Stanley Burgess, Gary McGee, and Patrick Alexander (Grand Rapids, MI: Zondervan, 1988).

Worshiping and the Spirit

forms, patterns, and understandings of worship. The ritual expressions, attitudes, and sensibilities—even the values and convictions—draw from historical sources. Early Pentecostal worship first flowed into the Pentecostal experience from a variety of peoples and worship traditions.

Early Pentecostals borrowed heavily from others. They adopted their cardinal theological themes from eighteenth- and nineteenth-century pietistic positions. Grant Wacker, a historian of Pentecostalism, identifies several pre-Pentecostal movements that shaped and influenced the early Pentecostal mix, bundling most of these together in a group that he calls "radical evangelicals."[6] Following the historian Donald Dayton's lead, Wacker looks to the theological roots of early Pentecostals to discover that Pentecostals bore deep into the strata of the Wesleyan–Holiness tradition among other so-called radical groups of the nineteenth century.

It was within the various permeations of these evangelical and holiness people that a "fourfold gospel" developed.[7] The fourfold gospel—often called the "full gospel" by Pentecostals—presented christological foci: Christ's role in personal salvation, Holy Spirit baptism, divine healing, and an early return/second coming of Christ. Both Dayton and Wacker recognize the fourfold gospel as a doctrinal

---

[6] Grant Wacker, *Heaven Below: Early Pentecostals and American Culture* (Cambridge, MA: Harvard University Press, 2001), 1. Those who migrated from many different religious streams into the Pentecostal ranks, according to Wacker, had in common their search for "new communions more visibly filled with the New Testament church's supernatural power . . . we might call them radical evangelicals, for they commonly insisted that the only true gospel is the four-fold gospel."

[7] Donald W. Dayton, *Theological Roots of Pentecostalism* (Metuchen, NJ: Scarecrow Press, 1987), 15–28. The fourfold gospel predated the Pentecostal movement in the U.S. and also the Evangelical Holiness movement in other nations. For an example of the place of the fourfold gospel in the early Korean Holiness Church, see Meesaeng Lee Choi, *The Rise of the Korean Holiness Church in Relation to the American Holiness Movement* (Lanham, MD: Scarecrow Press, 2008), quoted from webpage of "The Center for the Study of World Christian Revitalization Movements" [http://www.revitalizationmovements.net/books/70/the-rise-of-the-korean-holiness-church-in-relation-to-the-american-holiness-movementwesleys-scriptural-christianity-and-the-fourfold-gospel] accessed November 29, 2008. Choi argues that preaching the fourfold gospel was believed to be a "primary task" of the church from its inception.

Daniel E. Albrecht

configuration that the early Pentecostals borrowed from the Holiness/ Evangelical movement(s) and then "tweaked." Pentecostals preached the fourfold themes more frequently than any other; they took them as cardinal doctrines.

If the radical evangelical and holiness traditions brought a good deal of the theological content into the Pentecostal movement, then African tradition and culture conveyed much of the liturgical substance to Azusa Street and beyond. Walter Hollenweger insists that "Black" or "African" worship has been a primary influence in Pentecostalism.[8] While many traditions contributed to the liturgical footprint of Pentecostals, here I will focus briefly on the profound impact of African and African American traditions. The manners, practices, and values of African worship penetrated nascent Pentecostal worship and have continued to affect not only African American Pentecostal churches, but have shaped a variety of ethnic Pentecostal worship experiences, including white American Pentecostalism.

[8] Walter Hollenweger, *Pentecostalism: Origins and Developments Worldwide* (Peabody, MA: Hendrickson, 1997), 18–80. Hollenweger recognizes the influence of the Evangelical tradition and traces part of the Wesleyan tradition to Catholic impulses. Also, he posits three other roots: ecumenical, critical evaluative, and Black or African worship. For a fine explanation of Hollenweger's five "roots" see Amos Yong, *Discerning the Spirit(s): A Pentecostal-Charismatic Contribution to Christian Theology of Religions*, JPT Supplement Series 20 (Sheffield, UK: Sheffield Academic Press / Continuum, 2000), 207 ff. A number of Pentecostal scholars have recognized the important role of the African religious experience and its worship practices on Pentecostalism. See Cecil Robeck, Jr., *Azusa Street Mission and Revival: The Birth of the Global Pentecostal Movement* (Nashville: Thomas Nelson, 2006); and also Cox, *Fire from Heaven*, 133. Wacker notes African American formative influences through the African religious outlook and practices rooted in West Africa and shaped in Black Christianity in the U.S.; see Wacker, *Heaven Below*, 4 n14. For an example of an African liturgical practice—"tarrying"—and African influence in general, see David D. Daniels III, "'Until the Power of the Lord Comes Down': African American Pentecostal Spirituality and Tarrying," in *Contemporary Spiritualities: Social and Religious Contexts*, ed. Clive Erricker and Jane Erricker, 173–91 (New York: Continuum, 2001), and Alonzo Johnson, "'Pray's House Spirit': The Institutional Structure and Spiritual Case of an African American Folk Tradition," in *Ain't gonna lay my 'ligion down: African American Religion in the South*, ed. Alonzo Johnson and Paul Jersild, 8–38 (Columbia: University of South Carolina Press, 1996).

Worshiping and the Spirit

Among the African and African American influences, Hollenweger focuses especially on the strength of oral culture, and consequently the potency of orality within the Pentecostal movement. He asserts that the vitality and transferability of Pentecostal liturgy are mainly due to the oral (and kinesthetic) qualities of the Pentecostal worship practices and experience, insisting that "Black" (oral) sources and influences first helped to develop, and continue to sustain, Pentecostal liturgy around the world.

The historian Cecil Robeck agrees with Hollenweger. "Black" influences were felt on Azusa Street. Robeck, the preeminent scholar of the Azusa Street Revival, considers African American influences fundamental to the early worship of the revival. The mission was from the beginning interracial (an amazing fact in 1906 America). It was called by some "the old negro church." This identification, though not completely accurate, reveals the perceived African American ecclesiastical forms, spirituality, and worship. Robeck points to the general influence of African American ways of worship as shaping the Pentecostal liturgical ethos.[9] One other mark of the influence of African Americans on the early understanding of worship (and worshiping in the Spirit) lies in the prejudice directed toward the new Pentecostal revival. Robeck and others argue convincingly that the prejudice and harassment against the early Pentecostals was in great part a racial prejudice.[10] Whites and Blacks worshiped together, both moving, speaking, and expressing themselves in what were traditionally African American worship expressions.

Clearly, from the earliest moments of the twentieth-century Pentecostal revival, African Americans lent their heritage, liturgical sensibilities, and practices, along with their leadership, to the emerging movement. These elements, born in Africa, were drawn together and mixed with elements from the traditions and doctrines of the radical evangelical and holiness peoples. Sources of Pentecostal liturgy are important to understanding a Pentecostal liturgical vision and what

[9] Robeck, *Azusa Street*, 137–38. Some of the Black influences were mediated through the revivalist camp meetings of the times. The camp meeting formed the religious, cultural, and liturgical practices of both Black and white churches.

[10] Ibid., 137, and elsewhere. Robeck's extensive research in contemporaneous Los Angeles newspapers and other publications related to the early Pentecostal revival supports his claim.

Daniel E. Albrecht

"worship in the Spirit" means to Pentecostalism. I turn now to note some of the dynamics involved in worship becoming Pentecostal.

Revitalization, Communitas, Transmutation, and Becoming Pentecostal

Pentecostals and their ways of worship drew deeply from wells they did not dig. While Pentecostals tapped into the breadth of the historic Christian tradition, they drew selectively from rites, practices, attitudes, and sensibilities of particular strains of the spiritual aquifer. Detecting the variety of sources, however, does not explain how a new identifiably distinct liturgical vision took shape.

I will not attempt a comprehensive explanation of the processes by which Pentecostals and their worship gained a certain distinction. I will, however, present a few of the dynamics that I believe contributed to the appearance of a re-visioned understanding of life and liturgy. Dynamics of *revitalization*, *communitas*, and *transmutation*, were, I believe, in part responsible for what became distinctly "Pentecostal."

The participants in the Azusa revival believed that they had had an encounter with the living God by the Spirit in the midst of their worship. They said they "knew that they knew," that is, they knew the touch of God; they knew that they had been overwhelmed by the Spirit of God. Their experience in the Spirit informed their re-envisioning of worship. My attempt to understand and explain a Pentecostal view of worship in the Spirit and the Spirit's role in worship cannot and should not displace the testimonies, deep belief, and confidence of these early Spirit-filled believers. I do not discount their reality—they encountered God in the Spirit and they were dramatically changed. I do however seek to place their life-changing spiritual experiences in dialog with some pertinent categories from the human sciences. My attempt is an expression of Anselm's motto "faith seeking understanding." I seek to understand better and to give voice to the early Pentecostal experience of God in worship. In hindsight, it seems clear that early Pentecostal spirituality and worship represent revival and renewal within Christianity. Worship at Azusa Street and similar contemporary Pentecostal "hotspots" around the world marked the beginnings of a particular *revitalization* process.

Anthony Wallace's well-worn model of revitalization movements provides a starting point and direction for exploring the question of how the various streams that predated Pentecostalism combined and emerged as something unique. Wallace asserts that the inherent processes of a revitalization movement proceed according to certain patterns.[11] For the purposes of this work, I will focus on what Wallace identifies as the period of revitalization. The most fundamental change within the revitalization period is what Wallace calls "mazeway reformulation."[12] Mazeway reformulation marks a society's or group's new way of seeing and conceiving the world and how it works; it is a new vision of "reality." Early Pentecostals experienced a kind of mazeway re-envisioning that provided a newly coherent understanding of spirituality, liturgy, and life, a vision of life and worship in the Spirit that at least tweaked—if it did not radically revise—the vision that the sources provided. Below, in the second section, I will outline elements of this revised liturgical vision. Here I will note some of the dynamics at work during the original period of Pentecostal awakening.

One of the reasons I consider the Azusa Street mission and its revival so important is that it provided a context for a worshiping community.[13] It became an environment that drew a variety of religious and liturgical streams together and allowed mixing, merging, and experimenting in worship.[14] A fervent desire to encounter God fueled the

[11] See Anthony F. C. Wallace's seminal work, "Revitalization Movements," *American Anthropologist* 58 (1956): 264–81. Wallace's expansive research and the hundreds of studies that have followed his work posit five somewhat overlapping steps that surround a revitalization movement: (1) a steady state of the culture/group, (2) a period of individual stress, (3) a period of cultural distortion, (4) a period of revitalization, and (5) a new steady state.

[12] "Mazeway reformulation" is the first of six tasks of the revitalization period. The other five that Wallace identifies are: communication beyond the original group, organizing the "believers," adaptation to opposition/conflict, cultural transformation, and routinization of the new cultural system. To some extent each of these tasks can be tracked within the Pentecostal movement. (Ibid.)

[13] Numerous outbreaks of Pentecostal revival occurred around the world in the first decade of the twentieth century. Each revival has its own story and reflects its unique pattern of worship. Still the Azusa Street revival is an excellent lens through which to view emerging Pentecostal worship.

[14] Azusa's Pentecostal awakening functioned as a kind of "mixing bowl." As the revival mixed these religious traditions, it allowed and even encouraged a blending of worship expressions. Just as important, it provided a venue for the mixing of ethnic groups and their own styles of worship in the Spirit, and this provided an opportunity for something new and renewing. I see this merging of movements as a beginning, a transmutation, a revisioning of worship/liturgy. See Wacker, *Heaven Below*, 9, on the "mix."

Daniel E. Albrecht

exploration of the Holy. These ardent seekers committed themselves to hearing God's call and to living obediently in his service. They sought to worship in the Spirit, and in that worship to be sanctified and empowered by the Spirit. Such desires and attitudes shaped the environment of the mission—an environment that reflected elements of *communitas*. As the dynamics of communitas transpired, transmuting processes (rooted in an experience of worship) helped to develop a new liturgical vision, i.e., a re-visioning of the worship mazeway. The environment created within the Azusa Street revival produced a new vision of worship in the Spirit, a vision that flowed from the revitalization fountainhead of an unlikely venue.

The Azusa environment can be thought of in terms of Victor Turner's category "communitas."[15] Communitas refers here to the emergence of a particular kind of community where concentrated "feelings of social togetherness and belonging" arise. The togetherness at Azusa Street was reinforced by rituals, attitudes, and values that increasingly distinguished the community from the "outside" society and even other Christian traditions. In this somewhat liminal context of communitas Pentecostals began to stand together in a new manner.

The mission's communitas structure provided a convivial context for something new to transpire. The context itself was new, though the elements of the contributing traditions were old. The context of communitas set the stage for a new form and vision of worship, later to be known as Pentecostal worship. Communitas is a powerful environment; it certainly exerted its own influence on the burgeoning

[15] See Victor Turner, "Variations on a Theme of Liminality," in *Secular Ritual*, ed. Sally F. Moore and Barbara G. Myerhoff, 36–52 (Amsterdam: Van Gorcum, 1977), and his *The Ritual Process: Structure and Anti-Structure* (Ithaca, NY: Cornell University Press, 1977). See Bobby C. Alexander, "Pentecostal Ritual Reconsidered: Anti-Structural Dimensions of Possession," *Journal of Ritual Studies* 3 (1985): 109–28, on the use of Turner's categories when analyzing and interpreting Pentecostalism.

"Communitas" denotes strong feelings, a kind of social solidarity, a deep sense of togetherness and belonging, usually associated with rituals. In communitas members of the group stand together, outside society in some way. Communitas seems to move between standard social structure and communitas "structure," which is really an anti-structure. Communitas can be thought of as a "liminal phase" à la van Gennep's *rites de passages*. However, it is not necessarily confined to the liminal phase.

Worshiping and the Spirit

Pentecostal worship. Were there other factors that played a part in the *transmutation?*

When I speak of "transmuting" I refer to a process of change that re-arranges the elements of (an) experience and their relationship to each other. This reconfiguration is the consequence of the introduction and integration of a new element (e.g., concept, experience, belief, affec-tion, value) into the overall experience. The process of transmutation modifies the "experience's constitutive relational structure," yet the overall experience develops in continuity with the prior experience even as it integrates into itself the new element(s). Transmutations allow one to relate to reality differently.[16]

Undoubtedly, a number of elements played a part in the transmut-ing dynamics, in the changing of worship experience, at Azusa. Here I will propose a few that I believe acted in catalytic ways, causing trans-mutation of certain rites of worship, but that ultimately produced a new gestalt of liturgy, a new mazeway, a new vision of worship in the Spirit.

A deep desire for "revival" was an important contributing element to the transmuting effects. This deep desire marked a longing for au-thentic worship, a yearning for a religious awakening in the society and the church. The longing shaped even the way liturgical time was conceived of and practiced. It was common for the mission to have two and three main services a day, seven days a week; often these services blended into one ongoing service. Sacred time seemed to penetrate mundane time in this one continuous liturgy.[17] Worship, no

---

[16] The term "transmutation" refers to change on an "esthetic model," as when "an artist adds a dab of color to a painting; the result goes beyond the old painting plus the new dab. The added color changes the way the other colors relate to it and to one another. The whole painting changes because the felt, constitutive relationships of the colors that comprise it shift. In a world of transmuted experiences, something analogous happens in every change. The inclusion of a new feeling changes the entire experience into a different kind of experience. The difference in question is relational . . ." Donald L. Gelpi, *Grace as Transmuted Experience and Social Process, and Other Essays in North American Theology* (Lanham, MD: University Press of America, 1988), 48.

[17] Wacker, *Heaven Below*, observes that worship time and space were relativ-ized. "Days passed into weeks and weeks into months without any clear reck-oning of the date." Sacred space also seems more diffuse: "Saints reported that they received the Holy Spirit baptism wherever the fire fell—while praying in the belfry, sitting on the porch, shoveling coal at home, sitting on a coal pile

Daniel E. Albrecht

longer strictly contained in a temporal mode, introduced a new factor into the mix of the mission, which caused a transmuting effect.

Another element within the Pentecostal communitas that caused changes in the overall view of worship was the value placed on freedom. The meeting together and mixing of the diverse peoples and traditions was unusual. What was more astounding was the freedom given to all. Neither ethnicity, gender, nor even age remained a barrier in Pentecostal worship. This freedom was seen in the many participatory roles in the worship service. The communitas allowed experimentation and improvisation within the liturgy. Even leadership roles in the liturgy were experimented with, and they were open to all. The transmuting liturgy emerged as a democratization of worship roles, practices, and charisms.[18]

Perhaps unique and chief among the catalytic factors causing transmutation to the liturgy and overall spirituality was the teaching and experience of Baptism in the Holy Spirit. Spirit Baptism for early Pentecostals took the traditional elements of holiness/evangelical worship and transmuted them into a new understanding and experience of worship. This may have been the greatest of the new elements that were introduced into the mix of preexisting traditions. A new understanding of Spirit Baptism was introduced,[19] seen as a qualitatively different experience. Both speaking in tongues and Baptism in the Spirit had been experienced as a part of other spiritualities. Now that they

---

at work, talking on the phone, resting in bed, doing dishes." "The Almighty had lifted their worship out of the ordinary time and place and sanctioned it, just as Yahweh of old had sanctioned Israelite worship in the Holy of Holies" (103).

[18] See Margret Poloma, *Assemblies of God at the Crossroad* (Knoxville: University of Tennessee Press, 1989), where she uses Max Weber's categories. Behavior, of course, had boundaries. While enormous latitude for worship expression was recognized as legitimate, boundaries were necessary and "regulations" implicit and explicit were in play. See Wacker, *Heaven Below*, 103–11.

[19] The evolution of the concept of Spirit Baptism can be traced within the Wesleyan–Holiness movement of the nineteenth century. See Dayton, *Theological Roots*. At Azusa Street, participants adhered to Brother Seymour's teaching that he had received from Charles Parham. Both Seymour and Parham believed that the biblical book of Acts showed that Spirit Baptism is linked in some ways to the phenomenon of speaking in tongues. This experience erupted in many other places prior to Azusa, but this occurrence in 1906 soon overshadowed the others.

Worshiping and the Spirit

were thought of together in one experience, this particular rearrangement became a new element, and its introduction and integration into the overall worship experience modified the constitutive relational structure of the service and the spirituality in general. I must add that while Spirit Baptism had a major effect on the emergent Pentecostal liturgy, it was even more important to Pentecostal self-identity, the sense of empowerment, and spiritual vitality for daily living.

Pentecostal Revitalization Continues: Waves, Diversity, and Continuity

Clearly, Pentecostal worship didn't end (or even peak) with the turn-of-the-century revival that Azusa Street represents. What about Pentecostal worship beyond Azusa Street? In the next section I will highlight elements of Pentecostal worship that I believe bridge the early years of the movement, the intervening years, and our contemporary times. For the moment I note a few of the larger contours of the movement and its worship.

The Pentecostal/Charismatic movement has often been described with the metaphor of three waves. The first wave designates "Classical Pentecostalism" rooted in the initial moments of the new movement. The second wave signifies neo-Pentecostalism or charismatic renewal. This wave rolled in during the 1960s, mostly among historic Protestant churches and the Roman Catholic Church. In the 1980s and 1990s a third wave began to emerge. Its arrival was recognized in the Vineyard, Toronto Blessing, and Brownsville Revival. The third wave, or "Neo-charismatics," manifests more postmodern traits and/or reflects post-denominational (nondenominational/independent) impulses, with greater participation among the evangelical branches of Protestantism, historically hesitant to involve themselves in charismatic Christianity.[20]

[20] "'Neocharismatic' is a catchall category that comprises 18,810 independent, indigenous, post-denominational denominations and groups that cannot be classified as either Pentecostal or charismatic but share a common emphasis on the Holy Spirit, spiritual gifts, pentecostal-like experiences (*not* pentecostal terminology), signs and wonders, and power encounters. In virtually every other way, they are as diverse as the world's cultures they represent." Stanley M. Burgess et al., Introduction to *The New International Dictionary of Pentecostal and Charismatic Movements* (as in n. 2), xx. This "Introduction" sketches the three waves. Also see Phyllis Tickle's *The Great Emergence: How Christianity Is Changing and Why* (Grand Rapids, MI: Baker Books, 2008). She considers all three waves in the one term "Renewalists."

Daniel E. Albrecht

234

Each of these "waves" can be analyzed as a revitalization movement in its own right, but I consider here the three waves as parts of a larger movement of renewal within the church—a Pentecostal/Charismatic revitalization movement. There is a thematic continuity among the variations of Pentecostal/Charismatic worship. In the following section I will present some common and overlapping themes of the liturgical mazeway.

A PENTECOSTAL LITURGICAL VISION: UNDERSTANDING WORSHIP IN THE SPIRIT PENTECOSTALLY

While Pentecostal worship in the Spirit cannot be characterized as primarily a matter of the mind, still it has an internal logic, i.e., a set of assumptions, beliefs, and principles—a "theological vision." This theological vision informs, guides, and fuels Pentecostal worship and Pentecostals' freedom to move in the Spirit. When you ask Pentecostals "the most important thing about *Pentecostal* worship" you get a variety of answers, such as "the Holy Spirit," "Spirit-filled worship," "freedom of worship in the Spirit," "the Presence of the Holy Spirit," the hopeful expectations of "God's moving" in the service, "the gifts of the Spirit," and no doubt many others.[21] Imbedded in these answers are keys to understanding not only the general Pentecostal theological vision but also what I call a Pentecostal *liturgical* vision, i.e., a Pente-

[21] Scholarly textual research has yielded important insights into Pentecostalism, and much remains to be studied in this area. Complementary to work in texts is listening to Pentecostals themselves—hearing contemporary testimony, seeing the acts and rites of worship, and discerning the values, attitudes, and sensibilities that support and animate the worship and spirituality of Pentecostals. Pentecostals believe that many of their ways, including worship, are "better felt than telt." I have conducted several projects of a social anthropological type—including participant observation, survey/questionnaire, and ritual analysis—seeking to understand Pentecostal worship. In the fall of 2007 I conducted several surveys based on an ethnographic questionnaire. The survey data are the result of research in three Pentecostal or Pentecostal-like churches and in groups of students at a Pentecostal university. While the survey was narrow in scope, it agreed with previous findings. The results and preliminary analysis of these surveys, yet unpublished, confirm the importance of worship to the respondents, and the Spirit's role in worshiping pentecostally.

Worshiping and the Spirit

costal vision of worship.[22] I can identify here only selected elements of a liturgical vision, but a sketch of some of the elements of this "vision" can provide a glimpse into how Pentecostals "see" worship.

All Worship Is Worship in the Spirit

When Pentecostals envision worship, they see it as "worship in the Spirit." A Pentecostal might make the case that true worship is always in the Spirit. No other truly Christian worship can exist than worship in the Spirit. Having said that, at times Pentecostal parlance will include the predicate "in the Spirit," e.g., "praying in the Spirit," or "worshiping in the Spirit." Still, a Pentecostal liturgical vision sees all true worship as in the Spirit.

Worshiping in Prayer: Centerpiece of Pentecostal Liturgy

From the very beginning of the Pentecostal movement, prayer claimed a central position within a Pentecostal liturgical vision. Cecil Robeck does not overstate the importance of prayer to Azusa Street Pentecostals when he asserts that worship in prayer was so fundamental to the whole of the mission, liturgy, and life that it was the medium through which "all other activities of the Mission must be viewed."[23] While early Pentecostals highly valued all the elements of their emerging liturgy—including singing, personal testimony, preaching, and altar responses—prayer was the central characteristic. Even gifts of tongues were not valued as highly as prayer.

Later Pentecostal waves of renewal—e.g., the neo-Pentecostals (charismatics)—would continue to recognize the significance of prayer in corporate Pentecostal piety. For example, the Jesuit scholar and theologian Donald Gelpi believes that both the classical and neo-

[22] While a great variety of Pentecostal rites and liturgies exists among the many types of Pentecostals around the world, the following elements of a Pentecostal liturgical vision seem to me broad enough to encompass features that were present among Pentecostals at the turn of the twentieth century and have persisted through decades and across cultures. A generational persistence seems to have been supported by a recent limited survey made among college-age students. See my survey, mentioned above.

[23] Robeck, *Azusa Street*, 139ff. Robeck leaves little doubt that the Azusa Street Revival featured prayer as the "centerpiece" of the liturgy, the lifestyle, and the revival as a whole. The term "praying in the Spirit" can denote a prayer in tongues, but that is only one form of prayer in Pentecostal liturgy.

Daniel E. Albrecht

Pentecostal movements have fundamentally been prayer movements. That the Roman Catholic charismatic renewal adapted the setting of Pentecostal prayer meetings as its key venue—i.e., prayer groups—for its branch of Pentecostalism is no accident.[24]

Today, around the world, prayer continues to be recognized as the fundamental liturgical element with which Pentecostals worship in the Spirit. To pray is to experience God. Experience is primary for Pentecostals and their view of worship. The focus and desire of all worship experience is God. Prayer is the vehicle, the conduit; it is the interaction itself between the worshipers and God. It is the joining of the human and divine experiences.

A variety of types of prayer emerge within Pentecostal liturgy. I only mention three here.[25] Intense corporate and individual forms of prayer often center around the altar at the end of a Pentecostal service. This has been true since the beginning and remains so. Another nearly universal trademark of Pentecostal liturgy is praise. Praises ring out as the liturgy proceeds. Often "worship and praise songs" set the tone and give a channel for the congregation to give "offerings of praise." Congregational music has always been central to the vision and practice of Pentecostal liturgy. Pentecostals pray as they sing. Praise can take other forms too. A "concert of praise" gives voice to a harmonic cacophony of verbal praises as many members, if not all, lend their voices to simultaneous, sometimes spontaneous praises to God.

Pentecostals often call for whole services of prayer. These prayer services can involve music, sharing from the Word, testimony, and other rites, but they focus on prayer—mostly unwritten, spontaneous, fully participatory, and often loud. They are filled with sounds as believers' voices together crescendo and diminish in waves of corporate prayer. Whether at Azusa's altar service, a contemporary African weekly all-night prayer service, or the rocking musical prayers of Hillsong "down

[24] "Charismatic prayer groups" became the primary setting of the charismatic renewal. See T. Paul Thigpen, "Catholic Charismatic Renewal," 460–67, and Peter Hocken, "Charismatic Movement," 477–519, both in *The New International Dictionary of Pentecostal and Charismatic Movements*.

[25] Many forms of prayer are integral to Pentecostal liturgy, e.g., intercessory, "tarrying," healing, and deliverance prayers, prayers of petition, prophetic prayer, glossolalic prayer, songs of prayer including singing in tongues, and others.

Worshiping and the Spirit

under," to overemphasize the role of prayer in a Pentecostal vision of worship would be difficult.[26]

The Word and the Spirit

If prayer is central to the liturgical experience of God, complementing it is emphasis on the Bible. Pentecostals cannot envision worship without the Bible.[27] They draw directly from its images, narratives, and imaginative Spirit-filled message in "designing" and proceeding with their corporate worship. "Scripture both grounds and critiques their worship."[28] The Bible is God's word with ultimate authority for life, if not in a merely propositional way. The "Scriptures and the Spirit of the living God are in dialogical relationship" with the sphere of liturgy and daily life. Both are one realm, a world of "miracles and mystery, where healings, prophecy and divine serendipity are woven into the fabric of everyday life."[29]

[26] A poignant example of the characteristic of prayer among African Pentecostals is expressed by Tokunboh Adeyemo, a leader of the Association of Evangelicals in Nairobi, Kenya. He credits Pentecostalism's effectiveness in his country and on the African continent in large part to its emphasis on prayer; see Donald Miller and Tetsunao Yamamori, *Global Pentecostalism: The New Face of Christian Social Engagement* (Berkeley: University of California Press, 2007), interview, May 25, 2002, DVD accompanying the book; also see chap. 5 for a remarkable description of prayer among young socially engaged Pentecostals in Uganda and elsewhere. All-night prayer services are standard liturgical practice among Pentecostals around the world. Similar expressions of prayer abound in places such as Korea (e.g., "Prayer Mountains"), throughout Asia, and in Latin America. Hillsong's worship leader Darlene Zschech points to the yearning or "hunger" that drives the youth of Australia to Christ and prayer; see her paper, "The Role of the Holy Spirit in Worship," in this volume.

[27] The Pentecostal pastor and professor Jackie David Johns correctly asserts that "for Pentecostals the Bible is a living book in which the Holy Spirit is always active." Quoted by Margaret Poloma, "The Spirit Bade Me Go: Pentecostalism and Global Religion." Website: Hartfort Institute for Religion Research. <http://hirr.hartsem.edu/research/pentecostalism_polomaart1.html#TOP>. Accessed Dec. 18, 2008.

[28] Daniel E. Albrecht, "Pentecostal Worship," in *The Cambridge Dictionary of Christianity*, ed. Daniel Patte (Cambridge University Press, forthcoming).

[29] Poloma, "The Spirit Bade Me Go."

Daniel E. Albrecht

The liturgical expectation for a "word from God" runs deep in the tradition. God has spoken and still speaks, Pentecostals believe. Words of Scripture are taken at face value, which helps to explain some of the unique practices and beliefs of liturgy and life. The "Word of God" refers to the words of the Bible fundamentally, but it may also refer to how God yet speaks, especially within congregational narrative forms—sermons, testimonies, and charismatic words or utterances, for example. Such "words" must be discerned as genuine and are measured against the Bible.

Radical Receptivity: Sensitivity to the Holy Spirit

Pentecostals believe that God's Spirit should always be integrally involved in Christian worship. "The Holy Spirit is here," a pastor or a congregational member will often remark during a worship service or after the meeting as a "sanctified assessment." When giving a testimony or getting ready to pray for someone's healing, a Pentecostal worshiper will remind herself or himself as well as fellow worshipers that "the Spirit is here, right here, now; Jesus is here." The presence of the Holy Spirit then is fundamental to a Pentecostal perspective of worship. The conviction that the Spirit is present in worship is one of the deepest beliefs in a Pentecostal liturgical vision. The expectancy of the Spirit's presence is often palpable in the liturgy.

Yet, while Pentecostal congregants know that the Holy Spirit, the Spirit of Jesus, comes whenever and wherever "two or three gather in [his] name," they are also keenly aware that their attitudes and sensibilities make a difference in how God's presence is manifest and how it affects the worshipers. Pentecostals seek a radical receptivity to the Holy Spirit, i.e., openness, vulnerability, and docility before God. Their liturgical rites and sensibilities encourage becoming consciously present to God—even as God's presence is expected to become very real in worship. Such radical openness and sensitivity mark both their vision and their experience of worship in the Spirit and the Spirit's role in worship. To worship authentically and to experience the close presence of the Holy Spirit, worshipers must seek God with an open spirit toward God. A Pentecostal ideal in worship is to be progressing toward a goal of "radical openness" to God.[30]

---

[30] Signs of openness to the Holy Spirit as a key value for life and liturgy are ubiquitous. Pentecostals exhort one another during worship to be "open," to be "sensitive" to what God wants to do in the service, or what God wants to

In the midst of radical receptivity an encounter with the Holy may occur. Pentecostals envision such encounters as integral to the worship experience. While an overwhelming or overpowering experience of/in the Spirit is neither rare nor routine for a particular Pentecostal worshiper, the experiential dimension of worship is fundamental. The liturgical vision sees God as present in the service; consequently, Pentecostals reason that a direct experience of God is a normal expectation.

The Spirit's Work: More Than Mere Manifestations

All charisms, including the gift of tongues, function in part as signs of the Spirit's presence. Pentecostals see that the Lord is at work, is involved in, and is moving among the people in the service. Often the Spirit is manifest in the rites of the people. Liturgy may be the people's work in worship, but for Pentecostals it is also the Spirit's work, and the Spirit's work is more than mere manifestations. Of course, the Spirit speaks. Part of the Spirit's work in the liturgy, according to a Pentecostal liturgical vision, is to speak to God's people. Pentecostals look for the Word from the Lord. They hear the Spirit in the words of the Bible, through preaching, within testimonies, prophesies, and other charismatic words in and for the congregation. Consistent with their liturgical vision Pentecostals listen and look for the work of the Spirit in the liturgy. The focus, however, is on Jesus, not signs or manifestations in the Spirit. God's Spirit has purpose in the holy movements. God gifts and empowers people to do his work within the congregation and in the world.

The liturgical vision gives a prominent place to Spirit Baptism as described above. To be immersed in/filled with the Holy Spirit is to be empowered and sanctified for the work of ministry. The ministry is seen as threefold: ministry to God in worship, ministry of edification of the church and its members, and ministry to the world—evangelism in word and deed. Prayers to God for the overwhelming of the Spirit often occur in the liturgical setting, and the consequent empowering of Spirit Baptism flows in ministries. Worship seems sweeter and more

---

do in one's life. Training for ministry has long seen receptivity as a chief characteristic for Pentecostal leaders. Wacker relates the story of Ralph M. Riggs who finished his ministerial training in 1918 and later reflected on its value as "less in the intellectual training . . . [than in] how to 'open up' so that the Lord could work through him." (*Heaven Below*, 68)

Daniel E. Albrecht

"real," Pentecostals claim. Sharing of charismatic gifts for the building up of the Body of Christ edifies both individuals and the congregation as a whole, and Spirit-filled ministry to the world moves out, encountering the surrounding society in the power of the Spirit.

Working with the Spirit: Participation and Freedom

The Spirit moves, and the Spirit works, in their worship services, claim Pentecostals, but in their view people play an important role in works of the Spirit. Pentecostals quickly confess that the Spirit is sovereign and all-powerful. They know that they cannot manipulate the Holy, but they know too that the Spirit invites them to participate in the works of God. Pentecostals exhort one another to be sensitive to the Lord's leadings, to "step out in faith" and follow the Holy Spirit's lead. To "move in the Spirit" is to be sensitive to the Spirit's direction and desires within the more spontaneous moments in the service. That may mean speaking out "in the Spirit" with a message from the Holy Spirit, a gift for that moment in the service. It may mean laying hands on a fellow congregant and praying the "prayer of faith" for healing or deliverance. To move in and with the Spirit may be embodied in contemplative modes of adoration and love, or in exuberant worship filled with vocal praise and kinesthetic movement.[31] The liturgical vision of Pentecostals asserts that to move in and cooperate with the Holy Spirit in the liturgy takes faith, discernment, and obedience.

Above, I noted "freedom" as a catalytic factor in early Pentecostalism. Pentecostals continue to speak of "freedom" in worship.[32] The term has numerous overtones. Here I note but two that reflect this important element of a Pentecostal liturgical vision. First, freedom in

[31] Participatory forms of "praise and worship" are seen as fundamental to Pentecostal liturgy. Forms, or "vehicles," for Pentecostal praise include music, testimonies, concert prayer, sacred explicatives, and kinesthetic movement, e.g., hands uplifted in praise. See the appendix of micro-rites in Daniel Albrecht, *Rites in the Spirit: A Ritual Approach to Pentecostal/Charismatic Spirituality*, JPT Supplement Series 17 (Sheffield, UK: Sheffield Academic Press / Continuum, 1999).

[32] One surprising insight from my recent (yet unpublished) research on contemporary Pentecostal opinion was the repeated indication of the need for freedom within Pentecostal liturgical worship. Freedom ranks high as a contemporary value and is integral to a current liturgical vision among Pentecostals. This might be seen as a generational phenomenon, but it does run the gamut of ages in our limited survey.

Worshiping and the Spirit

worship identifies a sphere of (felt) freedom needed by worshipers to worship God most effectively and authentically. It means "having the room," not being "boxed in" by restrictive human structures. "Decently and in order" is a respected rule, but the order should be in line with the Spirit's work and direction; it should accommodate spiritual worship, not inhibit it. Second, and more important, freedom in worship means that God by the Holy Spirit is free to move in the ways that the Spirit wishes. God is sovereign, yet worshipers can inhibit God's desire for and movements in the service. A popular chorus begins, "Let the Lord have His way . . ." The Holy Spirit is the ultimate director of worship. The Spirit leads to Jesus, and directs worship to the Father.

Work of the Spirit: Transforming in the Liturgy

Pentecostals expect to be changed as a result of their liturgical moments. They envision experimenting in faith and experiencing the movement of the Holy Spirit in the liturgy. God is expected to move among and upon the people with transformative effects. Healings, deliverances, words from the Lord are seen as God's work among Pentecostal worshipers. They believe that the Spirit's work in the service is in part to change people, their lives, and their lifestyles. Self-identity changes too. Pentecostal liturgical experiences help to produce a new self-understanding. Pentecostals see themselves as children of God: saved, sanctified, filled with the Spirit, and called to follow the Lord in the work and purposes of God's kingdom.[33]

Beyond the Liturgical Setting: Worship Is for Living (and Serving)

Pentecostals know that the work of the Spirit and worship in the Spirit cannot be contained within the liturgical experience. Worship in the Spirit is not just a "Sunday thing." It is a daily thing. What begins

[33] The new awareness and growing identity that by the Spirit they are "children of God" works catalytically with the Spirit toward a change in personal identity; see Miller and Yamamori, *Global Pentecostalism*, DVD; also, Wacker, *Heaven Below*, 68–70. In Wacker's description of the importance and influence of testimony to Pentecostals he notes the impact of self-identity among early Pentecostals. Both personal and collective identity were shaped and strengthened as people testified. Pentecostals began to see their lives as "clothed with timeless significance," for the believer was involved in a cosmic, "magnificent drama."

Daniel E. Albrecht

in church unfolds into daily life. From their corporate worship Pentecostals move into the world, into their everyday lives. They live in the
"real world." Worship in the Spirit is real, but so is life beyond Sunday.
While Pentecostals see liturgy as worship that is due God and is mean-
ingful, necessary, and life changing, it must also be preparatory if it is
to be authentic worship in the Spirit. That is, Pentecostals view their
corporate worship services as a part of something much bigger—the
work of the Spirit in the world. Liturgy is not seen as an end to itself.
Worship continues in service to God in the world. It functions for Pentecostals as preparation and transformation for their ministry, for the
service to the world to which God calls and sends them. Part of the
Pentecostal liturgical vision, then, is the evangelism and cross-cultural
ministries that emerge from their worship services.[34]

A Mobile Liturgy: Worshiping Interculturally

Pentecostal liturgy is experienced as part of a movement, a Spirit
movement. Not surprisingly, then, Pentecostal worship and its rites
are mobile. Pentecostals can take their worship experience with them
everywhere. And they do. Mobility makes sense in a Pentecostal liturgical vision.[35] Pentecostals have discovered that their worship moves

[34] The Spirit's work in Pentecostal liturgy contextualizes and sensitizes
the worshipers to practical human needs—the needs of fellow Christians as
well as of nonbelievers. Pentecostals envision God's work in the liturgy as
sanctifying, gifting, and empowering them to serve/to minister. The liturgies
themselves reveal an intense desire for evangelism—to be God's witnesses.
Pentecostal worship services are envisioned as "witness." That is, in part, why
the liturgical setting and its rites involve testimonies and evangelistic messages. See Daniel Albrecht, "Witness in the Waters," in *Baptism Today: Understanding, Practice, Ecumenical Implications*, ed. Thomas F. Best et al., Faith and
Order Paper 207 (Collegeville, MN: Liturgical Press / Geneva: WCC Publications, 2008), 147–68.

[35] Hollenweger, as well as others, argue not only that Pentecostals' oral liturgy is largely responsible for the spread of Pentecostalism worldwide, but
that the Pentecostal movement at its heart is a missional movement. It is a
movement that has taken its rites, experiences in the Spirit, and liturgical vision along with the Gospel message around the world. In *Fire from Heaven*,
Harvey Cox calls Pentecostalism "a religion made to travel," claiming that its
"archetypal modes of worship" enable it to "root itself in almost any culture"
(101–2). Gary McGee points out that Pentecostals are "found on every continent and in every country, among almost all cultural and sociological groups

Worshiping and the Spirit

across cultural boundaries and that it flourishes in non-Western as well as Western cultures. It is adaptable and quickly takes on diverse inculturated forms. Pentecostals reason that Jesus is the same yesterday, today, forever, and everywhere; that Jesus still saves, heals, speaks by his Spirit; that by the Spirit he meets women and men wherever they seek him; and that he is no "respecter of persons." Thus, whoever they are, Pentecostals can take the message anywhere. They see the Holy Spirit "moving throughout the earth." It is the Spirit who calls followers to be mobile, too, to move with the Spirit. So Pentecostals have taken their liturgies everywhere, for their liturgies are an expression of who they are, how they see and relate to God—that is, how they worship in the Spirit. Pentecostal rites seem to be easily transported. If Pentecostal worship is not transcultural, it is certainly culturally adaptable. And Pentecostals have expected the Spirit to spread God's Word and work around the world. If God chooses to use them as a part of the transport, they pray that they will be ready to move with the Spirit.

> Pentecostal worship cuts across cultural boundaries. The Western world has neither designed nor dominated it. PW flourishes in nearly all non-Western cultures. Some credit these diverse *enculturated forms*, adaptable and mobile, to the oral nature of the liturgy. Others point to an entrepreneurial, creative, and pragmatic shaping of Pentecostal worship. Good explanations. But Pentecostals claim it is the work of the Holy Spirit in worship and the world.[36]

---

of the human mosaic" (citing David Barrett in "Missiology: Pentecostal and Charismatic," *The New International Dictionary of Pentecostal and Charismatic Movements*, 877; see also his "Missions, Overseas," ibid., 885–901).

[36] See Albrecht, "Pentecostal Worship."

Daniel E. Albrecht

13. The Spirit in Contemporary Charismatic Worship

One of the fascinating features of the story of Christianity in the twentieth century is the birth and rise of the Pentecostal movement. The importance of this movement for the spread and shaping of twentieth century Christianity across the globe cannot and must not be underestimated. For many of the historic denominations the major impact of Pentecostalism can be traced from the early 1960s, when the Pentecostal gifts and graces began to be expressed and experienced in what became known as the charismatic movement.

I would like to sketch briefly the story of the contemporary charismatic movement that I know best, and so turn to the U.K. There are two main eras: the first, spanning the 1960s and 1970s, is characterized particularly in its second decade by the dominant influence of the Fountain Trust; the second, running from the early 1980s to the present, is associated with the Vineyard church network. The first period was marked by a renewal called "baptism in the Spirit" accompanied in corporate worship by Pentecostal practices such as praying or singing in tongues, new musical styles that matched the more extemporary forms of prayer, and a new physical expressiveness in worship such as raising of hands. The charismatic movement and its style of worship were initially propagated primarily through two means: the large conference gathering (provided by the Fountain Trust in the late 1960s and throughout the 1970s) and the small midweek parish prayer group. The movement was ecumenical, and to an important degree catholic in spirit, as can be seen in the formative influence of Betty and Graham Pulkingham, High Church Episcopalians, for whom the new life of the Spirit was to be expressed most naturally in relation to the liturgical forms of the church.[1]

---

[1] See, for example, the three main songbooks edited by Betty Pulkingham in the 1970s (*Sound of Living Waters, Fresh Sounds*, and *Cry Hosanna!*) and their inclusion of musical settings to liturgical prayers.

1984 saw the beginning of the influence of John Wimber and the Vineyard network from California, launched by a series of large conferences across the U.K. This was much more than a relaunch of the charismatic movement. Prominent was a new emphasis upon the power of the Spirit for healing, expressed ritually in what is called the "Ministry Time" where the Spirit is called upon the assembly and participants receive prayer, often associated with visible and ecstatic demonstrations of the Spirit's presence in power. I use the word "demonstration" advisedly, since the Vineyard movement saw itself recovering the signs and wonders of the New Testament for the contemporary church. In the early and mid-1990s the "signs and wonders" element was to receive a fresh interpretation and expression when the Vineyard church in Toronto became the hub for international interest in an intensified form of ecstatic experience, which became known as the Toronto Blessing. Unlike the 1970s renewal, when the standard reference point was the Spirit at work among the body of Christ, as in 1 Corinthians 12–14, the Vineyard style was focused much more upon the healing ministry of Jesus and upon the book of Acts. The evangelical Quakerism of this movement (with its appeal to the need for individual transformation through the gospel combined with an emphasis upon the immediacy of the Spirit's action) meant that, compared to its 1970s precursor, it was less catholic and more revivalist in character.

Like Pentecostalism, the fundamental characteristic that makes the charismatic movement visible is its style of worship; indeed, it is the act of worship that both sustains and propagates charismatic identity. In the assembly the Pentecostal gifts and graces of the Spirit are actualized, recognized, and learned. As Don Williams writes, "the gift of charismatic worship to the church has been functionally to restore the Holy Spirit to our services."[2] This is not primarily a recovery of the Spirit that has come from the academy or church's doctrinal committees, which has subsequently affected patterns of worship. Rather the charismatic understanding of the Spirit has been formed by the experience of Pentecostal styles of ritual encounter in and with the Spirit. It is a good example of what has been called primary liturgical theology, where theological understanding is shaped by ritual realities.[3]

---

[2] "Charismatic Worship," in *Exploring the Worship Spectrum*, ed. Paul A. Basden (Grand Rapids, MI: Zondervan, 2004), 145.

[3] See for example David Fagerberg in *What Is Liturgical Theology? A Study in Methodology* (Collegeville, MN: Liturgical Press, 1992).

James Steven

My own research as a participant observer was based upon visits to Anglican parishes that had appropriated charismatic forms in their public worship. At the time of my visits in the early to mid-1990s the predominant form of charismatic expression in the parishes was that of the Vineyard, but the manner in which appropriation had taken place varied according to the prior liturgical tradition of the parish.[4] For example, the evangelical parishes that were less committed to Anglican liturgical forms tended to shape their worship around the three-fold pattern of the Vineyard assembly: Worship (a period of sung worship), Word (preaching), and Ministry (prayer for individuals in the worshiping assembly). An Anglo-Catholic parish however retained the liturgy and ceremonial of the Eucharist, and devised ways of incorporating charismatic expression. There was a time for public prayer ministry in the intercessions (complete with anointing with oil), new worship songs interspersed in the liturgy led by a worship band, and worshipers not only signing themselves with the cross but also raising hands in blessing, and laying hands upon others for prayer.

As I discovered from my case-study parishes, the interplay and relationship between historic liturgical traditions (in this case the Church of England) and Pentecostal styles and forms of worship generates important theological and liturgical issues. These can be discussed by focusing upon the threefold experience of the Spirit identified by Telford Work in his article on Pentecostal and Charismatic worship in the recently published *Oxford History of Christian Worship*: the spontaneous presence, the sovereign power, and personal mystical experience of Christ in the Holy Spirit.[5]

SPONTANEOUS DIVINE PRESENCE

From a historical and liturgical perspective one of the interesting questions raised by charismatic worship is in what sense is this form of prayer a revival of the "free prayer" tradition characteristic of the Dissenters?

---

[4] For the full discussion see James H. S. Steven, *Worship in the Spirit: Charismatic Worship in the Church of England* (Carlisle, UK: Paternoster Press, 2002), chap. 4, "Case Study Liturgies."

[5] "Pentecostal and Charismatic Worship," in *The Oxford History of Christian Worship*, ed. G. Wainwright and Karen B. Westerfield Tucker, 574–85 (New York: Oxford University Press, 2006).

In her book *Rituals of Spontaneity* Lori Branch offers a fascinating study of the rise of free prayer in late-seventeenth-century England following the restoration of the monarchy and re-imposition of the Book of Common Prayer in 1662.[6] She demonstrates that in this period of emerging modernity religious expression among Dissenters was defined by a rejection of liturgy's ritual repetition, and a replacement with forms of prayer that embraced and celebrated spontaneity and sudden inspiration. She summarizes the growth in the ideology of spontaneity:

> Concerned with the science of the soul and informed by emerging market and commercial logic, the cardinal points of this ideology were authentic and immediate sincerity (as opposed to performance or artifice), pure desire (as opposed to coldness, hypocrisy or a bifurcation between doctrinal knowledge and feeling), freedom (as opposed to form), and novelty and currency (as opposed to the repetitive, the boring and the out-of-date). . . . In the consolidation of the discourse and practice of free prayer, we see [how] spontaneity becomes a policy: not an option, but, for growing numbers of Protestants, paradoxically an obligation and the *sine qua non* of valid prayer and a saved subjectivity. (42)

Notice here not only the character of prayer in both positive and negative forms, but also its empirical function as demonstrating a "saved subjectivity." Branch describes the shift of the self-understanding of the religious subject, ushered in by the Reformation, from that centering on ritual participation, to the Cartesian *cogito*—self conceived without ritual, searching for a form of prayer that would nevertheless prove that the self has the necessary doctrinal knowledge for salvation.

Not surprisingly there was great investment in the manner and "performance" of prayer, the criterion for acceptable performance being mental and emotional intensity. Branch writes of the growth of a kind of emotional empiricism, which confirms the doctrinal knowledge of the praying subject, and which is also linked to the emerging commercial and economic values of the time in its appeals to novelty and variety. Spontaneity in prayer also becomes the ground for the

[6] Lori Branch, *Rituals of Spontaneity: Sentiment and Secularism from Free Prayer to Wordsworth* (Waco, TX: Baylor University Press, 2006). See especially chap. 1, "The Rejection of Liturgy, the Rise of Free Prayer and the Modern Religious Subjectivity."

James Steven

religious community in prayer: "[S]hared emotional intensity, arising spontaneously in the moment of extemporary prayer in the congregation . . . becomes the primary indicator of the promised presence of the Holy Spirit and of the unity among believers that Christ promised through that Spirit" (49).

In the light of Branch's analysis, to draw strong parallels between charismatic renewal and the "free prayer" tradition is not difficult. A participant in one of my case-study parishes highlights the authenticity of a charismatic prayer meeting in a way that mirrors the Dissenters' impatience with liturgical form:

> Thinking of our local churches, you feel that people are putting up fronts and you're just longing for the masks to fall away and for them to really be open to the Spirit . . . this frightfully formal traditional worship that they go to every Sunday morning . . . they may feel that it is meeting their need, but having experienced something like Evening Praise and I suppose the whole charismatic thing, one just knows that there's so much more they can have.[7]

The freedom in prayer is summarized by another participant, described in terms that echo the Dissenters' emphasis upon the measurable performance of true prayer:

> Seeing people freely express themselves in worship was another sign that to me they had gone past the group around them and they were actually focusing on God . . . the fact that Maggie knelt down and worshipped the Lord in front of the group was a big thing for her to do. She felt it was like a culmination of four years of what God had been doing in her. (Ibid., 62)

The language of desire permeates charismatic prayer and is often found in song lyrics, such as this meditative and devotional song that was very popular in the 1990s:

> To be in Your presence,
> to sit at Your feet,
> where Your love surrounds me,
> and makes me complete:
> (*Refrain*)

[7] Steven, *Worship and Spirit*, 59.

The Spirit in Contemporary Charismatic Worship

This is my desire, O Lord,
this is my desire.
This is my desire, O Lord,
this is my desire.

To rest in Your presence,
not rushing away,
to cherish each moment—
here would I stay.[8]

The sense of novelty in prayer is illustrated by the musical culture in charismatic worship which, either consciously or unconsciously, mimics the commercial trends in popular music.[9] The regular production of new songs is seen as the bona fide sign of worship that is "alive" and authentic. Being up to date, promoted and reinforced by the language of "anointing," can be employed to identify and mark the current song that God is giving to the church.

The examples cited could be supplemented with many others that give good grounds for concluding that the spirit and form of the free prayer tradition is very much alive in charismatic worship. It would be a mistake however to read charismatic worship as mere repetition of the Dissenting tradition, because there are some subtle transformations of this tradition within a liturgical context. One of the fascinating aspects of my research was to witness the variety of ways in which this contemporary form of free prayer was being related to the liturgical forms of the church. On the one hand I visited churches that were close in style and spirit to the Dissenting tradition; for them liturgical expression was a second-rate form of prayer, to be tolerated but given in small doses. Indeed freedom from a set liturgy, the flexibility to change the service structure and "go with what we discern to be the direction of God's Spirit," were regarded by one minister as highly valued features of his church's worship.[10] On the other hand, some parishes integrated the ethos of spontaneous prayer with liturgical forms. I think, for example, of the Anglo-Catholic parish cited above,

[8] From "My Desire to Be in Your Presence." Noel Richards. © 1991 Thankyou Music. All rights reserved. Used by permission.
[9] For a detailed treatment of this phenomenon see Pete Ward, *Selling Worship: How What We Sing Has Changed the Church* (Milton Keynes, UK: Paternoster Press, 2005).
[10] Steven, *Worship in the Spirit*, 65.

James Steven

and its priest whose liturgical presidency had been transformed through charismatic renewal from "saying Mass" to "praying Mass." In other words, the gift of the Spirit in prayer enabled him to enter more deeply, emotionally, and intentionally into the spirit and content of the prayer of the Mass. Here, it seems to me, is the gift of the Spirit in healing the modern division between subject and object, a division that the Dissenting tradition had embodied by locating true prayer, or spontaneous praises, in the realm of the subject. This catholic charismatic had brought together the spontaneous mode of prayer with the "objective" public prayer of the church.

Another way in which contemporary charismatic prayer marks a significant adaptation of free prayer in the late seventeenth century is in the priority it gives to theological interpretations of the action of prayer and worship. Of central concern to the Dissenters was the way in which prayer revealed the spiritual status of the praying individual. As Branch puts it, "The manner in which prayer is spoken may be taken as evidence of one's true spiritual condition, and a good heart— one saved or elect, sanctified by the grace of God—is both the source or cause of spontaneous, acceptable prayer, and the desired spiritual condition of which free prayer would ideally be evidence."[11] The theological account of spontaneous prayer complements this anthropological emphasis; it was a divine seal of approval in that such prayer was also enabled by, and a sign of, the Spirit of God at work. In charismatic prayer we notice a shift of focus, with the action of the divine Spirit brought to the foreground, and a comparative marginalization of concerns over the spiritual status of the individuals praying. Compared to the seventeenth-century Dissenting prayer, charismatic prayer is more concerned to establish free prayer as the sign of God's spontaneity, and less interested with free prayer being a sign of the spiritual status of those who pray.[12] In other words, the public perception is that prayer is more of a divine event than it is human.[13] This is not to deny that the human is important—worshipers are to be passionate, and the raising of hands, for example, signifies the intensity of engagement in

[11] Branch, *Rituals of Spontaneity*, 45.

[12] The early Pentecostal emphasis upon "baptism of the Spirit" as linked to the holiness of the Christian believer had all but disappeared by the late twentieth century in charismatic circles.

[13] For a discussion of the implications of this for the content of worship see Steven, *Worship in the Spirit*, chap. 7, "A Theological Appraisal."

The Spirit in Contemporary Charismatic Worship

prayer—but the prime significance of these so-called postural artifacts lies in their character as icons of God's presence in and through the Spirit. Hence the importance of the title to this section of my paper: spontaneous *divine* presence.

PERSONAL MYSTICAL EXPERIENCE

Like their seventeenth-century forebears, charismatic Christians have discovered that searching for authentic spontaneous prayer has ultimately led them to discover the logic of liturgical patterning.[14] A good example of this is the worship song sequence when songs are sung sequentially and without interruption for a length of time. These periods of sung worship exhibit all of Branch's characteristics of spontaneous prayer and are often designated as the "worship time"; this can and does cause consternation in liturgical traditions (for its implicit relegation and dismissal of all other traditional activities in worship). The significance of this form of worship lies in its character as a ritual pathway by which charismatics learn to encounter God. The chief goal of the ritual pathway is "intimacy" with God, achieved by a patterning and sequencing of songs, marrying musical style and lyrical content. In essence songs move from upbeat and confident declarations of praise to more devotional language, accompanied by popular ballad-style music. The worshiper is led into a personal mystical experience, characterized by an intimate and even romantic embrace of and by God.

A number of points must be made in relation to this ritual goal. The first is that the intimate encounter between worshiper and God is at the heart of the theology and ritual priorities of the Vineyard movement. Brian Doerkson, a leading songwriter and worship leader in the movement, describes intimacy as the highest value in worship:

> For most of my life, I remember singing songs in church about God, or singing songs that were exhortations to live better. But what I was hungry for, even as a boy, was to communicate directly with my Maker. *I wanted to sing to God. I wanted to reveal my heart to God and I wanted Him to reveal His heart to me.* In the summer of '85 I encountered the Vineyard at a Wimber conference where the worship leader began to sing songs that helped me express my heart to God. It was so simple.

[14] The creation of manuals giving instructions on how to pray spontaneously is the prime example of this for the Dissenters. See Branch, *Rituals of Spontaneity*, 52–56.

James Steven

Intimacy in worship is one of the foundations of the Vineyard movement . . .

And so for years, Vineyard worship around the world has been
marked by songs that are simple expressions of love and devotion. The
other thing that has marked Vineyard worship is our expectancy of
God's presence, *His heart revealed after we have revealed our heart to Him.*
This is real intimacy, a living relationship with God. What an incredible joy
when we discover that He is longing for these intimate times as well.[15]

Notice the language of the heart, which resonates again with the free
prayer tradition; worship is about the sincere heart (open heart) offering worship, to which God responds by opening his heart. Note that
this is not a moral heart, or a historical heart, but a romantic heart (a
human being who has fallen in love with God). Pete Ward, in his excellent study of song lyrics in contemporary charismatic worship, de-
tails how the heart in charismatic worship has been romanticized, the
consequence being that the climax of union with God is cast in terms
of the romantic self, and significantly, the individual romantic self.[16] A
good example of this is Matt Redman's song "The Heart of Worship,"
which portrays the worshiper and God in a "heart-to-heart" relationship: worshipers long to bring something of worth that will "bless"
God's heart, and God searches worshipers "deep within," looking into
their hearts:

> When the music fades
> All is stripped away
> And I simply come
> Longing just to bring
> Something that's of worth
> That will bless your heart
>
> I'll bring You more than a song
> For a song in itself
> Is not what You have required
> You search much deeper within
> Through the way things appear
> You're looking into my heart

---

[15] Brian Doerksen, "Intimacy: Our Highest Value in Worship," www
.vineyardboise.org/specialized_ministries/worship/doerksen_intimacy.htm.
[16] Ward, *Selling Worship*, 151–62.

The Spirit in Contemporary Charismatic Worship

I'm coming back to the heart of worship
And it's all about You
It's all about You, Jesus
I'm sorry, Lord, for the thing I've made it
When it's all about You
It's all about You, Jesus[17]

The second point is the topography of this ritual journey. Worship leaders that I met spoke of a threefold ritual structure of Invitation—Proclamation—Adoration. The Vineyard movement has a five-stage journey, and the musicians who lead the worship song sequence are trained to craft this ritual pathway.[18]

1. A Call to Worship

2. Engagement

3. Exaltation

4. Adoration

5. Intimacy

Others, who write, draw parallels with the journey of the Temple worshiper, who travels from the outer courts of the Temple (praise), to the inner courts, and even into the Holy of Holies, where there is an intimate encounter with God in Christ.[19]

How has this form of ritual been integrated in a liturgical church like the Church of England? A recent Grove booklet, entitled *Leading Others into the Presence of God*, illustrates how some Anglicans have appropriated this Vineyard tradition.[20] This booklet represents an approach that welcomes the tradition as the authentic model for public worship, and is revealing both for the way it faithfully exemplifies the

[17] From "The Heart of Worship (When the Music Fades)." Matt Redman. © 1999. Thankyou Music (admin. by EMI Christian Music Publishing). All rights reserved. Used by permission.

[18] Basden, *Exploring the Worship Spectrum* (n. 2), 143, and, for worship leaders, *Leading Worship: A DVD Training Experience* (Hull, UK: Vineyard Music Global, 2003).

[19] Mark W. G. Stibbe, *A Kingdom of Priests: Deeper into God in Prayer* (London: Darton, Longman and Todd, 1994).

[20] Chris Park, *Leading Others into the Presence of God: A Worship Leader's Guide* (Cambridge, England: Grove Books, 2004).

James Steven

Vineyard tradition, and also its critique of the patterns embodied in a liturgical tradition such as the Church of England. It does so by representing the flow of worship in diagrammatic form.

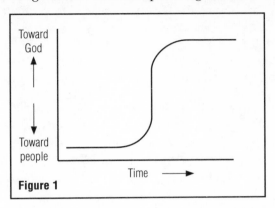

Figure 1

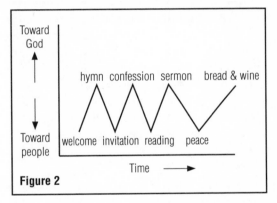

Figure 2

Diagrams from C. Park. *Leading Others into the Presence of God: A Worship Leader's Guide* (Grove Books, 2004).

The first of the diagrams represents the ideal Vineyard model, where worship is directed towards God for a sustained period of time; the second represents the more conventional liturgical experience of worship, where worship is a dialogue between the people and God. The author's preference for the Vineyard model is revealed in his comment that discovering charismatic worship has been a journey from what he calls "snacking" (figure 1) to "feasting" (figure 2). However the value of such diagrammatic representation is that it illustrates one of the major weaknesses of contemporary charismatic worship. The intimacy envisaged is characterized by the disappearance of the corporate dimensions of worship.

The Spirit in Contemporary Charismatic Worship

Two further observations are to be made. The first is that not all Anglicans would agree with this fairly uncritical absorption of Vineyard worship theology; many charismatic parishes use the ritual of worship song sequences in a way that honors the flow and sense of the liturgy. For example, a worship-song sequence may accompany and contribute to the thanksgiving of the Eucharist by songs being sung during the administration of communion, or alternatively, by replacing the Gloria to give voice to the congregation's praise. The second observation concerns the theology embedded in the Vineyard vision of worship: is this a faithful embodiment of worship in the Spirit? I have little doubt that the answer of the pioneers of the charismatic movement in the 1970s to that question would have been an unequivocal "No!" The important rediscovery of the early charismatic renewal movement was the *koinonia* of the Spirit, the church as the Body of Christ, where to come before God in public assembly was to realize that being in the presence of God meant discovering yourself in relation to others, giving and receiving in the Spirit. Worshiping in the Spirit should not be reduced to the intense personal mystical experience of a romanticized heart, but be a discovery of and celebration of the church, of being in community. As Irenaeus said, "Where the Spirit of God is, there is the Church and all grace."[21] So whereas at its best contemporary charismatic worship encourages a vision of liturgical worship as offering personal engagement in prayer, important questions need to be asked about the nature of the intimacy that is being promoted in its ritual.[22]

THE SOVEREIGN POWER OF THE SPIRIT

From a liturgical perspective one of the most interesting features of the Vineyard pattern of worship is the ritually enacted epiclesis that marks the beginning of the third stage of the Worship–Word–Ministry framework. The historical antecedents to this are to be found in the revivalist tradition of the American Frontier Camp Meetings.[23] There

---

[21] *Against Heresies* 3.24.1., trans. John Keble, A Library of Fathers of the Holy Catholic Church Anterior to the Division of the East and West (Oxford, England: James Parker and Co., 1872).

[22] For further discussion of intimacy and the individualism in charismatic worship see Steven, *Worship in the Spirit*, 118–34, 197.

[23] See James F. White, *Protestant Worship: Traditions in Transition* (Louisville: Westminster John Knox Press, 1989), chap. 10, for the classic historical discussion of the Frontier tradition.

James Steven

the final phase of a gathering would be the occasion for individuals to respond to the preacher, a tradition that was to develop into what is known as the altar call. Within Pentecostalism this was adapted to be the occasion in the gathering when those who wished to be filled with or baptized in the Spirit could come forward in order to "tarry" for the Spirit. In the Vineyard tradition there is a further reinterpretation of this. The service leader or preacher will call upon the Spirit with the words "Come Holy Spirit." This marks the beginning of a time of "Ministry" where individuals receive the Spirit's power. Typically some kind of physical expression identifies those upon whom the Spirit has come, and this is then "blessed" by members of a prayer team who wander amongst members of the congregation laying hands on people.

This ritually enacted epiclesis has had a significant impact upon the pattern of worship in charismatic Anglican churches.[24] In the 1990s some parishes molded their worship around the Vineyard structure, concluding with the Ministry; in one case the Sacrament was moved to the beginning of the service to allow this pattern to be followed. Other parishes integrated the Ministry into the regular liturgical pattern, for example by including public prayer ministry while intercessions were being offered: the intercessions began with an invocation of the Spirit, people then came forward for individual prayer, and meanwhile the parish priest led the congregation in public intercessions. An alternative pattern was to offer prayer ministry to individuals during the administration of communion (though this would not necessarily be linked with a public invocation of the Spirit). The widespread influence of this style of prayer can be witnessed in parishes that would not regard themselves as charismatic but now offer prayer at the end of a service for any who need it, and train up a prayer team to minister in this way.

Much could be said about this pattern and its implicit theology. Martyn Percy's sociological study of the Vineyard is illuminating for the way it makes explicit the underlying dynamics of the Ministry, and confirms my conclusion that it is a rite that is focused upon the spiritual empowerment of Christian worshipers.[25] In its original form this rite depends upon a radical openness and surrender of the individual

[24] See Steven, *Worship in the Spirit*, chap. 6.

[25] Martyn Percy, *Words, Wonders and Power: Understanding Contemporary Christian Fundamentalism and Revivalism* (London: SPCK, 1996).

The Spirit in Contemporary Charismatic Worship

to the purposes of God; public speech of those leading underlines and reinforces the need to be open to God, who is Lord and sovereign. Prayer asks God to "do whatever He wishes to do," even sometimes giving God "permission" to do what he wishes to do. Hence the ritual experience emphasizes the sovereignty of the Spirit and the corresponding willingness of the individual to submit or surrender to the Spirit's action.

Clearly plenty of antecedents exist in the history of prayer for the Spirit to bring about God's redemptive order and to empower Christians: through the laying on of hands Christians are empowered and commissioned for Christian ministries, and in sacramental action the Spirit is called upon to bring life to both people and sacramental elements. However, important issues are raised by the Vineyard style of epiclesis. For what purpose is the Spirit being called upon? At its best I see the Ministry as a form of pastoral prayer that undergirds members of the congregation as they make their own response to the call of Christ through the ministry of the Word. More problematic is the way the Spirit becomes a sacred performer whose activity, as witnessed by ecstatic behavior such as seen in the Toronto Blessing, is a mark of the degree to which the Spirit is present. By investing heavily in particular signs of the Spirit's presence, such as ecstatic physical patterns of behavior, church members define the Spirit by the empirical measurement of particular phenomena, which if absent imply that the Spirit has not "turned up." Liturgical leadership consequently becomes a serious matter of presiding over God's activity (hence a presider's running commentary, and requests of "more power") and liturgical participation becomes a matter of surrendering autonomy, being open to whatever the Spirit may do.

This raises important questions for those within a liturgical tradition.[26] Among the questions that need to be addressed are the following. First, does this not inevitably lead to a corporate anxiety over whether the Spirit has really been made present? Is this not the modern worshiper, shorn of assurance through sacramental means, searching for grounds for divine presence in measurable experience?[27] Second are concerns about the reality of the Spirit's personhood and

---

[26] See Steven, *Worship in the Spirit*, 201–7.

[27] See Ian Stackhouse, *The Gospel-Driven Church: Retrieving Classical Ministries for Contemporary Revivalism* (Milton Keynes, UK: Paternoster Press, 2004) for a recent discussion of this issue.

James Steven

freedom, tied both to empirical measurement and also to the direction of the liturgical leader, so that no longer does the Spirit "blow where he wills" but "it goes where it is sent."[28] This is ironic, given the movement's championing of the Spirit's freedom. Third are problems with the overwhelming emphasis on participants in or receivers of prayer ministry solely as recipients, with very little account made of their own powers of self-determination, or of their identity as moral actors who are seeking to make their own authentic response. "Surrender" is not the last word (and not the only word) in Christian existence before God!

It may be that these concerns have been recognized by the Anglican parishes that hosted the Toronto Blessing. Sustaining such public ritual performance has proved to be difficult. Revisiting churches ten years on from my research visits I have discovered that by and large energies have been channeled from the revivalist emphasis on the congregation's being "visited" by God toward a more missionary concern for the communities in which they are set. Even the influential charismatic flagship parish, Holy Trinity Brompton, had given up promoting "barking in the aisles" and instead invested significantly in their influential evangelistic Alpha Course.

CONCLUSION

Since its beginnings in the 1960s, the confluence of Pentecostal and historic denominations embodied by the charismatic movement has generated fresh discussion and perspectives on the nature of Christian identity and practice for Christians of all traditions. This study has illustrated how this is so with the practice of worship. Taking the key characteristics of Pentecostal prayer I have summarized the realities of charismatic worship in the historic liturgical tradition of the Church of England. In doing so some of the most fundamental aspects of Christian worship have been raised, concerning the character of prayer in the Spirit, the nature of communion with God, and the ritual expression of empowerment of Christian believers.

[28] Thomas Allan Smail, *The Giving Gift: The Holy Spirit in Person* (London: Hodder & Stoughton, 1988), 134, quoting Alasdair Heron.

The Spirit in Contemporary Charismatic Worship

Jonathan A. Draper

14. The Holy Spirit in the Worship of Some Zulu Zionist Churches

An aspect of modern South Africa after its transition to a nonracial democracy with a human rights constitution, one seldom noticed, is the quiet omission of the reference to the Holy Spirit in our national anthem. *Nkosi Sikelel' iAfrica* was written by Enoch Mankayi Sontonga in 1897 and became the de facto national anthem of black South Africans before being incorporated into the new composite national anthem in 1994. A casualty of the emergence of South Africa as a secular state, the line "Come down Holy Spirit" was dropped. I would like to cite in full the hymn as Sontonga composed it:[1]

Nkosi, sikelel' iAfrika;	Lord, bless Africa;
Malupakam'upondo lwayo;	May her horn rise high up;
Yiva imitandazo yetu	Hear Thou our prayers
Usisikelele.	And bless us.
Chorus	*Chorus*
Yihla Moya, Yihla Moya,	Descend, O Spirit,
Yihla Moya Oyingcwele	Descend, O Holy Spirit.

The hymn is remarkable for its vision of one Africa that transcends tribal divisions and calls for the restoration of the people. The reference to Africa's horn draws on a potent symbol in a Xhosa (and Zulu) culture based on cattle, which are associated with the ancestors and with power. Yet the hymn prays for the coming down of the Holy Spirit—not the ancestors—in order to heal, transform, and empower this national revival. I cannot think of an equivalent way of calling for the blessing of God in any other national anthem, and I believe

---

[1] I give here the original version with the English translation printed at Lovedale. The various versions, together with the modern, composite national anthem, are provided on the African National Congress website, together with a brief biography of Sontonga: http://www.anc.org.za/misc/nkosi.html.

it expresses something unique in African understanding of the Holy Spirit. First, the descent of the Spirit is understood corporately rather than individually. Second, the Spirit is not understood pietistically as related to worship alone, but as something that would transform all aspects of life with its power. Third, this Spirit of power is "holy" or numinous, by which I understand that it is not an aspect of "private religion" to be controlled or contained by a human will. When it descends it will effect something, and human beings either cooperate or stand in danger. Fourth, obedient submission to the Spirit brings blessing, and by this is understood the whole sphere of the life of the people.

These (submerged) aspects of the hymn are made clear in verses composed and added in 1927 by Samuel E Mqhayi:

> Bless our chiefs
> May they remember their Creator.
> Fear Him and revere Him,
> That He may bless them.
>
> Bless the public men,
> Bless also the youth
> That they may carry the land with patience
> and that Thou mayst bless them.
>
> Bless the wives
> And also all young women;
> Lift up all the young girls
> And bless them.
>
> Bless the ministers
> of all the churches of this land;
> Endue them with Thy Spirit
> And bless them.
>
> Bless agriculture and stock raising
> Banish all famine and diseases;
> Fill the land with good health
> And bless it.
>
> Bless our efforts
> of union and self-uplift,
> Of education and mutual understanding
> And bless them.

Jonathan A. Draper

Lord, bless Africa
Blot out all its wickedness
And its transgressions and sins,
And bless it.[2]

Blessing by the Holy Spirit is understood holistically: agricultural fertility, educational and economic development, the old and the young, the male and the female, rank alongside the gift of the Spirit in church and ministry. This is not accidental but is a feature of the way the Spirit is understood in African culture in general, and African Independent Churches of a Zionist nature in particular.

[2] Sikelela iNkosi zetu;
Zimkumbule umDali wazo;
Zimoyike zezimhlonele,
Azisikelele.

Sikelel' amadod' esizwe,
Sikelela kwa nomlisela
Ulitwal'ilizwe ngomonde,
Uwusikelele.

Sikelel'amakosikazi;
Nawo onk'amanenekazi;
Pakamisa wonk'umtinjana
Uwusikelele.

Sikelela abafundisi
Bemvaba zonke zelilizwe;
Ubatwese ngoMoya Wako
Ubasikelele.

Sikelel'ulimo nemfuyo;
Gxota zonk'indlala nezifo;
Zalisa ilizwe ngempilo
Ulisikelele

Sikelel'amalinge etu
Awomanyano nokuzaka,
Awemfundo nemvisiswano
Uwasikelele.

Nkosi Sikelel' iAfrika;
Cima bonk' ubugwenxa bayo
Nezigqito, nezono zayo
Uyisikelele.

The Holy Spirit in the Worship of Some Zulu Zionist Churches

While the widespread acceptance of *Nkosi Sikelel' iAfrica* shows how important and pervasive the notion of Holy Spirit is in South Africa and further afield, it has also occasioned considerable and ongoing debate in academic theology and anthropology. Bengt Sundkler, the pioneer of studies of African Independent Churches, unleashed a furor with his statement that Zionism "becomes the bridge over which Africans are brought back to heathenism."[3] His position was taken further in G. C. Oosthuisen's claim that "the most difficult theological problem in Africa [is] . . . the confusion that exists with regard to the ancestral spirits and the Holy Spirit."[4] James Kiernan points to the pervasive importance of the concept of Spirit and its links with power: "Zulu Zionists form small-scale curing communities in which reserves of spiritual power (*umoya*), are ritually built up and expended to offset the effects of human and mystical agents which afflict the individual. *Umoya*, meaning air, breath or spirit, suffuses a whole range of powers which Zionists fashion and transmit in the course of the healing rite."[5] Spirit is "conferred" by rituals such as laying on of hands, and defined in a strictly maintained hierarchy of rank and office. Kiernan also points to the agonistic nature of the deployment of Spirit to protect members and to ward off "impending mystical attacks" by Satan, sorcery, or witchcraft. Symbolic media such as clothing, staff, and flags are then understood as "weaponry" (*izikhali*).[6]

Allan Anderson has taken the discussion further in his fine study *Zion and Pentecost*, despite characterizing the discussion as "now an old and a 'white', rather irrelevant debate."[7] Coming from a Pentecostal background, he is keen to point to commonalities between

[3] Bengt Sundkler, *Bantu Prophets in South Africa* (London: Oxford University Press, 1948), 297.

[4] G. C. Oosthuizen, *Post Christianity in Africa* (London: C. Hurst, 1968), 120.

[5] James E. Kiernan, *The Production and Management of Therapeutic Power in Zionist Churches within a Zulu City* (Lewiston, NY: Edwin Mellen, 1990), 111.

[6] Ibid., 111–12.

[7] Allan Anderson, *Zion and Pentecost: The Spirituality and Experience of Pentecostal and Zionist/Apostolic Churches in South Africa*, AICM 6 (Pretoria: University of South Africa Press, 2000).

Jonathan A. Draper

African Pentecostals and Zionist/Apostolic churches.[8] He argues quite rightly for the importance of the creative inculturation of Christianity in Africa, and for the central role of the Holy Spirit in this reformulation of a religion received at the hands of an imperial culture both alien and alienating to Africans. Anderson comes to the conclusion that no confusion exists between the Holy Spirit and ancestors: "It seems that the alleged confusion between the ancestors and the Holy Spirit in AICs was a Western 'storm in a teacup' with no real foundation. Quite the contrary, many of the Pentecostal and Zionist churches have challenged the traditional spirit-world by their message of the power of the Holy Spirit to liberate from oppression of malevolent and capricious spirits that daunt their people's everyday lives."[9]

As sympathetic as I am with Anderson's overall project of revaluing the contribution of Zionist/Apostolic churches to the evolution of Christianity in South Africa and their links with global pentecostalism, I do not believe that the evidence he presents concerning the alleged "confusion" is convincing. In this essay I test Anderson's theory by looking again at two of the movements covered by Bengt Sundkler in Zulu Zion:[10] the Church of the Saints of George Khambule (1884–1949), and the Church of Jericho of Eliyasi Vilikati. I have also engaged in limited fieldwork with a number of churches in KwaZulu-Natal and Swaziland.[11]

---

[8] This concern is clear also in his important new book Spreading Fires: The Missionary Nature of Early Pentecostalism (Maryknoll, NY: Orbis, 2007), which charts the global influence of the Pentecostal movement from its beginnings with Charles Parnham, William Seymour, and the Azusa Street Revival.

[9] Anderson, Zion and Pentecost, 195–96.

[10] Bengt Sundkler, Zulu Zion and Some Swazi Zionists (London: Oxford University Press, 1976).

[11] Churches I examined with a small team of three postgraduate student fieldworkers (Kenneth Mtata, Queen Masondo, and Bongani Gumbi) were the Zion Combination Church of South Africa, the Christian Catholic Apostolic Holy Spirit Church in Zion, the Jericho Church, and Amabidiya. Some of the churches I approached were unwilling to participate because of bad experiences with previous researchers. All interviews in this study were conducted in accordance with the University of KwaZulu-Natal's strict ethical guidelines for research; participants signed release agreements after being carefully

The Holy Spirit in the Worship of Some Zulu Zionist Churches

Before continuing I wish to point out the complexity and problem of speaking about "Africa" in general rather than in specifics. For instance, the distinction made in 1948 by Bengt Sundkler in his *Bantu Prophets in South Africa*[12] between what he terms "Ethiopian" and "Zionist" independent churches is important. Sundkler distinguishes churches that broke away from their missionary parent bodies in rebellion against the racist domination of white missionaries and church leaders, and churches that have a specific configuration dominated by a particular understanding of the Holy Spirit. I wish to keep this debated distinction as a "useful indicator," although it may apply only in South Africa, and as modified by James Kiernan.[13] Major cultural differences exist from one part of Africa to another—even within South Africa—that need to be taken into account even if commonalities enable us to speak of an "African style of worship" that may continue to operate even among African Americans.

One further remark: the division between "mainline" churches and "independent" churches with regard to the Spirit may also be misleading. I have observed and experienced many if not most of the characteristics of Zulu Zionist worship in the Spirit in the context of the worship of Zulu Anglicans over many years. Indeed, there is a movement, *iViyo loFakazi bakuChristu* (the Legion of Christ's Witnesses), begun by Bishop Alphaeus Zulu and Canons Philip Mbatha and Peter Biyela as early as the 1940s, that bears many of the hallmarks of Zulu Zionism and has had a pervasive influence on Zulu

---

informed of their right to withhold information and to receive copies of any tapes.

[12] Sundkler, *Bantu Prophets*, 53–59.

[13] *Production and Management*, 1–10. Kiernan argues for a typological rather than historical distinction on the basis that most independent churches lean either toward the Word/Book or the Spirit, even though there is significant overlap. Nevertheless, as Kiernan himself observes, most of the Zionist churches—and this has been true of those I have interviewed, with the possible exception of Vilikati's *AmaJericho* Church—trace their origins to the mission of Pieter Le Roux, Daniel Nkonyane, and Fred Lutuli, which began in the Apostolic Faith Mission in 1904–5, but splintered thereafter into various African Zionist churches. The influence of Dowie's Chicago Zionist movement was significant (see *Production and Management*, 170–71; Sundkler, *Zulu Zion*, 13ff.; Anderson, *Spreading Fires*, 149–90).

Jonathan A. Draper

Anglicanism, at least in KwaZulu-Natal and the Eastern Cape.[14] My suspicion is that common underlying understandings of the Holy Spirit are operative among Zulu Christians of all denominations and can emerge at key moments, even though congregations usually follow the liturgies and formularies of their denominations in normal Sunday worship. Nevertheless, I will limit myself to the Spirit in some Zulu and Swathi Zionist churches, to use the terminology of Sundkler's second book, *Zulu Zion*, which was the starting point of my own studies.

UMOYA

In his interesting monograph on the Jericho Church of Eliyasi Vilakati, Anders Fogelqvist rightly notes the importance of "power, prophecy, and purification" at the center of the community life, but devotes merely two pages to the Spirit, noting only that the word *umoya* to refer to spirit and soul is "of missionary origin."[15] After that he uses only the word "power." This is a misconception, I believe. The Holy Spirit in Zionist life and worship is more than power; it stands at the center of their thought and praxis. Fogelqvist cites Alfred T. Bryant[16] as his authority for this, but the observation was already made by Bishop John William Colenso in the first Zulu dictionary, which he published in 1861,[17] and Bryant undoubtedly took it from him. Were Colenso and other missionaries consciously or unconsciously trying to preserve their monopoly of the interpre-

---

[14] See Richard Shorten, *The Legion of Christ's Witnesses: Change within the Anglican Diocese of Zululand 1948–1984*, Communications 15 (Cape Town: Centre for African Studies, 1987); Stephen Hayes, *Black Charismatic Anglicans: The Iviyo loFakazi bataKristu and Its Relations with Other Renewal Movements*, Studia Specialia 4 (Pretoria: University of South Africa, 1990). I have personally witnessed Zulu nuns of the Community of the Holy Name sniffing out demons in an afflicted prostrate woman during a revival service before they and the priest exorcised them in a manner very close to that of the Zionist healers.

[15] Anders Fogelqvist, *The Red-Dressed Zionists: Symbols of Power in a Swazi Independent Church* (Uppsala, Sweden: Uppsala Research Reports in Cultural Anthropology, 1986), 124–25.

[16] Alfred T. Bryant, *A Zulu-English Dictionary* (Pinetown: Marionhill Mission Press, 1905).

[17] John W. Colenso, *Zulu-English Dictionary* (Pietermaritzburg: P. Davis, 1861).

The Holy Spirit in the Worship of Some Zulu Zionist Churches

tation of *umoya*? The claim of *izangoma*[18] to possess the Holy Spirit also, noted in a complaint of one of Sundkler's Zionist informers,[19] may have its roots in cultural traditions older than the missionaries.

The importance of the issue of the vernacular in the development of African Christianity has been forcefully raised by a number of African theologians in recent years, most notably Lamin Sanneh and Kwame Bediako. They argue that the "translatability of the Word" is a central aspect of the Christian faith as opposed, for example, to Islam. In this way the Word has incarnated itself in Africa beyond the control of the missionaries who brought it. Word and words were contested from the beginning.

Thus the meaning of *umoya* was also contested from the start. Whether or not the word was first used by missionaries to refer to a personal or divine spirit, rather than to the wind, *umoya* carried and carries a weight of cultural and religious meaning that cannot be reduced to power, even if power is central to the concept of spirit. Nor can the meaning of the term be confined by trinitarian formulations as these were hammered out in Western culture. Clearly, various technical words have been used for a number of good and evil spirit(s)—as we would term them in English—and the traditional understandings have interacted and fused with understandings of *umoya* deriving from the missionaries. For instance, Paulina Nomguqo Dlamini was a member of King Cetshwayo's *isigodlo* (harem) and was ignorant of Christianity until her conversion. Interviewed in 1939 as an old woman, she gives a detailed account of the various spirits invading people (*ufufunyane*). These include *umoya wezwe* ("world spirit") and *imimoya wezizwe* ("spirits of the nations"), which "did not exist at the time of the old Zulu kings," and she opposes them to the Holy Spirit.[20] This is characteristic. Fundamentally, the division is between good and evil spirit(s). Human beings are at the center of a spiritual contest that never ceases and that affects everything they do—not just in terms of "spiritual life" but also in terms of success, prosperity, physical health, and a general sense of well-being. Unless proper care

---

[18] The *isangoma* is the spirit medium who serves as the "doorway" for commerce between people and their ancestors.

[19] Sundkler, *Bantu Prophets*, 242.

[20] H. Filter and S. Bourquin, ed. and trans., *Paulina Dlamini: Servant of Two Kings* (Pietermaritzburg: University of Natal Press, 1986).

Jonathan A. Draper

268

is taken, the careful balance can be destroyed, and a person's life may be in danger.

Finally, spirit cannot be "disembodied" the way it can be in Western culture. Spirit invades a body and possesses it. If a harmful spirit invades a person, physical means must be taken to expel it, such as induced vomiting, voiding, or bleeding. The spirit must be named, identified by its nature and by its location in the body. Drinking treated water, taking emetics or suppositories, inhaling smoke, and beating affected parts of the body are not unspiritual activities but intimately related to spirit. Spirit cannot be compartmentalized either, as if we can have an ecclesiology separate from a pneumatology, or a christology separate from a pneumatology. In interviews about the nature of the Holy Spirit in their life and worship, Zulu Zionists commonly say that "the Spirit is everything." In other words, the world is infused with spirit, and God is immanent within God's creation. We cannot say that at one point or another the Holy Spirit must be at work, since the Holy Spirit is the ground of, the starting point of, the purpose of, and the power of worship and liturgy, as it is also of life outside worship. Nevertheless, particular objects and activities may be intended to invoke that power in a service of protection or healing.

PROFILES OF SOME ZULU ZIONIST CHURCHES

The Church of George Khambule

I begin my exploration with early texts coming from the Church of George Khambule (*iBandla Abancwele*) in the 1920s. These were obtained by Sundkler and used in his description of the movement in *Zulu Zion*, but were written entirely for internal use.[21] Khambule was from rural Nqutu in Zululand. His father came from a well-established Methodist family in Edendale, in Pietermaritzburg, and had taken advantage of the Zulu civil war of the 1880s to obtain land from

---

[21] I have studied this church over a number of years and published my findings in a number of publications. The most recent are: "The Bricoleur from Oral Performance to Written Text: Early Christian Prophets and African Prophets," in *Performing the Gospel: Mark, Orality and Memory*, ed. R. A. Horsley, J. A. Draper, and J. Miles Foley, 44–63 (Minneapolis: Fortress, 2006) and, drawn from this research, "The Bible and Culture in Africa," in *Blackwell Companion to the Bible and Culture*, ed. J. Sawyer, 176–97 (Oxford: Blackwell, 2006), (a small section on Khambule).

The Holy Spirit in the Worship of Some Zulu Zionist Churches

Chief Hlubi. George Khambule fought in the South African Native Labour Corps and became an "exempted native," a legal status given to educated and Westernized Zulu people under Natal colonial law. While he was working in the mines Khambule experienced a "death" from Spanish flu in 1919 and had a vision that called him to return to Nqutu, where he founded his church. Initially it appeared to be a Methodist revival movement, but the revelations of the Spirit soon changed its direction. Some references to the Spirit in the texts of his church show trends that continue to appear in other Zionist churches. In a 1925 prophecy precisely dated and recorded, the prophetess Joanna Ndlovu (General of the Lord and Prosecutor) receives the following words from the angel Gabriel:

> 4th June 1925 6 pm–9.30 pm
> The General of the Lord and Prosecutor
> That which is hidden shall be exposed to the light now. St. Gabriel says this carrying the sword in his right hand and in his left hand the palm branch, saying that, "The morning star, which led the Wise men to the child. When they had seen the child they gave him a gift of gold. And so it is with them, that they gave him the gift of the Spirit by their hearts, says the Lord. Y.-S.P.A.J.Z.J. F.B.T.M.J.A.L.T.S.K.-S.O.S.: These are the names that were written on the Glorious Morning Star." Big, black stoles are needed rather than the ones that we have. They shall be fastened on the right hand side. They shall be written with silk cotton, which is known by the Bearer of the Ark. They shall be white ones, written with black or red. They are for the seven spirits of God. (Diary 1:7B-9A)[22]

What is significant is that the prophecy, heavily influenced by the language of Revelation and Matthew, is delivered by an angel. Gabriel

[22] Photocopies of these Zulu manuscripts are located in the Sundkler Archives in the Carolinum Library, Uppsala University. The originals were destroyed in the fire that swept through the house of Archbishop Sikakane, the last leader of the church. They have been transcribed and translated by myself with a team of postgraduate students who also conducted fieldwork with me on this church, in accordance with the university's ethics policy, and whose names are recorded here with gratitude: B. M. Mkhize, M. K. Ntuli, and B. Maseko. The texts are cited here and in what follows according to the titles and page numbers given them by Sundkler. In this early book of texts the prophecies are described as "words of Jehovah."

Jonathan A. Draper

says that just as the Morning Star led the wise men to give gifts of gold to Jesus in the past, symbolic of the gift of the Spirit to Jesus, so now that gift is given to Khambule. Also important is that the writing and garments seen in the vision are actually reproduced exactly in the garments of the prophet and his two prophetesses. The gift of the Spirit is also characterized as receiving the seven spirits of God, as in Revelation, that are named on the garments from Isaiah 11: "The spirit of the LORD, the spirit of wisdom, understanding, counsel, might, knowledge, fear of the LORD." This is followed up in a ritual for tending the seven candles of the seven churches and for the going out of the seven angels, a practice continued until the end of the church (and reputedly beyond its formal demise), as can be clearly seen in a photograph in the Carolinum in Uppsala, taken by Bengt Sundkler, of worship led by Archbishop Mordekai Sikakane. The angel also revealed that the prophet should establish an *isigodlo* or royal harem of virgins for the new Jerusalem, which all members, male and female, of the church would enter through the "marriage of the Lamb." They forsook marriage and settled together in the new Zion built on Khambule's land (when he was expelled from this land by the government he bought a farm elsewhere to rebuild Zion).

Khambule's church was focused on healing; the sick were brought to his Zion to stay until they were healed or died. They were prayed for by the "hospital" (*isibhedlela*), or praying healers, who stood in cross-and-circle formation. Khambule and his church used the physical media of stones, understood to be weapons (*izikhali*, the crossed spear and stick of traditional Zulu soldiers) passed over the affected part of the body, and water mixed with ash over which Khambule had prayed. Traditional *izangoma* or mediums also carried symbolic sticks as "weapons" in their spiritual contest. The stones, like the cross, are understood to be objects of power and danger, conveying the numinous. For this reason they are wrapped with cloth and handled carefully. They convey healing and power but can also convey death.

Healing is part of an ongoing battle between the Spirit and the angels on the one hand and Satan on the other, played out in the lives of the small community and its members. Satan is at work in the example that follows through one, Reuben Mncube.[23] Reference is made

[23] Informants told me that sinners, or those believed to be possessed by Satan, were severely beaten in the church—one told me that when she was

The Holy Spirit in the Worship of Some Zulu Zionist Churches

to one of the church's foundational healing events when evil spirits were exorcised from the daughters of Sithole, who then left home and joined Khambule's *isigodlo*, something that displeased Sithole and others in the community (such as prospective husbands):

> Truly the devil has no power over the faithful except he first asks God. And he is allowed only by Him alone. If the angel speaks about difficult places where he fights with Satan, he conquers. Pho! So how can it be that he cannot mention Sithole's place, where he fought with an engine and where he fought with a mighty legion and where he chased them away? It is really indeed that the devil has no power over an angel. Pho! So what is it that the devil can use to conquer? It is really so. The devil has no power upon the innocent, because Jehovah is there, who will fight for us by the power of an angel and Satan is conquered together with his *impi*! The Spirit himself descended and settled down. I praise my God who conquered Satan for me in the person of Reuben Mncube. (Diary 1:27B-28B)

Every movement of the battle between the angels and Satan is directed by the Spirit. For example, "if the Spirit is willing you Nazar can also go" (Diary 1:31A); "They talked and they concluded, the Spirit agreeing. Pho!" (1:33A). The members of the church "volunteers" are divided into "labour gangs" overseen by a "captain." The healing gangs are called "the hospital"; they participate in the worship of the church in a special way:

> The Hospital (*Isibhedlela*): "Khambule would pray for many who were sick and they would be healed. If they did not get healed, Khambule would ask them to confess their sins. Besides Khambule there was an *isibhedlela* (hospital) consisting of those who were chosen to pray for and visit the sick. They used water and prayer (*ngesiwasho nangomkhuleko*). Ash (*umlotha*) is put in the water over which prayer has been said and is used to ward off all diseases, casting out demons and ending fits of insanity (*asebenza izifo zonke ngawo bakhipha amadimoni nezipoliyana*). The days for prayers of the *isibhedlela*: Tuesday and Friday after the *isibhedlela* had fasted for two days and prayed all night. They wear blue long dresses and hats. They go and preach in the houses among the unbelievers, even at

---

twelve she was beaten so badly that her hip is permanently damaged, which is why she left the church (though she continued their worship and healing practices on her own account!).

Jonathan A. Draper

Msinga where the unbelievers abound." . . . The Hospital sits separately in church gatherings: "The *isibhedlela* prays for the sick. One
stands and the other sits down. All buy clothes for themselves since
the money of the church does not come by compulsion but as a vol-
untary gift." (Mhlungu 1941)[24]

While this movement had begun with a fervent eschatological hope,
in which Khambule named a specific day for the return of the Lord
described in detail by members interviewed by Philip Mhlungu, it
was determined on that day that Jesus (one side black and the other
side white) had come in the Spirit by means of a prophecy by one of
the members (Mhlungu 1941:25–26).[25] On another occasion Khambule
prophesied that manna would come down from heaven to feed the
people miraculously, and he forbade them to plough their fields for a
year, causing much hunger (ibid., 27)—the manna came in some form
in the worship of the church.

It is not only members who are mysteriously in contact through
the Spirit with the angels, even inhabited by them. Khambule himself, whose angelic medium name is "Nazar," is understood as in
some sense having the same contact with Jesus, in some way in-
carnating him in the community: "You must know this. You have
taken upon you the likeness of the Lord Jesus" (Diary 1:7A). It is not
simply a matter of an "imitation of Christ," nor the "black messiah"
idea that was proposed, but the idea that an ancestor can come on a
person, often by means of the name given to the person, and can in
some sense "become that person" without that being defined very
precisely.

The theme of prayer or thanksgiving for the coming down of the
Holy Spirit is a recurrent theme of the liturgical texts of the community, including this beautiful pair of hymns composed on the same day
in 1928:

[24] This interesting account of *iBandla Labancwele*, while Khambule himself
was still alive, was provided to Sundkler by Philip Mhlungu while a student
at Umpumulo Lutheran Seminary in 1941. Mhlungu subsequently became a
bishop in the Evangelical Lutheran Church of Southern Africa.
[25] Ibid.

The Holy Spirit in the Worship of Some Zulu Zionist Churches

Wednesday 22/2/28 2pm
The Hymn of the Saints through
St. Itengirrah of the Descending
of the Holy Spirit
Joel 2:28
A.
Come to us
Holy Spirit
Come with your power
Holy Spirit.
B.
Let it be known to me
Let it be true
That name of yours, O Father
Saying Abba.
C.
They were of one heart
In prayer
When the day of Pentecost
came.
D.
They were all overtaken
By the great noise
Which was from heaven
As if it was a gale.
E.
He filled
The whole house
Which they were in.
They saw different tongues.
F.
They were like fire
They were all overtaken by it
They all began to speak
In other tongues.

Wednesday 22/2/28 7pm
A Hymn of the Coming down
of the Holy Spirit through
St. Itengirrah of the Church of
the Saints
A.
Come Holy Spirit
Who is with the life of the Lord
Come and preach to us
Come and remind us of all
Your words Lord.
B.
Father what you have given us
Let it be multiplied here in us
The fruit of holiness
Let them sprout here in us
May we see your beauty.
C.
Come Holy Spirit
Make our heart
To love the Saviour
Let there be nothing in us
Which displeases him.
Amen.

Few Christians of any persuasion would quarrel with these hymns.
Yet they are revealed through St. Itengirrah, the angel of a departed
member of the church, as evidenced in a "new song" of 30 May 1926
after the death of Ndlovu: "It happened on a certain day that St.

Jonathan A. Draper

Itengirrah entered Paradise. Today St. Itengirrah is present. She sang and said, 'Blessed are they, the holy ones in heaven.' Itengirrah overcame death" (Liturgy 3:75–78).

I have argued this point at some length because it seems that the Holy Spirit, the seven spirits of God, the angels, and even Jesus as the "other Comforter" whom he sends, are not clearly distinguished conceptually or in worship: "Hail, Lord who sends us the Holy Spirit, the Counsellor. We see a person coming through him. We see the Church receiving" (Liturgy 3:7). What is critical is the immanence of God among his people, and the bridge between heaven and earth established by faith in Jesus and enabled by the gift of the Holy Spirit, mediated by angel-ancestors through dreams and visions. This enables the church, guided every step of the way, to fight evil and to know that it will prevail and receive blessing and healing in an uncertain and dangerous world.

The Church of Jericho

While Khambule's church failed in the end, the Church of Jericho (*AmaJericho*), also featured in Sundkler's *Zulu Zion*, not only survived but continues to grow, not only in Swaziland, where it is probably one of the largest churches, but also in South Africa. Founded by the late Eliyasi Vilikati, the rather secretive[26] Church of Jericho has a number of features not characteristic of other churches; for instance, in the use of red (and many other colors!) in its robes rather than white and blue/green. *AmaJericho* was the subject of a major study in 1986 by Anders Fogelqvist,[27] who argued that the use of the ambivalent color red indicated that the church attempts a transitional state between "traditionalists" and modernity. Vilikati's church has a strong association with the king today, and has a majority of men as members, unlike most Zionist churches.[28] Vilikati had no formal education, and was unchurched prior to his conversion in prison in Johannesburg. For our purposes, his two seemingly contradictory accounts of his conversion,

[26] Members are not supposed to disclose anything to outsiders. Local Jericho members had to consult the Spirit (and the archbishop) before Queen Masondo was allowed to speak—and then only after a process of testing.
[27] *The Red-Dressed Zionists* (Uppsala, Sweden: Department of Cultural Anthropology, Uppsala University, 1986). His main hypothesis has not won much support and will not form part of our analysis.
[28] For a discussion, see Fogelqvist, *Red-Dressed Zionists*, 44–46, 106–10.

The Holy Spirit in the Worship of Some Zulu Zionist Churches

given to Fogelqvist, are significant because they merge God, the Spirit, and angels in a rather undifferentiated way:

> In 1948 I was put in jail in Germiston because I was going between Johannesburg and Pretoria without a pass. I stayed four days in jail. God then came with his angels. They said that I must obey the law. They said that I must sing a song. I then did what I was told. I then cried. When I woke in the morning I had power. God asked me what I wanted there. He said that I must go and preach among his people . . . (61)

In the second account we hear:

> The spirit of God came to me while I was in jail. The old angels who were men came to me in the jail in Johannesburg, and they took me away from the jail. They had large wings. They told me that they were *kerobhi* [cherubs]. They were three. They said: "Go out! You are not a criminal. You are free. You are one of the kings of the Christians in the world". . . (62)

In both accounts Vilikati is given a vision of water pouring through his hands. A third version was given by his son to Queen Masondo in field interviews.

His period of searching and of visions before beginning his church is replete with angelic messages and voices. He has a vision of a "man with one leg" (*Mlente ngamunye*, also called *Mantikwene*) who is somehow associated with God. This is also associated with the snake with many—usually seven—heads (*inyoka emakhandakhanda*), which appears in a pool or *isitiba*. His converts have to enter the pool for purification, but only after the snake has left. Power and danger go together. In fact, Queen Masondo, who is not a Zionist, was taken to the pool, which no one else would approach, where she had a terrifying experience she could not account for:

> This place is deserted and frightening. The men who were with me said that they would not go near the dam, but I went forward without a word. While I was just about a hundred meters from the dam, the water rose up about ten to fifteen meters above me. I stood still and heard a voice saying, "Do not look up. I will go out of the dam." I did as it had said. After that I can only remember that I was standing on the bank of the dam in the water. I called them and they started washing themselves and people from the nearby homes shouted saying,

Jonathan A. Draper

276

"Don't move. We also want to come and have *isiwasho* [sacred water] (8ᵗʰ December 2007).[29]

The snake is discussed by Fogelqvist in terms of its associations with traditional patterns of divination in Swazi (and for that matter Zulu) divination (105–6). While he is correct in this, he does not see the connection with Moses and the healing snake, explicit also in Khambule's church ("You are Moses," Diary 1:51B), where the prophet's staff is headed by a snake, and understood to be the staff of Moses that mediates healing.

In the Church of Jericho all decisions are taken on the basis of dreams or visions from the spirit(s) and the angels, which are to be tested by the archbishop or a duly appointed pastor. Archbishop Bhekibandla stated:

> The spirits or angels, which appear to *amaJericho*, are either a big white bird with the face and voice of a human, and is either female or male. Or it is a voice that comes from the wall if it is in the house, while outside no one is certain where it comes from. Again it is either a female or a male voice.[30]

Queen Masondo was told in interviews with Archbishop Bhekibandla that *AmaJericho* has no problems if members have an ancestral spirit (*ubungoma*) possessing them, as they can convert it into a Jericho spirit. Likewise, they make sacrifices for the dead on the mountain, where the entire carcass is burnt. Then they pray for rain or burn incense during droughts. They may sacrifice sheep (not goats as in traditional rites) in the temple for special requests. With regard to healing, informants stated that:

> The healing angels stay in a certain place called *iLadi* (altar). The owner of the altar should give offerings and sacrifices to the spirits, which are present in that altar. As they are taken to be the babies, a chicken or a lamb sacrifice or offering is suitable, except when the altar needs to be cleansed (a cow is needed there). There are no times stipulated to do

---

[29] This account, taken from a report of fieldwork from November 2007 to February 2008, was provided by Queen Masondo and based on her tape transcripts.

[30] Fieldwork report of Queen Masondo.

The Holy Spirit in the Worship of Some Zulu Zionist Churches

this, but at times the spirits/angels demand the sacrifice or offering for an immediate reason.[31]

The sick person may be placed on the altar for the laying on of hands while the spirits/angels reveal the cause of the problem. Various media are used in healing (e.g., ashes, salt, seawater) as the spirits reveal. An offering to the church is then made of money, work, or food. New members usually join as a result of such healing.

In interviews the archbishop outlined a total of thirty-two spirits, each with particular colors and associated uniforms, symbols, powers, and purposes. He emphasized that the *AmaJericho* believe in one triune God and recite the Apostles' Creed at the beginning of each service, but that they also believe in the indwelling of each member by the Holy Spirit and by the particular spirits of power that work with the Holy Spirit. The Bible is important in the worship of the church (where it seems it may be used as an oracle to determine someone's future), but church members are more concerned with direct revelation.

Zion Combination Church of South Africa

The Zion Combination Church, like the next one we will discuss, traces its origin to Daniel Nkonyane, the first Zulu leader to break away from the white Pentecostals and Zionists at the beginning of the twentieth century. Its pastor, Reverend (*Mongomeli*) Samson Luthuli left school at Standard 5 and completed his Junior Certificate by correspondence. He retired after working all his life for a local furniture company. After his mother was healed by a Zionist minister he was converted and joined the Zion Combination Church, becoming a local minister, general secretary, and finally president of his church. The congregation is relatively small, but looks forward to the grand annual gathering of the church in Newcastle at Easter every year, a feature of all of the Zionist churches. In an interview Luthuli saw the Spirit as being first and foremost involved in healing and prophecy (with which it is related). Church members heal by prayer and laying on of hands, but also use *isiwahso sokuthelwa*—water mixed with ashes. Identifying illness is the first priority, and the healing will depend on that. Pouring or drinking water treated with ashes (sometimes salt) is important; so too is "shaking" the person afflicted with evil spirits, to chase them out.

[31] Ibid.

Jonathan A. Draper

278

In this church the minister indicated a considerable amount of freedom in what ministry in the Spirit persons exercise and when—it depends on persons and their gifts and how they are led on a particular day. The reception of the Spirit follows baptism and directs persons from then onward in the way they should go: "They are baptized with water. Let me say the person repents first, then s/he is baptized with water in the river. After being baptized, s/he is enlightened by the Spirit in the way s/he is supposed to go (*indlela okufanele ahambo ngayo*), because the word of God says that the Spirit is the one which is the way in which we should walk. It is the one which shows us the way."[32] There is no special prayer for calling down the Spirit, only prayer and fasting for God to send it. The gifts of the Spirit depend on the "commitment" of the person and what path the Spirit leads. When asked about the role of the angels, Luthuli confirmed that "the angel works in the church but by means of dreams; others see visions, as I have said. They can see ailments. We consider the angel as the Sent One (*isithunywa*) of God, who shows you the way to see such things." The terminology is the same as the visit of an ancestor in traditional Zulu culture. Luthuli confirmed that the church members sacrifice animals and undertake the traditional *umsebenzi* or work of honoring the ancestors: "We remember them as, for instance, what they used to do in church or at home doing various things, but we do not worship them. We do serve them."

This discussion showed Luthuli's keen awareness of the debate about the "orthodoxy" of Zionists and whether they "worshiped" the ancestors, and his intention to firmly reject this idea. On the other hand, he acknowledged that he and the members of his church do continue to be visited by ancestors: "they come through dreams and speak to us concerning various matters." His church does not prevent people from going to traditional healers or mediums of African traditional religion, but he did not think many people did because there was no need for a member to do this when healing and access to the ancestors was possible within the church: "There is no need for us to go to the mediums (*ezangomeni*) because we are mediums (*siyizangoma*) in our own sense. Many of our people do not go to the mediums (*ezangomeni*). We see things according to our own way. But there is no restriction against those who want to go consult the mediums

---

[32] Translation of a transcript of an interview with Reverend Luthuli conducted by K. Mtata and myself on 16 January 2008.

The Holy Spirit in the Worship of Some Zulu Zionist Churches

(*izangoma*)." The ancestors come to church members in the form of angels or "sent ones" (*izithunywa*) and give dreams to tell people what to do, which is the traditional role played by the ancestors.

On my first visit to the worship of the Zion Combination Church of South Africa in Sweetwaters, near Pietermaritzburg, the Creed was sung—something clearly not done often, since it was read by members of the congregation from a photocopied page. However, it was also not entirely unfamiliar since it was sung with hesitation but some competence. It was done, I am sure, to emphasize the church's orthodox credentials—which I am not concerned to question—to outsiders. The service was devoted to consoling the pastor, *umongomeli* (an area supervisor of the church—he had been secretary of the whole church at one stage), and Luthuli, whose wife had just died. The seating arrangement was unremarkable, with a white and blue-clad "captain," or lay minister, and four women members in uniform, seated behind a table covered in white linen on which two white candles were burning. The table had a white frontal with the blue cross and stars characteristic of Zionism, which I was told was revealed in a dream.[33] A white rope stretched the length of the church above the congregation. The minister, dressed in reformed manner, except with his gown in green, sat a little higher on a dais, with a desk. When the minister looked across, he suddenly noticed that there were only the two candles, and he immediately instructed the captain to bring out and light a third, yellow candle between the two others. After the service we asked what the significance of this candle was, and were told it was for the angels. On further discussion the minister revealed that the angels were also the ancestors. It had seemed inappropriate to him to continue with a service devoted to his deceased wife without the candle for the angels burning on the table.

The importance of candles in spiritual warfare found here matches that in Khambule's church and is important in St. John's Apostolic Church too. This church also uses the sevenfold candles of the Apocalypse, as Linda Elaine Thomas emphasizes. One of the bishops she

---

[33] The Zulu language traditionally makes no distinction between green and blue. This "blue" is regarded as the color of heaven, and traditionally as the color of the heaven queen/*Nomkhubulwana*. Her identity is a matter of debate, but not her significance in traditional culture. See Axel-Ivar Berglund, *Zulu Thought-Patterns and Symbolism* (Bloomington: Indiana University Press, 1976), 63–64.

Jonathan A. Draper

interviewed explains: "Candles and water are the main things at St. John's. We must always have candles so that we can see what we are doing."[34] In all the churches this project examined candles were important ritual objects related to the release of the power of the Spirit and of the angels.

In an interview, Rev. Luthuli, when asked to describe how he knew the Spirit's power was at work, understandably found it difficult to put into words, but said:

> You will feel it. You will have power to preach . . . it does not arise out of nowhere . . . you know . . . you do not prepare to preach. There is something that . . . I don't know how to explain . . . there is something inside you which tells you, speak like this, do like that . . . you don't prepare . . . it is not like at school where there the teacher says, I am preparing what I will teach tomorrow . . .[35]

Interestingly, although he did not prepare the sermon, nevertheless the regular daily reading of the Bible was crucial to him: "the Bible is my life . . ." This is a common theme among the Zionists, even though they are so insistent on the constant guidance of the Spirit. In any case, everything is sung from the beginning to the end of the service except the preaching, and even that is constantly interspersed with the congregation's breaking out into singing with the constant beat of the drum. The coming of the Spirit may be dramatic, evidenced in trance-like states and sometimes violent movements.

The Christian Catholic Apostolic Holy Spirit Church in Zion

This church also sprang out of the Zulu Zion movement of Reverend Daniel Nkonyane in 1906. In this case its pastor was not a convert like Luthuli but grew up in the church, and took over as minister when his predecessor, Reverend Mkhize, who had trained him, died. Reverend Maphumulo is currently also vice president of the church as a whole. He has a Standard 8 education, worked as a builder, and was not embarrassed to say that "I was not successful in many things, including education, but this church is led by the Spirit and not by people with high academic achievements." When asked to describe

---

[34] Linda E. Thomas, *Under the Canopy: Ritual Process and Spiritual Resilience in South Africa* (Columbia: University of South Carolina Press, 1999), 89–90.
[35] Interview by Draper and Mtata, 8 February 2008.

The Holy Spirit in the Worship of Some Zulu Zionist Churches

how the Spirit works in the life and worship of the church he said: "This is the way the Holy Spirit works; if there is something that the Spirit is not happy with in the church, s/he[36] cries (*uyakhalaza*) against it. If there is sickness, the Spirit will cry about it. Even if there is something going wrong in someone's life or if the person says it, the Holy Spirit reveals it . . . S/he only comes at particular times and says what s/he wants to say."

When pressed on the question of angels and the Spirit he said, "The Spirit and the angels just work according to what the Bible says. S/he speaks with anyone, as if one is listening to the telephone. We can also have some who will be led by the Spirit to speak in other tongues that people who are listening will not know. Someone will then say what the Spirit has been saying."

As with all the informants, prophecy is an important aspect of the work of the Spirit: pointing out what is the problem, the sickness, the location of Satan, the way to heal, the way to achieve success, and so on. As has often been observed, whether in friendly or hostile reports, this is close to the way the ancestors operate through mediums in African traditional religion, even when most of the churches see themselves as doing something quite different, something uniquely Christian. When pressed on the question of the ancestors, Maphumulo said that the continuing use of traditional rites for the ancestors was the result of the members' participation in the normal life of the neighborhood, where it would be wrong not to share. Some Zionist churches, he argued, continued these practices so that "sometimes they invite us for church services to remember their dead, but in the midst of all these services people do their own kind of things one cannot control."

Secondly, Maphumulo emphasized the importance of healing by laying on of hands and by the use of water and ashes. This was borne out in the services of the church where the climax was the "hospital" where healing was carried out. Again, beating and shaking of the afflicted person was practiced to drive out the spirit afflicting her or him. In worship, singing is practiced from beginning to end; everything is sung. All members of this group carry reed sticks as "weapons" in the contest with Satan and evil spirits, and the minister specifically pointed out to us in the course of the service that in Exodus 4:17 Moses

---

[36] Gender is not signaled grammatically in Zulu, and it is impossible to tell except in context whether a male or female is referred to.

Jonathan A. Draper

used a staff to achieve miracles: "Take in your hand this staff, with which you shall perform the signs." So every member, by carrying the rod, was equipped to work miracles. Maphumulo also preached on John 8:36 in the service, deliberately in the context of our visit: "So if the Son makes you free, you will be free indeed." This was a deliberate pointer to the origin of the church in resistance to white control and domination, directed at me I am sure!

CONCLUSION

None of the churches I examined here thought they placed limitations on the presence and activity of the Spirit in worship or worship in the Spirit. The Spirit is everywhere and in everything. On the other hand, little real distinction is made between the Holy Spirit in its Christian doctrinal definition and spirit in its usual Western understanding as a human property, nor between angels understood as those sent from God to give messages or to intervene on specific occasions, and ancestors, understood as those family members who have passed on and are now with God, who have been brought back to the homestead, and who have become like angels of God as Jesus said they would. Basically, there is good Spirit and bad spirit in various expressions. No doubt the Zulu Zionist churches examined here understand the Spirit, as sent by Jesus, as the one who is present among them, but the delineation of this presence and its various ramifications is much fuzzier than most of us would be comfortable with. The endless wrangling over the exact definition of the moment of the Spirit's presence, the Spirit's relation to the Father and to Jesus, the relation of the Spirit to angels and ancestors, so significant in Western Christianity, is not their concern. Their concern is receiving power from God to overcome the life-threatening insecurities of existence so that believers may obtain life, healing, and well-being in every aspect of life.

While I appreciate the attempt of Anderson and others to make Zionist worship conform to the safe limits of Western Pentecostalism, I am skeptical that this is moving in the right direction. Perhaps fuzziness is inherent in the Christian faith from the beginning, and is bound up with the question of culture. I believe that the Christian Scriptures are inherently self-contradictory with regard to the Spirit. Paul can talk of the Spirit of Christ as if the Spirit is the earthly presence of Christ now, but at other times in a much more hypostatic way. John's view of the Spirit being "another Paraclete," hence another Jesus in some way, lends itself without careful creedal protective barriers to the idea of

The Holy Spirit in the Worship of Some Zulu Zionist Churches

another person embodying Jesus—Khambule, Shembe, or whoever—not as replacing him, but as the coming Spirit. The book of Revelation confuses Jesus, the Angel of God, the Spirit, the Seven Spirits of God, and the Seven Angels of God, in a rich and wonderful kaleidoscope of color and light that would be difficult to reduce to a creedal statement—and why would one want to?

All the churches examined in this essay were and are in transition. Churches born out of resistance to Western imperial and missionary control have awakened in a new independent South Africa in which the African National Congress rules, and in which the hymn for the coming of the Spirit has passed into the national anthem, albeit without the epiclesis! These churches are changing and will continue to change. They will continue to be Christian in impulse and understanding. They all declare the Bible to be "their backbone" and use it in every corner of what they do in a way that puts Western Christianity to shame. But on the issue of the Holy Spirit and pneumatology, why should they conform to the councils and creeds of Western Christianity, born out of a Western worldview, defined in terms of the Logos? The concept of "orthodoxy" is in some respects an attempt by the West to continue to exercise its imperial hegemony over the world!

Jonathan A. Draper

Darlene Zschech

15. The Role of the Holy Spirit in Worship: An Introduction to the Hillsong Church, Sydney, Australia

I want to begin with some personal reflections: I certainly have not come to the table as an academic. I was invited to share from my experience as worship pastor of Hillsong Church, an Assemblies of God church in Sydney, Australia, over many years. We are unashamedly a vibrant, Pentecostal church full of young people whose desire is that their heartfelt praise and worship touch heaven and change earth. Our worship seeks to influence the praises of people throughout the earth, and, to the best of our ability, exalt Christ with powerful songs of faith and hope. We are one of the strands of churches that God is using across the earth in this season of history.

I personally had a powerful conversion experience at the age of fifteen, and from that day to this I have been humbled and over-whelmed by the great love of God. My hunger for truth continued to escalate, I guess culminating in an unrelenting dissatisfaction with life as it was and a longing for the promised life as the Word of God described it in Acts 1:8: "But you will receive power when the Holy Spirit has come upon you, and you will be my witnesses . . . to the ends of the earth." As my personal understanding of worship increases—of its power, its necessity, its value, its fruit, its cost—I have come to understand that God is complete without us, and yet he chooses not to be complete without us. Exodus 7:16, where God tells Pharaoh, "Let my people go, so that they may worship me," starts to give us an inkling into God's heart for connection. That this highest priority, "to love the Lord your God with all our heart, soul, mind, and strength," actually matters—well, as far as ministry goes, this unfolding revelation is what I decided to give my life to. Truthful worship is the goal, fueled by revelation of Christ and sustained by relationship in Christ. Yielding to the Spirit of God in my own life has been uncomfortable and has required me to continue to change, but at the same time it has defined and equipped me to stand and to be comfortable in the skin I was born in.

I have also become captivated by the presence of God. An awareness of his being near, the Person of the Holy Spirit filling me, teaching me, leading me, and comforting me, has absolutely ruined me for anything less, and even messed with my own initial "safer" understanding of worshiping in spirit. In actual fact, as we are people of spirit, soul, and body, I find that worship without the Spirit can be reduced to a merely religious, two-dimensional activity. I have found that without the Spirit there is no way forward to our worship being in truth. First Corinthians 12:3 says, "Therefore I want you to understand that NO ONE speaking by the Spirit of God ever says 'Let Jesus be cursed!' and no one can say 'Jesus is Lord' except by the Holy Spirit." Bishop Graham Cray, the bishop of Maidstone in the United Kingdom, said this in January 2008: "I believe the power of the Holy Spirit is the foretaste of the power of what is to come. All ministry, genuinely in the power of the Holy Spirit brings the power of the new heaven and the new earth into the here and now . . . the old becoming new." This is simply stunning.

As a nation, Australia is just over two hundred years old. In 1605 the Spaniard Pedro Fernandez de Quiros sailed from South America in search of the great south land, the mythical *terra australis*. Upon arriving, in 1606, at Vanuatu in the islands later called New Hebrides, he declared that "this region of the south as far as the Pole" is to be named "La Australia del Espirito Santo." The name means roughly "the south land of the Holy Spirit." We are now beginning to see glimpses of what this can mean for our land when true worship is a lifestyle that embraces the entire spectrum of life. Our worship is not based on ritual or tradition but is a real expression of our intimate relationship with God. The contemporary music and freedom of worship are reasons why the younger generation is being drawn to Jesus Christ, and our churches are seeing explosive growth in the number of young people in our congregations.

When we at Hillsong Church started worshiping together as a church over twenty-five years ago, we were around one hundred eighty strong—not filled with a great deal of musical talent, but certainly with wonderful potential, and always an intense hunger for more than just another church service. Our pastor, Brian Houston, has always been a great believer in people, and through much trust and a lot of hard work we developed over time a great team of musicians and singers who dedicate themselves to writing and leading songs of

Darlene Zschech

286

worship in a local church context—passionate and genuine, played and written by very imperfect people, but all with an authentic relationship with God.[1]

We desired all along that, with great celebration, we would always approach God's throne with awe and reverence at the wonder of our God. Matt Redman, a great composer of worship songs from the U.K., calls his understanding of the presence of God "the otherness of God."[2] The great A. W. Tozer said, "I could not exist very long as a Christian without this inner consciousness of the presence and nearness of God."[3] Psalm 2 says, "Serve the Lord with reverent awe and worshipful fear—rejoice and be in high spirits with TREMBLING" (my translation). In worship we become part of the great manifesto of song, the eternal song—every nation, tribe, and tongue being gathered and included, not scattered and excluded. And so, over years our goal has been to develop a Spirit-infused culture—revealed in our day-to-day lives, bringing with it an unfolding revelation of the Father, Son, and Holy Spirit in our midst.

Many key things have developed and continue to define our worship culture at Hillsong Church. The journey has been fun, interesting, intense, and more than fulfilling, but hunger and unashamed passion have been the underlying bass notes that cannot be put on a chart but are definitely the continuing thread of our music. The opposite of hunger, which Western society promotes, is comfort.

Our pastor always spoke Psalm 100 over our church: "to serve the Lord with gladness and joy, my mouth will praise You with joyful

---

[1] Today Hillsong Church operates from a twenty-one-acre site in a modern business park in the Hills District, and from a facility in Waterloo near the heart of Sydney's central business district. With a total attendance of over twenty thousand on any given weekend, the church is continually becoming better known, having a dynamic impact in Australia and many other nations. Hillsong also has churches in London, Kiev, Stockholm, and Cape Town, South Africa. The live praise and worship albums produced by Hillsong Music have achieved gold status in various countries, and the songs are sung in churches around the world. For more information see the church's website: http:// wwww2. hillsong.com/church/.

[2] For Matt Redman see *The Unquenchable Worshipper: Coming Back to the Heart of Worship* (Ventura, CA: Regal, 2001).

[3] A. W. Tozer, Sermon "Astonished Reverence." http://www.sermonindex .net/modules/articles/index.php?view=article&aid=4955.

The Role of the Holy Spirit in Worship

lips" (his translation)—and so we have, glad and thankful. One of the saddest moments regarding worship in the Scriptures is found in Lamentations 5:14-15: "The old men have left the city gate, the young men their music. The joy of our hearts has ceased; our dancing has been turned into mourning." No joyful hearts, no joyful songs.

But laying down our lives? What does that look like in Sydney, Australia? "For me to live is Christ and to die is gain"—the words of Paul echo in our hearts. We started to study the glory of God—and the word in the Old Testament was that we could not see his glory and actually survive. We started to study about service—what was actually required by heaven? We decided early on to be a "whatever it takes" kind of people. Radical service led us to Mother Teresa, to whom is attributed the saying, "You'll never know Jesus is all you need until Jesus is all you have!"

As a leader I realized that we had many, many first-generation Christians in our team of worship leaders, singers, and musicians. As little as I knew about worship, they knew even less. So we started to correspond with others, glean from experts, and teach a theology of worship in order to create a biblically based *why* behind the *what*. We still ensure that this is taught—raising ministers of music rather than simply facilitators of music. This is discipleship 101! We studied the psalms for many years, every week delving into the lives of the psalmists and what a lifestyle of worship looks like. I personally was very intent about doing my best to ensure this was real in us—not rhetoric, not reduced to creating good music and a pleasant time for parishioners.

We developed a culture that understands the power of prayer—that it is a very presumptuous people who would stand for a life as a Christ-follower, and stand off afar when it comes to prayer. James 4:8 says to "draw near to God, and he will draw near to you." Putting the prayers of the saints to music has been one of life's greatest privileges, one none of us ever takes for granted. Being a prayerful people has always been a critical priority. In Revelation the word speaks of a glory-filled scene in heaven as the prayers of the saints and worship reach the nostrils of God.

We developed a strong culture of community, of family, as again we were very aware that we were leading a parentless generation, and often the church family is the only family many ever know. I started out myself as a very insecure person, and my heart and the culture of our church are committed to people's knowing that they are valued for more than what they can do, for who they are. In the church in

Darlene Zschech

Acts a strong community had one heart, one mind, great power—a great awakening of the Spirit—a united team, a sense of belonging, and a commitment to each other's success. In Psalm 133 unity is held up as a pathway to true blessing.

We decided early on that our finest moments of worship would not be reserved for a public gathering, not just for corporate worship, but on our knees, carved out in a 24/7 life, the moments that only the Lord himself would ever know about—and for teaching individuals to know how to bring praise, how to develop lives of thanksgiving. Then, in moments of adversity, or moments when God feels very far away, when heaven seems silent, Spirit-inspired worship, truly by faith through grace, will release some of the sweetest fragrances of all before our Lord. This was learning to sing in the storm or in a night season. Isaiah 54:1: "Sing O Barren woman . . . you who had NOT YET BROUGHT FORTH a child" (my translation).

We are passionate to live with a legacy in mind—that our lives of devotion will inspire those who follow with a faith they can live for and die for if need be: "throughout all generations" (Ps 145:13). Young people today are not interested in passive, plastic music. They want to play music that moves people—they want more than their mind and body to be involved when they play. They want to create, and to play the part of the psalmist who asks us over forty times to sing, and to sing a new song at that! It will take a lifetime to discover the depth of what that new song is, how it sounds, and the gathering of like-minded hearts it will invoke.

Music, being such a powerful language, is created to give voice to the human condition; it is a powerful vehicle of expression for the human heart. It communicates the cries, the elation, the anguish, the joys, the highs and the lows: "when language is insufficient, the music speaks on." In Psalm 71 from the Messabe Bible, David says, "When I open up in song to You, I let out lungs full of praise— my rescued life a song." But Matthew 7 says, *"Don't be flip with the sacred."* Nicholas Wolterstorff of Yale once said that "each people group, each generation, needs to be able to express its sense of worship in its own voice, in a way that resonates deep in the soul." As our culture keeps changing, these are not issues that the church can pretend will go away. Just because a sound is not our style does not mean that it is not sacred.

Music and the arts have at times been distorted and perverted, but I see again and again Spirit-filled young people reclaiming their inheritance. The earth we live in today has one in five people between the ages of fifteen and twenty-four. Nearly 40 percent of the world is under twenty-five years of age. In Southeast Asia, over 50 percent of the population is under twenty. If the sound doesn't change, our ways to relate become incredibly minimized.

I humbly say that I feel that our whole journey has been Spirit inspired—knowing that obedient worship fuels us for this life journey, as the Spirit of God infuses us with life and life in all its fullness (John 10:10).

HILLSONG MUSIC[4]

So what about the songs, the passionate Hillsong Music, for which our church is famous?

> We have just kept writing songs from the heart
> Songs about the faithfulness of God
> Songs that are the Word of God put to music, rather than our opinions of the word
> Songs that would gather and songs accessible to the ordinary
> Songs that would sincerely serve the heartbeat of the local church and her passion for Christ
> Songs relevant to today
> Songs that reflect the internal struggle
> Songs that would simply be our prayers put to music
> Songs that would be childlike in approach yet Spirit inspired
> Songs that would LIFT people and encourage them to seek the Lord, to look beyond ourselves and our own inadequacies and look to the promises of the word of God.

Throughout history songs have become theological signposts for every generation, and we see them crossing over many of the denominational barriers that have traditionally been barricades rather than differences. In my experience the worship of this generation seems simply to serve as many denominations as is possible—could this be part of the new song? We have been questioned about our approach, condemned for it, but I say we have never claimed to be the experts; it has never been "out with the old, in with the new." Just "Lord, this is my heart song." As we risk looking foolish and comical to some, our

---

[4] More information and music downloads can be found on our website: http://www.hillsong.com/music/.

Darlene Zschech

music continues to be a lifeline to so many. Every one of our writers receives many letters from people saying that "the songs cause what in my heart is in the distance, and strains to become close by way of songs that are slightly more intimate in content." Changing a song from "We love you" to "I love you" is for many a powerful and confronting journey.

Without the Spirit of God it is simply all just noise, but with a heart awakened to the great love of God worship becomes a part of the great eternal anthem. Our songs become part of that wonderful human experience we engage in here on earth, an experience that actually matters in heaven. But it is no use singing the songs and going through the motions and simply living life our own way from Monday to Saturday.

About Spirit and Truth worship—enabled by the Spirit, offered in truth: I do know that you cannot encounter Christ and genuinely seek him and remain the same. This journey has taken us from loving and adoring our King to getting honest about imperfections and shortcomings, receiving grace and forgiving others, to dealing with big life disappointments, and yet still finding a sweet joy only known by the redeemed—this song is just our starting point.

Mark Labberton, in his book entitled *The Dangerous Act of Worship*, asks, "Will we worship God with the whole of our lives, so that the work of justice becomes our bedrock testimony to the presence and power of Jesus Christ, whom we serve and worship?"[5] This question resonates with Micah 6:8: "To do justice, and to love kindness, and to walk humbly with your God." This is what is required. Hebrews 13:15-16 says: "through him . . . let us continually offer a sacrifice of praise to God, that is, the fruit of lips that confess his name. Do not neglect to do good and to share what you have, for such sacrifices are pleasing to God."

As we are changed in his presence, our role as his hands and his feet in this hurting world becomes so very prevalent. To worship him in Spirit—be fuelled in his presence and in truth—is to take the love of Christ to the earth. So, our lives continue on this journey of faith, the working out of our salvation, and our commitment to truthful worship being the central fact remains.

[5] Mark Labberton, *The Dangerous Act of Worship* (Downers Grove, IL: IVP Books, 2007), 188.

The Role of the Holy Spirit in Worship

In saying all this my heart and quest are the same as they were when I first encountered Christ—to love the Lord my God with all my heart and my soul and my mind and my strength—and to love my neighbor as myself. My top priority in life is to take responsibility for this always ringing true—whether leading others in worship during services, loving the broken, and serving the poor—or in the secret place that only God and I ever know about.

I wish to close my reflections simply with the lyrics of this song, written in our church many years ago for a Communion service, for, in the end, this grace we have found is all about the power of the cross—and to that end we will ever worship.

> WORTHY IS THE LAMB
> Thank you for the cross Lord
> Thank you for the price You paid
> Bearing all my sin and shame, in love You came
> And gave amazing grace
>
> Thank you for this Love Lord
> Thank you for Your nail pierced hands
> Wash me in Your cleansing flow,
> Now all I know,
> Your forgiveness and embrace
>
> Worthy IS the Lamb
> Seated on the throne
> I crown You now with many crowns
> You reign victorious
>
> High and lifted up
> Jesus Son of God
> The Darling of heaven crucified
> Worthy IS the Lamb
>
> By Darlene Zschech

Darlene Zschech

Contributors

Daniel E. Albrecht is professor of church history and Christian spirituality at Bethany University in Santa Cruz, California. He received his PhD from the Graduate Theological Union, Berkeley. His scholarly work focuses on the intersection of human development and experience with spiritual experience and development. His publications include *Rites in the Spirit: A Ritual Approach to Pentecostal/Charismatic Spirituality* (1999).

Teresa Berger is professor of liturgical studies at the Yale Institute of Sacred Music and Yale Divinity School. She is a Roman Catholic, with experience in the charismatic movement, and holds doctorates in both dogmatic theology and liturgical studies. Her publications include *Women's Ways of Worship: Gender Analysis and Liturgical History* (1999), *Dissident Daughters: Feminist Liturgies in Global Context* (2001), and *Fragments of Real Presence* (2005). In 2008 she produced, with Mystic Waters Media, the interactive CD-ROM *Ocean Psalms*.

Matthew Myer Boulton is assistant professor of ministry studies at Harvard Divinity School. He earned his PhD from the University of Chicago, and is the author of *God Against Religion: Rethinking Christian Theology through Worship* (2008) and a co-editor and contributor to the volume *Doing Justice to Mercy: Religion, Law, and Criminal Justice* (2007). He is an ordained minister in the Christian Church (Disciples of Christ).

Paul F. Bradshaw is professor of liturgy at the University of Notre Dame. Ordained in the Church of England, he received his PhD in liturgical studies from the University of London in 1971, and in 1994 was awarded the degree of Doctor of Divinity by the University of Oxford for his published works. He has published extensively on the subject of Christian liturgy, having written or edited more than twenty books, together with over ninety essays or articles in periodicals. From 1987 to 2005 he was editor in chief of the scholarly journal *Studia Liturgica*.

Simon Chan is professor of systematic theology at Trinity Theological College in Singapore. His special interest is in the relationship between dogmatics, spirituality, and the liturgy, from a global Pentecostal perspective. He is an ordained minister of the Assemblies of God of Singapore. His recent publications include *Liturgical Theology: The Church as Worshipping Community* (2006).

Melva Wilson Costen, an elder in the Presbyterian Church (USA), is the Helmar Emil Nielsen Professor of Worship and Music *emerita* at the Interdenominational Theological Center in Atlanta, Georgia. She earned her PhD from Georgia State University and holds two Doctor of Humane Letters honorary degrees. Her publications include *In Spirit and in Truth* (2004), *African American Christian Worship* (rev. ed. 2007), and *African American Worship: Faith Looking Forward* (2000).

Jonathan A. Draper is a professor of theology at the University of KwaZulu-Natal, South Africa. He earned his PhD from the University of Cambridge, U.K., and has published widely in the areas of Christian origins and of contextual exegesis.

Peter Galadza is Kule family professor of liturgy at the Sheptytsky Institute of Eastern Christian Studies in the Faculty of Theology, Saint Paul University, Ottawa, Canada. He earned his PhD in theology from the University of Saint Michael's College in the University of Toronto in 1994. Among his publications are *The Theology and Liturgical Work of Andrei Sheptytsky* (2004); *The Divine Liturgy: An Anthology for Worship* (2004); and *Unité en division: Les lettres de Lev Gillet ("Un moine de l'Eglise d'Orient") à Andrei Cheptytsky 1921–1929* (2007).

Maxwell E. Johnson is professor of liturgical studies in the Department of Theology at the University of Notre Dame and a pastor in the Evangelical Lutheran Church in America. He is a graduate of Augustana College, Sioux Falls, South Dakota (BA), Wartburg Theological Seminary (MDiv), Saint John's School of Theology, Collegeville, Minnesota (MA), and the University of Notre Dame (MA, PhD). Widely published in the field of liturgical studies and a frequent presenter to diverse audiences, Johnson's interests include the rites of Christian initiation, the feasts and seasons of the liturgical year, Christian liturgy in the first centuries of Christianity, as well as contemporary liturgical-ecumenical issues.

Contributors

Simon Jones is chaplain and research fellow at Merton College, Oxford. He teaches liturgy in the theology faculty of the University of Oxford and at St. Stephen's House, Oxford. His doctoral dissertation at the University of Cambridge investigated the liturgical implications of the doctrine of the Spirit for the Syrian baptismal tradition. More recently he has written the introduction to the sixtieth anniversary edition of Gregory Dix's *The Shape of the Liturgy* and edited a collection of some of Dix's unpublished works.

Habtemichael Kidane was born in Eritrea and received his PhD in Oriental liturgy from the Pontifical Oriental Institute in Rome with a dissertation on the Liturgy of the Hours in the Ethiopian Orthodox Rite (1990). His major publications include *L'Ufficio divino della Chiesa etiopica* (1998), *Origin and Development of the Ge'ez Liturgy in Tegregna*, a language widely spoken in Northern Ethiopia and Eritrea (2005), and, most recently, *La Bibliografia della liturgia etiopica* (2008). He is currently preparing a book on the first part of the Divine Liturgy (Śərə'atä Qəddase) and eucharistic prayers (Akʷatetä Qʷərban) of the Ethiopic Eritrean liturgical tradition.

Ruth Langer is associate professor of Jewish studies in the Theology Department and associate director of the Center for Christian-Jewish Learning at Boston College. She received her PhD in Jewish Liturgy in 1994 and her rabbinic ordination in 1986 from Hebrew Union College–Jewish Institute of Religion in Cincinnati. She is the author of *To Worship God Properly: Tensions between Liturgical Custom and Halakhah in Judaism* (1998) and co-editor of *Liturgy in the Life of the Synagogue: Studies in the History of Jewish Prayer* (2005).

Bryan Spinks is professor of liturgical studies at the Yale Institute of Sacred Music and Yale Divinity School. He holds a DD from the University of Durham (U.K.) and is an ordained presbyter of the Church of England. Spinks is the author of numerous books and articles, and is coeditor of the *Scottish Journal of Theology*. He is a former consultant to the Church of England Liturgical Commission, president emeritus of the Church Service Society of the Church of Scotland, and a fellow of the Royal Historical Society.

James Steven is lecturer in theology and ministry at King's College, London, where he teaches contemporary worship and ecclesiology and runs the Doctorate in Ministry program. He studied natural sciences at Cambridge (M.A.) and theology in Durham (B.A.), was ordained

Contributors

in 1987, and completed a Ph.D. at King's College while in parish and chaplaincy posts. His doctoral dissertation was published in 2002 as *Worship in the Spirit: Charismatic Worship in the Church of England* (Paternoster). He is membership secretary of the British Society of Liturgical Studies, and a member of the editorial board for the Grove Book worship series.

Bishop N. T. Wright obtained his DPhil for a thesis on Saint Paul, and his DD for books on the New Testament and, in particular, Jesus in his historical context. He has taught New Testament studies at Cambridge, McGill, and Oxford Universities, and worked as a college chaplain before becoming Dean of Lichfield in 1994, Canon of Westminster in 2000, and Bishop of Durham in 2003. He has written over forty books and hundreds of articles at both scholarly and popular levels, and has broadcast frequently on radio and TV.

Darlene Zschech is an internationally known singer, songwriter, worship leader, and speaker, who spearheads the music of Hillsong Church in Sydney, Australia. She has achieved numerous gold albums, and her songs are sung in many parts of the world. As a songwriter Zschech is best known for the chorus "Shout to the Lord," a song that is sung by an estimated twenty-five million churchgoers every week and has been covered by at least twenty other artists. In 2000 she received a Dove Award nomination for Songwriter of the Year.

Contributors

General Index

Abelard, 150
active participation, 55–57
Adam, Karl, 80
Adeyemo, Tokunboh, 238 n 26
African American Spiritual, xi
African American worship, 207–20,
    227–28
African spirituality, 208–11
African traditional religion, 208–20,
    279
Alcuin, 152
AmaJericho, 275–78
Ambrose, 170
ʿamidah, 6, 36
anabathmoi, 132–35
anamnesis, 145–46
ancestors, 279
Andəmta Qəddase, 183
Anderson, Allan, 264–65, 283
Anglican Prayer Book, 84–86, 248
anointing, 146–48
Aphrahat, 104–5
Apostolic Constitutions 8, 81
Apostolic Tradition, 41–42, 81, 88, 91,
    153, 170
Aqiva, Rabbi, 30
Argenti, Cyrille, 120
Arranz, Miguel, 116, 122
ascesis, 138–39
ascetic Christianity, 68
Augsburg Confession, 155
Augustine, Saint, 52
Australia, 286
Azuza Street Mission, 216–17, 223,
    225, 228–31, 233 n 19, 234, 236,
    265

Babel, 71, 72
Balicka-Witakowska, Ewa, 202–3
Bandrés Urdániz, José L., 187
baptism, xvii, 10–11, 107–13, 118–27,
    144–46, 147, 170–72, 189–91, 279
  as birth, 144
  as dying and rising with Christ,
    145
  infant, 147
  in the Spirit, 216, 233
  of Jesus, 6, 66, 103
  of the Spirit, 251 n 12
Baptism, Eucharist, Ministry, xvii,
    93–94
baptismal font, 8
baptismal *ordines*, 110–12
Barth, Karl, 45–46, 60, 73–76, 80
bat qol (heavenly voice), 26–27
Beck, Edmund, 104 n 16
Bediako, Kwame, 268
Bernard, J. H., 100
Bhekibandla, Archbishop, 277–78
Bible, 238–39, 284
Bishop, Edmund, 81
Blessing of Baptismal Waters, 144–46
Bobrinskoy, Boris, 115, 119, 122, 123,
    138–39
Bouyer, Louis, 88
Bradshaw, Paul, 3
Branch, Lori, 248–49
Brightman, F. E., 86
Brock, Sebastian, 99–100, 116, 161
Brown, Raymond, 44
Brownsville Revival, 234
Bruner, Frederick Dale, 157
Brunner, Peter, 90, 166–67
Bryant, Alfred T., 267

Bulgakov, Sergius, 115, 129–30
"Byzantinization," 176–77

Camp Meetings, American Frontier,
    256–57
Casel, Odo, 79, 82
Catechism of the Catholic Church, 95,
    142–43, 153
charismatic Anglican churches,
    257–59
Charismatic Movement, 91
Charismatic worship, 225, 245–59
Chirovsky, Andriy, 135
Choi, Meesaeng Lee, 226 n 7
chrismation, 171–72, 176
    Byzantine, 117, 119–27
Christian . . . Church in Zion, 281–83
Chrysostom, John, 118 n 13, 120,
    128–29
Chung, Hyun Kyung, xviii
Church of England, 84–86, 245–59
"Church of Fools," xix–xx
Church of George Khambule, 269–75
Church of Jericho, 265, 267, 275–78
Church of the Saints, 265
Coakley, Sarah, 99
Colenso, John William, 267
"communitas," 231–32
Cone, James, 216
confession of faith, 146
confirmation, 117, 146, 171–76
Congar, Yves, xii, 54, 91, 99 n 1
Connolly, R. H., 82
Corbon, Jean, 142 n 3
Council for World Religions, 209
councils, North African, 151
Cox, Harvey, 224 n 2, 243 n 35
Cray, Graham, 286
creatio ex nihilo, 62 n 2
creation, 61–64
Creed, third article, 50
Crichton, J. D., 88
cyberspace, xix–xx, 141

Cyriacus of Bələnsa, 198–99
Cyril of Jerusalem, 122, 125

Davies, J. G., 91
Davis, Cyprian, 212
Day, Juliette, 122 n 31
Dayton, Donald, 226, 229 n 19
Dead Sea Scrolls, 26
Dəggʷa, 191
Del Colle, Ralph, 48–49
demonic opposition, 69
Dêr Balyzeh Papyrus, 165
Dictionary of Liturgy and Worship, 3
Dissenters, 247–52
Dix, Gregory, 91, 117 n 11
Dlamini, Paulina Nomguqo, 268
Doerkson, Brian, 252–53
doxology, 146
Drijvers, H. J. W., 102
Du Bois, W. E. B., 215
Duchesne, Louis, 83

Eastern Orthodox worship, 115–39
ecumenical conversations, xvi–xviii
ecumenical pneumatology, xiv,
    xvi–xviii
"Egyptian Church Order," 81
Ehrlich, Uri, 34 n 23, 37 n 31, 38 n 36
Elazar ben Pedat, Rabbi, 30–33
Eliezer ben Hyrcanus, Rabbi, 36 n 28
England, charismatic movement,
    245–59
Enuma elish, 61–63
Ephrem of Nisibis, 103–7
epiclesis of the Spirit, 53–55, 59–60,
    77, 79–96, 142, 146, 152, 155–57,
    274
    and the Church of England, 84–86
    and the Roman Canon, 80–84,
        156–57
    in Lutheran worship, 155–70
    in the Ethiopian tradition, 187–89
    in the Syrian tradition, 156

General Index

General Index

General Index

General Index

General Index

Trembelas, Panagiotis, 118 nn 11 & 14, 125 n 38
trinitarian economy, 42
trinitarian mission, 42
Trinity, 64 n 6, 83, 91, 102
    equality of, 198–201, 203
Trisagion, 181–82
Turner, Max, 44
Turner, Victor, 231
Tyrer, J. W., 82

umoya (spiritual power), 264, 267–69

Vagaggini, Cipriano, 87, 91, 167 n 28
Vasileu ouranie, 131–32
Vatican Council II, 141
    Lumen Gentium, xvi
    Sacrosanctum Concilium, xx–xxi, 86, 152
    Unitatis Redintegratio, xvi
Velkovska, Elena, 132
Veni Creator Spiritus, 54, 141, 144, 154, 197 n 75
Veni, Sancte Spiritus, 150
Verona Sacramentary, 147
Vilikati, Eliyasi, 265, 275–76
Vineyard network, 234, 245–47, 252–58
Vischer, Lukas, 92
von Allmen, J.-J., 90
von Deutz, Rupert 148–50
    Liber de divinis officiis, 148–50
von Rad, Gerhard, 63 n 5

Wacker, Grant, 226, 232 n 17, 242 n 33
Wallace, Anthony, 229–30
Ward, Graham, xx
Ward, Pete, 253
Welker, Michael, xiv
Williams, Don, 246
Wilmore, Gayraud, 207–8
Wimber, John, 246

Winkler, Gabriele, 96, 102 n 12, 104 n 15, 113, 143 n 5, 156 n 3, 161, 188 n 36
Wolterstorff, Nicholas, 289
womb imagery, 101–13, 144–45
Woolfenden, Gregory, Hieromonk, xxv
World Council of Churches, xvii–xviii, 92
    Athens assembly, xviii
    Baptism, Eucharist, Ministry, xvii, 93–94
    Canberra assembly, xviii
worship, xviii–xxiv, 65–66, 71–75
    African American, 207–20
    charismatic, 225, 245–59
    Eastern Orthodox, 115–39
    epicletic character, 59–60, 77
    in the New Testament, 3–24
    in the Spirit, 223–44
    Pentecostal, 223–44
Worship-Word-Ministry, 256–57
"Worthy is the Lamb," 292
Wright, N. T., 42–43

Xhosa, culture, 261–62

Yeago, David, 51
YHWH, 8–9, 13, 20, 43
Yonas, Abba, 196 n 70
YouTube, 141

Zahan, Dominique, 208–9
Zä-mika'el, 189
Zschech, Darlene, 238 n 26
Zion Combination Church, 278
Zizioulas, John, 48, 115, 130–31
Zulu Anglicanism, 266–67
Zulu culture, 261–62
Zulu Zionism, 266–67
Zulu Zionist churches, worship, 261–84

General Index

303

Scripture Index

Hebrew Bible

Genesis
1	61–64, 70
11:1-9	71, 72
32:22-32	59, 77
50:20	68 n 9

Exodus
4:10-15	183
7:16	285
20:20	32
23:2	27
25:8	36 n 29
31:3	26 n 2
35:31	26 n 2

Numbers
24:2	26 n 2
28–29	29

Deuteronomy
30:12	27
33:2	38

1 Samuel
10	26 n 2

1 Kings
8:28	31

Psalms
2	287
19:15	29
40:6-8	65
50:9-15	61, 65, 66, 76
51:13	26 n 2
71	289
74:12-14	61, 63
82:1	31
91:7	38
100	287
113–18	35
118:22	67
130:1	37
133	289
145:13	289

Isaiah
1:11ff	65
2:4	67
51:9-10	61
53:1	8
54:1	289
61:1ff	66
63:10-11	26 n 2

Jeremiah
6:20ff	65
7:21ff	65

Lamentations
5:14-15	288

Ezekiel
47	9

Daniel
7:2	63 n 5

Hosea
6:6	65, 66

Joel
2:28-32	43, 70

Scripture Index